CONTEMPLATION NATION

CONTEMPLATION NATION:
HOW ANCIENT PRACTICES
ARE CHANGING THE WAY WE LIVE

Papers from
THE STATE OF CONTEMPLATIVE PRACTICE IN AMERICA
Fetzer Institute
Kalamazoo, Michigan
June 10-13, 2010
Co-Hosted by
The Center for Contemplative Mind in Society

Foreword by
Rob Lehman

Introduction by
Mirabai Bush

FETZER INSTITUTE
WWW.FETZER.ORG

Available from the Fetzer Institute.

Fetzer Institute
9292 West KL Avenue
Kalamazoo, MI 49009-9398

www.fetzer.org

Printed in the United States of America

First Edition
ISBN 978-1461118411

CONTENTS

Grateful Acknowledgments ix
Mirabai Bush

Foreword..xi
Rob Lehman

Introduction...1
Mirabai Bush

Assessing the State of Contemplative Practices in the
United States..9
Maia Duerr

The Blue Sapphire of the Mind: Christian Contemplative
Practice and the Healing of the Whole 35
Douglas Burton-Christie

Action and Contemplation: A Christian Perspective............53
Richard Rohr

Contemplative Practice in Seminaries and with Clergy........59
Andrew Dreitcer

Christian Centering Prayer in America:
A Contemplative Practice for Contemporary America.........75
David Frenette

State of Contemplative Practice: Contemplative Living.......89
Robert Toth

Islamic and Islamicate Contemplative Practice
in the United States..97
Zia Inayat-Khan

Socially Engaged Buddhist Contemplative Practices:
Past and Potential Future Contributions at a
Time of Cultural Transition and Crisis 109
Donald Rothberg

The Growth of Contemplative Practice in
Contemporary Jewish Life..131
Rachel Cowan

Contemplative Practice and the Enrichment, Formation,
and Training of Spiritual Directors 143
Liz Ellmann

Contemplative Practice and Online Communities 163
Mary Ann Brussat

The Role of Contemplative Practice in
Transforming Conflict..175
Dena Merriam

Contemplative Practice in a Frantic World 183
Michele Gossman

Naming, Connecting, Nourishing, Illuminating:
How the Shambhala Sun Foundation is serving the
Contemplative Movement..189
Barry Boyce

Contemplative Practice in America:
Retreat Center Trends..205
Michael Craft

Contemplative Higher Education
in Contemporary Life...221
Mirabai Bush

Contemplative Higher Education:
A Case Study of Naropa University 237
Susan Burggraf

Envisioning the Future of K–12
Contemplative Education...247
Patricia Jennings and David I. Rome

Contemplative Practice and Healing Trauma....................259
Deborah Rozelle

Mindfulness-Based Interventions:
An Emerging Phenomenon 293
Margaret Cullen

Contemplative Practice and End-of-Life Care:
A Preliminary Discussion 315
Judy Lief

The State of Contemplative Practice in the USA and
Globally: Integrating Contemplative Practice and Leadership
Development in Diverse Sectors of Society and
Around the World...323
Walter Link

Contemplative Leadership in Organizations.....................343
Janet Drey

Contemplative Practice in Law: An Overview 361
Rhonda V. Magee

"Point Vierge" (The Virgin Point):
The Contemplative Intention in Community....................373
Bobby William Austin

Contemplative Practice and Social Activism 387
Claudia Horwitz

Appendices

Appendix I: The State of the Contemplative Movement 399
Tom Callanan

Appendix II: Participant Biographies 411

Grateful Acknowledgments

Special thanks to all the authors of these papers, who revised and edited their own work and agreed to have them included. We had given them permission to write what seemed most relevant for the meeting, so the styles are not consistent. They agreed to be included in this collection anyhow, hoping that the combined wisdom would benefit others who are interested in the diverse ways in which contemplative practice is evolving in America.

Convening a meeting of 27 contemplative leaders from across the country required sustained effort, creative thought, discriminating wisdom, deep equanimity, and a sense of humor. Fortunately, such people existed at Fetzer Institute and the Center for Contemplative Mind in Society. Eric Nelson led the meeting effort with grace and discipline, drawing on his friendships and collaborative history with many of the participants. Linda Grdina's insight into personal chemistry and communication helped transform the meeting into a connection of both minds and hearts, and she guided this book into being. David Addiss inspired the team. Arthur Zajonc helped with meeting facilitation and spoke about contemplative knowing and learning. Tom Callanan reported on the meeting for *Shambhala Sun*. The Seasons staff fluffed the pillows and stocked the refrigerators in each of our rooms. Tamar Miller advised us on meeting process.

And the deepest appreciation to Rob Lehman, who has held the vision and encouraged the work of the contemplative society since the founding of Fetzer Institute. Rob once said that the cultivation of contemplative practices would have as significant an impact on society as literacy did in the 15th-16th centuries.

May the good work of these many teachers and leaders continue to relieve suffering and increase joy for many beings. May their work—and yours— help create a more peaceful, just, compassionate, wise, and loving society.

Mirabai Bush

FOREWORD

Often when we define ourselves we ask what makes us distinct or unique. This book reports on a meeting of contemplative leaders who gathered to ask a different question: What is the larger purpose we share with others? What is the nature of the emergent movement or awakening in which we are participating?

An interesting thing happens when we experience our identity in terms of our relationships to others. The Copernican shift that takes us out of the center of our universe allows us to see together what none of us can see separately—the true form of our mission becomes visible.

Seeing from a perspective of what unites, instead of what separates, us—experiencing the wholeness of life—is for me the heart of contemplative awareness. The beautiful symmetry of this gathering was that the outward unity the meeting sought was to be found in the inward experience of each of the contemplative practices represented. Authentic contemplative practice awakens in us a deeper unity.

This meeting was about working together, about collaboration. Collaboration, on the surface, is about bringing together resources, both financial and intellectual, to work toward a common purpose. But true collaboration has an inner life; collaboration that draws on the outer without integrating the inner life will only rearrange the furniture. True collaboration is about a transformation of consciousness that is a radical opening to what unites us. The practices of true collaboration are contemplative practices.

Each participant in this meeting came with an independent identity and each left strengthened through an understanding of a common purpose. This certainly has been our experience at the Fetzer Institute where our mission is to foster awareness of the power of love and forgiveness in the emerging global community. Larry Sullivan, Fetzer's new president, points to the centrality of the word "awareness" in our mission. He sees our mission as calling for a priority of awareness, a phase change in awareness that opens us, in our full humanity, to the power of love; the love that breaks through the walls of separation.

As I read through the wonderful offerings on the pages of this book, the question that focused my attention was simply, "Is not the experience of love, after all, a gift of contemplative awareness?"

Rob Lehman
Chair, Board of Trustees
Fetzer Institute
February 14, 2011

CONTEMPLATION NATION:
HOW ANCIENT PRACTICES
ARE CHANGING THE WAY WE LIVE

Introduction

Mirabai Bush

"Wake up, you of clear vision, you who see beingness. Beingness is all there is! It is the underlying unity!" Rabbi Rachel Cowan was speaking, giving a contemplative rendition of a Hebrew prayer and its reminder that "the truth shall set you free," and 40 people in a circle were listening. She was riveting. She was telling us a story of how contemplative practices were lost and then regained in Judaism. One part of her story was about a radical and transforming 1990 journey of rabbis to visit the Dalai Lama in Dharamsala, India, where they talked about how to keep tradition alive while in exile, and how many young Jews had looked to Buddhism for contemplative practice. In her talk were themes that would resonate for the rest of this meeting, including the re-emergence of the contemplative in American religious and secular society, the influence of the East on Western spirituality, the common values reached through diverse practices, and the opportunities for some contemplatives to return to the religions of their birth.

The meeting was a gathering of contemplative leaders from religious and spiritual traditions and secular arenas, including business, law, leadership, social and environmental justice, education, healthcare, trauma healing, and end-of-life care. We were looking for the unique contemplative expression of each tradition or sector and our shared understanding of the sacred. For three days, we sat in a circle in a beautiful room filed with natural light, and everyone was encouraged to be fully engaged, even though many had not met before arriving. We were invited to take risks, speak from the heart, share what is useful or important with others, listen mindfully, be open to changing the agenda as the meeting needed, and have fun. We saw our work as naming, catalyzing, thinking and practicing together, building a field, and doing research.

The papers in this collection were prepared by the meeting participants to be read by each other before the meeting. They were not originally written for publication, but after reading them all we felt that their diversity makes a unique statement about Contemplative America and ought to be more widely available. The writers were asked to respond to, or be inspired by, a set of questions:

1. How do you define the term, "contemplative practice?"
2. Describe the development of contemplative practice in your sector over the past twenty-five years.
3. What organizations have developed to support contemplative practice in this sector?
4. Describe the demographics: who is participating?
5. What are the key trends, opportunities and challenges facing contemplative practice in your sector in the coming decade?
6. To what extent do you agree with the notion that a contemplative movement is emerging in America? What will be needed to nurture its growth?

The meeting was held in June 2010, and I was facilitating, having directed the Center for Contemplative Mind in Society for 15 years. During that time the Center provided opportunities for ordinary people, from litigators at the Federal Trade Commission to environmental leaders at the Wilderness Society and engineers at Google, to explore and experience practices like meditation, yoga, and mindful listening. We created space for them to ask questions about their work and their lives not asked in other contexts. Many people were profoundly affected by those experiences. At this meeting, I knew many but not all of the people in the room and knew that there was likely to be a rich discussion because of their diversity of backgrounds. I also knew that most religious and secular contemplatives didn't know each other's work and might be surprised by it. One of the issues that I was sure would come up because of this particular intermingling of secular and religious participants was what happens to practice when it is taken out of its original context, as when mindfulness practice is taught in the workplace or *lectio divina* in the classroom. When we interviewed leading contemplative teachers at the start of the Center, not all thought that practice had to be contained by religion, but most spoke of the need for at least a context, an ethical framework, and community. Parker Palmer had said, "Well, that's a fascinating question... Quakers would say, no, this comes from deep within the human self, the human psyche. On the other hand, to hold the paradox, I also think that traditions have much value to offer, and that among other things, tradition represents communities of people who can both help guide us in these practices and hold us accountable."

The meeting was in Kalamazoo, Michigan, at the Fetzer Institute, whose work for years has been to encourage love, forgiveness, and compassion in the world. While we were meeting, as if to remind us of the need, there was a rocket attack on a nationwide peace conference in Afghanistan, and the BP oil executives were deciding on their dividends while people in Louisiana were jobless and brown pelicans were dying on the shores of the Gulf. Recognizing that love, forgiveness, and compassion rarely flourish without practices to encourage them, Fetzer partnered with the Center in hosting this gathering to discuss the state of contemplative practice in America. Practices that are specifically designed to open the heart and deepen connection to others work directly to foster love and compassion. Others practices cultivate the capacity for asking forgiveness as well as giving and receiving forgiveness for oneself and others; supporting these are practices of letting go, grieving, and reconciliation. And yet other practices, which cultivate capacities from simple stillness to insight and wisdom, also develop awareness of the interconnectedness of life from which the actions of love and forgiveness can grow. Maybe there could be fewer dead pelicans in the future.

Contemplative practices are as old as the world's religions, part of the human heritage. They are practical, radical, and transformative. Every major religious tradition includes forms of contemplative practice, such as meditation, contemplative reading, silent time in nature, and yoga and other physical or artistic practices. Many practices remain rooted in their religions, and others have flourished in secular settings. Various kinds of ritual and ceremony designed to create sacred space and increase insight and awareness are also considered contemplative.

Until the past 40 years, when Westerners—from Thomas Merton and Allen Ginsberg to Ram Dass and Pema Chödrön—arrived home from Asia having learned practices in monasteries there, lay people rarely engaged in meditation and yoga and other contemplative practices. Even in Western monasteries they have been uncommon since the Reformation, when spiritual practices were washed away by the new currents that swept through Europe. And as Father Thomas Keating writes, "The Inquisition would send contemplation to hide fearfully in the corners of a few convents and monasteries." Now it is back, and at this meeting we had gathered to reflect on what was happening.

There were participants who had been introducing mindfulness practices into end-of-life care, trauma therapy, and the military. There was a journalist asking whether a mindful society was emerging. A Sufi leader, who was carrying on the work of his father and grandfather, sat next to a Catholic priest. A professor of contemplative psychology shared her methods with a law professor from San Francisco. Together, we set about exploring the lay of the contemplative land in America, and on the way we meditated and prayed together, listened to De Profundis ("Out of the depths I cry to you O Lord"), tried to listen to each other with beginner's mind, without judgment, and even laughed a lot.

The over-arching question for the meeting was: Is there a contemplative movement (or alliance or awakening) in America, and, if so, what is it? And what is its appropriate role? It's pretty clear that it is emerging from the grass-roots. As Dena Merriman said, "We're responding to something that is moving in society. We can't force it. It has to naturally unfold." In a traditional social or political movement, people typically have some awareness that they are part of that movement and make strategic (or not-so-strategic) choices in order to advance its cause. In the case of contemplative practice, even though there is a spontaneous emergence of contemplative practices and values across diverse fields, and it has moved from being inspired by a few charismatic teachers to finding its place in the mainstream of America, it is likely that many of the people and institutions involved wouldn't identify themselves as part of a larger whole and/or seek to work with others. One thing we were asking was whether that could be helpful. And whether our work can be simultaneously emergent and strategic.

Each participant shared some of his or her work and talked about why contemplative practice is important. Doug Burton-Christie talked about the importance of withdrawal before emerging to "inhabit the mind of Christ," the mind that knows and receives all things. Pir Zia spoke about Sufi beliefs: "There is no reality except the One Being." Arthur Zajonc, who teaches at Amherst College, asked us to reflect on how a contemplative context affects our knowing. Judy Lief talked about providing contemplative space for young nurses in a pediatric oncology center to talk to each other. Bobby Austin, who is a radio host, returned many times to how contemplative practice can cultivate "public kinship." Tom Callanan told us about his first experience of contemplative knowing: he was 10, he was in the woods, and he just *knew*. Someone quoted John of the Cross: "Let that quiet darkness be your whole mind."

Many questions suggested that more conversation would be fruitful: What is the relationship of this movement to indigenous spirituality? What is the shadow side of contemplation and the contemplative movement? How does the contemplative perspective relate to political views? What is the role of the arts? Of science?

We learned from each other. We were living witnesses to a contemplative America. We shared our stories. As Richard Rohr had recently written, "The only authority we have in other people's lives is what we ourselves have walked and what we know to be true." That is what we shared. We didn't write a manifesto. We didn't organize committees. We agreed to reflect on what we had learned.

A number of ideas emerged about how to encourage contemplative practice to grow in America. Maia Duerr had suggested four trends in her white paper, and our discussions expanded them:

1. Start with the end in mind; focus on the vision.
2. Design for depth.
3. Build bridges.
4. Make the linkages more apparent.

Start with the End in Mind; Focus on the Vision

We should consider shifting from encouraging the use of contemplative practices to emphasizing a vision of a society based on contemplative values, which offers people many avenues for participation. The Earth Charter and the Charter for Compassion are examples of this approach.

We acknowledged that people use diverse methods for cultivating contemplative qualities, some of which look traditional and others of which are defining new practices, especially in the areas of family, leadership and organization, and politics and activism. Here, we need to be ready to let go of fixed ideas and be receptive to new possibilities. The Tree of Practices on the Center's website illustrates diversity of practice. At the same time, everyone there supported "authentic" practice, but there are questions about who decides what is authentic.

Some thought that the election of President Obama was an indication that many people are hungry for a more compassionate, just, and respectful society. What might a society based on contemplative values look like? Suggestions included "marrying a rich inner life dedicated to the cultivation of loving-kindness and compassion with the practice of new forms of politics, economics and public policy" (Claudia Horwitz) to build a society committed to—

- Awareness of our inescapable mutual interdependence and its implications for the politics of a global society, "public kinship"
- Fulfillment of basic human needs and human rights for all
- Business with a bottom line that is not exclusively driven by power and profit but that promotes ethical, spiritual, compassionate, and ecologically responsible life

- Technology that is appropriate, sustainable and eco-friendly
- A medical profession committed to healing, wholeness, and compassionate decision making
- A justice system that encourages a lawyer to have compassion for his adversary while still being a zealous advocate for his client
- A military system that actively works to build constructive relationships and foster resilient human communities in the face of adversity
- An economics that looks carefully at the relation between consumption and the pursuit of happiness
- Sharing of religious and spiritual wisdom among traditions without attempts to convert.

Design for Depth

Many people expressed concern that the depth and integrity of practices could be lost when they are taught in secular settings, in short timeframes, without the support of experienced teachers and a community of practitioners. As people enter through the secular doors of stress reduction, emotional intelligence, or pain relief, can the practices resist become merely instruments toward these ends?

Arthur Zajonc spoke about depth in the Center for Contemplative Mind in Society's Academic Program: "In higher education, it's clear to me that there is a longing for a deepening of the spiritual dimension. But people don't know what that looks like. We've said, 'Here are the design principles of contemplative pedagogy, of contemplative inquiry.' These are terms we invented. We began to articulate in a public language what people are reaching for but for which they don't yet have a clear vision. They have a longing, and we had an idea and a practice that allowed that idea to come to realization." Three elements contribute to the success of the Academic Program, he noted: persistence, focus, and people. "If you just drop in and do one or two years of work [in a sector] and then leave, you're not likely to build anything of sustaining value…You need to be able to provide support, services, networking opportunities. This takes time, maybe 10 or 20 years to build a coherent movement." And the practices need to be taught in a way that allows people to begin with a specific need but to continue into places of depth and meaning.

Build Bridges

Another finding was the importance of the first rule of community activism, "meeting people where they are." In other words, it is essential to find the appropriate language and format for presenting contemplative practices in each context and to be willing to creatively adapt one's teaching goals and style. This flexibility has enabled contemplative practices to be successfully introduced to diverse groups of people, from grade school students to corporate executives to incarcerated men and women. At the same time, it is important to maintain the integrity of the practices so that they remain powerful methods for accessing the truth.

The pressing social needs of today ask us to go beyond the use of practice for individual liberation. During the meeting, Claudia Horwitz talked about how activists are transforming organizations and resolving conflict based on contemplative values and perspectives, which encourage one to choose new responses to old and familiar questions. Such practices have the capacity to heal the deep divisions that have built up over time (and have been manipulated for political gain) between people with different religious and political beliefs, and across economic classes and ethnic groups. Contemplative facilitators can bring together people on many sides of an issue and help them be heard, feel heard, and stay connected across differences.

Make the Linkages More Apparent

Continue to organize meetings that bring together people from diverse sectors so there is more awareness of how contemplative practices and values are being taught and more opportunity for creative collaborations. Some of the most interesting developments in the growing field of contemplative practice have come at the intersection of two or more sectors, such as health and politics, as when Rep. Tim Ryan (Ohio) spoke to the U.S. Congress in 2009 about the role that mindfulness practice could play in health care.

The meeting ended with a meditation led by Pir Zia and a prayer by Father Richard Rohr.

Only those who risk going too far
can possibly find out how far one can go.
—T.S. Eliot

Assessing the State of Contemplative Practices in the United States

Maia Duerr

> *There is an inner revolution taking place in our culture in which great numbers of people are becoming aware of the relationship of their inner lives to their outer lives.*
> — Rob Lehman, 1999

I. Introduction

A Powerful Silence: The Role of Meditation and Other Contemplative Practices in American Life and Work, published by the Center for Contemplative Mind in Society (Duerr, 2004), summarized the findings of a qualitative research project called "The Contemplative Net," sponsored by the Center from 2001 to 2004. This project was, to our knowledge, the first systematic effort to map the use of contemplative practices across a diverse group of secular settings including business, healthcare, education, law, social change, and prison work. In-depth interviews were conducted with 84 professionals who incorporated contemplative practices in their work. The data was then analyzed for recurring patterns and themes.

The report confirmed the growing use of contemplative practice in non-religious settings and that it was a phenomenon worthy of further study. Findings included:

- The use of contemplative practices in professional settings is on the rise.
- At the time *A Powerful Silence* was written, at least 135 companies, nonprofit organizations, and government agencies offered their employees classes in some form of meditation and/or yoga. The number of hospitals and medical clinics that provided Mindfulness-Based Stress Reduction training for patients had increased from 80 in 1993 to 250 in 2003.
- Individuals who regularly meditate or have other contemplative practices reported a difference in the quality of their work experiences and personal relationships.

- In addition to well-documented stress reduction benefits, interviewees described how contemplative practices helped to increase self-awareness and served as a vehicle for forgiveness and reconciliation. They reported a renewed sense of commitment to their work, improved workplace communication, and an increased ability to deal with organizational challenges. In addition, they spoke of how these practices enhanced their personal relationships with family, friends, co-workers, and significant others.
- The emergence of a new organizational paradigm: the "Contemplative Organization."
- Thirty-eight of the 84 interviewees (32%), many of them in leadership and/or managerial positions, described bringing contemplative practices into their workplace with the intention of creating a more reflective environment. Analysis of these interviews revealed a new organizational paradigm, one that uses contemplative awareness as an organizing principle for the workplace. In these companies and organizations, meditation and other practices are not simply add-on benefits but are incorporated into the structure of daily work and decision-making processes (Duerr, 2004).

Since *A Powerful Silence* was published, the use and integration of these practices in non-religious sectors has continued to grow. The purpose of this paper is to review the developments in this field over the last five years and to consider their implications.

For the purposes of the Contemplative Net project as well as for this paper, contemplative practices are defined as practices that quiet the mind in order to cultivate a personal capacity for deep concentration and insight. Examples include sitting in silence but also many forms of single-minded concentration including meditation, contemplative prayer, mindful walking, focused experiences in nature, yoga and other physical or artistic practices. Various kinds of ritual and ceremony designed to create sacred space and increase insight and awareness are also considered forms of contemplative practice.

In this framework, contemplative practices are distinct from more active forms of prayer (such as petitionary prayer), though not mutually exclusive. Active prayer and faith-based approaches tend to reinforce pre-existing religious, spiritual, and psychological beliefs. Contemplative practices, in contrast, emphasize direct experience and cultivate receptivity and openness.

II. What's Happened Since 2004?

A. Polls and Surveys on Contemplative Practices, 2005–2010

In the past five years, a number of polls and surveys have explored the role of religion and spirituality (including contemplative practices) in American life. Viewed collectively, the data from these studies indicates that the use of contemplative practices such as meditation and yoga continues to increase.

General Population

- The 2007 Pew Religious Landscape Survey found that "four-in-ten adults (39%) [say] they meditate at least once a week, compared with three-quarters of Americans who say they pray at least once a week. But meditation is a regular practice among most Buddhists (61% meditate at least once a week) and is also practiced on a weekly basis by majorities of Jehovah's Witnesses (72%), Mormons (56%) and members of historically black churches (55%)" (Pew, 2007).
- Among younger people, the Pew Survey found that "One-quarter of adults under 30 say they meditate on a weekly basis (26%), compared with more than four-in-ten adults 30 and older (43%). These patterns hold true across a variety of religious groups" (Pew, 2007).
- "The number of Americans who practice yoga at least twice a week jumped 133 percent, to 3 million this year [2006] from 1.3 million in 2001, according to a survey conducted by Mediamark Research" (Moran, 2006).

Health Care

- Among U.S. adults, the use of deep breathing exercises, meditation, and yoga for health purposes increased between 2002 and 2007 (Barnes, Bloom, & Nahin, 2007, p. 4).
- "A 2007 national Government survey that asked about CAM [complementary and alternative medicine] use in a sample of 23,393 U.S. adults found that 9.4 percent of respondents (representing more than 20 million people) had used meditation in the past 12 months—compared

with 7.6 percent of respondents (representing more than 15 million people) in a similar survey conducted in 2002. The 2007 survey also asked about CAM use in a sample of 9,417 children; 1 percent (representing 725,000 children) had used meditation in the past 12 months." (National Center for Complementary and Alternative Medicine website)

- The Garrison Institute's Initiative on Transforming Trauma (ITT) is currently conducting a mapping survey of the field of contemplative trauma care, led by Garrison Institute Senior Fellow Deborah Rozelle, Psy.D. and University of Michigan researcher Anthony King, Ph.D.

B. Cultural Observations

In addition to data from the above research, I suggest that there are some cultural markers to indicate this "movement" of applying contemplative practices in non-religious contexts is approaching a tipping point:

1. Mainstream Media Coverage of Contemplative Practices

Stories about the benefits of meditation and other practices are no longer published primarily in specialty publications, but appear with increasing frequency in venues such as *USA Today, The Huffington Post, The Wall Street Journal,* and *The New York Times.*

The 2010 PBS documentary "The Buddha" also played an important role in introducing many Americans to meditation, as well as its applications to fields such as health care, death and dying, law, and more. The film was viewed on its first PBS screening by 1.6 million people across the country. The show's companion website, which provided resources for learning to meditate, had more than 1.6 million hits by mid-April, 2010, and its Facebook page had 31,642 fans.

Media outlets that have traditionally focused on contemplative practices have also seen growth. For example, subscriptions to *Shambhala Sun* magazine grew 56% from 2004 to 2009. The March 2010 special issue called *A Guide to Mindful Living* was the bestselling issue in the magazine's entire history (Boyce, 2010).

2. Election of President Obama

Setting aside political affiliations, the election of President Obama in 2008 is one of the most interesting indicators that the American public has a strong yearning for a more contemplative way of being (albeit perhaps on an unconscious level). Mr. Obama embodies a number of qualities that are developed with contemplative practice: reflection, thoughtfulness, equanimity, and an emphasis on collaboration and interconnection. When he searched for his first Supreme Court nominee, for example, he looked for a "candidate with empathy." In a time when Americans seem to becoming more polarized, Mr. Obama's ability to respect points of view different than his own and to hold multiple truths—also dimensions of a contemplative perspective—is refreshing to many people.

3. Institutional Strength

A number of institutions devoted to the study and application of contemplative practices have been established in the past five years, including the Mindfulness Awareness Research Center (based at UCLA), the Association for Contemplative Mind in Higher Education, and the Center for the Investigation of Healthy Minds. Institutions that existed prior to 2005 have grown and extended the reach of their work, such as the Mind & Life Institute, the Center for Mindfulness Medicine, Health Care, and Society, the Center for Contemplative Mind in Society, and the Garrison Institute.

Collectively, the events and publications being put forth by these institutions are reaching a critical mass that is raising public awareness of the benefits of contemplative practices. See Table A on the following page for a list of selected key events from the past decade.

4. New Generation of Contemplative Leaders

Compared to five years ago, there are more people in leadership positions with contemplative backgrounds, and they are no longer primarily spiritual teachers. These leaders are making their own unique contributions to the contemplative process and its dissemination. Two examples in the world of technology are Meng Tan and Greg Pass. Both are engineers who are also students of meditation; they have applied their skills to design tools and structures that can support reflection and insight. (For more on this, see the Technology section below.)

5. Contemplative Responses to Current Events

Table B (on the following pages) presents a timeline that juxtaposes some of the major socio-political-historical events of the last decade with some of the key events in the "contemplative movement."

TABLE A
Selected Key Events in the "Contemplative Movement"
2000 – 2010

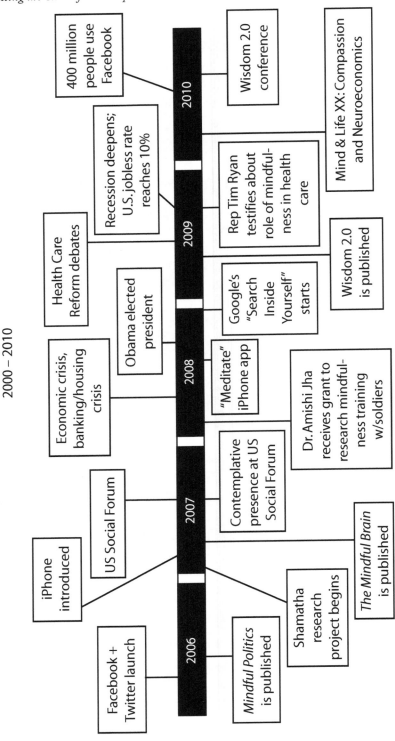

It would appear that we are becoming more skilled in creating relevant contemplative responses to contemporary situations—for example, a program of mindfulness retreats for military veterans and their families was developed in response to the many vets who returned home suffering from PTSD. And, compared to previous years, these responses are garnering more press coverage and public attention.

2000

- The Center for Contemplative Mind in Society organizes two retreats for Yale Law School faculty and students.

2001

- *Mindfulness Based Cognitive Therapy for Depression: A New Approach to Preventing Relapse*, by Zindel Segal et al, is published
- Mindfulness in Education Network (MiEN) starts

2002

- UC Davis Center for Mind and Brain established
- "Law and Contemplative Awareness: An Exploratory Gathering" held at the Fetzer Institute

2003

- Thich Nhat Hanh leads a retreat for U.S. Congress members
- First annual International Scientific Conference on MBSR
- *Time* magazine publishes entire issue on "The Science of Meditation"
- "Inviting the World to Transform: Building a Community of Change," gathering for social activists organized by the Center for Contemplative Mind in Society
- "Survey of Transformative and Spiritual Dimension of Higher Education" completed by the Center for Contemplative Mind in Society, for the Fetzer Institute

2004

- First Annual Mind & Life Summer Research Institute
- Mind & Life awards first round of grants for the Francisco J. Varela Research Award

TABLE B: Timelines
Key Socio-Political Events and the "Contemplative Movement"

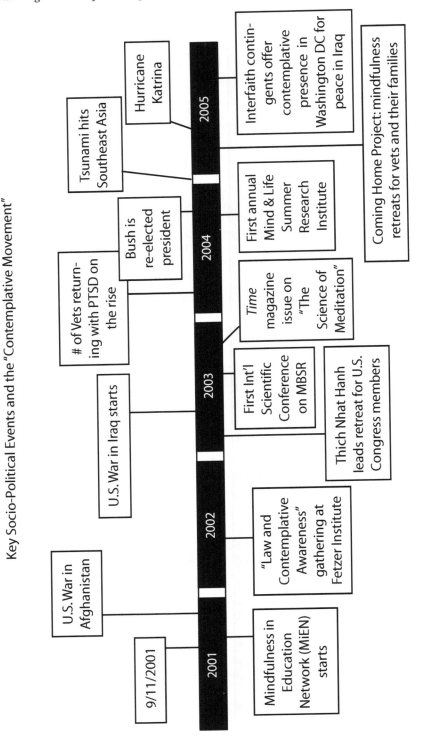

- Publication of *A Powerful Silence* by the Center for Contemplative Mind in Society

2005

- Coming Home Project begins; provides mindfulness retreats for military vets and families
- Publication of the Garrison Institute's *Contemplation and Education: Current Status of Programs Using Contemplative Techniques in K – 12 Educational Settings: A Mapping Report*
- Mind & Life XIII: The Science and Clinical Applications of Meditation
- Mindfulness Awareness Research Center (MARC) at UCLA is launched
- Interfaith religious contingents offer a contemplative presence at a Day of Action at the White House to call for peace in Iraq
- *Presence: An Exploration of Profound Change in People, Organizations, and Society,* by Peter M. Senge, C. Otto Scharmer, Joseph Jaworski, and Betty Sue Flowers, is published
- "Transforming the Culture of Organizing: A Gathering for Emerging Leaders," held at the Garrison Institute

2006

- Mind and Life Education Research Network (MLERN) starts
- *Mindful Politics, A Buddhist Guide to Making the World a Better Place,* edited by Melvin McLeod, is published
- *Radical Amazement: Contemplative Lessons from Black Holes, Supernovas, And Other Wonders of the Universe*, by Judy Cannato, is published

2007

- Shamatha Project launches—the most comprehensive attempt to scientifically study the effects of meditation
- The Stone House starts in Mebane, NC; retreat center dedicated to spiritual activism

- Contemplative presence at US Social Forum, organized by stone circles and others
- Mindfulness, Courage, and Reflection for Educators program launched by Center for Mindfulness
- Buddhist monks march in Myanmar/Burma in a mass nonviolent protest for human rights
- *The Mindful Brain: Reflection and Attunement in the Culture of Well Being,* by Dr. Daniel Siegel, is published
- *Making Waves and Riding the Currents: Activism and the Practice of Wisdom,* by Charles Halpern, is published

2008

- First "Zen Brain" event at Upaya Zen Center, bringing together neuroscientists and Buddhist teachers in a retreat for the general public
- Center for Compassion and Altruism Research and Education (CCARE) at Stanford launches
- Association for Contemplative Mind in Higher Education (ACMHE) starts
- "Meditate," a meditation timer iPhone app, is released
- Google's "Search Inside Yourself Program" starts

2009

- Mind & Life XIX meeting: Educating World Citizens for the 21st Century
- "The Contemplative Heart of Higher Education" conference, organized by ACMHE
- Symposium on Contemplative Practices for Army Care Providers held in Washington, DC
- Rep. Tim Ryan (D-OH) testifies in U.S. Congress about the role of mindfulness practices in health care, as part of Health Care Reform debates
- *Wisdom 2.0: Ancient Secrets for the Creative and Constantly Connected,* by Soren Gordhamer, is published
- *Mindful Teaching and Teaching Mindfulness,* by Deborah Schoeberlein and Suki Sheth, is published
- Soren Gordhamer starts regular blog on mindfulness and technology for *Huffington Post*

- Barry Boyce's "Mindful Society" column begins in *Shambhala Sun* magazine

2010

- "The Buddha" documentary airs on PBS, with companion website
- Mind & Life XX meeting: Altruism and Compassion in Neuroeconomic Systems held in Zurich, Switzerland
- Wisdom 2.0 conference on the mindful use of technology held in Silicon Valley

C. The Use of Contemplative Practices by Sector

The 2004 *Powerful Silence* report covered five sectors: Business, Medicine/Science, Education, Law, and Prison Work. In a paper of this brief length we are not able to cover all the developments in these areas, but a review of key events over the past five years shows that two sectors from the original report are of particular significance: Medicine/Science and Education. And we see the emergence of contemplative practices applied in two new sectors: Technology and the Military.

1. Medicine / Science

The proliferation of scientific research on contemplative practices (particularly meditation and mindfulness) is one of the most remarkable trends of the past five years.

As recently as 2007, a report commissioned by the National Center for Complementary and Alternative Medicine (NCCAM) found that, "…firm conclusions on the effects of meditation practices in healthcare cannot be drawn based on the available evidence…It is imperative that future studies on meditation practices be more rigorous in design, execution, and analysis, and in the reporting of the results" (Opsina et al., 2007, p. 210).

However, a number of high caliber research designs have been carried out more recently by university-based, well-respected scientists such as Dr. Clifford Saron (UC Davis), Dr. Richard Davidson (University of Wisconsin/Madison), and Dr. Amishi Jha (University of Pennsylvania). The Shamatha Project is of special note. Based at the University of California Davis, it is the largest and most comprehensive attempt to study changes brought about by meditation.

Overall, the number of studies on contemplative practices has increased dramatically during this time period (see Table C). The quality of these studies, larger sample sizes, and more comprehensive findings are dramatically raising the profile and utility of this research. Combined with previous findings from research on MBSR (Mindfulness Based Stress Reduction), this wealth of data is creating legitimacy for contemplative practices, and is providing people in leadership positions with excellent data to justify the application of these practices, not only in health care but in other fields as well.

Two of the most important institutions dedicated to the scientific study of contemplative practices and health care marked significant milestones in these past five years.

The Center for Mindfulness in Medicine, Health Care, and Society (also known as CFM, and founded by Jon Kabat-Zinn) celebrated its 30th anniversary in 2009. In the 24 years from 1979 to 2003, 13,000 people completed MBSR courses. In the five years from 2003 to 2008, an additional 5,000 people completed MBSR courses. As of May 2001, 563 MBSR practitioners are listed in the CFM directory. MBSR continues to have a prominent presence in health care, but also now in business, education, prisons.

The Mind & Life Institute, which held its first meeting between His Holiness the Dalai Lama and scientists in 1987, experienced a decade of phenomenal growth. Mind & Life annual meetings on topics such as "The Science and Clinical Applications of Meditation" (2005) have gained increasing notice in the media and among the general public. In 2003, the Institute launched the Mind and Life Summer Research Institute (MLSRI), and has held the MLSRI annually since then. More than 200 graduate students, post docs, junior and senior faculty, contemplatives and philosophers have attended each of the MLSRIs, with attendance at the 2009 meeting topping 300. Along with the Varela Research Awards, the MLSRI has become a powerful catalyst for developing the emerging field of Contemplative Neuroscience and Clinical Science.

Table C: PubMed Search of Published Studies Related to Selected Contemplative Practices

Category/Intervention	Years	Number of Articles
All articles		
Mindfulness meditation	2000 - 2004	69
Mindfulness meditation	2005 - 2009	252
MBSR (Mindfulness-based Stress Reduction)	2000 - 2004	44
MBSR	2005 - 2009	122
Clinical Trials		
Mindfulness meditation	2000 – 2004	12
Mindfulness meditation	2005 – 2009	72
MBSR	2000 – 2004	11
MBSR	2005 – 2009	35

And finally, two closely related memes have emerged in popular culture during the last few years: neuroplasticity and mental fitness. The concept of neuroplasticity is becoming part of the common parlance now, receiving coverage in mainstream media such as *The Wall Street Journal* (Begley, 2004) and *The New York Times* (Holt, 2005; Aamodt and Wang, 2007). From 2000 to 2004, three articles in the *New York Times* referenced neuroplasticity; from 2005 to 2009, the *Times* published 12 articles on the topic. In December 2007, PBS aired a documentary titled "Brain Fitness Program and Neuroplasticity." The Canadian Broadcasting Centre aired *The Brain that Changes Itself* in January 2009, based on the best-selling book of the same title by Dr. Norman Doidge (2007). The work of Drs. Richard Davidson and Antoine Lutz has been especially instrumental in demonstrating the relationship between meditation and neuroplasticity.

2. Education

Seismic shifts are happening in the integration of contemplative practices at both K–12 and higher education over the past five years. Naropa University (founded in 1974) and the California Institute of Integral Studies (founded in1980) helped to pioneer contemplative education; then institutions like the Center for Contemplative Mind in Society and others built on that foundation. Several research studies have helped in recognizing this phenomenon and documenting the individuals and organizations that have played a role in it:

- "The Survey of Transformative and Spiritual Dimensions of Higher Education" (Duerr, Zajonc, and Dana, 2003), funded by the Fetzer Institute, documented academic programs and other initiatives in North American universities and colleges that incorporated transformative and spiritual elements of learning, including contemplative practices.
- A mapping survey conducted by the Garrison Institute (2005) identified 33 K–12 schools and educational institutions that incorporated a contemplative approach into their pedagogy.
- UCLA's Spirituality in Higher Education Survey, conducted from 2003 – 2010, found that students show the greatest degree of growth in five spiritual qualities if they actively engaged in self-reflection, contemplation, or meditation. The survey also found that these kinds of practices have uniformly positive effects on traditional college outcomes. The study included interviews and focus groups with 14,527 students attending 136 colleges and universities nationwide.

The Mindfulness in Education Network (MiEN), which began in 2001 as an informal group of educators who were students of Buddhist teacher Ven. Thich Nhat Hanh, has grown into a more formal organization and has hosted annual national conferences since 2008. MiEN has been instrumental in building relationships between teachers, parents, students, and others who are interested in the integration of mindfulness in education.

A landmark national conference on "Contemplative Practices in Education: Making Peace in Ourselves and in the World," held at Teachers College, Columbia University, in February of 2005, may have been the first event to put this framework on the national map. Other major events in recent years have included:

- "Mindfulness as a Foundation for Teaching & Learning: A Conference for Educators, Counselors and Administrators," organized by MiEN (2008)
- Mind & Life XIX meeting: "Educating World Citizens for the 21st Century," featuring His Holiness the Dalai Lama (2009)
- "The Contemplative Heart of Higher Education," organized by ACMHE (2009)

In 2006, *the Teachers Record* (published by Columbia University), regarded as one of the leading publications in educational research and scholarship, devoted an entire issue to the theme of "Contemplative Practices and Education," with articles by Robert Thurman, Arthur Zajonc, Steven Rockefeller, and Mirabai Bush, among others. A research paper by Shapiro, Brown, and Astin (2008) helped to link neuroscientific findings on meditation with potential benefits in education.

A number of organizations and networks dedicated to the intersection of contemplative practices and education have emerged over the past five years. These include:

- Association for Contemplative Mind in Higher Education (ACMHE)
- Association for Mindfulness in Education
- Between Four Eyes
- The Hawn Foundation
- The Impact Foundation
- The Initiative on Contemplation and Education (The Garrison Institute)
- The Inner Kids Foundation

Other organizations that place a high value on contemplative practices as part of a vision for transformative learning for both students and teachers include the Academy for the Love of Learning, Passage Works, HeartMath, ChildSpirit Institute, and the Center for Courage and Renewal.

Thanks in large part to the work of the Center for Contemplative Mind in Society's Academic Program and its Contemplative Fellowships, "contemplative knowing" is now seen as a serious complement to critical thinking in the field of higher education. There are initiatives and academic institutes dedicated to contemplative studies at Brown University, City University of New York, and the University of Michigan in Ann Arbor, to name a few examples.

3. Military

Global violence and U.S. military action has been the backdrop for much of the past decade, starting with the September 11, 2001, attacks on the World Trade Center and the Pentagon, and progressing to wars in Afghanistan and Iraq as well as the unbounded "war on terrorism."

The financial, physical, and emotional costs of combat have been high. A study from the U.S. Army Surgeon General's office estimated that 15% to 20% of all soldiers fighting in Iraq and Afghanistan show signs of depression or post-traumatic stress disorder (PTSD) (Zoroya, 2008). *The Huffington Post* reported that the suicide rate among 18- to 29-year-old men who've left the military went up 26% from 2005 to 2007, according to the Veterans Affairs Department (Hefling, 2010). Caregivers for these soldiers and their families are also experiencing deleterious effects (Duerr, 2009).

In this climate, contemplative practices are emerging as an effective intervention. In 2005, Zen Buddhist teacher Joseph Bobrow started the "Coming Home Project" to offer mindfulness retreats and counseling services to returning veterans and their families. Yoga classes offered at Walter Reed Army Medical Center helped soldiers find some reprieve from PTSD symptoms (Rivers, 2008).

A number of research and treatment projects utilizing meditation and other contemplative practices has been commissioned and funded by the U.S. Army. Some of these include:

- Chaplain (MAJ) Robert Williams began working with the Center for Contemplative Mind in Society on the "Military Care Providers Project" in 2008. In 2009, the U.S. Army and the Center co-organized a symposium in Washington, DC, that brought together military personnel and contemplative teachers (including Norman Fischer, Mirabai Bush, and Sharon Salzberg) to discuss how to deliver mindfulness to Army chaplains, medics, and other care providers. Retreat participants will be measured for increases in attention and compassion by the Center for Compassion and Altruism Research and Education at Stanford University.

- The Army's RESPECT-Mil program incorporates meditation, tai chi, qi gong, and other modalities to address physical symptoms and PTSD, according to Brigadier General Loree K. Sutton, M.D., who is the highest ranking psychiatrist in the U.S. Army and director of the Defense Centers of Excellence for Psychological Health and Traumatic Brain Injury (Steele, 2010).
- In 2009, principal investigator Dr. Amishi Jha, of the University of Pennsylvania, and Elizabeth Stanley, Professor at the Walsh School of Foreign Service and Dept. of Government at Georgetown, received $2 million from the Department of Defense to determine whether mindfulness training could help soldiers going into combat to stay focused and make good decisions. Findings from the pilot study show improvements in mood and working memory (University of Pennsylvania, 2010). The study is now training 240 soldiers at Schofield Barracks Training and Research Center on Neurobehavioral Growth.

Engagement with military institutions raises interesting ethical questions for contemplative practitioners about the nature of peace, war, and practice. There is no easy answer to these questions, but it's clear that a high level of physical and emotional suffering are present in this sector, and the need for skillful interventions will be ongoing for years to come.

4. Technology

According to the 2004 Pew Internet and American Life Project, 64% of online Americans use the Internet for faith-related reasons—nearly 82 million people. (Hoover, Clark, and Rainie, 2004). This appears to be the most recent demographic research on the use of the Internet and religion/spirituality, but we can surmise that this number has increased in the last five years.

During this same period of time, we have become increasingly dependent on technology to interface with many daily tasks (the iPhone is a case in point), and many of us have been part of the meteoric rise of social networking in the form of applications like Facebook and Twitter.

The emergence of a contemplative perspective in the technology sector has been percolating in the last few years. It has taken the form of tech tools that have the potential to support contemplative practices, such as the "Meditate" and yoga applications for the iPhone and on-line audio and video meditation sessions, as well as a larger conversations on the topic. As meditation teacher and writer Soren Gordhamer puts it, "The great challenge of our age is not only to live connected to one another through technology, but to do so in ways that are beneficial to our own well-being, effective in our work, and useful to the world" (Wisdom 2.0 website).

Leading executives and engineers in several high profile Silicon Valley companies who have studied meditation are now bringing this perspective into their work. Greg Pass, the Chief Technology Officer of Twitter, is a longtime student of meditation and leads a weekly qi gong class for employees. Bradley Horowitz, the Vice President of Product Management at Google, has practiced meditation for 25 years.

Perhaps most famous of all is Meng Tan, an early employee of Google who worked as a software engineer at the company and is now head of Google University's School of Personal Growth, where he oversees the mindfulness-based program called "Search Inside Yourself." Meng originally thought of offering MBSR to Google employees, but found that no one registered for the course. Then he began to work with Mirabai Bush, Norman Fischer, and Daniel Goleman to develop a curriculum on "Mindfulness Based Emotional Intelligence" which launched in 2009. One hundred and forty employees signed up right away. There have also been lectures by a number of well-known Buddhist teachers, including Sharon Salzberg, Lama Surya Das, Matthieu Ricard, and Jon Kabat-Zinn.

The basic practices in the course are mindfulness, lovingkindness, and compassion, but, as Meng said, "We also intended for it to be an effective Emotional Intelligence curriculum for adults (perhaps the first of its kind in the world) that can be applied in the workplace and that is helpful both to increasing businesses profits and to people achieving more success in their careers."

In April 2010, Soren Gordhamer organized the "Wisdom 2.0" conference, the first large-scale event to bring together two previously disparate topics: technology and mindfulness. The two-day event, held at the Computer History Museum near San Jose, CA, drew more than 300 people and featured business and technology leaders such as Tony Hsieh (CEO of Zappos), Meng Tan, and Greg Pass, as well as contemplative teachers such as Roshi Joan Halifax. There are plans to hold the event again in 2011.

At a Wisdom 2.0 talk on the aesthetics of Twitter, Greg Pass described Twitter as an invitation to experience a moment in time more deeply, to give "extraordinary attention" to something in our lives that might otherwise pass us by. Of course not everyone will use Twitter in this manner, but the fact that a leading engineer has the aspiration for it to be used in this way is remarkable.

Although there is often a tendency to view technology as an obstruction to a mindful life, Roshi Joan Halifax reminded the audience that it has a great capacity to connect us, to give us new modes of expression, and to mobilize us to act from compassion. However, technology can also lead to dissociation and isolation if not used with mindfulness.

III. What Will Nurture the Growth and Development of a Contemplative Movement in America?

Is there really a "Contemplative Movement"? In a traditional social or political movement, people typically have some awareness that they are part of that movement and make strategic (or not-so-strategic) choices in order to advance its cause. In this case, even though there is a spontaneous emergence of contemplative practices and values across diverse fields, it is likely that many of the people and institutions involved wouldn't identify themselves as part of a larger whole. Sociologist Paul Ray's theory about "Cultural Creatives" (2000) might be a useful analogy here:

> While Cultural Creatives are a subculture, they lack one critical ingredient in their lives: awareness of themselves as a whole people. We call them the Cultural Creatives precisely because they are already creating a new culture. If they could see how promising this creativity is for all of us, if they could know how large their numbers are, many things might follow. These optimistic, altruistic millions might be willing to speak more frankly in public settings and act more directly in shaping a new way of life for our time and the time ahead...When we discovered the great promise of this new group, we set out to hold up a mirror for them, so they could see themselves fully (Cultural Creatives website).

As in the case of Cultural Creatives, by naming this phenomenon we are helping people to become aware of it, perhaps thereby facilitating the next steps in its evolution.

The data and anecdotal evidence from these past five years suggests that contemplative practices are being used by more people and they are finding a normative place in American life. But are contemplative values actually being internalized or is this a more superficial level of adoption? What are the indicators that these values are being internalized?

I would suggest that we are not just looking for an increase in the numbers of people who meditate, but rather for indications that the qualities nurtured by contemplative practices are taking deeper root and supporting a cultural shift. What would a society based on contemplative values look like? Some of the elements of it might include (Bush, 2010):

- Awareness of our inescapable mutual interdependence and its implications for the politics of a global society
- Fulfillment of basic human needs and human rights for all
- Business with a bottom line that is no longer exclusively power and profit but one that promotes ethically, spiritually, compassionate, and ecologically responsible human life
- A medical profession committed to healing, wholeness, and compassionate decision making
- A justice system that encourages a lawyer to have compassion for his adversary while still being a zealous advocate for his client
- An economics that looks carefully at the relation between consumption and the pursuit of happiness

In the process of working toward this deeper level of integration, some of the challenges we need to be aware of include:

- The American propensity toward consumerism; the tendency to turn everything into a commodity, and to look for an "easy fix."
- Fear and misunderstanding of what contemplative practices are; suspicion that someone is trying to "take away" one's religious beliefs or convert one to another religion.
- Our own tendency to be evangelistic about these practices. (The case of a 2003 "anti-stress" ballot measure in Denver, Colorado, is instructive. The initiative would have required the city to implement community-wide steps such as mass meditation sessions, piping soothing music into public buildings, and serving natural foods in school cafeterias. The measure was soundly defeated and was the object of much ridicule.)

Here are four suggestions for addressing these challenges and for taking this nascent movement forward to the next stage of evolution:

1. Start with the End in Mind

This may seem counterintuitive, but it may help to focus on our end goal, on our biggest vision, rather than the specific means to get there. We can consider shifting the framework from encouraging the use of contemplative practices and instead emphasize a vision of a society based on contemplative values, which offers people many avenues for participation. The Charter for Compassion, sponsored by the Fetzer Institute, is an excellent example of this.

Again, the election of President Obama may be seen as an indication that many people are hungry for a kinder, gentler, and more respectful society. How can we use this strong desire to inspire people? Paul Gorman, former director of the National Religious Partnership for the Environment, suggested that, "The values and qualities that we love so much about Obama need to be named and more broadly owned." As Gorman defines it, the challenge for us is to identify and claim these values in our own lives rather than project them onto a person or an organization.

Related to this, it will be important to recognize that people have diverse ways of cultivating these qualities, some of which may look like "traditional" contemplative practices and others of which will help to define new kinds of practices. Here, we need to "walk our talk" and be ready to let go of fixed ideas and be receptive to new iterations of contemplative practice.

2. Design for Depth

The Center for Contemplative Mind in Society's Academic Program (established in 1997) provides a good case study on how to make a systemic impact.

Arthur Zajonc, the program's director, said, "In higher education, it's clear to me that there is a longing for a deepening of the spiritual dimension. But people don't know what that looks like. I think this is where the Center [has provided] leadership. We've said, 'Here are the design principles of contemplative pedagogy, of contemplative inquiry.' These are terms we invented, and now I am hearing them everywhere. You begin to articulate in a public language toward which people are reaching but for which they don't yet have a clear vision. Where they have a longing, you have an idea and a practice that allows that idea to come to realization."

According to Zajonc, three elements have contributed to the success of the Academic Program: persistence, focus, and people. He noted, "If you just drop in and do one or two years of work [in a sector] and then leave, you're not likely to build anything of sustaining value...You need to be able to provide support, services, networking opportunities. This takes time to build, over 10 or 20 years, to build a coherent movement."

The Center's Academic Program has created a wide-range of activities that serve this constituency including: conferences on both regional and national levels, summer sessions on curriculum development, academic fellowships, an e-newsletter, monthly webinars, publications, practice retreats, and a professional membership-based organization (the Association for Contemplative Mind in Higher Education). The program has also worked in partnership with well-respected educational organizations such as the American Council of Learned Societies, an effective strategy for establishing legitimacy with more traditional institutions.

The result has been a growing number of academic institutions that are embracing the idea of contemplative education and supporting their faculty in this endeavor. Because of the Center's long-term commitment to this goal and diversity of strategies to meet it, the concept of contemplative education is now deeply rooted in higher education.

3. Build Bridges

Another finding from the original Contemplative Net study was the importance of "meeting people where they are." In other words, it is essential to find the appropriate language and format for presenting contemplative practices, and to be willing to creatively adapt one's teaching goals and style in the service of the context. This has enabled these practices to be successfully introduced to a diverse group of people, from grade school students to corporate executives to incarcerated men and women. Google's Meng Tan has been extremely successful at doing this. When asked if he was introducing Buddhism into corporate life, Meng said, "I'm not interested in bringing Buddhism to Google. I am interested in helping people at Google find the key to happiness."

The 2009 Symposium on Contemplative Practices for Army Care Providers brought together members of two different cultures: the military and the contemplative. The dialogue that transpired was very informative about how to begin building bridges between two cultures. Both groups agreed that it was crucial that mindfulness trainers understand the world view and language of the military participants. For example, military culture places a high value on being a "Warrior" and the language often emphasizes strength. In contrast, contemplative teachers frequently present practices like meditation in the context of "opening up to pain" and accepting the condition of things "just as they are." The potential for resistance and misunderstanding is high if we do not take these differences into account and plan for them. As Norman Fischer noted, contemplative practice is not value-neutral. We need to be aware and respectful of the differences in our backgrounds in order to effectively work together.

Perhaps one of the most pressing needs in the U.S. today is the capacity to heal the deep divisions that have built up over time (and have been manipulated for political gain) between people with different religious and political beliefs, and across economic classes and ethnic groups. There is a great need for facilitators who can bring together a room full of people on "both" or all sides of an issues and help people to be heard, to feel heard, and to stay connected across differences. These skills can be developed and supported through the use of contemplative practices. One interesting funding area to consider would be a project to support a cadre of facilitators with a contemplative perspective who can work in "hot spots," e.g., the immigration issue in Arizona, the health care debates around the United States.

In such situations, a great deal of intention and effort is required to understand each other's point of view and to truly respect differences. But the payoff can be great. By being willing to cross borders, as it were, to work with people we might not normally imagine as contemplative practitioners, we may realize a whole new dimension of contemplative practice and stretch our own boundaries in the process.

4. Make the Linkages More Apparent

Continue to organize meetings like this June 2010 Fetzer gathering that bring together people from diverse sectors so there is more awareness of how contemplative practices and values are being applied, and opportunities for creative collaborations. Some of the most interesting developments in this "movement" have come at the intersection of two or more sectors, such as when Rep. Tim Ryan spoke to the U.S. Congress about the role that mindfulness practice could play in health care in 2009. This represented a contemplative presence in politics, health care, and science, simultaneously.

Notes

Barnes P.M., Bloom B., Nahin R.L. (2008) "Complementary and alternative medicine use among adults and children: United States, 2007." *National health statistics reports; no 12*. Hyattsville, MD: National Center for Health Statistics.

Begley, S. (November 5, 2004). "Scans of Monks' Brains Show Meditation Alters Structure, Functioning." *The Wall Street Journal* (Washington D.C.): p. B1. Accessed online: http://psyphz.psych.wisc.edu/web/News/Meditation_Alters_Brain_WSJ_11-04.htm

Boyce, B. (May 12, 2010). Personal correspondence.

Bush, M. (April 19, 2010). Personal correspondence.

Davidson, R. and Lutz, A. (2008). Buddha's Brain: Neuroplasticity and Meditation. *IEEE Signal Processing Magazine,* January 2008. p 176.

Doidge, N. (2007). *The Brain That Changes Itself.* New York: Viking.

Duerr, M. (2009). *The Use of Meditation and Mindfulness Practices to Support Military Care Providers: A Prospectus.* Center for Contemplative Mind in Society.

Duerr, M. (2004). "The Contemplative Organization." *Journal of Organizational Change Management,* Volume 17, Number 1, 2004, pp. 43–61(19).

Duerr, M. (2004). *A Powerful Silence: The Role of Meditation and Other Contemplative Practices in American Life and Work.* Center for Contemplative Mind in Society.

Garrison Institute (2005). *Contemplation and Education: Current Status of Programs Using Contemplative Techniques in K – 12 Educational Settings: A Mapping Report.*

Hefling, K. (January 11, 2010). "Suicide Rate of Veterans Increases Significantly for Former Soldiers 18–29". *The Huffington Post* website. Accessed online: http://www.huffingtonpost.com/2010/01/11/suicide-rate-of-veterans-_n_418780.html.

Holt, J. (May 8, 2005). "The Way We Live Now: Of Two Minds". *The New York Times* (New York City, NY). Accessed online: http://www.nytimes.com/2005/05/08/magazine/08WWLN.html?scp=12&sq=neuroplasticity&st=nyt.

Hoover, H. M., Clark, L. S., & Rainie, L. (2004). "Faith online: 64% of wired Americans have used the Internet for spiritual or religious purposes." *Pew Internet & American Life Project.* Retrieved November 14, 2006 from http://www.pewinternet.org/pdfs/PIP_Faith_Online_2004.pdf.

Moran, S. (December 28, 2006). "Meditate on This: Yoga is Big Business." *The New York Times* (New York City, NY). Accessed online: http://www.nytimes.com/2006/12/28/business/28sbiz.html.

National Center for Complementary and Alternative Medicines (NCCAM) website: http://nccam.nih.gov/health/meditation/overview.htm.

Ospina M.B., Bond T.K., Karkhaneh M., Tjosvold L., Vandermeer B., Liang Y., Bialy L., Hooton N., Buscemi N., Dryden D.M., Klassen T.P. (2007)/*Meditation Practices for Health: State of the Research. Evidence Report/Technology Assessment* No. 155. (Prepared by the University of Alberta Evidence-based Practice Center under Contract No. 290-02-0023.) AHRQ Publication No. 07-E010. Rockville, MD: Agency for Healthcare Research and Quality.

Pew Forum on Religion & Public Life (2007). *U.S. Religious Landscape Survey, Summary of Key Findings*, page 13. Accessed online: http://religions.pewforum.org/reports#.

Pew website: http://pewforum.org/Age/Religion-Among-the-Millennials.aspx.

Ray, P. (2000) *Cultural Creatives.* New York: Harmony Books.

Rivers, E. (2008). "A Breath of Hope: Walter Reed Tries Yoga to Counter PTSD." *The Washington Post,* May 6, 2008. Accessed online: http://www.washingtonpost.com/wp-dyn/content/article/2008/05/02/AR2008050203426.html.

Shapiro, S., Warren, K. and Astin, J. with Duerr, M. ed. (2008). *Toward the Integration of Meditation into Higher Education: A Review of Research.* Prepared for the Center for Contemplative Mind in Society.

Steele, D. (2010). "Brain Injuries Require Systematic, Holistic, Integrated Treatment: An Interview with BG Loree Sutton" *Army USA,* May 2010, 39–48.

University of Pennsylvania (February 15, 2010). Press release: "Building Fit Minds Under Stress: Penn Neuroscientists Examine the Protective Effects of Mindfulness Training." Accessed online: http://www.upenn.edu/pennnews/news/building-fit-minds-under-stress-penn-neuroscientists-examine-protective-effects-mindfulness-tra.

Wisdom 2.0 website: http://www.wisdom2summit.com/About.

Zoroya, G. (2008). "A Fifth of Soldiers at PTSD Risk." *USA Today,* March 6, 2008. Accessed online: http://www.usatoday.com/news/world/iraq/2008-03-06-soldier-stress_N.htm.

The Blue Sapphire of the Mind: Christian Contemplative Practice and the Healing of the Whole

Douglas Burton-Christie

See everything
and ourselves in *everything*
healed and whole
forever.[1]
— Rainer Maria Rilke

To crave and to have are as like as a thing and its shadow. For
when does a berry break upon the tongue as sweetly as when one
longs to taste it, and when is the taste refracted into so many
hues and savors of ripeness and earth, and when do our senses
know anything so utterly as when we lack it? And here again is
a foreshadowing—the world will be made whole. For to wish
for a hand on one's hair is all but to feel it. So whatever we may
lose, very craving gives it back to us again. Though we dream
and hardly know it, longing, like an angel, fosters us, smooths
our hair, and brings us wild strawberries.[2]
— Marilynne Robinson

In his treatise *On Thoughts*, the fourth century monastic writer Evagrius of Pontus likens the experience of contemplation to dwelling in a kind of place. "When the mind has put off the old self and shall put on the one born of grace," says Evagrius, "then it will see its own state in the time of prayer resembling sapphire or the color of heaven; this state scripture calls the place of God that was seen by the elders on Mount Sinai."[3] This description of contemplation is, like many accounts of spiritual experience in early Christian monastic literature, an approximation of something utterly mysterious and ultimately beyond expression. And yet, as is so often the case in the Christian contemplative tradition, language and images are brought to bear upon the

A version of this paper originally appeared in Sewanee Theological Review, *54:3 (Pentecost 2011), published by The School of Theology of The University of the South in Sewanee, Tennessee.*

task of articulating what cannot, at least not fully, be said or imagined. One of Evagrius's most important contributions to the discourse of early monastic spirituality is his insistence that pure prayer is "imageless," an indication of how seriously he took the challenge of penetrating beyond ideas and images of God for the sake of God. In this account, however, he employs both geography and color to describe the true character of contemplation. These images are drawn from the Exodus account that describes the extraordinary experience of Moses and the Jewish elders on Mt. Sinai. There, we are told, they "beheld the God of Israel. Under his feet there appeared to be sapphire tilework, as clear as the sky itself" (Exodus 24:10).

This account and others like it played a crucial role in shaping the early Christian understanding of contemplation. Evagrius, like his contemporary Gregory of Nyssa, configured the mountain as an imaginative space, a symbolic landscape capable of evoking and illuminating the contemplative's deepest experience of God. In transposing the geographical image of Moses' encounter with God on Sinai to the inner life of the monk, the "place of God" became almost indistinguishable from the "place of prayer."[4] And yet, in a move that reflects Evagrius' vigilance to guard against any literal reading of these images, he insisted that dwelling in this "place" required a radical renunciation of all images, even the image of the "place of God." This is the meaning of Evagrius's claim that: "The mind...when it is in prayer...is in a light without form, which is called the place of God."[5] Here and elsewhere in Evagrius's writings one encounters what feels like an impossible paradox: the experience of contemplation at its deepest level is utterly imageless; and yet the mind in prayer seems like a space saturated with light the color of sapphire or like a place— "the place of God." Still, this is a paradox that Evagrius insists must be accommodated if the monk is to remain open to an experience of prayer that is true and deep.

*   *   *

This vision of the monk completely subsumed into the life of God, living *in* God, is one of the most sublime and compelling expressions of contemplative experience in all of early Christian monastic literature. Its specific character is rooted in Evagrius's particular perspective on the monastic journey, especially his insistence on the need to seek God in a place beyond all images and language. Still, it is consistent with the testimony about the ultimate end of monastic life that has come down to us from so much of the early Christian monastic tradition. And it is rooted in an image of place, a place that has existence both in the physical world and in the world within. It is a vision of the whole, suffused by a sense of God's presence, and it is consciousness of this whole that the early Christian monks sought to cultivate through their contemplative practice.

If we consider the sense of place out of which this contemplative vision arose, it becomes necessary to acknowledge two related truths. For Evagrius and many other early Christian monks, Mt. Sinai was less important as an actual place than it was as a symbol of a certain intimacy with God the contemplative might hope to realize on the inner journey. Even so, the evocation of the mountain and the sapphire-blue tiles remains an important reminder of the intricate relationship that exists between the outer and inner landscapes, and of the way the physical landscape can spark thought, open the imagination, deepen awareness. The mountain became a place toward which the monk could direct his gaze, a point of orientation, an emblem of the awesome and charged space of his own inner life. Still, it was not only a symbol. Many of Evagrius's monastic contemporaries lived under the shadow of the great mountain. For them, Mt. Sinai existed not simply as a place of the imagination, part of an inner landscape, but also as a place of concrete specificity, the particular landscape in which their lives unfolded. It is here that they gave themselves over to the daily rhythm of monastic living that served as the ground out of which the contemplative vision articulated by Evagrius and others arose.

This contemplative vision arising from the ancient Christian monastic world expresses a hunger still present and familiar to us at the dawn of the twenty-first century: the longing to live with an awareness of the whole. And it speaks to the promise inherent in all great spiritual traditions of the world, that the human mind (or heart or soul) is capable of expanding and deepening to such an extent that it becomes possible to incorporate everything and to be incorporated into everything: to exist and know oneself as existing within the whole. To dwell in the place of God, as Evagrius puts it, is to live with a particular intense awareness of this reality, to know oneself not as a solitary, autonomous being but as one whose identity can only be conceived of as existing within an encompassing web of intricate relationships. The primary work of contemplative practice is to become more aware of this web of relationships, to learn to live within it fully and responsibly and to give expression to it in one's life. That such awareness is understood to be the fruit of long practice, an expression of a gradual transformation of consciousness that can only come about through a sustained process of self-reflection and a gradual relinquishment of the ego's tenacious attachments is one of the most valuable insights arising from contemplative traditions of spiritual practice.

Nor should the potential contribution of such contemplative traditions to the work of reknitting a broken, fragmented world be underestimated. To retrieve a vision of the world as whole—through sustained attention to the underlying unity that connects all beings to one another and to the root causes in our thought and practice that contribute to the deepening fragmentation of self, community and world—is necessary to the work of healing that is at the heart of any sustained ecological renewal.

*   *   *

We are now facing the very real possibility that such a vision of the whole has been rendered unimaginable and unrealizable by the sheer range and extent of the ecological degradation afflicting the world. One of the most potent and enduring images of our precarious condition to have emerged from the literature of ecology during the past twenty five years—of the natural world as an archipelago of ecologically impoverished islands—suggests that fragmentation is *the* fundamental reality with which we must now contend.[6] This image of widespread ecological fragmentation—one that reflects the growing loss of biodiversity and ecological integrity that is increasingly evident throughout the world—raises serious questions about whether it is still meaningful to speak of cultivating a vision of the whole, and whether any spiritual practice can help to mend this torn fabric.

The contemplative tradition in which Evagrius and the other Christian monks stand was itself formed in an historical moment of intense and widespread loss, in which the social and cultural fabric that had long bound life together in the ancient Mediterranean world had begun to fray to the breaking point. This particular tradition of spiritual practice emerged in part as a response to this tearing of the fabric, and represented an a sustained effort to face it with courage and honesty, all the while remaining open to the possibility that paradise—a world whole and untarnished—might yet be rediscovered. The blue sapphire of the mind of which Evagrius speaks—that condition of serene and encompassing awareness of being immersed in the all—did not arise spontaneously in the life of the monk in a kind of blissful ignorance of suffering and loss, but emerged through long struggle, through a sustained practice of examining the sources of the alienation and fragmentation that afflicted the monks and their society. Contemplative practice meant opening oneself to the long, difficult process of relinquishing one's attachment to the ego's isolating and alienating power and realizing in oneself a more encompassing, whole vision of reality. It was thus, the monks believed that they could best contribute toward the reknitting of the torn fabric of the world. This contemplative vision resonated profoundly among their contemporaries in Late Antiquity, for whom these monks came to be known simply as: "T[hose] by whom the world is kept in being."[7]

This is an audacious claim. But it echoes similar claims found in many other spiritual traditions regarding the significance to the wider community of those who devote themselves to such contemplative work. In its most profound expressions, such contemplative work can be understood as undertaken on behalf of the world and as contributing toward its healing and restoration. Indeed, the aim of contemplative living, in its widest application, is to address the fragmentation and alienation that haunts existence at the deepest possible level and, through sustained practice, come to realize a different, more integrated way of being in the world. Here, amidst the inevitable fragmentation of existence, the contemplative seeks to recover a vision of the whole and a new way of living in relationship to the whole.

*　　　　　*　　　　　*

It was a little more than thirty years ago that I first visited the Cistercian monastery of Our Lady of New Clairvaux, located amidst walnut and prune orchards near the Sacramento river in Central California. Sometime before, I had come across a copy of Helen Waddell's translation of the sayings of the Desert fathers. What I read there so moved me that I knew, without quite understanding why, I had to find my way to an actual monastery. My experience during the four days I spent at New Clairvaux changed everything for me, most significantly my understanding of prayer. I had been raised to think of prayer as a discursive activity, a conscious form of communication between the human person and God. The prayer I was invited into during those days certainly included such discursive expression. But it went much deeper, into a place of silence and mystery I had never encountered before. It also included, I realized, not simply the liturgical life of the monks centered in the church, but every aspect of their life in that place—manual labor, common meals, study, sleep, everything. It also encompassed the place itself. To stand in silence before God in prayer and then to move out into the fields to harvest walnuts and then to return once again into the space of prayer was to participate in the ancient Benedictine rhythm of *ora et labora*—prayer and work. I did not fully grasp the utterly integrative, sacramental character of this experience at the time, but I began to intuit even then that here was an approach to living that was whole and undivided. There was no inner life, no outer life, but simply a life lived in the presence of God in which everything was included, nothing excluded.

I speak of an ideal of course. Over the years, as I have come to know and participate in the life of different monastic communities, and given myself over to careful study of the classic texts of this tradition, I have realized more fully than I did at the time what it is to give oneself over to the contemplative life as a *project*, and how this project remains ever unfinished, always unfolding. Still, it is a vision of life that I continue to find immensely compelling, and I have devoted much of my life to the task of interpreting the contemplative traditions of Christianity in terms that can be retrieved and adapted for contemporary use. It is has been a source of unending astonishment to me to discover how many and various are the possible adaptations of these contemplative traditions. Far from being of interest only to monks, the contemplative vision of life, I have discovered, speaks in a compelling way to a wide range of persons seeking to live their lives with a greater sense of authenticity and purpose. To live contemplatively, in this sense, can be understood simply as a certain intense way of being alive, grounded in a conscious awareness of the depth and beauty of one's own soul and one's relationship to God and the whole of existence.

Still, the Christian contemplative tradition, in particular the primitive tradition of ancient Egytian monasticism, is insistent that the acquisition of such awareness is a long, difficult process, requiring a disciplined attention to the sources of our own fragmentation and alienation and a commitment to a kind of therapeutic process whereby the soul can be remade in God, restored to its original image and likeness. Part of what makes the contemplative approach to spiritual renewal so compelling is its honesty about the depth of our alienation and the effects of this alienation on our lives and on the world. Renewal is possible, the contemplative tradition maintains, but for it to be sustained and meaningful it must touch into the very roots of our being.

I confess that for a long time I understood this renewal process largely in personal, even individual terms. But through an ongoing participation in the lived experience of actual contemplative communities—initially with the monks at New Clairvaux, then with a group of Cistercian nuns at Redwoods monastery near the California coast, and eventually with monks on Mt. Athos, at St. Catherine's near Mt. Sinai and at St. Antony's monastery in the remote Red Sea desert of Egypt—my sense of the *wholeness* of contemplative experience began to grow and deepen. And I began to realize that this sense of wholeness was there from the beginning of the Christian monastic tradition. By wholeness, I mean not only the ancient contemplatives' feeling for the living world—although the stories evoking the monks' simple awareness of the beauty of the desert, or appreciation for its deep silence, or wonder at the prospect of kindling intimate reciprocity with other living beings give important expression to the paradisal dream which was so central to their lives. I also mean the monks' intense commitment to *pay attention*, out of which emerged a sense of compassion and responsibility for the broken world.[8] The desert tradition understood the contemplative as one who opened himself to a long, difficult process of purification, not only for his own sake but for the sake of the larger community. Here, I began to see, was an utterly compelling vision of *koinonia*, in which the work of personal renewal was inextricably bound up with a vision of renewal of the whole.[9]

The ancient monks had a sober and honest understanding of how extensively the fabric of their world had become torn and frayed. The brutality of the late Roman empire had reduced entire communities to fragmented, impoverished places and this apocalyptic reality profoundly shaped the monks' understanding of their contemplative vocation. To engage in an act of *anachoresis* or withdrawal was to seek in solitude not an escape, but a means of reconstituting a broken whole. The images that became so central to the early monastic vision—of monks engaged in a fierce struggle against nameless forces within and without, and of others dwelling in a still-fresh paradise—suggest how encompassing their contemplative practice was for them and what it meant for them to work toward such a restoration in their lives, and the life of the society and world of which they were a part.

*   *   *

Still, the question of whether such a vision of contemplative renewal is still viable for us, can inform efforts to reweave the frayed fabric of *our* world, is real. Nowhere, I think, is this question more pressing for us in the present moment than in relation to the growing ecological degradation whose presence now pervades nearly every aspect of our lives, permeating both conscious and unconscious dimensions of our being.[10] Gradually it is beginning to dawn on us that we are living through a time when our very sense of the integrity of the living world is being shaken to the core. Biologists have helped us to see more clearly than ever before that the fabric of life has been torn deeply, perhaps irrevocably, and we now face the prospect of living in a permanently degraded world.[11] This is in almost every sense an utterly overwhelming prospect, one that is immensely difficult to absorb into our consciousness, much less respond to. Even finding language to account for all we are losing is often beyond us; it is too painful. Still, it is becoming clear is that whatever else may be said of the loss we are experiencing, it has become for many part of an acute spiritual crisis. We are losing not only species and places in the natural world. We are losing the Beloved Other.

I have come to believe that it is precisely our growing awareness of the immensity and preciousness of what we are losing that makes a retrieval of contemplative thought and practice so urgent in the present moment. Nowhere else in our common spiritual discourse do we find thought and practice so oriented toward helping us open up our awareness to the immensity of the whole and to its meaning for our lives. And it finds striking echoes in the emergence among contemporary writers of a spiritual vision that poet Denise Levertov suggests is rooted in "a more conscious attentiveness to the non-human and…a more or less conscious desire to immerse the self in that larger whole."[12] It is here, in the "affinities of content" between ancient contemplative discourse and the still-emerging poetic vision of the natural world that the seeds of what I am calling "contemplative ecology" can be found.[13] To orient oneself towards the non-human world in this way, to give one's conscious attention fully and deeply to a place, an animal, a tree or a river is already to open oneself to relationship and intimacy with another. It is to see and feel the presence of the other not as an object, but as a living subject. To experience this other as part of "a larger whole," part of a vibrant and complex ecology, and to seek to immerse oneself in that larger whole, is to open oneself completely and without reservation to what Thomas Merton called the hidden ground of love, that encompassing mystery within which we live and move and have our being. "[B]y being attentive, by learning to listen (or recovering the natural capacity to listen which cannot be learned any more than breathing)," Merton said, "we can find ourselves engulfed in such happiness that it cannot be explained: the happiness of being at one with everything in that hidden ground of Love for which there can be no explanation."[14] Openness to this ground involves risk, an acceptance of the kind of vulnerability and the merging of identities that contemplatives often speak of in relation to God. I believe the recovery of such intimacy and reciprocity may well turn out to be foundational to any genuine and lasting restoration of the natural world.

Still, the question of what kind of response this experience will call forth in us, and how we can transform an intuition, a moment of awareness, into a way of living, remains. This is not far from the central question with which the great ecological writer Aldo Leopold struggled in his *Sand County Almanac*, a question he ultimately answered in a kind of credo. "We can be ethical," he said, "only in relation to something we can see, feel, understand, love, or otherwise have faith in."[15] Leopold had a contemplative's sense of the importance of coming to see and know a place intimately and deeply and became convinced that without a real effort to cultivate such intimacy, our efforts to learn how to live in the natural world thoughtfully and ethically will not be sustainable. He came to think of this as the work of cultivating what he called an "ecological conscience." This idea, that ecology must include the human struggle to see and understand the world as part of an encompassing whole, became one of Leopold's most important and enduring insights. This meant not simply following an ethical code (as important as this is), but searching out the deepest sources of our relationship with the natural world, opening ourselves to a new awareness of who we are in the world. To achieve a deep and lasting change in our awareness and our practice, Leopold understood, would require a willingness to engage in the equivalent of what contemplative spiritual traditions have commonly referred to as an "examination of conscience."

In a justly famous section of the *Sand County Almanac* called "Thinking Like a Mountain," Leopold memorably recounts a painful experience as a young man that provoked in him a profound examination of conscience and brought him to the threshold of a new awareness of his own relationship to the whole. He was traveling with friends in the rimrock country of Arizona, when a wolf with several cubs suddenly appeared below them crossing a river. "In those days," he says, "we had never heard of a passing up a chance to kill a wolf. In a second, we were pumping led into the pack…when our rifles were empty, the old wolf was down, and a pup was dragging a leg into impassable slide rocks." What happened next completely undid him.

> We reached the old wolf in time to watch a fierce green fire dying in her eyes. I realized then, and have known ever since, that there was something new to me in those eyes— something known only to her and to the mountain. I was young then, and full of trigger-itch; I thought that because fewer wolves meant more deer, that no wolves would mean hunter's paradise. But after seeing the green fire die, I sensed that neither the wolf nor the mountain agreed with such a view.

Leopold's experience suggests how important the transformation of one's awareness can be to the work of cultivating a meaningful ecological ethic. Also how mysterious it is. The unexpected force of the "fierce green fire" in the wolf's eyes seems to have unnerved him. But what did it mean? He could not say, at least not precisely. "There was something new to me in those eyes—something known only to her and to the mountain." Leopold takes care to honor the mystery of this encounter. And nothing in his subsequent reflections on the ecological significance of wolves in their environment undermines this sense of mystery. He wants to understand how the ecosystem works, and what intricate pattern enables wolves and deer and mountains to exist together. But there is something in this pattern that eludes and will always elude precise explanation, something to do with its wild character. "Perhaps this is the hidden meaning in the howl of the wolf," suggests Leopold, "long known among the mountains, but seldom perceived among men." It cannot be fully known; it is too deep and mysterious. Still Leopold makes it clear that we have a greater capacity to open ourselves to this mystery than we have acknowledged or expressed, and that until we learn to open ourselves more fully to wild world, until we learn to "think like a mountain," we will have nothing but "dustbowls, and rivers washing the future into the sea."[16]

*   *   *

To "think like a mountain." Few ideas have come to resonate more deeply in our emerging ecological consciousness than this one. The sense that we possess the capacity for cultivating a more encompassing awareness of the wild world and of living from the center of this awareness is alluring and exciting. Nor is it difficult to imagine how a deepening of such thinking might contribute to the work of repairing the world. The task of integrating such awareness into our individual and collective lives clearly remains unfinished. But as way of understanding what it might mean to inhabit the world more fully and thoughtfully, Leopold's vision remains crucial. It is, I believe, a fundamentally contemplative vision of the world. And its contemplative character is one of its most important contributions to the ongoing work of engaging our broken fragmented world. Leopold understood, as the early Christian monks did, that the simple act of gazing, of paying attention—one of the most ancient and enduring ways of understanding contemplative practice—can open up a space in the soul, a space where the world may live and move in us.

In the midst of a deepening ecological crisis, do we still have the capacity to cultivate an authentically contemplative way of living? Can we learn again to experience and express our deepest sense of affinity with the living world, to develop both the sensibilities and practices that allow us to engage the living world not merely as an object but as a subject—as Beloved Other? I believe such a vision of living is still possible for us. But we have yet to acquire the kind of moral and spiritual honesty required to bring it into being. Perhaps we do not really want to see the world and take it in so deeply, or tend to it as if it were part of the fabric of our soul. It would be too costly. Still, the alternative is too bleak to imagine. Nor will superficial responses suffice. We stand at a critical threshold, in which nothing less than the whole of our being will need to be poured into the task of tending to the broken world. The retrieval of ancient traditions of contemplative thought and practice can play a critical role in helping us do so. The Christian contemplative tradition has its own distinctive contributions to make to this common work, especially through its recognition of the value of the long, purifying struggle in which the self can rediscover its own authentic ground, a ground shared with God and all living beings.

Certainly the Christian contemplative tradition is not unique in its commitment to such radical spiritual transformation. But it has developed its own idioms and practices oriented toward helping persons and communities live with a more encompassing awareness of the sacred ground of all things. This distinctive contemplative sensibility is not only taking hold within the Christian community, but is also finding echoes and resonances in diverse places beyond the Christian community. Indeed, there is evidence that something like a shared contemplative idiom is beginning to emerge in contemporary thought and practice, especially in response to the growing threat to the natural world.[17] Simply finding language adequate to account for all we are losing has become immensely difficult. And while part of this task no doubt involves describing, intricately and carefully, the characteristic features of places and species that are under threat, another part of the work involves finding language that can begin to express the *value* of these beings to us, language strong and resonant enough to provoke a meaningful response.

*   *   *

Consider, for example, how the language of *ultimacy* and *necessity* has entered into our discourse about the meaning of the natural world in contemporary experience. Often these ideas have no explicit religious meaning. But increasingly they are coming to be associated with the sense of the sacredness of nature. Their use in contemporary ecological discourse signals, I believe, a growing sense that we cannot do without language and symbols that touch into the depths of our common experience. We are still struggling to find a shared language of the sacred that can ground and galvanize the work of community building, political resistance, and ecological preservation. Such contemplative language—supple, fluid and open—might provide a good place from which to begin.

How, for example, can we learn to express the deepest or most ultimate ground of our shared concern? The twelfth-century Dominican mystic Meister Eckhart famously employed the image of the *grunde* or ground to express the deepest dimension of the soul, that enables human beings to recognize and dwell within the divine. It is, Eckhart claimed, "the purest thing that the soul is capable of…the noblest part…indeed…the very essence of the soul which is the soul's most secret part…. Here God's ground is my ground and my ground is God's ground."[18] For Eckhart, the ground of the soul stands at the center of everything that exists, in us, in God and in the world. Contemplative living is nothing more or less than a simple awakening to this ground. This is a beautiful and capacious idea that can help us grasp the underlying unity of all being and the intimate relationship that exists between and among all living beings. Still, if we ask what it might mean to bring this classical spiritual ideal to bear upon our contemporary efforts to create a stronger and more enduring sense of connection with the living world, we may need to attend more carefully to the concrete reality of the ground in our lives, that is the places where we actually live. This is what Scott Russell Sanders attempts to do in his thoughtful meditation on place, *Staying Put,* offering a kind of bioregional reading of this ancient spiritual ideal. "The likeliest path to the *ultimate* ground," says Sanders, "leads through my local ground. I mean the land itself, with its creeks and rivers, its weather, seasons, stone outcroppings, and all the plants and animals that share it. I cannot have a spiritual center without having a geographical one…. If our interior journeys are cut loose entirely from…place, then both we and the neighborhood will suffer."[19] There are clear echoes here of the old philosophical-mystical idea of the ground of being. But Sanders wants to extend and broaden the way we understand this ground, and invite us to reconsider where we look for it. There is always a danger among spiritual practitioners of detaching the soul's quest from the actual material world. Thinking about this ground in relation to our singular, embodied existence in place can help us reclaim the radical immanence of the divine that was certainly implicit in Eckhart's teaching, even if it has not always been taken seriously in the subsequent contemplative tradition. Detach our ultimate concerns from the gritty details of our actual world, as we have too often done, and "both we and the neighborhood will suffer." Instead, this contemplative vision suggests, it is here in the life and texture of particular places—noticed, cherished, cared for—that this *ultimate* ground can and must be discovered.

Reorienting contemplative practice in this way toward the local and the particular is also helping us retrieve a sense of the utter preciousness of the living world. We are learning again how to value particular places, particular living beings, and how to consider more deeply what is essential and *necessary* in our lives. The ancient Christian contemplative tradition meditated long and hard on Jesus' teaching on the need to value and attend to what he called "the one thing necessary (Luke 10:42)." Indeed, acquiring the gift of discernment—learning to distinguish what is crucial or necessary from what is extraneous or secondary—has always been understood as one of the hallmarks of mature contemplative thought. But what is "the one thing necessary?" To what are we called to attend with our whole heart and soul? The classical response to this has always been "God" or "the soul." This is still a meaningful response. But in an historical moment of increasing spiritual diversity, in which a shared understanding of neither "God" nor "soul" can always be assumed, we continue to struggle ways to account for the source of our deepest values and allegiances. The contemplative idiom is coming alive again in the present moment, but in surprising and unlikely forms that its ancient practitioners would hardly have imagined. But like them, are coming to recognize in our own way the importance "one thing necessary," the cultivation of a simple, spacious awareness of the whole that may yet help us rediscover what it is to live in the world with purpose, meaning and depth.

Montana writer William Kittredge touches on this question in his simple articulation of the meaning of the sacred. "To me," he says, "sacred means necessary." At its root, he acknowledges, this necessity may be primarily biological or psychological. "We evolved in nature, with other animals.... Isolate us from nature too long, as individuals, as societies, and we start getting nervous, crazy, unmoored, inhabited by diseases we cannot name, driven to thoughtless ambitions and easy cruelties."[20] He echoes here the diagnosis of Paul Shepard, who argues in his book *Nature and Madness* for "the necessity of a rich nonhuman environment" as crucial to healthy psychological development in human beings.[21] But Shepard freely acknowledges the rich, inclusive character of the human relationship with the natural world, in particular its importance for helping us form a meaningful spiritual life, and a connection with the living world that is both deep and encompassing. "[E]cological reality (flowers-bees, bears-salmon) become satisfying otherness in their own right and metaphorical sign images or messages about the inner world, the binding forces of human society, and the invisible spiritual realm."[22] It is in response to this rich, relational reality, in profound poetic response, through play, storytelling, song, and dance that we come to know who we are in the world, that we come to know the ground of our own being, the ground of the world, ultimate ground. Becoming aware of this rich ecological reality, coming to feel it as part of one's own being and learning to live in reciprocal relationship to it is, to use Kittredge's term, so necessary. A sacred task.

*   *   *

These pointed allusions to the *ultimate ground* of our existence as rooted in our encounter with the living world, to the *necessity of the sacred* found in and through our relationships with other living beings, reveal the growing importance of contemplative thought and practice in contemporary experience. The ancient traditions of contemplative practice will continue to haunt and inform our own efforts to attend thoughtfully and deeply to "the one thing necessary." But increasingly, we will need to find a means of integrating the teaching of these ancient traditions into our own emerging sense of the living world as sacred and necessary. We know, intuitively, what it means to dwell in the "place of God," to "think like a mountain," to "see everything/and ourselves *in* everything/healed and whole/forever." But our ability to do so has become severely diminished and must be renewed if we are to have any hope of reversing the patterns of neglect and destruction that have come to characterize our attitudes towards the natural world. A sustained commitment to contemplative practice may well be crucial if we are to discover again an authentic way of living in the world, rooted in attitudes of reverence, reciprocity and responsibility.

Notes

1 Rainer Maria Rilke, *Duino Elegies (Eighth Elegy)*. This version is cited by Pierre Hadot in his essay "The Sage and the World," in *Philosophy as a Way of Life*, edited and with an introduction by Arnold I. Davidson (Oxford, Blackwell, 2005), p. 258. Hadot draws upon Rilke's intuitive sense of the whole (or the "Open") to illuminate, by analogy, the meaning of the contemplative vision through which some ancient philosophers sought to locate themselves fully within the cosmos. "The contemplation mentioned by Seneca is…a kind of unitive contemplation. In order to perceive the world, we must, as it were, perceive our unity with the world, by means of an exercise of concentration on the present moment." (p. 261). For another rendering of Rilke's notion of what can come of dwelling in what he calls the "Open," see: *Duino Elegies and the Sonnets to Orpheus*. Translated by Stephen Mitchell (New York: Vintage, 2009), pp. 50–51: "It sees all time/and itself within all time, forever healed."

2 Marilynne Robinson, *Housekeeping* (New York: Farrar, Strauss and Giroux, 1980), p. 152.

3 Evagrius, On Thoughts, 39. *Evagrius of Pontus: The Greek Ascetic Corpus*. Translated by Robert E. Sinkewicz. Oxford and New York: Oxford University Press 2003), p. 180. See also Reflections 2: "If someone would want to behold the state of the mind, let him deprive himself of all mental representations, and then he shall behold himself resembling sapphire or the color of heaven (Exod. 24: 9-11). It is impossible to accomplish this without impassibility, for he will need God to collaborate with him and breathe into him connatural light." (Sinkewicz, *Evagrius*, p. 211).

4 See Evagrius, On Prayer, 56 and 57, where "place of God" is juxtaposed to "place of prayer." Sinkewicz, *Evagrius of Pontus*, p. 198.

5 Evagrius, Reflections, 20. Sinkewicz, p. 213. Columba Stewart, "Imageless Prayer and the Theological Vision of Evagrius Ponticus," p. 197, notes: "The place of God is, by definition, 'unimaged,' meaning that the mind itself, when it becomes the place of God, is free of self-created imagery."

6 This image and much of the discussion of island biogeography contained in this essay comes from the work of David Quammen, *The Song of the Dodo: Island Biogeography in an Age of Extinctions* (New York: Scribner, 1996).

7 *Lives of the Desert Fathers*, Trans. Norman Russell (Kalamazoo: Cistercian Publications, 1981), p. 50.

8 On the practice of prosoche or attention within ancient philosophical practice and early Christian monasticism, see: Pierre Hadot, *Philosophy as a Way of Life* (Oxford: Blackwell, 1995), pp. 126–144.

9 Athanasius's *The Life of Antony* is the most significant of the early monastic texts to reflect on this question. See: Athanasius of Alexandria, *The Life of Antony and the Letter to Marcelinus*. Translation and Introduction by Robert C. Gregg (New York: Paulist, 1980). For a thoughtful historical analysis of the monk's role in reconstituting society, see: Peter Brown, *The Making of Late Antiquity* (Cambridge, MA: Harvard University Press, 1978); "The Rise and

Function of the Holy Man in Late Antiquity," in *Society and the Holy in Late Antiquity* (London: Faber and Faber, 1982).

10 Increasingly, we are becoming aware of the unconscious depths of our current environmental predicament, the sense in which the broken, unhealed dimensions of our inner lives is contributing to the destruction of the world. There is a striking affinity between the reflection on this question arising from ancient Christian monasticism and the work of contemporary psychoanalytic thinkers. See: Harold Searles, "Unconscious Processes in the Environmental Crisis," in *Countertransference and Related Subjects* (New York: International Universities Press, 1979). Shierry Weber Nicholsen, *The Love of Nature and the End of the World: The Unspoken Dimensions of Environmental Concern* (Cambridge, MA: MIT, 2002).

11 David Quammen, *The Song of the Dodo: Island Biogeography in an Age of Extinctions* (New York: Scribner, 1996).

12 Denise Levertov, *New and Selected Essays* (New York: New Directions, 1992), pp. 4–6.

13 "Contemplative Ecology" can best be understood as one expression of a diverse and wide-ranging body of thought and practice—including what is sometimes referred to as "spiritual ecology" or "ecological spirituality"—that has come to occupy an increasingly important place in contemporary thinking about the natural world. They point to a growing recognition that there is a dimension of the human experience of nature, perhaps a dimension of the natural world itself, that transcends simple, materialistic explanations, that requires an honest attempt to create a wider field of discourse in which natural phenomena and the experience of the transcendent (however it is construed), can be understood as part of a single, unbroken reality. See for example, David Kinsley, *Ecology and Religion: Ecological Spirituality in Cross-Cultural Perspective* (Englewood Cliffs, NJ: Prentice Hall, 1995); Sallie McFague, *Super, Natural Christians: How We Should Love Nature* (Minneapolis: Fortress Press, 1997); Mark I. Wallace, *Finding God in the Singing River: Christianity, Spirit, Nature* (Minneapolis: Augsburg Fortress, 2005); Sarah McFarland Taylor, *Green Sisters: A Spiritual Ecology* (Cambridge, MA: Harvard University Press, 2007).

14 Thomas Merton, *The Hidden Ground of Love: The Letters of Thomas Merton on Religious Experience and Social Concerns*, ed. William H. Shannon (New York: Farrar, Strauss and Giroux, 1985), p. 115. [letter to Amiya Chakravarty, April 13, 1967] .

15 Aldo Leopold, *A Sand County Almanac* (New York: Oxford University Press, 1949), p. 214.

16 Leopold, *A Sand County Almanac*, pp. 129–132.

17 One of the most intriguing signs of a the revival of contemplative practice and ideals in the present moment that takes it far beyond the confines of monastic practitioners is something that is coming to be known as the "slow living movement." The progeny of this still-developing movement are many—slow knowledge, slow food, slow design, slow cities, slow travel and slow thought among others. See Carl Honoré, *In Praise of Slowness: Challenging the Cult of Speed* (New York: HarperOne, 2005). Carlo Petrini, *Slow Food Nation: Why Our Food Should be Good, Clean, Fair* (New York: Rizzoli, 2007); David Orr, "Slow Knowledge," in *The Nature of Design: Ecology, Culture and Human Intention* (New York: Oxford University Press, 2004), pp. 35–42.

18 Meister Eckhart: *Sermons and Treatises, Vol I.* trans. and ed. M. O'C. Walshe (Longmead: Element, 1987), pp. 3, 117.

19 Scott Russell Sanders, *Staying Put: Making a Home in a Restless World* (Boston: Beacon, 1993), chap. 5.

20 William Kittredge, *Who Owns the West* (San Francisco: Mercury House, 1996), p. 108.

21 Paul Shepard, *Nature and Madness* (San Francisco: Sierra Club, 1982), p. 129.

22 Shepard, *Nature and Madness*, p. 112.

Action and Contemplation:
A Christian Perspective

Richard Rohr

The terms active and contemplative became classic Catholic and Christian language in the twelfth and thirteenth centuries with the rise of the new mendicant Orders in the church, particularly the Franciscans, Dominicans, and Carmelites, who were called "friars" because they were making a clear structural break with the older monastic orders, like the Benedictines and Cistercians, or even from the eremetical communities like the Camaldolese or the Carthusians.

St. Thomas Aquinas had to do a major "Defense of the Mendicant Orders" at the University of Paris in 1252. The regular, or "diocesan" clergy, who took care of the parishes and the sacramental life of the people, were always considered the "active" ministers in the church, and those who went off to monasteries were the "contemplatives" who separated themselves from the people and active ministry.

Now St. Francis and St. Dominic initiated a new form of ministry in the church that was supposed to be both! This seemed like a compromise on both ends, and of course, some turf wars were going on too. The monks resented our popularity with the people, and our mobility. The clergy also resented our popularity with the people, because we were carrying an aura of "contemplation," education, and depth that they did not always enjoy. Plus we wore classy outfits, called religious habits, which have lasted to this day. Give men a fancy uniform, and they will come!

What we were seeing in the history of spirituality in the West, is that the older tradition of wordless, silent, apophatic prayer that was found, for example, in the Desert Fathers and Mothers, in Celtic Christianity, and still taught at many monasteries for centuries, was beginning to be lost, in favor of the daily chanting of psalms, religious devotions, and often elaborate processions, para liturgies, and the major liturgy of the Mass. The kataphatic tradition was coming to totally dominate the church, and suddenly we have men like Francis of Assisi spending more than half of his year in caves, hermitages, and wandering in nature. This was new and dangerous.

No longer were religious men (it would take the women a few more centuries to be freed from their enclosures, starting with groups like the Ursulines,

Daughters of Charity, and the Sisters of Mercy) bound to chanting office from huge copied Psalters in choir stalls. Now we were on the move, and had to find a way to maintain inner silence and prayer while being in the midst of everything. Friaries were ordinarily built right in the middle of the cities, whereas monasteries were always outside of town. You will tend to see Franciscan and Dominican churches to this day in the heart of most older European cities, soon joined by Servites, and then Augustinians and Carmelites, who modified their older heremetical or coenobitical traditions to the new "friar" model. These five groups were known as the Mendicant Orders, and began the practice of what was called "the mixed life" of active service and yet contemplative practice.

The very words give away the change, a monk lived monachus or alone, with the emphasis on solitude, silence, even in community. The friar was a form of the Latin based word for brother. He was no longer alone but was supposed to be a brother to the people, and not necessarily a cleric either. The great bound psalters of the 150 psalms were not abbreviated into what are still called "breviaries" that could be carried around in one's pocket.

But now the real task began. How do you actually achieve it? One wonders if it was still not a rare achievement to be engaged and yet centered, active and yet contemplative, working in this world and yet living, as it were, in another. I have always said two things, when people ask me about the long, cumbersome name of our center in Albuquerque, The Center for Action and Contemplation.

- I deliberately put the word action first because I do not believe you have anything to contemplate until you have been in the field for a while and personally experienced your own lack of integration, and how very hard it is.
- The most important word in our name is not action nor is it contemplation, but it is AND! That is the great art form, to be grounded, peaceful, and operating from your positive Center when you are working, and when you are sitting to be holding with God the pain and suffering and concerns of the world—consciously!

In our 23 years of existence, we have sponsored at least four internships a year, in which we take 6 – 12 people on an immersion experience living with the poor in Juarez, Mexico. They are prepared not just with very practical logistics, but also there is training and practice of contemplation before, during, and after the experience.

I imagined when I began the Center in 1987 that we would teach contemplative practice 50% of the time, and we would then teach liberation theology and do some solid social analysis the other 50% of the time. Now 23 years later, we probably do 80% of our teaching on contemplative mind, practice, and "fallout," and we increasingly find that the requestioning of our politics, economics, and American foreign and military policy takes care of itself, because people are slowly detached from both their ego positions, their fear, and the American dominant consciousness, which largely reinforces an uncritical attitude toward capitalism, war, and our gross consumerism.

We also emphasize an experiential form of education, which allows people by moving out of middle class America, to come to many of their own conclusions. We never need to push or persuade people. Simply changing positions does the teaching, much better than any ideological harangue.

I would like to largely spend the rest of our time explaining to you our vision and mission statements, along with our 8 Core Principles. I think this will be as good an analysis of the integration that we seek as anything.

The Center for Action and Contemplation Supports a new reformation From the inside!

- In the spirit of the Gospels
- Confirming peoples' deeper spiritual intuitions
- Encouraging actions of justice rooted in prayer
- With a new appreciation for, and cooperation with, other denominations, religions, and cultures

Our mission:

"We are a center for experiential education, encouraging the transformation of human consciousness through contemplation, equipping people to be instruments of peaceful change in the world."

Our core principles:

- The teaching of Jesus is our central reference point (criterion[1]).
- We need a contemplative mind in order to do compassionate action (process).
- The best criticism of the bad is the practice of the better. Oppositional energy only creates more of the same (emphasis).
- Practical truth is more likely found at the bottom and the

edges than at the top or the center of most groups, institutions, and cultures (perspective).

- We will support true authority, the ability to "author" life in others, regardless of the group (non tribal).
- Life is about discovering the right que stions more than having the right answers (primacy of discernment).
- True religion leads us to an experience of our True Self and undermines my false self (ultimate direction).
- We do not think ourselves into a new way of living, but we live ourselves into a new way of thinking (praxis over theory).

As far as an overview of how this is happening in general, I would say that it is professed as an ideal by many, many groups, but the art form as such is seldom achieved structurally. Organizations have to be active, working, engaged to survive, even economically. And when people are paying salaries, they want a job description followed.

Some teachers and follows of Spiral Dynamics, in their 9 level understanding of human consciousness, believe that institutions as institutions can rarely rise above the lower levels, the tribal level of mythic membership, or perhaps the order driven authority structure, or perhaps the strategic enterprise level striving toward excellence and success.

In other words, it is hard for an organization that pays salaries, and has policies, procedures, and concerns for precedent and consistency, to fully be contemplative in our sense. They can hopefully work for a workplace style that is not too goal driven, and that deals with human resources in a prayerful, just, patient, and respectful way. On the other side, these organizations often find that if the "spiritual" or "contemplative" hand is played too up front, you frankly, gather people who are not that interested in working! Non profit organizations deal with this constantly in terms of people expecting a "faith based" organization not to be that demanding, that accountable, with little supervision or concern for any "quality control."

Many groups and communities I have worked with spend much of their time with human resources issues, because spiritual people often have a very real resistance to any language of criteria, accountability, competence, skill sets, work hours, and concrete supervision or management. In my opinion, there is an anti-structuralist bias inside of many folks who would like to name themselves "contemplatives."

Answers to specific questions:

- We would first of all speak of contemplative practice as a lifestyle, an alternative consciousness, a way of addressing issues in a more egoless and open horizoned way, than mere goal agendas, or emphasis on performance. Secondarily, we would teach and recognize that at least one, preferably two, specific contemplative sits each day, are going to be required for this to happen at any depth.
- Answered above, I believe. The main addition has been the practice of walking meditation, and practicing awareness by focusing in nature.
- Although many truthfully use the language and work for the synthesis in community and institutional setting, and many surely achieve it better than we do, I am not aware of another groups that puts its two biases right out in front as the Center for Action and Contemplation.
- Our demographics tend to be mostly young idealists between 20 – 30, and retired folks over 55, usually white and middle class. Largely North American, with a few Europeans, and some returning missionaries from all countries.
- With the decline and disillusionment with organized religion, our conferences have become very large, anywhere from 500 – 1,400 attendees at our three to four yearly sponsored events in Albuquerque. The desire is huge and growing, it seems, to find an actual interior practice since ritualized and verbal religion has so disappointed people.
- Thomas Keating's Contemplative Outreach, and John Main/Laurence Freeman's World Community for Christian Meditation have grown exponentially in the last 15 years. I have spoken to both of their conventions, and they seem to have a very solid commitment level and practice level among their many circles of meditators. They are, of course, being resisted and opposed by very conservative groupings within the Catholic Church, and some mainline churches too. They tend to resist anything that is interior, or wants to move beyond the mind and doctrines and words. This is our challenge, to open up the balancing apophatic Biblical and mystical tradition, which was

largely lost after the Reformation and the Enlightenment
in Western Christianity.

In general, although it is the great art form, our dualistic thinking has kept us from making the linkage on the mental level first of all, and then also for the emotional level, and the lifestyle levels.

My last book was on this subject of non-dual thinking. It is called *The Naked Now: Learning to See as the Mystics See*, and I have been amazed at the strong positive response from Christians, which tells me we are moving to higher levels of consciousness, which now do not resist, but even seem to be ready for non-dual thinking. So my hope is that the linkage we hope for is emerging around the world in our time. Maybe still a minority position, but that is enough.

Notes

1   http://www.cacradicalgrace.org/aboutus/core_principle_1_
    criterion.pdf.

Contemplative Practice in Seminaries and with Clergy

Andrew Dreitcer

In developing this "white paper" on Christian "Contemplative Practice in Seminaries and with Clergy" it seems prudent to organize its content around the "guiding questions" that were formulated to assist us in focusing our writing. And so, grateful for a handy framework on which to hang my thoughts, I will begin this essay by addressing how I am using and defining the phrase "contemplative practice," and will move through the guiding questions in the approximate order in which they were given, freely expanding or redefining them as necessary.

1. Describe how you define or use the term "contemplative practice."

Certainly, the phrase "contemplative practice" has a long and multi-dimensional history within Christianity. Other white papers in this collection will present surveys of the past and present definitions and uses of the phrase in its theoretical and practical aspects. With this in mind, I will focus my working definition around what seem to me to be those meanings and uses of "contemplative practice" that show up most fully and commonly within current seminary and clergy-related contexts. That is, rather than offering a definition governed primarily by historical uses of the phrase or my own desires for how it ought to be used, I am trying to let the past 25 years of Christian seminary and clergy usage frame this essay's working understanding of "contemplative practice."

I turn first to a definition of the word "contemplative." In its current usage among clergy and in seminaries, it seems to me that "contemplative" carries a number of key characteristics:

- *Open Receptivity.* Rather than being centered in *directing* something to God[1] (e.g., prayers of petition), or *acting* for or on behalf of God (e.g., service projects, ministry activities, social justice work), "contemplative" points to a stance of being open to receiving from God whatever emerges. Such a stance often highlights capacities of awareness, waiting, listening, and noticing.

- *Non-judgmental Beholding.* Walter Burghardt, in his 1989 essay on contemplation, coined a phrase that has become perhaps the dominant defining aspect of contemplation for contemporary clergy and for seminary contexts (at least within the mainstream churches): "a long loving look at the real."[2] Mainstream seminary programs in spirituality have consistently used Burghardt's essay in their teaching, so much so that his definition now often appears in conversation, presentations, and written material without attribution. Burghardt's definition (known or not, correctly attributed or not), accurately captures (and probably helped form) the current, common understanding that contemplation has to do with a stance toward the world that doesn't simply receive, but receives things, sees things, for what they are, without imposing on them agendas, judgments, or critical analyses. In non-judgmental beholding, the capacities of attending, "gazing," and appreciation are especially activated.
- *Effortlessness.* This aspect of the contemplative way emphasizes letting go of human control and effort and allowing God to "do the work." The capacities of surrender and release are particularly activated. (Some contrast this with "meditation," which has classically been associated with intentional, effort-filled practices of attention, awareness, and thoughtful consideration.)
- *Dwelling in and with the sacred.* This is spoken of as simply "being there," "soaking," or "resting" in and with God. It is described as a relational experience of no-time in which self-awareness and awareness of surroundings drop away. In their place comes a rich experience of intimate connection[3] with God—which may come to consciousness only after the contemplative moment (and, perhaps, much time) passes.

Within contemporary Christian seminary and clergy circles, to live a "contemplative life" or to follow a "contemplative path" is commonly understood as being grounded in (or at least be engaged in trying to cultivate) the characteristics described above. "Contemplative practices," then, are commonly understood as intentional activities in which persons seek to experience and cultivate a receptive, effortless, non-judgmental stance of dwelling intimately with God.

2.a. Describe the development of contemplative practice in this setting over the past twenty-five years.

In answering this set of questions, I will offer two windows into the developments in contemplative practice in seminaries and among clergy across the country. The first, San Francisco Theological seminary, exemplifies the progress of contemplative practice within "oldline/mainstream" Protestant Christianity in the United States. The second, "Lighthouse Trails Research Project," points to developments within conservative Evangelical expressions of Christianity.

"Oldline/Mainstream" Seminaries and Clergy

San Francisco Theological Seminary (SFTS) is a 125-year-old seminary of the Presbyterian Church, USA. Historically, Presbyterians have resisted anything that went by the name of "spirituality," "spiritual formation," or "contemplative" because (it was said) such practices and perspectives may be dangerously Roman Catholic, dangerously Buddhist, not doctrinely pure, too tied to the emotions, not intellectually rigorous enough, or too suggestive of an other-worldly spiritualism or escapism that does not take seriously the Reformed tradition's call to work for justice and peace in this world.

In 1979, in the face of this apparently solid wall of resistance, SFTS accepted (over the objections of many powerful faculty members) a $500,000 gift to establish a center for spirituality, the first such program in a Presbyterian seminary. By 1981, the Center had established an ongoing series of contemplative retreats, lectures by contemplative leaders such as John Sanford, spiritual direction opportunities for students, and courses in "Reformed spirituality" that included contemplative practices.

Faculty resistance to the contemplative programming of the Center grew along with the activities of the Center, which came to be renamed the Program in Christian Spirituality (PCS). But growing support from pastors and laypersons prompted the PCS to continue to increase its activities in spite of faculty resistance. Five developments at SFTS exemplify the force of the contemplative movement that was growing through the 1980's and 1990's:

1. After the founding director of the PCS retired in 1985, he was replaced by a member of a Catholic women's religious order, who

was the only academic the school could find who could teach contemplative practices, and the first Catholic faculty member ever hired by a Presbyterian seminary. The fact that the school was willing to "resort" to a Catholic religious (favoring contemplative expertise over denominational affiliation) points to the pressure exerted by the cultural shift toward a demand for training in contemplative practice.

2. In 1991, in response to student requests for more PCS programming, a contemplative-practice-based concentration in spirituality was established as part of the M.Div. curriculum. Similar concentrations in the D.Min. and M.A. soon followed.

3. In 1992, as the school was shedding programs and laying off employees due to financial stress, the PCS added an employee (one of the ones who had been laid off) and (much to the chagrin of most of the faculty) started a contemplative-practice-based spiritual director training program. The program attracted enough students (from a wide range of denominational traditions) to operate using only tuition moneys—a necessity, since the faculty would not allow general funds or endowment money to support the program in any manner.

4. In 1997, a $760,000 Lilly Endowment grant established the Youth Ministry and Spirituality Project, a program within PCS that trained persons and congregations in a form of youth ministry grounded in contemplative practice. Faculty resistance continued, but national support was very strong: 15 congregations from many denominations and from every region of the country participated; the program was featured in a multi-page, color-spread Wall Street Journal article and on Peter Jennings's evening news show; publishers welcomed books that flowed from the project; and church leaders from this country and beyond contacted the project for contemplative ministry resources that might be available.

5. By the late 1990's, 40% of M.Div. students were enrolled in the spirituality concentration. By 2010, the spirituality program in general, and the spiritual direction training program that was established as part of it in 1993, have become SFTS's most impor-

tant tool for recruiting students. In fact, for almost 15 years now, SFTS M.Div. students have listed the spirituality program as one of the two most important reasons they enroll at the seminary. The other top reason: location.

Beginning in the mid-nineties, clergy and lay demand for training in contemplative practices has sparked the establishment of contemplative-practice programs and/or courses in every Presbyterian (PC USA) seminary in the country. Since a case could be made that the PCUSA has been constitutionally more resistant to contemplative practice than any other mainstream denomination, the PCUSA shift suggests a sea change across all mainline churches (including Roman Catholic). In fact, the seminaries (perhaps all of them, though time did not permit a full survey) of every other mainstream denomination have established contemplative-practice courses, programs, and/or faculty positions. And that Roman Catholic contemplative religious hired by SFTS 25 years ago as a "last resort"? She is now Dean of the seminary.

Conservative Evangelical Seminaries and Clergy

The Lighthouse Trails Research Project was established in 2002 for the sole purpose of "exposing the dangers of contemplative spirituality."[4] The Project's web site describes what prompted the founding of Lighthouse Trails:

> In the year 2000, we learned that a mantra-style meditation coupled with a mystical spirituality had been introduced to the evangelical, Christian church and was infiltrating youth groups, churches, seminaries, and Bible studies at an alarming rate.
>
> In the spring of 2002, we began Lighthouse Trails Publishing with the hope of exposing this dangerous and pervasive mystical paradigm….As we learned more about contemplative spirituality (also known as the spiritual formation movement), we came to realize it had entered the church through a number of avenues—Willow Creek, Purpose Driven, and the emerging church just to name a few of the more prominent ones.
>
> Because the premise of this spirituality is both pantheistic (God is all things) and panentheistic (God is in all things),

thus refuting the gospel message of the Cross, we are compelled to address this issue.[5]

And address it they do. Lighthouse Trails offers an astonishingly comprehensive treasure trove of meticulously compiled research on the state of Christian contemplative practice in the United States—particularly within, but not limited to, evangelical circles. Further, the web site appropriately quotes, among others, Thomas Merton and Thomas Keating in order to define the territory the research project is attacking.[6]

Among its many offerings, Lighthouse Trails presents a helpful summary of the breadth of contemplative practice in the church, with evidence to support its research[7]:

Purpose Driven Life—one of the major avenues through which contemplative spirituality is entering the church
The Emerging Church—emerging, but not with the Gospel of Jesus Christ.
Willow Creek—Bill Hybels church another major influence in bringing contemplative/emerging into the church
Christian Seminaries & Colleges—leading our future pastors and Christian leaders into the new spirituality
Christian Publishers —succumbing to the temptation to publish books promoting contemplative and emerging spirituality
The Spiritual Formation Movement—another way of saying contemplative spirituality
Mystical Rituals—labyrinths, contemplative prayer, *lectio divina*, breath prayer, yoga, Taize and other rituals

For our purposes, the "Christian Seminaries & Colleges" page, noted above, is particularly useful. It offers an A-Z listing of dozens of educational (and other) institutions that promote contemplative practice. The following examples suggest how widespread contemplative sensibilities have become:[8]

Assemblies of God Theological Seminary
Professor Earl Creps
Doctor of Ministry Program Associate Professor of
Leadership and Spiritual Renewal

Azusa Pacific University
Haggard School of Theology
Azusa, CA
Example: Transitions in Ministry

Biola University
(Institute of Spiritual Formation)
aka: Talbot School of Theology
ISF 532 Developmental Spirituality & Contemplative
Prayer

Hope International University (AKA: Pacific
Christian College)
Spiritual Formation with Professor David Timms
Fullerton, CA

Indiana Wesleyan University
(mentoring program)
Division of Religion & Philosophy with Youth Specialties

Intervarsity Christian Fellowship NW
Portland, OR

With most of the institutional listings come examples of courses or programs that qualify as contemplative. The website also offers a "database of articles[9] on Christian [institutions] that promote contemplative" practice,[10] as well as an A-Z listing of twenty-one that do not.[11]

From its analysis of the "emerging" church's use of silence-filled ritual, to Rick Warren's advocacy of "breath prayer," to Youth Specialty's "contemplative retreats for pastors," and beyond, The Lighthouse Trails Research Project makes a compelling, well-documented argument for how contemplative practices have come to be embraced by virtually every dimension of the evangelical movement over the past decade. The project's research leaves little doubt that the contemplative way has moved off the fringe and closer to the center of Christian life in this country than might have been expected 25 years ago.

2.b. What specific contemplative practices are most commonly used in this setting? How have these evolved or been adapted over the past twenty-five years?

My experience, reports from clergy and my former students, and the research of Lighthouse Trails suggests that Centering Prayer, Ignatian imaginal meditation, Taizé-style prayer, *lectio divina*, and labyrinth walking are especially common contemplative practices within seminaries and churches. As suggestive of the way contemplative practices have become more common-place and have evolved (or not), I will briefly describe my own experiences of the growth in Taizé prayer, *lectio divina*, and labyrinth walking that has occurred over the past 30 years.

- Taizé prayer: In 1982, I returned to Yale Divinity School after a year-long internship volunteering at the French monastic community of Taizé. At the time, the community had published its first volumes of music in this country, and had maintained a virtually-unknown presence in the Hell's Kitchen district of Manhattan for approximately a dozen years. Upon my return I discovered that outside of a few pockets of Taizé groupies, mostly collected on the East Coast and the San Francisco Bay Area (especially the Mercy Center in Burlingame) and within certain circles of professional church musicians and liturgists, few people knew of the community or its music and prayer style. In 1984, I entered doctoral studies in Berkeley, and began to attend the once-a-month Taizé services at the Mercy Center. Twenty to thirty people gathered in a small circle in the sanctuary for those services. By 1994, the sanctuary was filled to over-flowing with hundreds of worshipers. In the intervening decade a similar expansion of Taizé-style prayer had taken place throughout the country. The community had published more music, the publisher (GIA) was making it more easily available, and seminaries had begun using it more often in their regular campus worship services and in special programs. For instance, San Francisco Theological Seminary's spirituality program made Taizé-style prayer the foundational worship experience for all of its contemplative events, thus influencing hundreds of clergy and, subsequently, their congregations. Now, in 2010, it is

difficult to find a clergy person or seminarian of any mainstream denomination who has not sung Taizé music and
participated in some form of Taizé-style prayer. Lighthouse
Trails reports that even congregations of the conservative
evangelical Presbyterian Church of America are offering
Taizé worship.[12]

- Labyrinth walking: In January, 1994, San Francisco Theological Seminary offered the first intensive courses of its
spiritual director's training program. Lauren Artress, who
had founded Grace Cathedral's Labyrinth project in 1992,
was invited to teach in the intensive and help lead meditative labyrinth walks. None of the students of the seminary
or in the spiritual direction program had walked a labyrinth. Very few had even heard of such a thing. Rev. Artress
helped the staff construct a labyrinth by affixing masking
tape to the wood floor of the lecture hall (ruining the floor,
it turned out), and instructed the students in contemplative walking. Several years later Grace Cathedral's labyrinth
project began selling labyrinth-making kits. By the middle
of this past decade the cathedral had inlaid a 45-foot-diam-
eter stone/tile labyrinth in its sanctuary and a similar patio
labyrinth near the entrance to the sanctuary. Labyrinths of
a variety of sizes and designs have been installed in Christian churches and seminaries throughout the United States.
I no longer meet mainstream clergy members and seminarians who have no knowledge of contemplatively walking
labyrinths. Lighthouse Trails is very concerned.[13]

- *Lectio divina*: In 1984, following the advice of one of my
academic advisors, I began my Ph.D. studies in Christian
spirituality by researching the practice of *lectio divina*.
A world-wide search for books and articles on the topic
yielded one English-language essay in a Japanese journal,
a single article in a Spanish monastic journal, a chapter in
the book my advisor had loaned me, and...nothing more.
By 1990, a book had been published that reformulated
the private practice of *lectio divina* as a group practice. In
1991, the staff of the spirituality program at San Francisco
Theological Seminary began teaching the "new" practice of
lectio divina (including the recently-formulated group ver-

sion) to gatherings of laypersons, seminarians, and pastors who had never heard of it. Evidently, that was one point of light in a million, since by 2010, it is safe to say that *lectio divina* (in whatever form) is the contemplative practice that is most commonly engaged by Christians across this country. I just now Googled "lectio divina" and received "about 425,000 results," while Amazon shows 385 results. None are in Japanese journals.

3. What organizations have developed to support contemplative practice in this setting?

- In 1995, only three years before the Lilly Endowment (LEI) gave the "contemplative Youth ministry" grant to the San Francisco Theological Seminary, Lilly was supporting not a single project in contemplative practice, nor did it have plans to (according to a survey I did for LEI at the time). LEI has gone on to support a series of books on contemplative practices, as well as many more contemplative-practice-based projects. It has become a key resource in U.S. Christianity for spiritual formation grounded in contemplative practices.
- The Association of Theological Schools, while not explicitly stating a preference for contemplative practice, does now include a requirement for spiritual formation within the M.Div.—prompting the establishment of contemplative practice in clergy training programs throughout the country.
- A number of Ph.D. programs have arisen that tend to train future professors (many of whom will train seminary students) in forms of Christian spirituality that are based in contemplative practice. For example, in 1978, the Graduate Theological Union established a Ph.D. in Christian Spirituality, while in 2009, Southern Baptist Theological Seminary established a Ph.D. in Biblical Spirituality.
- The Fetzer Institute, of course, has funded events and projects that support Christian contemplative practice connected to seminary/clergy settings, including the Merton Institute and the 2008, Claremont School of Theology conference "Neuroscience and Contemplative Practices."

I know of no other organizational support for contemplative practices that explicitly targets this setting in significant ways. Of course, this is not counting the plethora of retreat centers, spiritual formation centers and programs, spiritual direction programs, and contemplative training programs that have arisen in the past 25 years. (Other participants in this gathering will report on these.)

4. Describe the demographics of those who participate in contemplative practice in this setting. Please include, where available, information on the number of practitioners as well as their age, gender, education, and ethnicity. Have the demographics changed over the past twenty-five years? Please provide citations if references are available.

My experience, as well as reports from others around the country who are involved with leading programs in contemplative practices, suggests that those who participate in such practices have been predominately (perhaps, overwhelmingly) middle-aged, middle-to-upper-middle-class, Anglo-American women, both clergy and laity. As far as I know, no demographic studies have been done to confirm or contradict this impression. Studies would be welcomed.

5.[14] To what extent do you agree with the notion that a larger contemplative movement is emerging in America? What does contemplative practice in your setting contribute to such a movement?

Based on the 25-year-long explosion of contemplative practice within seminary settings and among clergy members (as well as lay persons), I think it is clear that a Christian contemplative movement is contributing to a broader movement that is also visible across the country. This broader movement is being magnified by significant government and foundation funding for scientific and medical studies that are examining how contemplative practices might contribute to health and wellbeing. Interestingly, however, virtually none of these studies have focused on Christian contemplative practices; overwhelmingly the focus has been on Buddhism-based practices.

Absent information about the possible benefits to wellbeing offered by Christian contemplative practices, it makes sense to consider their wider cultural impact. In fact, I suspect the very fact that more and more Christians have embraced the contemplative way, has legitimated contemplative practices in the collective mind of our (subtly or not-so-subtly) Christian-dominated national sensibility. That legitimizing influence has, I can imagine, made it easier for governmental and non-governmental organizations to offer financial and other support for the Buddhism-based studies that, in turn, may benefit us all.

6. What are the key trends, opportunities and challenges facing contemplative practice in this setting in the coming decade? What in your opinion will be needed to nurture the growth and development of a contemplative movement in America?

It appears to me that contemplative practice has reached a plateau of sorts within seminary and clergy circles. By this I do not mean that a saturation point has been achieved; no, there are plenty of opportunities to introduce or expand contemplative practices. Rather, the plateau has to do with the *purpose, constituency,* and *understanding* of the practices. All three need a re-working, I believe. I will conclude this paper with suggestions toward such a re-working.

1. Possibilities for a shift in *purpose.* By far, the dominant reason people embrace contemplative practices, it seems to me, continues to be for rest, retreat, and rejuvenation. The characteristics of the working definition[15] I presented at the beginning of this essay certainly reflect this sense of the purpose of the practices. Certainly there are individuals and organizations that promote contemplative practice as being not only for spiritual rejuvenation, but as essentially the foundational building blocks for transformative action in the world (Richard Rohr and the Center for Action and Contemplation come to mind here), but in general the movement has not found a way to move this purpose to the fore. I think we do ourselves, our world, and the traditional purpose of Christian contemplative practice a disservice if we do not find a way to show more fully how contemplative practices are not only meant for, but deepened by, the formation of lives of "engaged compassion"[16], lives that engage in compassionate social transformation from a stance of contemplative presence. If the movement does not find ways to rework the practices for a contemporary sensibility of social engagement, I suspect there will be at best a growing flatness or at worst a withering.

One possibility for beginning to nurture this shift: Drawing together individuals and organizations that have been focused on the connection between contemplation and action, and inviting them to envision how to establish a new direction.

2. The issue of *constituency*: The Christian contemplative movement faces a demographic challenge. The questions, put simply, are these: Can younger persons and persons of ethnic/cultural contexts other than Anglo-American be attracted in greater numbers to contemplative practice? Should that be a goal of the movement? If so, what would it take to realize such a goal?

Addressing these questions would take concerted efforts in social, cultural and demographic analyses, as well as a collection of persons focused on the considering whether or not this issue actually matters.

3. A new *understanding*: As I have suggested above, Buddhist practices are being heavily studied in medical, psychological, and neuroscientific laboratories across the country in order to understand how they may contribute to human wellbeing, both in terms of personal health and wellness and in terms of how compassionate behavior is formed for the benefit of communities, society, and the world. It is becoming ever-clearer that particular practices form particular ways of being. Or at least, it is becoming clearer that *Buddhist* practices form particular ways of being.

But what about Christian contemplative practices? Surely, they bring their own flavor to the table. And perhaps they form persons in a unique way of being. Consider, for example, the definition of contemplative practice presented in the essay we were sent: "Executive Summary of: *A Powerful Silence: The Role of Meditation and Other Contemplative Practices In American Society.*" That definition (on page 12)—"*A practice undertaken with the intention to quiet the mind and to cultivate a personal capacity for deep concentration, presence, and awareness*"—seems to be less focused on practice as formative of life-giving, world-transforming human relationships than the definition that could be grounded in more explicitly Christian sensibilities. In fact, I would say that the definition presented in the "Executive Summary" (and formulated from survey responses) leans in a Buddhist direction. In contrast, a Christian-leaning definition might assume "quieting the mind" is simply one contemplative practice among many (including the practice of deepening concentration, the practice of presence, and the practice of deepening awareness), rather than the intended fruit of contemplative practice, as the Executive Summary's definition suggests. Along with other practices, "quieting the mind" would intend primarily to cultivate an intimate relationship with God in order to cultivate compassionately transformed relationships with oneself and others (i.e., loving God, and loving your neighbor as you love yourself).

If, in fact, Christian contemplative practice contains its own uniqueness, I believe the movement needs to encourage the exploration of the intricacies of the subjective experiences and lived outcomes of the practices with the same sort of care that has (fortunately!) been brought to bear on Buddhist contemplative practices. With an understanding of Christian contemplative practice that is deepened and expanded by medical, neuroscientific, and psychological studies, the Christian contemplative movement may have something even more profound, beneficial, and enduring to contribute to the larger contemplative movement than it has to date.

Notes

1 Within the varied world that is Christianity, there are many names and formulations for the divine, the eternal, the presence of the sacred. For simplicity's sake, I will use "God" in this essay.

2 Burghardt, Walter J., "Contemplation: A Long Loving Look at the Real." *Church.* Winter, 1989.

3 Of course, this experience of rich intimacy is described in many ways, including "absence" and "fullness," but the key element here is the sense of simply "being."

4 http://www.lighthousetrailsresearch.com/NewsletterJanuary.htm. I thank my research assistant, Anne Walker, for directing me to Lighthouse Trails.

5 http://www.lighthousetrailsresearch.com/aboutus.htm#mission. htm.

6 http://www.lighthousetrailsresearch.com/cp.htm.

7 http://www.lighthousetrailsresearch.com/index.html, http://www.lighthousetrailsresearch.com/warren.htm, http://www.lighthousetrailsresearch.com/emergingchurch.htm, http://www.lighthousetrailsresearch.com/publishers.htm, http://www.lighthousetrailsresearch.com/spiritualformation.htm, http://www.lighthousetrailsresearch.com/researchtopics.htm#cprituals.

8 http://www.lighthousetrailsresearch.com/Colleges.htm .

9 http://www.lighthousetrailsresearch.com/blog/?cat=71 .

10 http://www.lighthousetrailsresearch.com/Colleges.htm.

11 http://www.lighthousetrailsresearch.com/collegesgood.htm .

12 http://www.lighthousetrailsresearch.com/blog/?s=pca.

13 http://www.lighthousetrailsresearch.com/blog/?s=labyrinth&search =Search.

14 I am re-ordering the questions as they were given within #5 and #6.

15 "…intentional activities in which persons seek to experience and cultivate a receptive, effortless, non-judgmental stance of dwelling intimately with God." Above, page 2.

16 "'Engaged compassion' is the process of turning the feeling of empathy into well-considered actions that benefit every dimension of life [and are] formed through a grounding in contemplative practice." http://centerforengagedcompassion.wordpress.com/about/.

CHRISTIAN CENTERING PRAYER IN AMERICA: A CONTEMPLATIVE PRACTICE FOR CONTEMPORARY AMERICA

David Frenette

Summary

Centering Prayer is a Christian contemplative practice that has been taught over the last 35 years, initially in the United States to Roman Catholics and then more broadly in many countries, in several Christian denominations and in diverse secular settings. Contemplative Outreach—the organization founded by Father Thomas Keating to support Centering Prayer practitioners—now has about 46,000 informal members. Many more people practice Centering Prayer who are not affiliated with this organization.

Centering Prayer has also more generally affected Christian spirituality in America by helping to renew the contemplative dimension of Christianity. Because Christianity is the dominant religion in the United Sates, Centering Prayer and the renewal of contemplative Christianity has indirectly contributed to a larger contemplative movement in America. Both challenges and opportunities exist for Centering Prayer's growth in the next decade.

Background and Definitions

In Christianity, the term *meditation* (from the Latin, *meditatio)* traditionally meant the active use of the intellectual faculties to reflect upon God or truth, while the term *contemplation* (from the Latin, *contemplatio*) meant the non-conceptual experience of "resting in God," or truth itself. In contemplation or *contemplative prayer*, one relates to God not through words, specific prayers or thoughts but through direct experience beyond thought and concept and, as contemplation deepens, through living in God as the ground of experiencing itself. The fruit of contemplation is greater selfless service, as the living Christ gradually becomes the source of the practitioner's activity in quiet, simple and often unseen ways. As one's relationship deepens with God, the practitioner begins to discover a new sense of identity and purpose. As Paul says in the Christian scriptures, "I live, not now I, but Christ lives in me." (Gal 2:20)

In the twentieth century, as the spiritual traditions of Asia were brought to the West, the terms meditation and contemplation began to be used in ways opposite to their traditional meanings. *Meditation* now is used, even in Christianity, to describe the activity that leads towards nonconceptual experience, and *contemplation* is often used to describe the mental activity of self-reflection.

Christian Contemplative Practice

In line with the ancient Christian understanding, in this paper the term *contemplative practice* refers to the interior actions, skills and methods that open one to the nonconceptual experience of God. The Christian understanding of contemplative practice intertwines inner actions with a deepening relationship with God. In the traditional Roman Catholic spiritual theology that defines much of Christian contemplative practice, inner actions were made through the *memory, intellect,* and *will*—a traditional three-fold Christian psychology of the human person, who was seen as being created in the image of the Trinitarian life of God. Contemplative practice includes acts of *forgetting* all thoughts of the past, present or future, the *unknowing* cognition of God, and the deepening *surrender* of the will to God in all things.

As the inner life of the human person has been described more fully by contemporary psychology, the actions that comprise contemplative practice can also be better described. I find that contemplative practice involves the training of the inner psychological capacities of intention and motivation, attention and awareness, reflection and concentration of mind, devotion and the shifting or transformation of the subjective self-sense, receptivity and being in pure consciousness, and the ways these interior actions are expressed exteriorly, in behavior and relationships with others. A specific method of contemplative practice usually focuses on one of these (pairs of) actions more than the others. As a practitioner progresses on the spiritual path, skillful teaching and spiritual direction brings the other secondary actions into contemplative practice as well.

Although contemplative practice has quantifiable physiological effects in the person—as in affecting brain wave activity and blood pressure—the primary effects of Christian contemplative practice are more interior and qualitative: affecting one's sense of meaning, faith, and relationship with God.

It is not clear what contemplative practices Jesus of Nazareth may have taught to his followers. As in Judaism and Islam, rather than providing concrete instructions on how to train or practice for the contemplative experience of God, parts of Christianity's scriptures point towards the contemplative experience of God, and how to orient oneself towards this experience. For example, the invitation to "Be still and know that I am God" (Psalm

46:10) draws the practitioner into an inner quietness, an inner stilling of effort, in order to experience God. Similarly, Jesus' instructions on how to pray in Matthew's Gospel, "If you want to pray, go to your inner room, close the door and pray to your Father in secret, and your Father who sees in secret will reward you" (Matthew 6:6), has been interpreted by many spiritual teachers across the centuries as an invitation to the inwardness and hiddenness of contemplative practice.

The first written records of Christian contemplative practice begin in the third century C.E. with the desert fathers and mothers (*abbas* and *ammas*), the forerunners of Christian monasticism who lived in present day Egypt and Syria. As the famous desert father Abba Isaac said, "We need to be especially careful to follow the Gospel precept which instructs us to go into our private room and shut the door, so that we may pray to our Father. And this is how we do it. We pray in our private room whenever we withdraw our hearts completely from the tumult and noise of our thoughts and our worries and when secretly and intimately we offer our prayer to the Lord."[1] Abba Isaac offers his own contemplative practice for doing this: interiorly repeating a scriptural phrase.

Centering Prayer

Building upon this early tradition in Christianity, over the years other practices were articulated that dispose practitioners to the grace or gift of contemplative "resting" in God. Based on traditional teachings in Christianity, especially the anonymous fourteenth-century classic text *The Cloud of Unknowing*, Centering Prayer as a contemplative practice presents a method that many contemporary Americans use as a basic contemplative practice.

The practice of Centering Prayer is fairly simple. Beginning practitioners use a symbol of consent to the presence and action of God within, usually a word of one or two syllables. The technical term in Christian spiritual theology for this is *monologistic prayer*: the prayer of one (*monos*) word (*logos*). This sacred word can be the name of God, such as *God, Jesus, spirit,* another euphonious spiritual term, like *shalom,* or a nonreligious word, like *peace* or *be.* However, as taught by Father Thomas Keating, the practitioner of Centering Prayer can also use their breath or a simple inward glance as a sacred symbol. The essential practice is that whenever one is engaged with thoughts, one returns, ever-so-gently, to this sacred symbol. As the mind settles, one lets go of the form of the symbol and receives that to which it points: God. Such is the essence of the practice of Centering Prayer: simple, receptive and nonconceptual.

One takes time to prepare oneself for the simplicity of this practice, and assumes a comfortable, relaxed and alert posture. One engages in the practice for a set, committed period of time (e.g. 20 minutes), and takes a couple of minutes at the end of this period to integrate the effects of Centering Prayer and transition back into active life.

Centering Prayer is primarily a practice of intention and receptivity—renewing inner consent to the nonconceptual relationship with God as one lets go of thinking about thoughts. The other essential actions of contemplative practice—motivation, attention, awareness, reflection, concentration of the mind, devotion, the shifting or transformation of subjective self-sense, being in pure consciousness itself, and the ways these interior acts are expressed exteriorly, in behavior and relationships with others—are not directly included in the beginning instructions of this basic introductory method of Christian contemplative practice. These can be—and usually need to be—cultivated in the Centering Prayer practitioner's life as the spiritual journey unfolds through the traditional stages of purification, illumination and union with God. The teachings of Centering Prayer are currently being expanded to assist maturing practitioners in the deepening of their practice.

The Development of Centering Prayer

Centering Prayer was originally formulated in the 1970's by three Roman Catholic Cistercian (Trappist) monks at Saint Joseph's Monastery in Spencer, Massachusetts: Father Thomas Keating, Father Basil Pennington and Father William Menninger. Each wrote books on Centering Prayer and taught in ways that reflected their own gifts and experiences. An abbot for twenty years and a psychologically astute teacher, Father Keating articulated the psycho/theological teaching that surrounds the practice.

These animators of Centering Prayer began teaching it at the Spencer monastery's retreat house to groups of Roman Catholic Religious—priests, nuns, brothers and monks. However, as each continued in their work in the early 1980's, they found that it was laypeople who were most interested in learning and, most importantly, in continuing the practice of Centering Prayer.

With this audience in mind, in 1983 Father Keating gave an experimental two-week Intensive Centering Prayer Retreat to a group of twelve laypeople at the Lama Foundation in New Mexico. The first such event offered to non-monks, this intensive retreat was inspired by the Zen sesshins that he had attended when, as abbot, he regularly invited Zen masters to teach at his monastic community. The intensive, silent retreat, in which teaching was given along with five hours of Centering Prayer each day, proved to be a "watershed" event, solidifying participants in the practice of Centering Prayer for ordinary life. Seven of those twelve people who attended that event, myself included, went on to form and serve full-time in Contemplative Outreach, an organization Keating founded to support Centering Prayer in ordinary life.

With the support of these people and others, Father Keating began offering intensive retreats monthly at St. Benedict's Monastery in Snowmass, Colorado, where he was living since retiring his abbacy. These intensive retreats quickly became a key ingredient in supporting Centering Prayer practice. In the late 1980's Father Keating's retreat teachings were videotaped. People with a few years experience of Centering Prayer practice were trained to present a one-day introductory workshop and to facilitate weekend and ten-day intensive retreats at which Father Keating's videos were shown.

Centering Prayer's spread was slow, steady and organic. For example, someone who went on retreat at the Snowmass monastery would feel inspired to bring Centering Prayer into his or her home church. Through Contemplative Outreach, they were put in contact with a trained presenter from their region to come and give an introductory workshop. The local person would then facilitate a follow-up class with the videotapes. Afterwards, a Centering Prayer support group often formed. When enough local interest developed, the region would host its own intensive retreat or invite Father Keating, Pennington or Menninger to give a presentation, which would in turn generate more interest in the area.

Thus, a grassroots spiritual movement developed in the late 1980's and 1990's. Centering Prayer spread to other Christian denominations. Some Centering Prayer people who were in the twelve-step recovery programs began to experience that Centering Prayer fit well as their 11th Step: "Sought through prayer and meditation to improve our conscious contact with God as we understood Him." Now there are workshops and retreats given by trained people in "Centering Prayer As An 11th Step Practice." Some people felt inspired to bring Centering Prayer into prisons. There have also been initiatives offering Centering Prayer to young people, low-income, Hispanic, and ethnically-diverse populations.

As people progressed in Centering Prayer, they naturally experienced a need for deeper spiritual training. In 1985, a retreat center was formed in New York State, Chrysalis House, at which advanced training practices and programs were developed and exported into the larger Contemplative Outreach "network." For example, a practice for embracing God in emotions, the Welcoming Prayer, was developed there in the late 1980's. Thus, over

25 years, Centering Prayer developed in the United States according to the emerging needs of those who were engaged in its practice.

In this way, I believe that Centering Prayer represents an important part of a contemporary contemplative renewal in Christianity. Spiritual renewals grow across generations, like the way ocean waves build upon each other. In the 1950's and 1960's, spiritual writers like Thomas Merton created a *first wave* of contemplative renewal in Christianity in America, as his writings articulated the Christian contemplative message for modern readers. A generation later, in a *second wave,* teachers such as Keating, Pennington and Menninger built upon this message, offering a basic contemplative practice so that people living in active non-monastic life could have a way to practice what monastic authors like Merton had written about. Now, in a *third wave* of this spiritual renewal, people well trained in Centering Prayer are developing additional practices and resources to support maturing practitioners, and are translating the message of contemplation for a new generation of seekers drawn to, and by, Christ.

Organizations that Support Centering Prayer

- Contemplative Outreach Ltd. is the primary organization that supports Centering Prayer by providing resources (books, videos, and a website), maintaining a mailing list and offering introductory workshops and intensive retreats in Centering Prayer. The international resource center of Contemplative Outreach, located in Butler, New Jersey, also nurtures contacts with Centering Prayer groups outside of the United States in places such as Canada, the United Kingdom, South Korea, the Philippines, South Africa, and the Dominican Republic. While originally sponsored in the mid-1980's by spiritually progressive Roman Catholic dioceses (in New York City and Denver) Contemplative Outreach has remained ecumenical and independent from church or monastic institutions, and continues to look at ways to ensure that spiritual wisdom informs its decision-making when Father Keating is no longer available to it. The organization sustains a spiritual relationship with St. Benedict's Monastery in Snowmass, Colorado.
- Extension Contemplativa is the organization that supports Centering Prayer in Spanish-speaking churches in the United States and in other countries. This organization, a

cousin to Contemplative Outreach Ltd, is especially strong
in the Dominican Republic, Mexico and Central America.

- Contemplative Outreach of Colorado is a sister organization to the international resource center, and offers monthly ten-day intensive retreats at the Snowmass monastery,
  has a center for classes and community in Denver, and
  sponsors a program that I run, Incarnational Contemplation, that researches and develops contemplative practices,
  and trains people in deepening Centering Prayer.
- The Mastery Foundation is the organization Father Basil
  Pennington worked with in the 1980's and 1990's that has
  taught Centering Prayer to ministers, in conjunction with
  techniques for psychological growth.
- Father William Menninger has a website, www.contempla-
  tiveprayer.net, that lists events and resources for his
  work with Centering Prayer, which he also calls The
  Prayer of the Cloud, as a way of highlighting this practice's
  sources in the medieval spiritual classic text, *The Cloud of
  Unknowing*.

Many other organizations teach or incorporate Centering Prayer as part
of their curriculum, including Christian spiritual/social justice networks like
Father Richard Rohr's Center for Action and Contemplation, online interspiritual organizations like Ken Wilber's Integral Institute, and academic institutions such as Naropa University.

Demographics of Centering Prayer Practitioners in America

Contemplative Outreach itself has no formal membership. The mailing list
for its biannual newsletter has stabilized at about 46,000 since the year 2000.
Currently there are nearly a thousand active small Centering Prayer support
groups loosely affiliated with Contemplative Outreach in churches, homes,
prisons and twelve-step groups, with 32 chapters in the United States and 20
other countries.

The number of Centering Prayer practitioners is difficult to quantify with
any certainty, as many people learn and practice it on their own, without
any direct connection with Contemplative Outreach. If the Centering Prayer
market can be surmised by the number of books in print about it, Amazon.
com now lists 122 titles on Centering Prayer. Father Keating's classic book
Open Mind, Open Heart remains the most prominent of these titles, having
sold more than 600,000 copies.

Within Contemplative Outreach in the United States, varying according to region, Centering Prayer workshops and retreat participants are now approximately 40% Roman Catholic and 30% Protestant. Another 30% are unaffiliated with any denomination. These event attendees tend to be predominantly female (approximately 66%), predominantly Caucasian (approximately 75%) and predominantly middle-class (70%). I estimate that more than 50% are college-educated. There have been initiatives to reach out to other populations, yet these have not significantly changed the demographics of Centering Prayer. On a normal workshop or retreat, 80% of the participants are in their 50's, 60's or 70's. Also, approximately 80% of the leadership of Contemplative Outreach is 65 or older.

Key Trends, Opportunities and Challenges

In the coming decade, there are both challenges and opportunities for Centering Prayer's development in America.

Broader Societal Trends

Changes in the face of Christianity and in American society in general will affect Centering Prayer in many ways:

- *The fundamentalist critique.* Around 1990, some Catholic and Christian groups began publicly criticizing Centering Prayer. Currently, two of the top ten sites in a Google search of "Centering Prayer" link to websites that warn of its un-Biblical/ New Age dangers. Their central criticism is that Centering Prayer opens one to Satan's influence. Some religious authorities in the denomination from which Centering Prayer emerged in the 1980's—the Roman Catholic Church—are less supportive of the practice. The conservative cable TV network, EWTN, remains critical of Centering Prayer as being "un-Catholic." This criticism, because it is based in misunderstanding and a fundamentalist mindset fearful of contemplation, is likely to continue, and may even increase when the priest-monks who founded Centering Prayer have died. Centering Prayer's presence and growth in conservative Catholic and evangelical churches may then be reduced.
- *The emerging church.* As criticism of Centering Prayer in some Christian circles has increased, receptivity to it in

other parts of Christianity has grown. The movement known as the *emerging church*, a diverse evangelical movement united in its disillusionment with organized religion, is more receptive to this, and other, forms of Christian contemplative practice. Also, some segments of the Episcopal Church (for example, in Denver, Tennessee and Washington, D.C.) are very supportive of Centering Prayer, as many of their bishops, clergy and lay members are practicing it themselves. Centering Prayer's opportunities in the next decade may likely be in different, more "progressive" Christian churches.

- *Non-institutionalized spirituality*. In the last several decades, more and more Americans self-identify as "spiritual but not religious." Many sociologists expect this trend to continue. Because more participants on recent Contemplative Outreach events express similar views, the growth of this group will be an opportunity for the growth of Centering Prayer.

- *The hyper-stimulated technological future*. A question exists in my mind about how young people raised on the current and future technologies will relate to Centering Prayer in the next decade, or to any contemplative practice. Will they burn out on multi-tasking and seek the peaceful interior silence that Centering Prayer invites? Or will they be unable to sit still long enough to practice it? Will they seek a different form of contemplative practice that integrates thoughts and interior freedom directly, rather than orienting towards a transcendent inner stillness and then integrating this experience in life? Have the effects of the information age already influenced Centering Prayer's potential to impact young people, or is the practice one that more naturally appeals to those who have gone through midlife? It will be interesting to observe if and how all the contemplative practices of "inward stillness" will need to be adapted for future highly stimulated generations.

Seminaries and Academic Training

In the 1980's the founders of Centering Prayer recognized that one way for it to spread in Christian churches was if it were part of the spiritual/academic training of ministers and priests. Yet, surprisingly, in 25 years, Centering Prayer has never found a solid place in any seminary training. The only educational institutions that offer real training in it that I know of are the University of San Francisco, Creighton University, and Naropa University. None of these are Christian seminaries. Although this situation remains a challenge for Centering Prayer's growth in mainstream churches, the leadership of Contemplative Outreach has remained committed to sharing Centering Prayer based on the interest of individuals, rather than through promotion or institutional training. As seminary attendance declines in many churches, other institutions that value contemplative education may include Centering Prayer in their curriculum.

Research

Scientific research on Hindu and Buddhist forms of meditation such as TM and mindfulness has greatly advanced their acceptance and practice in American society in the last decades. Relatively little research has, of yet, been done on Centering Prayer. In a notable exception, a study published last year[2] found that daily Centering Prayer practice reduced participants' stress and increased their collaborative relationship with God. The Mind and Life Institute has also done preliminary explorations on Centering Prayer research topics. As these endeavors continue, the quantifiable benefits of this practice may increase Centering Prayer's acceptance in secular settings, as well as raise consciousness about the Christian contemplative tradition and its benefits for contemporary Americans.

Developing a Living Tradition

The graying of Contemplative Outreach's leadership and membership present a challenge to the primary organization that has supported this practice, if not to Centering Prayer itself. There are initiatives currently underway to provide ongoing spiritual wisdom for the organization with Father Keating's retirement. At age 87, he has withdrawn from his formerly active traveling and teaching schedule. As mentioned, outreach attempts to younger generations continue to be made.

Contemplative movements, both Western and Eastern, in order to remain vibrant, have to continue developing their contemplative practice, vision and organizational presence in changing societies. History is full of examples of spiritual movements that failed to adjust their practices to changing times, whose dynamic interior and communal life became institutionalized, or who did not transmit their vision to a new generation of elders and teachers once their founders died. By its nature, the transformation of consciousness and behavior that contemplative practice initiates cannot be programmed for the future or packaged in bureaucracy. Developing a living contemplative tradition for Centering Prayer is a major challenge, as it is for every spiritual movement.

Contemplative Outreach is responding to this challenge by:

- Incorporating into its vision statement an institutional commitment to expand in new ways, and experimenting with structures that will encourage this adaptation;
- Developing advanced teachings and trainings for its long-time practitioners, so that the contemplative presence of Christ is more embodied in their teaching of Centering Prayer;
- Building bridges with initiatives (such as the project on Incarnational Contemplation) and with teachers (such as Cynthia Bourgeault) that seek to translate the message of Centering Prayer in new ways.

Whatever happens with the forms and the populations that have comprised the first generation of Centering Prayer practitioners, I believe that the essential vision of this contemplative practice will continue, perhaps through adaptation, well into the future.

A Larger Emerging American Contemplative Movement

As Maia Duerr writes in *A Powerful Silence: The Role of Meditation and Other Contemplative Practices in American Society,* I think there are signs that a larger contemplative movement is emerging in America.

Centering Prayer contributes to this larger contemplative movement because Christianity is the dominant religion in America, and because Centering Prayer has helped renew the Christian contemplative tradition. Particularly since Centering Prayer helps recover the Christian contemplative tradition from the inside out, through inner practice rather than through intellectual study, it helps create a context for the larger contemplative movement described so well in Duerr's article.

The following are a few brief thoughts about what will be needed to nurture the growth of this larger contemplative movement in America, from my perspective as a Christian contemplative practitioner who has worked since

1983 with Father Keating and Contemplative Outreach on the development of Centering Prayer:

- As mentioned, the significant traditions of contemplative practice that contribute to the larger contemplative movement in America can be supported to develop their teachings, institutional structures, and practices to meet the needs of new generations of seekers, by training long-term students and developing an organizational commitment to change with changing times. Gratefully, the Fetzer Institute is supporting Centering Prayer in just this way. All the Western traditions should continue recovering their own unique contemplative practices. Support needs to continue for an American form of Buddhism, as Buddhist teachers and practitioners so discern. Ways that the different traditions could inform each other about their progress in these areas should be better established.
- Applications of these contemplative practices to the secular world through scientific research, psychological dialogue and translations to non-religious settings (like prison work and the 12 steps) need to continue. These ventures should preserve the integrity of the religious/spiritual character of the practices by, for example, adapting them to secular use but distinguishing the adaptations from traditional religious usage.
- Networking events, such as the Future of Contemplative Practice in America gathering, could continue, so that the traditions can support each other in the light of the broader perspective that academic input provides. Appropriate networking structures, institutes and publications can be developed from such gatherings.
- The common themes that comprise and foster the larger contemplative movement could be identified and explored further, such as: interspiritual sensitivity, lay-oriented practice, and the different styles and forms of contemplative practice from various traditions.

We are now living in a time and place when information about the contemplative traditions is more accessible than ever before. But information is not enough. What needs to be strengthened, sustained and translated for contemporary American life are the communities and structures that embody and transmit the heart of the contemplative experience. Due to the commitment of many practitioners of good heart and institutions of great vision, this support is happening.

There will always be a place for the enduring path of contemplative practice in America; may it continue to illumine the lives of all who seek it.

Notes

1   John Cassian. (1985). *Conferences; The Classics of Western Spirituality*. New York: Paulist Press.

2   Ferguson, J.K., Willemsen, E.W., & Castaneto, M.V. (June 2009). "Centering Prayer as a Healing Response to Stress" *Pastoral Psychology*, Springer, Netherlands. Retrieved from http://www.springerlink.com/content/8253111mj1223930/.

State of Contemplative Practice: Contemplative Living

Robert Toth

> *Wherever man and society exist: where there are hopes, ideals,*
> *aspirations for a better future; where there is love—and where*
> *there is mingled pain and happiness—there the contemplative*
> *life has a place.* — Thomas Merton

Five years ago as The Thomas Merton Foundation Board of Directors was reviewing its mission and strategic direction we were challenged by one of our members to consider what the organization could do that will continue to have an impact on culture and society for the next fifty to one hundred years. That led to a year long process of identifying what, at the core of our mission, would have long term impact. Considering the insights of Thomas Merton and others, we concluded that something fundamental to resolving the major issues confronting humanity needed to be addressed, that is, repairing the disintegrating relationships that are essential for any enduring progress in improving the human condition. Those essential relationships are with oneself, others, nature and God.

With a focus on relationships, we defined contemplative living as "living in unified relationship with oneself, others, nature and God, free of the illusion of separateness." We revised our mission statement to, "awaken interest in and develop resources for contemplative living through the works of Thomas Merton and others in order to create a more just, peaceful and sustainable world." In 2006 we changed our name to The Merton Institute for Contemplative Living to better represent the nature of our work.

Bridges to Contemplative Living

The Institute's initial program in this area, *Bridges to Contemplative Living*, was designed to engage individuals in a more reflective approach to daily life through contemplative dialogue leading them to understand the unity of these relationships and to take greater responsibility for deepening them.

The words contemplative and contemplation describe an important dimension of human nature that is necessary for personal balance and integration particularly in a culture that is addicted to activity and external stimulus and are complementary, not antithetical, to active life in the secular world.

Contemplative living is a way of listening and responding to our everyday experiences by consciously attending to our relationships with self, others, God, and all of nature. The goal of contemplative living is not merely the personal fulfillment of those who pursue it. Its ultimate goal is a global society that is profoundly just and at peace.

Bridges is a small group resource that guides participants toward a more contemplative and peace-filled life. Using Merton's writings as a starting point, it seeks to mine the life experience and spiritual depths of those who use it. The series' themes are based on key principles from Merton's thought:

- Our everyday life is our spiritual life.
- It is every person's primary vocation to be fully human, aware of who we are and how we relate to others.
- Our spiritual formation cannot take place in isolation. It is grounded in the experience of relationships and community.
- Personal transformation is the foundation for societal and cultural transformation.

Each of the eight booklets of the *Bridges* series contains eight sessions with a reading from Merton paired with another on the same theme from a different spiritual writer.

Bridges does not provide lesson plans or blueprints, but is simply a springboard into contemplative dialogue and living. Contemplative dialogue in the context of *Bridges* involves reflecting deeply on each of the themes in the context of everyday life, listening to others without judgment or evaluation and sharing with them one's own experiences, thoughts, and questions as they flow from the session themes. Its goal is to help one consider how what is being shared applies to the current context of one's life—what one believes and values, how one spends time, and how one decides what is really important. Contemplative dialogue is an effective way for a group of diverse people to talk without dissention when they have differences of beliefs or opinions.

Since launching *Bridges* in the fall of 2007, an estimated 3,000 groups have formed in the United States and throughout the English speaking world. It is being used in many places including churches, colleges and universities, prisons, retreat centers and the US House of Representatives.

Contemplative Leadership and the Contemplative Family

While developing *Bridges,* we saw that the complex problems facing nations, organizations, communities and families are rooted in the way the members who comprise those entities experience the four core relationships. The logical extension of *Bridges,* a program that starts with self-relationship, was to address specific areas of relationship with others. This led to developing two new initiatives: Contemplative Leadership and The Contemplative Family.

The Need for Contemplative Living

In 2006 New West Public Relations conducted focus groups and an online survey for The Merton Institute. Here is a summary of the results.

Focus Group Results

"Spirituality is simple—but hard." Members in each group acknowledged the importance of religion in helping them pursue their own spirituality since the core of all religions is the acceptance that there is "something larger than myself." But to a person, each group made a distinction between being a spiritual person and being a religious person.

"Religion is the knowledge of God. Spirituality is the experience of God." Spirituality was described as something very personal—"finding God within me," "a journey," "joyful." On the other hand, religion was easier for people in both groups to define. It is an "external affiliation" where one becomes a member of a group, follows rules and participates in rituals.

"Contemplative living is not passive." Both groups concurred that contemplative living is more closely aligned with the spiritual than the religious. Contemplative living was described as a filter to help block out the noise of daily life so a person can appreciate the rhythms of the world; find his or her place in it; and the actions he or she should undertake to improve it. There was considerable agreement that while being contemplative can lead to "surprise awareness" in the simple joys of life—the consensus was that contemplative living takes planning and preparation and then "translating the internal state to external practice for peace and justice."

Several members in both groups attended retreats—guided and unstructured. The unstructured model was seen as the preferred model for experiencing the "surprise awareness" of spirituality.

"I think that Merton and contemplative life come together and cause great sparks." The groups see Merton as a teacher who helps educate people on how to explore and express spirituality. His works provide a menu of ideas to help a person live a contemplative life and shows a breadth of vehicles one can use to express the spirituality he or she discovers while being contemplative. In that sense, Merton's work underscores the fact that the spirituality one discovers should be shared with others—through art (writing, painting, poetry) or through other action, from being a caring parent or spouse to being a peace activist.

Online Survey Results (515 responses)

An overwhelming number, approximately 95%, have a desire to live more contemplatively. The descriptors selected most to define contemplative living were "spiritual discovery," "self-awareness," "more focused" and "quiet." Improved relationships rank high as a benefit of contemplative living.

The age mix is reflective of those participating in the two focus groups. More than half are in the 50-65 demographic and about a quarter in each demographic group above and below. The educational level of the respondents is impressive—84% hold Baccalaureate degrees and above. More than 50% hold postgraduate degrees. Sixty percent of the respondents identify themselves as Catholic, although 95% say Thomas Merton's work is not specific to any particular religion.

The most requested deliverable was resources to be used in personal spiritual discovery. These resources were further defined to be access to inspirational materials and a spiritual guide. A majority of respondents (64%) make retreats although there is no preferred frequency.

The Contemplative Living Movement

The Contemplative Living Movement stems from a realization that the pursuit of a higher and higher materialistic standard of living is antithetical to the ultimate expectations of that pursuit—happiness, peace and joy—and that such a pursuit by individuals has detrimental consequences to the relationships that are fundamental to personal happiness and joy and to the welfare of the human community.

Our culture equates the standard of living with wealth, power, prestige, pleasure, and extravagance. There comes a time when some people reach a saturation point, when they have their fill of things, technology, entertainment, food, alcohol, drugs, sex, etc., and seek some other approach to life that satisfies their need for greater meaning and purpose.

Others are also seeking a different way of life in the context of their personal spiritual journeys.

There are many examples of the collective power of individuals to influence the direction of society. By addressing the primary source for resolving the issues confronting humanity, that is, humankind's core relationships, the Contemplative Living Movement can slow down and reverse the negative aspects of our culture's current direction. This movement represents a significant shift from merely addressing symptoms to addressing root causes of the effects of alienation in our personal lives and in our society. It involves a shift from institutional responsibility to personal responsibility, from self-serving leadership to other-centered leadership. It is also so fundamental that it transcends all the barriers that traditionally impede progress—religion, politics, nationalism, age, and sex.

As we work on our initiatives we better understand the extent to which they fit into this broad and growing movement toward a contemplative way of living. We encounter many individuals and organizations concerned with some aspect of contemplative values and practices. For the most part they are working independently and have not seen themselves as part of a movement leading to some result much greater than their personal objectives or those of their particular project or program. This can be attributed to a lack of definition and a well-articulated, common, "ultimate" objective. If this is indeed a movement, its objective must be universally compelling. It must address recognized personal and institutional needs that affect great numbers of people.

The Merton Institute believes the ultimate objective of this movement is to improve the human condition.

The Merton Institute's goal is to make a significant contribution to the movement by:

- Focusing on strengthening the relationships (with oneself, others, nature and God) that are fundamental for personal and cultural transformation
- Concentrating on three specific initiatives: personal development; leadership and family life
- Applying the contemplative values of monastic traditions to these initiatives
- Developing resources for widespread use that are accessible and affordable
- Collaborating with other organizations and individuals to form a mutually supporting network that shares a common vision

- Building constituency through a national communications campaign that creates awareness of The Institute's/Collaborative Network's initiatives and resources.
- Planning a new center for Contemplative Living and Leadership on forty acres given to the Institute by the Abbey of Gethsemani.

Contemplative living may never move from being entirely counter-cultural to being mainstream culture, but the principles and values of contemplative living can be a powerful influence—a brake for the out-of control pace of life; a way of seeing the illusions we unconsciously accept; a way to integrate active and contemplative life; and a way to discover the peace that comes from trusting, loving relationships.

Thomas Merton could be starkly realistic about the human condition:

> I think what I need to learn is an almost infinite tolerance and compassion because negative thought gets nowhere. I am beginning to think that in our time we will correct almost nothing, and get almost nowhere: but if we can just prepare a compassionate and receptive soil for the future, we will have done a great work. I feel at least that this is the turn that my own life ought to take.

And as he counseled peace activist, Jim Forest:

> Do not depend on the hope of results. When you are doing the sort of work you have taken on, essentially an apostolic work, you may have to face the fact that your work will be apparently worthless and even achieve no result at all, if not perhaps results opposite to what you expect. As you get used to this idea you start more and more to concentrate not on the results but on the value, the rightness, the truth of the work itself (*The Hidden Ground of Love*, p.294).

But he also saw the possibilities for humanity:

> I have the immense joy of being human, a member of a race in which God himself became incarnate. As if the sorrows and stupidities of the human condition could overwhelm me, now that I realize what we all are. If only everybody

could realize this! But it cannot be explained. There is no way of telling people that they are all walking around shining like the sun (*Conjectures of a Guilty Bystander*, p. 157).

Islamic and Islamicate Contemplative Practice in the United States

Zia Inayat-Khan

1. Describe how you define or use the term, "contemplative practice."

The word "contemplation" derives from the Latin roots *cum* ("with") and *templum* ("a consecrated space"). In antiquity a *templum* was "a vast space, open on all sides, from which one could survey the whole surrounding landscape as far as the horizon."[1] The practice of contemplation therefore suggests the widening of one's field of vision.

In the Christian tradition, contemplation is frequently contrasted with meditation. Whereas meditation is defined as deep reflection on a sacred theme, contemplation denotes an act of direct intuitive perception. St. John of the Cross identifies meditation with *sense* and contemplation with *spirit*. The former mode of knowing, he says, must eventually be renounced in favor of the latter.[2]

In the tradition to which I belong, the Sufism of Hazrat Inayat Khan, the words contemplation and meditation mean the opposite: contemplation (*muraqaba*) refers to the process of deepening reflection, while meditation (*mushahada*) refers to awareness without thought content. Spiritual study on the Sufi path comprises four basic stages: concentration, contemplation, meditation, and realization.[3] Concentration involves stilling the body and focusing the mind on a single object. Contemplation involves shifting one's attention from the form of an object to its essence, or subtle "signature." In meditation the seeker learns to transcend subject and object entirely and experience the pure ground of undifferentiated consciousness. Realization is achieved when the seeker is able to maintain "stereoscopic" awareness, encompassing the whole range of perception from form to formlessness.

In mainstream contemporary parlance, "contemplative practice" is often used in a general sense to denote various disciplines of practice concerned with the elevation, expansion, and deepening of consciousness. Often it is used interchangeably with the words "mysticism," "spirituality," and "mindfulness." I find, however, that it has certain distinct advantages over these words. For many, mysticism evokes the specter of arcane mysteries that are intrinsically obfuscatory and incompatible with rational thought. Spirituality is closely associated with religiosity, and might be assumed to exclude secular methodologies. It also suggests a spirit/matter split, and the privileging of spirit over matter. Mindfulness is limited by its reference to the mind. In some contemplative traditions, the "heart" is more central than the "mind." For all of these reasons, "contemplative practice" seems to me the most satisfactory rubric under which to discuss the wide array of contemporary methodologies concerned with the transformation of consciousness.

2. Describe the development of contemplative practice in this sector over the past twenty-five years. What specific contemplative practices are most commonly used in this sector? How have these evolved or been adapted over the past twenty-five years?

The sector that has been assigned to me is Islam. I would like to extend the scope of my discussion to include, in addition to Islamic practice, Islamicate practice. The term Islamicate was coined by Marshall Hodgson, who wrote, "'Islamicate' would refer not directly to the religion, Islam, but to the social and cultural complex historically associated with Islam and the Muslims, both among Muslims themselves and even when found among non-Muslims."[4]

The contemplative dimension of Islam and Islamic culture is largely synonymous with Sufism. Sufism is a widespread and diverse phenomenon, embedded in nearly every Muslim society in the world. It emerged as a mystical worldview in the ninth century and over time transformed into a dynamic social and intellectual movement driven by organized orders spread across the Afro-Eurasian *oikumene*.

In 1910, the Indian philosopher-musician Hazrat Inayat Khan (1882-1927) introduced Sufism to the United States and Europe. He first taught within a traditional Islamic framework, but soon adapted his teaching to accommodate the religious and cultural orientation of his students. Later, in the 70s and 80s, a wave of Sufi teachers from the Islamic world introduced their orders in the United States. These included Bawa Muhyiuddin (Qadiri), Dr. Javad Nurbakhsh (Nimatullahi), Shaikh Fadhlalla Haeri (Shadhili-Darqawi), Suleyman Dede (Mevlevi), Shaikh Muzaffer Ozak (Jerrahi), and Shaikh Nazim al-Haqqani (Naqshbandi). Many of these teachers taught Sufism within the context of formal Islamic practice.

Surveying the "garden" of Western Sufism, Marcia Hermansen divides contemporary groups into the categories of transplant, hybrid, and perennial.[5] Transplants are Islamic Sufi groups that make only minimal concessions to their new Western environment. Hybrids adapt to the Western cultural landscape while maintaining a close identification with an Islamic source and content. Perennials, by contrast, downplay their Islamic moorings and emphasize the mystical unity of all religions. Dr. Hermansen's three categories provide a useful framework within which to track the development of Islamic and Islamicate contemplative practices in the United States over the last twenty-five years.

Transplants are the least visible of the three kinds of groups, but they are also, I suspect, the largest and fastest growing. According to the Pew Research Center, there are 2.5 million Muslims in the United States and (based on data collected in 2007) 65% of adult Muslims in the U.S. were born elsewhere.[6] Muslim immigrants from Asia, Africa and Eastern Europe frequently bring with them practices and affiliations rooted in their homelands. When immigrant communities reach a critical mass in urban centers they become capable of supporting religious leaders and institutions. Transplant Sufi groups generally display a strongly religious and devotional character. The dividing line between religious and devotional practice and contemplative practice is often difficult to delineate, particularly when the former modes reach a high level of psychological and spiritual intensity. Beyond the obligatory and supererogatory rituals of Islam, the core practices of transplants are *zikr* (*dhikr*), the rhythmic intonation of the Islamic profession of faith (*la ilaha illa'llah*, "no god but God"), and *awrad*, orisons incorporating verses from the Qur'an.

Transplant groups depend upon the internal cohesion of immigrant communities for their continuity. As second-generation Muslims merge into the general population and adapt to its norms, a new idiom is needed, and this is what hybrid Sufi groups provide. Whereas transplants are for the most part ethnically and culturally homogenous, hybrids accommodate greater diversity. Because they tend to utilize contemporary information technologies, hybrid groups are more visible. They are also better positioned to promote their teachings and practices in a manner capable of attracting the attention of general spiritual seekers. Despite the greater accessibility of these groups, however, their practices often do not differ significantly from the practices of transplant groups.

Perennials may be divided into two categories: traditionalist and universalist. Traditionalist perennials follow the legacy of the early twentieth-century French esotericist Renee Guenon (1886-1951), who condemned the ideologies of modernity and sought to revive the "perennial tradition" that he discerned underlying all classical civilizations. Guenon's followers, a number of them Sufis, formed an intellectual circle that has made significant inroads in academia. While numerically small, the perennialist movement has been effective in focusing attention on the aesthetic and spiritual value of traditional cosmologies and disciplines of sacred practice.

Universalist perennials display perhaps the greatest propensity for adaptation of all Sufi groups. Their lack of emphasis on normative Islamic practice manifests in some cases as indifference to religious forms and in other cases as a commitment to interfaith reconciliation and solidarity. The practices of these groups include *zikr*, but Arabic recitations are fewer, and the "yogic" element of Sufism is more pronounced.[7] These groups also tend to be more receptive to new ideas in the fields of science and psychology, with the result that their contemplative methods have in some cases become informed by the insights of quantum physics, cell biology, ecology, object relations theory, transpersonal psychology, etc.

The legacy of Hazrat Inayat Khan is a case in point. Inayat Khan maintained a policy of inclusiveness that was in keeping with the traditions of the South Asian Chishti Order to which he belonged. His object was not to proselytize, but to transmit esoteric teachings and practices conducive to "the awakening of the consciousness of humanity to the divinity of man."[8] Members of the leisured class figured prominently in Inayat Khan's original Sufi organization. The large circle of belle-epoque aristocrats who surrounded him were drawn to contemplative practice as a means of deepening and interiorizing their own inbred romantic aestheticism. Their gilded subculture was, however, not to last; when the next major wave of Sufi activity arose, in the late 60s and early 70s, a very different generation took up the torch of Sufism. This was the heyday of the countercultural movement, when political and social disaffection prompted young adults to distance themselves from mainstream culture and explore alternative lifeways, including the practice of Eastern religions.

The elaboration of Inayat Khan's contemplative teachings has taken various directions in the last twenty-five years. Two notable developments emerged in the late 60s. The first was the spiritual teaching of Samuel Lewis (1896-1971), a student of Inayat Khan who created a series of interfaith contemplative circle dances called the Dances of Universal Peace. These dances attracted a loyal following among young counterculturals, and in succeeding decades spread internationally. According to the website of the International Network for the Dances of Universal Peace: "From the early days and his original body of about 50 dances, the collection has grown since his passing to more than 500 dances which celebrate the sacred heart of Hinduism, Buddhism, Zoroastrianism, Sikhism, Judaism, Christianity, Islam, and the Aramaic, Native American, Native Middle Eastern, Celtic, Native African, and Goddess traditions. Since the late 1960's, the Dances have spread throughout the world, touching more than a half million people in North and South America, eastern and western Europe, the former Soviet Union, India, the Middle East, Africa, Pakistan, Australia, and New Zealand. New grassroots Dance circles are continually springing up around the globe, with over two hundred dance circles meeting weekly or monthly in the United States alone."[9]

Another significant development was the teaching of Hazrat Inayat Khan's son Pir Vilayat (1916-2004). Like Lewis, Pir Vilayat drew extensively on non-Islamic spiritual sources, including yoga, Buddhism, Kabbalah, and Christian mysticism. But he also invoked a number of contemporary disciplines; most prominently, the depth psychology of Carl Jung, the evolutionary theology of Teilhard de Chardin, and the quantum physics of David Bohm and Ilya Prigogine. Pir Vilayat conceived of meditation as a science that requires continuous updating as the human condition evolves. He described "the new spirituality" as, "the validation of the bounty of life instead of asceticism; awakening in life rather than evasion; arousing the qualities of the cosmos lying in wait in one's being so as to become a more bountiful personality; mastery through achievement; and building a more beautiful world by becoming more beautiful people."[10]

Pir Vilayat established strong Sufi organizations in a number of countries in North America and Europe. His students have developed various aspects of his work. Some have emphasized the alchemical process that he created as a model for spiritual retreat, working with breath, sound, and light to "modulate consciousness beyond the middle range." Others have stressed the psychological element in meditation, downplaying ritual forms and giving precedence to internal self-reflection.[11] Others have focused on physiology, studying the interplay of respiration and circulation.[12] Another group has amalgamated Sufi healing with concepts from somatic psychology.[13] As Pir Vilayat's designated successor, my own contribution has been the creation of an esoteric school called The Suluk Academy, which offers a two-year experiential course focused on Inayat Khan's original methodology of concentration, contemplation, meditation, and realization.

3. What organizations have developed to support contemplative practice in this sector?

The Bawa Muhaiyaddeen Fellowship: Lineage of Bawa Muhaiyaddeen. Mosque in Philadelphia. twww.bmf.org

The Golden Sufi Center: Lineage of Irina Tweedie. Currently led by Llewellyn Vaughn-Lee. Emphasis on dreamwork. www.goldensufi.org

The Halveti-Jerrahi Tariqa: Lineage of Shaikh Muzaffer Ozak. Currently led by Shaikh Tosun Bayrak. www.jerrahi.org

The Ibn al-'Arabi Society: Study group dedicated to the teachings of the 13th-century philosopher Ibn al-'Arabi. www.ibnarabisociety.org

The International Association of Sufism: Affiliated with the U.N.; organizes an annual inter-order symposium. www.ias.org

The Mevlevi Order of America: Lineage of Suleiman Dede. Currently led by Shaikh Jelaluddin Loras. Emphasis on turning. www.hayatidede.org

The Naqshbandi-Haqqani Sufi Order of America: Lineage of Shaikh Nazim al-Haqqani. Currently led by Shaikh Hisham al-Kabbani. Wide global reach. www.naqshbandi.org

The Nimatullahi Order: Lineage of Dr. Javad Nurbakhsh. Currently led by Dr. Alireza Nurbakhsh. www.nimatullahi.org

The Nur Ashki Jerrahi Sufi Order: Lineage of Shaikh Muzaffer Ozak. Currently led by Shaikha Fariha al-Jerrahi. Mosque in New York City. www.nurashkijerrahi.org

The Shadhiliyya Sufi Center: Led by Sidi Jamal al-Shadhili. Emphasis on healing. www.suficenter.org; www.sufiuniversity.org

The Sufi Foundation of America. Led by Adnan Sarhan. Emphasis on dance. www.sufifoundation.org

The Sufi Movement International. Lineage of Hazrat Inayat Khan. Currently led by Murshid Hidayat Inayat-Khan. www.sufimovement.org

The Sufi Order International. Lineage of Hazrat Inayat Khan and Pir Vilayat Inayat-Khan. Currently led by Pir Zia Inayat-Khan. www.sufiorder.org; www.theabode.net; www.sulukacademy.org

The Sufi Ruhaniat International. Lineage of Hazrat Inayat Khan and Murshid Samuel Lewis. Currently led by Pir Shabda Kahn. Emphasis on Dances of Universal Peace. www.ruhaniat.org

The Threshold Society. Led by Kabir and Camille Helminski. Emphasis on the teachings of the 13th century poet Jalal al-Din Rumi. www.sufism.org

4. Describe the demographics of those who participate in contemplative practice in this sector. Please include, where available, information on the number of practitioners as well as their age, gender, education, and ethnicity. Have the demographics changed over the past twenty-five years? Please provide citations if references are available.

Unfortunately statistics on participation in Sufi activities among Americans is not available. My response, therefore, will have to be a reflection of my personal perceptions.

As noted above, members of transplant groups are almost exclusively Muslim immigrants. Public roles in these organizations are generally reserved for men. Hybrid groups usually consist of a combination of immigrants, second-generation Muslim Americans, and converts to Islam. Women play a somewhat more visible role in these organizations. In perennial groups, women often hold positions of authority, and frequently outnumber men. Participants in perennial groups historically have been white middle-class Americans, but this is beginning to change in recent times as second-generation American Muslims are drawn to these groups in their search for a spiritual path that is at once Islamicate and pluralistic. Generation X was not attracted to Sufism to the degree that Baby Boomers were, but there are signs of a resurgence of interest among young adults.

5. What are the key trends, opportunities and challenges facing contemplative practice in this sector in the coming decade?

The perception of a "clash of civilizations" between Islam and the West, intensified by the terrorist attacks of 9-11 and the wars in Iraq and Afghanistan, has heightened public awareness of Islam among Americans. While much of the attention directed toward Islam has been negative, numerous attempts have been made to present a more balanced picture, and Sufism in particular has frequently been highlighted as an example of Islam's capacity for progressive, pluralistic discourse. At the present juncture, when the implications of the relationship between the Islamic world and the West are so far-reaching, Sufism has a crucial role to play in facilitating cultural exchange and bearing witness to the universal moral and spiritual values at the heart of the human experience.

Technology is propelling social change with amazing rapidity, particularly in the area of communication. Face-to-face conversations and printed books are becoming obsolete as Millennials turn to computers, cell phones, and other digital devices for information, entertainment, and friendship. Like almost all segments of society, Muslim and Sufi groups are availing themselves of the opportunities that the Internet presents. Most organizations have websites, and there are email listserves and social networking groups dedicated to various paths. The Naqshbandi-Haqqani site invites seekers to take initiation with their shaikh via email.[14] Other sites offer web courses in contemplative practice. These developments mean that Sufism is more accessible than ever before to people throughout the world. Amidst this profusion of *representations* of Sufism, however, the nonverbal transmission of *presence*, which traditionally has been considered the sacred essence of the Sufi path, is in danger of being diminished or lost.

Human societies across the world are likely to experience increasingly significant disruptions in the coming century due to the effects of climate change. The continued degradation of Earth's living systems will further reduce already limited natural resources, producing droughts, conflicts, and the dislocation of populations. Limits on emissions to reduce the rate of global heating combined with oil depletion will substantially raise energy costs, undermining the economic foundations of globalization. Sustainable energy and local agriculture and community will consequently take on renewed importance. The religious and contemplative groups that will have a relevant and constructive voice in the flow of events will be those that are able to frame these profound changes within a coherent cosmological story and provide useful contemplative tools for navigating shifting structures.

6. To what extent do you agree with the notion that a larger contemplative movement is emerging in America? What does contemplative practice in your setting contribute to such a movement? What in your opinion what will be needed to nurture the growth and development of a contemplative movement in

America?

Certainly there is anecdotal evidence that contemplative practice is entering the mainstream. The airport that I regularly use, Albany International, has a Meditation Room. In cities and towns across the U.S., yoga centers are ubiquitous. Deepak Chopra is a familiar guest on Larry King Live, the Beastie Boys practice Tibetan Buddhism, and Madonna advocates Kabbalah.

More importantly, in conversations with friends, colleagues, and new acquaintances working in various sectors of society I have often had the impression that a convergence seems to be taking place, a deepening nexus between the fields of ecology, psychology, healing, spirituality, education, and action for social, political, and economic change. When I think of the potential for a contemplative movement, I think of it as an inextricable strand of this larger pattern of burgeoning consciousness of interdependence and wholeness.

Though my primary work is in the domain of Sufism, I have felt called to participate in the larger interspiritual and transdisciplinary movement for the transformation of consciousness that I see taking shape. Toward this end, with a group of friends and colleagues, in 2008 I founded Seven Pillars House of Wisdom (www.sevenpillarshouse.org). The four areas of Seven Pillars' mission represent my understanding of what is needed at the present time, and how my collaborators and I can contribute.

The first area is *Cosmology*. The task here is to assimilate the monumental discoveries of modern science within a living cosmological narrative that speaks meaningfully to the spiritual imagination and awakened conscience of contemporary people, enabling nature to function as a meta-scripture.

The second area is *Revelation*. The task here is to explore revelation as a planetary phenomenon in which all religions have a share but of which none has a monopoly. The perspective that emerges honors all faith traditions as historical expressions of the ongoing human encounter with the divine, and seeks to make a place for them all at the table.

The third area is *Mysticism*. The task here is to responsibly explore faculties of perception beyond the ordinary diurnal range, and on the basis on this widening vista of experience, to promote awareness within public discourse of the authenticity and accessibility of contemplative states of consciousness.

The fourth area is *Chivalry*. The task here is to translate consciousness and conscience into direct action at the individual and collective level by creating and enacting a contemporary chivalric code premised on the virtues of justice, forgiveness, truthfulness, generosity, courage, and hope.

These four areas have been the subject of extensive discussion in Seven

Pillars, and our goals and strategies are progressively becoming clearer. I look forward the upcoming gathering hosted by the Fetzer Institute as a splendid opportunity to further hone my understanding of what is needed.

Notes

1   Henry Corbin, *Temple and Contemplation*, trans. Philip Sherrard (London: KPI, 1986), p. 386.

2   St. John of the Cross, *The Dark Night of the Soul*, trans. E. Allison Peers (Westminster, MD: The Newman Press, 1964), I, pp. 108–111.

3   Inayat Khan, *The Sufi Message* (London: Barrie and Jenkins, 1972): IV, pp. 154–156.

4   Marshall G.S. Hodgson, *The Venture of Islam* (Chicago: The University of Chicago Press, 1974), I, p. 59.

5   Marcia Hermansen, "In the Garden of American Sufism," in *New Trends and Developments in the World of Islam*, ed. Peter Clarke (London: Luzac Oriental Press, 1997), pp. 155–178.

6   http://pewresearch.org/pubs/483/muslim-americans.

7   In South Asia, from the 13th century onward Chishti Sufis and Nathpanthi yogis maintained collegial relations, and a body of shared esoteric lore took shape. This lore is concerned with mastery of breath and the awakening of subtle organs of spiritual perception (*chakrein, lata'if*).

8   Inayat Khan, *The Sufi Message* (London: Barrie and Rockliff, 1963), IX, p. 249.

9   http://dancesofuniversalpeace.org/about.htm.

10 Pir Vilayat Inayat-Khan, "Hazrat Pir-o-Murshid Inayat Khan's Message for Our Time," in Zia Inayat-Khan, ed., *A Pearl in Wine* (New Lebanon, NY: Omega Publications, 2001), p. 372.

11 This tendency has been reinforced by the influence of the Diamond

Heart method of A.H. Almaas.

12 See, for example: http://www.appliedmeditation.org/index.php.

13 See, for example: http://www.theraphaelitework.com/.

14 http://naqshbandi.org/about/baya.htm.

Socially Engaged Buddhist Contemplative Practices: Past and Potential Future Contributions at a Time of Cultural Transition and Crisis

Donald Rothberg

I would like, in this short essay, to survey the state of socially engaged Buddhist practice, outlining (1) what I take to be the key developments in this field in the last twenty-five years, (2) some of the field's contributions to the emergence of "contemplative practice in America" (including questions and challenges about some of the main ways that contemplation and meditation have been understood and popularized), and (3) some of the potential future horizons and contributions of socially engaged Buddhist practice.

First, though, I would like to situate my reflections in relationship to the practical and theoretical contexts out of which they have grown, reflecting on my own background and training. This will also begin to identify a number of the organizations and programs in which the development of socially engaged Buddhist practice has occurred. Secondly, I want to offer some initial reflections on some of the core concepts framing my discussion (all but the last of which are central to our conference): "*contemplation*," "*action*," "*meditation*," and "*engaged Buddhism*." As we will see, some of the contributions of socially engaged Buddhism, coupled with an examination of the meaning and historical origins of these concepts, may lead us to question the historically dominant Western duality of contemplation and action, and to explore its influence in contemporary contemplative practice.

The Background for This Essay: Personal, Organizational, and Historical

A short exploration of my personal journey and work in socially engaged Buddhist practice may help point to some of the main organizations, trends, developments, and challenges of the last 25 years in this field, which I will then explore in more depth in later sections.

I began Buddhist practice in 1976, while a student (receiving a B.A. from Yale and a Ph.D. in Philosophy from Boston University), while spending two summers at Naropa Institute. There I met Joseph Goldstein and Jack

Kornfield, with whom I started the practice of insight meditation (a practice that has continued to this day), as well as Chogyam Trungpa Rinpoche, Maezumi Roshi, and others. At the time, I was very involved with responding to social issues, studying social and political theory, psychology, and the Greek and German philosophical traditions, and felt deeply committed to working for social justice while also drawn to mystical traditions and transpersonal psychology

Upon beginning Buddhist practice, I put some of my interest in social justice on the back burner, so to speak, being drawn to participate in silent retreats at the newly-formed Insight Meditation Society in Barre, Massachusetts, where, from 1977 to 1980, I did numerous 10-14 day retreats, as well as a 6-7 month stay in 1979 and 1980. After my first retreat, I felt a deep kind of homecoming, and felt strongly drawn to the powerful explorations and transformations possible in retreats (even as I was continuing my other studies).

At first intending to become a monk in Asia, I came to see my own vocation as more integrative, connecting the Buddhist practice that had become so important, with practices in other parts of my life, including everyday life, relationships, and social justice work, asking what forms of spirituality would be appropriate to help us respond to the needs of the times. I then chose to go into the "heartland" of America, in my case, rural Ohio and Kentucky, to teach at universities and colleges for seven years, and to pursue such an integration personally and theoretically.

Eventually, I chose to continue this work in the San Francisco Bay Area, where there was a critical mass of people sharing my perspectives, moving there in 1988. I began working with the Buddhist Peace Fellowship (BPF), based in Berkeley, serving on the Board and helping to organize workshops and summer institutes, bringing together such major teachers and figures as Robert Aitken, Roshi; Dr. A. T. Ariyaratne; Joanna Macy; Sulak Sivaraksa; and others. I traveled to Thailand several times for meetings of the International Network of Engaged Buddhists (INEB), meeting many like-minded colleagues from Asia and the West; in 1997, many of us formed the "Think Sangha," to support the development of the theoretical basis of socially engaged Buddhism.

I had myself begun, in the early 1990s, publishing essays on socially engaged Buddhism. But I was especially drawn to helping to articulate a kind of *practical path* of socially engaged Buddhism, eventually helping to organize a series of training programs for those doing social service or social action work, including the development of a curriculum of study and practices, that might help clarify such a path.

Since 1995, I have worked with three training programs. The first, founded by my good friend, Diana Winston, currently Director of Education at the Mindful Awareness Research Center at UCLA, is the *BASE (Buddhist Alliance for Social Engagement)* program; we've had about 30 of these six-month training programs, typically structured by weekend retreats to begin and end the programs, one or two monthly daylong retreats, and weekly meetings.[1]

I also started, with the help of my colleagues Jürgen Kremer and Ann Masai, an interfaith program in *Socially Engaged Spirituality* in 2001, at Saybrook University in San Francisco, where I was a core faculty member up until 2009. These were 18 to 24 month programs, focusing more on study—of the Jewish prophets and Jesus, Gandhi and King, liberation theology and Dorothy Day, indigenous traditions, socially engaged Buddhism, and contemporary emphases on gender and ecology, among others. We took as foundational resources (1) contemplative practice, particularly mindfulness practice from Buddhist tradition; (2) social justice perspectives from the Abrahamic traditions; and (3) the focus on ecology and community in indigenous traditions.[2]

The third program is the *Path of Engagement Program* at Spirit Rock, where I teach as a member of its Teachers Council. This two-year program, running from 2007 to 2009, had 50 initial participants, over 20 mentors and guest teachers (as well as three core teachers—myself, Ann Masai, and Adrianne Ross), and a structure of five seven-day retreats, monthly group meetings, monthly work with a mentor, and a monthly "study and practice" curriculum.

While this focus on connecting more "inner" and more "outer" transformation has remained central, there have been cycles, reflected in both my personal journey and in the curriculum, in which either the inner or the outer is more emphasized. I have found myself drawn regularly toward longer periods of more intensive silent practice, toward more solitude, moving away from a focus on everyday life and action, once for a year and commonly for one to two months a year. Understanding and respecting such cycles and our own deep intuitions for "what comes next," and what is required for long-term sustainability, are crucial.

A Clarification of Key Terms—"Contemplation," "Action," "Meditation," "Engaged Buddhism"—and the Historical Separation of Contemplation and Action

In exploring "socially engaged Buddhism," I have come to a deepened understanding of the advantages, ambiguities, and challenges associated with terms like "contemplation," "meditation," "action," and "engaged." Giving attention to these terms in fact helps us to understand a lot about "the [present and future] state[s] of contemplation in America."

Contemplation (or Meditation) and Action

Take the terms, "contemplation" (or "meditation," often used as a synonym for contemplation, despite their different meanings in Christian contemplative tradition) and "action." "Contemplation" has its conceptual origins in a strong *separation of contemplation and action*, with a basis in Western philosophical and religious traditions. When we use the term, there are numerous resonances, of history and meaning, which condition us to continue that separation when we speak of contemplative traditions "entering the mainstream" at the current time. This separation certainly is problematic in a number of ways; many socially engaged Buddhists, as well as many Western contemplatives, have pointed out some of the issues and attempted to overcome the separation, speaking of the need for "meditation in action" (socially engaged Buddhists generally have not used "contemplation" as a central term).

The dominant Western philosophical and religious traditions of the last 2500 years, stemming especially from ancient Greek traditions, have rested on this separation. The spiritual (or "contemplative") realm is distinguished from the political or practical realm (the activity or action of *praxis* in the *polis*), with the former often seen as. timeless, absolute, and other-worldly, and the latter understood as time-bound, historical, contingent, and this-worldly.[3]

The opposition goes at least back to the fourth century B.C.E. At that time, Aristotle systematized the distinction between "theory" (*theōria*) and "practice" (*praxis*), i.e., "political" discussion and decision-making. The superior contemplative life of *theōria*, in which we come to know the eternal truths both conceptually and experientially, requires a suspension from the duties and constraints of practical, active life. The philosopher, Plotinus, who would provide much of the intellectual framework for later Jewish and Christian contemplation and mysticism, explained the need for this separation a few centuries later: "The point of action is contemplation . . . Contemplation is therefore the end of action."[4] For Plotinus, furthermore, the contemplative knows the eternal apart from ordinary human life: "Such is the life of the divinity and of divine and blessed men: detachment from all things here below, scorn of all earthly pleasures, the flight of the lone to the Alone."[5]

We find contemporary secular forms of the distinction between theory and practice, or contemplation and action, in the separation between science and ethics, knowledge and values, objective and subjective, and intellectual and activist. With modernity, the split between contemplation and action has, if anything, been exacerbated, because of the "anti-religious" and "anti-metaphysical" origins of this epoch, with modern critiques of religion and metaphysics clearing public space so that scientists could study the "objective" world and advocates of rights and democracy could structure the "social" or "intersubjective" world, both without the constraints of religious authorities and dogma.

As spirituality and contemplation have re-emerged from the margins of the contemporary world, they have typically appeared in the "subjective" world (the distinction between these three worlds come especially from the work of Max Weber and Jürgen Habermas[6]), radically distinguished from the "objective" and "social" worlds. For example, Kierkegaard directed the spiritual aspirant away from the public realms of science, ethics, and public discourse: "Subjectivity," the private world, "becomes the truth . . . To seek objectivity is to be in error."[7] Authenticity is not possible in the social world: "The public is a monstrous nothing."[8] Max Weber summarized this privatization of spirituality: "The ultimate and most sublime values have retreated from public life either into the transcendental realm of mystic life or into . . . direct and personal human relations."[9]

Indeed, the origins of recent interest in meditation and contemplation have been closely linked with the renewal of access to deep *subjective* experiences, linked with the human potential movement, psychedelics, humanistic and transpersonal psychology, and the Western discovery of Asian contemplative traditions, and increasingly Western contemplative traditions as well. And yet, when, in the last 40 years, Westerners in larger numbers began engaging in such contemplative, they were set up for a kind of conflict. In the context of the structure of modernity and the 2500-year old separation of contemplation and action, they were primed to approach meditation or contemplation as a subjective exploration leading to often life-transforming experiences. Yet many had just come through a highly volatile period of major social turmoil, deep awareness of many social problems, and commitment to social change. Some of us seemed to have to choose between the two. Or we could, with considerable effort, reject such a choice as a false one, following the call to connect contemplation and action, inner and outer transformation.

Engaged Buddhism

Interestingly, the very term, "engaged Buddhism," can be interpreted as a concept first expressed in a contemporary Asian setting to question the *Buddhist* separation of contemplative practice and action, while drawing the actual term from a Western philosopher similarly questioning the separation of (philosophical) contemplation and action.

As far as I know, "engaged Buddhism" was a concept first articulated by the Vietnamese teacher, activist, and writer, Thich Nhat Hanh, in the 1960s, in the context of war. Nhat Hanh brought together with one concept three distinct movements of Vietnamese Buddhism, dating from the 1930s, each with particular Vietnamese terms linked with them, translated as (1) "Buddhism for everybody" (moving Buddhist practice from the monasteries to be available for all), (2) "going into the world" (particularly offering service to meet the needs of people suffering in the war), and (3) "getting involved" (attempting, through demonstrations and other means, to stop the war).[10] Thich Nhat Hanh later wrote:

> When I was in Vietnam, so many of our villages were being bombed. Along with my monastic brothers and sisters, I had to decide what to do. Should we continue to practice in our monasteries, or should we leave the meditation halls in order to help the people who were suffering under the bombs? After careful reflection, we decided to do both—to go out and help people and to do so in mindfulness. We called it engaged Buddhism. Mindfulness must be engaged. *Once there is seeing, there must be acting.* . . . We must be aware of the real problems of the world. Then, with mindfulness, we will know what to do and what not to do to be of help.[11]

The term "engaged" itself was central to Jean-Paul Sartre's existentialism, influential in post-World War II Vietnam, and came out of an affirmation of the importance of enacting one's deeper values in one's actions, linked with a critique of a separation of a more contemplative and intellectual life from moral and political action, particularly in the context of the Nazi occupation. As "engaged Buddhism" has developed in both Asia and the West, particularly in the last thirty years, it has brought together, as is evident in the origins of the term, Buddhist teachings and practices, on the one hand, and perspectives often drawn from Western moral and social justice traditions, on the other.

Yet even after some 50 years of engaged Buddhism, the term, "engagement," has remained at times ambiguous. What is "engagement" and what is not? Some have preferred the terms, "*socially* engaged Buddhism," to point toward particular types of *social* involvement. In developing the BASE program, for example, we have sometimes used the shorthand of "social service or social action," understanding by "service" a broad range of activities in which there is a direct response to those in need.

The Development of Socially Engaged Buddhism in the United States in the Last Thirty Years

While recognizing the ambiguity about "engagement," I want to focus especially on the development of *socially* engaged Buddhism, particularly in the United States, given the scope of our conference. However, one way of making some sense of the ambiguity is by seeing some of the ways that the Vietnamese development on engaged Buddhism itself followed a progressive sequence. The more explicit social activism of the third phase depended on the broadening of contemplative practice to lay life generally in the first phase, and on the second phase of contemplative practice applied broadly to service. In the actual development of socially engaged Buddhism in the U.S., there has similarly necessarily been attention to many areas that are foundational to Buddhist practice in everyday life, such as cultivating mindfulness, wise speech, generosity, and all of the many other traditional virtues: lovingkindness, compassion, ethics, equanimity, wisdom, and so on. What do these mean in many contexts—such as those of relationships, family, and work, as well as service and social action—that were not explored in monastic contexts that were often the place of origin of the practices and associated teachings?

Organizations

The main socially engaged Buddhist organizations in the U.S. developed especially within about a ten-year period, starting in the late 1970s. The Buddhist Peace Fellowship, probably the most prominent socially engaged Buddhist organization, is based in Berkeley, California. It was founded by Robert Aitken Roshi and five others in Hawaii in 1978 as a membership organization, and generally grew steadily for some 25 years, reaching a membership peak of some 5000 members. It publishes an influential journal, *Turning Wheel*, and has developed various programs, including the BASE program, mentioned above, a Prison Program, various collaborations with affiliated programs, and material support for a number of Asian projects.

Some of the affiliated programs have included the Karuna Center for Peacemaking, founded in Massachusetts by Paula Green, a former BPF board member, which has led worldwide trainings in such areas as peacemaking, conflict transformation, and reconciliation; the Green Sangha, a collection of local groups founded by Jonathan Gustin in the San Francisco Bay Area; the Gay Buddhist Fellowship, initiated at a BPF Summer Institute in the early 1990s; the Prison Dharma Network, developed by Fleet Maull (present at this conference and a former BPF board member); Sakyadhita, an international organization of Buddhist women guided by an American nun, Karma Lekshe Tsomo, which holds annual conferences; and others.

Thich Nhat Hanh began to teach in the West in 1982, after a five-year retreat at his community in France, Plum Village. He immediately had a very strong influence through his talks, retreats, and many books, published mostly through Parallax Press in Berkeley. His umbrella organization, "The Community of Mindful Living," has had many affiliated local groups throughout the U.S.; some have participated in the "Order of Interbeing," founded in Vietnam in 1964, with more rigorous contemplative demands of its members.

Bernie Glassman, who received Zen transmission from Maezumi Roshi, has also been a main organizer. In the late 1980s, he founded the "Greyston Mandala" in Yonkers, New York, a set of projects to benefit people in need, including serving the homeless both through a bakery employing them and through a housing construction initiative, and serving those with AIDS. He has developed a series of innovative retreats "bearing witness," including a "street retreat" in which retreatants spend five days living (and meditating) without a place to sleep, and regular retreats at Auschwitz. He has also guided the Zen Peacemakers, an organization that presents retreats, trainings, and, in August 2010, will offer a "Symposium for Western Socially Engaged Buddhism."

A number of Buddhist centers have also had active socially engaged programs, many of them more recently. What follows is a small sample, to get the flavor of these widespread kinds of programs. For many years, the San Francisco Zen Center, through Frank Ostaseski, has run the Zen Center Hospice, a highly influential program for volunteers. The Upaya center, led by Roshi Joan Halifax, has many programs related to death and dying, helping the homeless, Buddhist chaplaincy, and service. Manzanita Village, a retreat center in near Los Angeles, founded by Caitríona Reed and Michele Benzamin-Miki, links mindfulness with concerns related to deep ecology, diversity issues, and nonviolence. The Insight Meditation Center in Redwood City,

California, near San Francisco, guided by Gil Fronsdal, a vipassana and Zen teacher, has a one-year chaplaincy program. The East Bay Meditation Center, in Oakland, California, has had a particular focus on diversity related to ethnicity, sexual orientation, and class, in both its programming and teachers. The Spirit Rock Meditation Center, north of San Francisco, has the two-year, "Path of Engagement" training program, mentioned above, and, like many centers, has many retreats and other gatherings intended specifically for People of Color, women, and men.

There are also numerous Buddhist-based organizations focused on specific concerns, such as Burma, Tibet, global climate change, prison work, diversity issues, and humanitarian relief. There are also a number of academic programs where one can study socially engaged Buddhism.[12]

Demographics

In many ways, the examples given in the last two paragraphs show what we might call a "mainstreaming" of socially engaged Buddhist approaches and practices, often supported by the organizations founded in or around the 1980s. The influence of these latter organizations has increased, just as related work has developed in many local communities and centers.

Such a growth of socially engaged Buddhism in Buddhist communities may in part also represent a maturing of the vision of contemplative practice, a willingness to widen one's sense of practice from the emphasis on personal healing, peace, and self-discovery that continues to be perhaps the predominant motivation for practicing meditation in the U.S. Still, this latter emphasis is typically by far the most common and very understandable, given the levels of stress and the relative loss of the inner dimension of life for many in the United States.

Socially Engaged Buddhist Contemplative Practices: An Overview

Socially engaged Buddhists tend to broaden the vision of practice considerably from the primary emphasis of Western (non-ethnically-based) Buddhism on sitting meditation at home and in retreats, classes, and weekly community groups. Interestingly, this broadening is in part a kind of return to the original teachings of the Buddha, in which training is divided into (1) ethics and action, (2) meditation, and (3) wisdom. Due to many of the deep structural and historical factors mentioned above related to the distinction of contemplation and action, "convert" Buddhism in the United States has developed with a narrowing of this traditional training, with practitioners primarily focusing on the second training in meditation.[13]

In presenting this overview of practices, I have two qualifications to mention. First, I cannot in such a short space be comprehensive. Secondly, although I have in some of my writings, training programs, and published compilations of resources attempted to be comprehensive, seeking out knowledge of approaches with which I am not familiar, here, I will tend to highlight practices with which I have the most acquaintance.[14]

Socially Engaged Buddhist Retreats: Innovations in Design and Settings

Many if not most socially engaged retreats have departed from the more "standard" form of many (but not all) Buddhist retreats in the West, that are conducted in silence, solitude (i.e., without interpersonal interaction), and simple comfort, in secluded settings in which retreatants typically carry out contemplative practices 10 to 15 hours a day. Rather, there is often a mix of silent practices and more interactive practices (including discussion), with an emphasis on the interplay of the two forms and the ways that qualities such as mindfulness, lovingkindness, compassion, ethical sensitivity, and wisdom can be developed in the midst of action and interaction.

Retreats can be thus be seen in part as training periods, giving support for learning how to practice "contemplation in action." The interplay of the two forms, however, is not simply one-way, as it were, bringing contemplation into action. What emerges in action and interaction can also both give material that then arises in contemplation, and can suggest new and innovative forms of contemplation that meet the needs of action and interaction (more on this below). For example, a socially engaged retreat of seven days duration might have the first full day be devoted to silent practice, and then have three to seven hours per day of silent practice for the remainder of the retreat.

While many socially engaged retreats take place in secluded and beautiful settings, at retreat centers and monasteries, some retreats have occurred in more gritty circumstances. Perhaps best known are the retreats offered by Bernie Glassman and others. The "street retreat" takes place typically in a run-down urban environment, in which the retreatants have no housing and limited money for five days, while carrying out regular periods of meditation. Glassman has also led retreats at the Auschwitz-Birkenau concentration camp in Poland, at which retreatants practice meditation at a place associated with great suffering, while carrying out dialogue and inquiry.[15] Similarly, BPF co-organized a retreat at the Los Alamos National Laboratory in New Mexico, where nuclear weapons are produced, with periods of meditation, conversations with Los Alamos scientists, and evening "councils" to explore the retreatants' experiences.

Bringing Traditional Contemplative Practices into New Settings

Introducing traditional contemplative practices into these innovative retreats points to a more general contribution of socially engaged Buddhists—to bring contemplative practices into a variety of engaged settings. Basic mindfulness practice can also be brought into meetings and into organizational life in general, and, in some organizations, be made a standard feature of the workday. When there are challenging situations, there may be the option of practicing in various ways with difficult emotions, or summoning the resources of lovingkindness, compassion, joy, equanimity (the brahmavihara in Theravada tradition, or four immeasurables in Mahayana), or wisdom teachings.

Meditation has been widely used in recent years at demonstrations. For example, at the several demonstrations in San Francisco against the invasion of Iraq in 2003, BPF organized large group meditations, both *before* the actual demonstrations—to help clarify intentions and support a sense of practice—and *during* the demonstrations. (These give a glimpse of the power of the very large group meditations that have been used in Sri Lanka, with as many as 650,000 people, to support the peace process ending the civil war.)

"Inner" and "Outer" Contemplative Practices at the Same Time

The nature of socially engaged retreats also points generally toward a more innovative type of contemplative practice in which there is *both inner and outer attention at the same time*, rather than the much more common application of exclusively *inner* attention in contemplative practice. One of the most basic and foundational forms of such practice is contemplative speech practice, in which one both speaks and listens interactively or "externally," and also can listen "internally" for any responses, reactions, or commentaries (more on this in the next section). In other words, there can be an inner mindfulness (or some other practice) at the same time that one engages externally, also as practice, with another person or in some more complex social reality.[16]

The need for contemplative practices that combine inner and outer attention also points to three features of socially engaged contemplative practices. One is that some of these practices may be, relatively speaking, more intermediate or advanced practices, and presuppose stabilized competences in traditional inner practices. This may also be one of the reasons why some of those initially drawn to contemplative practice may not be attracted to socially engaged practices.

A second is that the kinds of contemplative practices that are or would be most helpful are for the most part relatively newly developed or undeveloped. We can think of possible practices carried out in a variety of settings: in various kinds of communications, spoken, written, or electronic; in meetings, public forums, or work in organizations and offices; in the complex settings of service in hospitals, clinics, and community centers; in places of conflict, violence, and suffering; or in demonstrations, vigils, and other forms of public witnessing. In other words, tremendous creativity is needed to develop socially engaged contemplative practices.

A third feature is the understanding of the radical interdependence of "inner" and "outer." Indeed, when we consider "inner" practices in more depth, we can see that there can be many kinds of *inner* practices in which we work with our internalized *social* (or external) conditioning and the inner effects of social events, and there can be several kinds of *outer* practices in which we support individuals to do *inner* work.[17]

Speech and Communication Practices

In this context, it is clear that developing contemplative speech and communication practices is central to socially engaged contemplative practice, and also, of course, to any kind of more relational contemplative practice. From a Buddhist perspective, these practices can build on the primarily ethical teachings of the Buddha, to have one's speech follow four guidelines, to be: (1) true, (2) helpful, (3) warm or kind (even if firm), and (4) timely and appropriate.

In retreats that I have co-led, we connect these guidelines with an inner mindfulness during speech, and with the discipline of Nonviolent Communication (NVC), which can be interpreted as a form of focused mindfulness during speech. In 7-day retreats, we train people to take their periods of speech and interaction as opportunities for a rigorous contemplative practice, that for many of us can lead to having many hours a day for contemplative practice! For most Western practitioners, grounding in awareness of the body during speech is particularly helpful to keep both inner and outer attention during speech, although it generally takes some time to develop.[18]

Somewhat similarly, Greg Kramer has developed Insight Dialogue to bring the teachings and practices of Insight Meditation to speech.[19] Others in Buddhist settings have refined methods of community dialogue in a form called "Council," with its origins in Native American practices, and parallels in many traditions, such as that of the Quakers.[20] Many have focused on the importance of cultivating careful listening to the other. Thich Nhat Hanh's "mindfulness bell," when rung, invites a few moments of silence and return to awareness of the present moment; it is commonly used in various kinds of gatherings, as a way of encouraging contemplative presence in the midst of speech and interaction.

Cultivating such speech practices may have a large impact. Practitioners may learn speech practices in classes, programs, or retreats, and then bring these practices into their personal, community, and work lives, where they may inform the norms and practices of many others, and perhaps even of whole communities, groups, and organizations.

Other Relational and Interactive Contemplative Practices

There have also been a number of other relational and interactive practices developed in the context of socially engaged Buddhism.

Some of the most influential practices have been those of Joanna Macy and her colleagues, collected in recent years as "The Work that Reconnects."[21] She has developed dyadic practices of the Buddhist brahmavihara—the "divine abodes" of lovingkindness, compassion, joy, and equanimity. There are also a number of practices to help participants in her workshops or retreats enter into the pain felt in relationship to social realities, whether the pain is felt in relationship to a community or organization or to the wider world. In the "Despair Ritual" or the "Truth Mandala," participants have the chance to express, in a contemplative setting, various difficult emotions, often permitting them to surface material that has long been stuck or lived inaccessibly beneath the surface. Macy has also helped develop a number of ecologically-based ritual forms, such as the Council of All Beings, and forms that invoke our relationship to past and future beings. These practices and rituals work very well in a contemplative setting, supported by other contemplative practices. They have been widely used by others in workshops and retreats, and function well as practices conducted periodically. In a related way, many have explored bringing Buddhist teachings and practices to ecological issues.[22]

In many socially engaged settings, an attention to the normative community framework of groups and organizations has been important. Having a clear set of intentions and norms can provide relative safety, guidelines for helping group interactions (whether in a spiritual community, a group, or an organization) to become themselves forms of contemplative practices, and a basis for working with challenges and difficulties.[23] Making use of some of the secular field of group dynamics has also been central.

Some have used primarily contemplative approaches for helping to work with challenging areas related to social issues, typically integrating contemplative practices, exercises and practices developed in other settings, and Buddhist-based principles and guidelines. For example, several have developed contemplative ways of working with *conflict*, including Thich Nhat Hanh, Paula Green, Lawrence Ellis, and myself. In Nhat Hanh's community, Plum Village, members sign a "Peace Treaty," in which they agree to work out all conflicts using a sequence of guidelines, based on mindfulness practice. In my work together with Lawrence Ellis, we have combined mindfulness practice, particularly connected with transforming difficult emotions, thoughts, and body-states, with non-dual perspectives drawn from Buddhist principles, and the work of peacemakers, mediators, and organizational consultants.

Similarly, contemplative tools have been brought to help work with issues of gender, diversity, and sexual orientation, with retreats specially designed for women, men, People of Color, and gay, lesbian, bisexual, transgender, and queer practitioners. While many of these retreats have been traditional in terms of silence and lack of interaction, some have involved the combination of silent practice and group interactions mentioned above. Mindfulness, lovingkindness, and wisdom teachings become powerful tools to work with the residual pain of trauma and oppression, and the often less accessible issues related to privilege, yet these concerns often require somewhat different settings and approaches than found in typical Western Buddhist retreats.[24] Considerable attention has also been given to the very framework of contemplative centers and groups, and the ways that many factors in the ways that centers are developed, and retreats or meetings are held, can lead to contemplative resources becoming difficult to access for members of certain groups.[25]

In all of these areas, as we can see, it has been important to make use of secular materials from the social sciences, psychology, philosophy, and Western social movements, as this is where insights into social realities have been developed and articulated in great detail. Similarly, the resources of other spiritual traditions—the nonviolence of Gandhi and King, the life and work of the Jewish prophets and Jesus, liberation theology (the BPF BASE program was named to refer to this approach), and aspects of indigenous traditions, to name a few—have often been inspiring and energizing for socially engaged Buddhists.

Guiding Principles for Socially Engaged Practice

We can find a number of sets of principles offered to guide socially engaged contemplative practice as a whole. One of the earliest is the list of fourteen principles developed by Thich Nhat Hanh in Vietnam for the Order of Interbeing (presented in *Being Peace* and other places). Bernie Glassman has developed a shorter list of guiding principles in his work in the 1990s (found in *Bearing Witness*). In my own work with Diana Winston, we developed a framework of ten principles that provides the structure of *The Engaged Spiritual Life.*[26] Others have been deeply inspired by the traditional figure of the bodhisattva, a being dedicated to help liberate others, and by the traditional set of ten practices for the bodhisattva.[27]

Future Directions and Challenges for Socially Engaged Buddhist Practice

These reflections show the promising but, I believe, early development of socially engaged Buddhist contemplative practices. Here I want to point what I take to be some key trends, future directions, and challenges.

1. Further Development and Clarification of Socially Engaged "Paths"

There remains great creativity invited of those with socially engaged perspectives. In Buddhist contemplative centers, even with some "mainstreaming" of engaged approaches, very traditional contemplative models are, if not the norm, then highly influential. Indeed, many teachers and students are very sympathetic to socially engaged practices and approaches, but don't have a clear sense of how to practice, or how such an approach relates to traditional practices.

Hence, it is crucial to develop further a range of practices suitable to fill out a sense of how deep transformation (hopefully of *both* inner and outer confusion and suffering) is possible, and can follow a coherent path and curriculum. There are very helpful frameworks in some of the sets of guiding principles mentioned above, and in their associated practices. There are also a number of varied socially engaged communities where one can receive support and training over different lengths of time.

A crucial aspect of the development of these paths is ensuring that socially engaged contemplative approaches retain the *depth* of the best of traditional contemplative paths—the emphasis on liberation, nirvana, and Buddha Nature, to use Buddhist language—even as such depth may be expressed in new and creative ways. A major challenge of socially engaged practice is to keep focused on the depth dimension, and be aware of any tendencies for such a depth dimension to be lost or obscured.

2. Further Development of Socially Engaged Buddhist "Theory"

Related to the articulation of socially engaged paths is the need to clarify socially engaged Buddhist ways of understanding the world. The articulation of a Buddhist "social theory" that would let us connect an understanding of institutions (economic, political, social, etc.) and social issues from spiritually-grounded positions is at an early stage of development. We can point especially to the wonderful, pioneering work of David Loy, and the work of the Think Sangha linked with the International Network of Engaged Buddhists.[28] Related to such a social theory is a need for clearer grounding of such theory in Buddhist ethical values and wisdom teachings. In general, developing such an approach in any spiritual tradition is demanding of much work and creativity, as the prevailing frameworks of social analysis are almost entirely secular; still, we find generally more articulation of spiritually-grounded social theory among many Christian and Jewish socially engaged writers.

3. Further Development of Socially Engaged Buddhist Strategy and Social Action

Not surprisingly, the relative lack of a clear Buddhist-based social analysis makes strategy and social action more difficult, particularly in terms of helping to respond to suffering rooted in the "normal" working of our institutions and cultural ideologies. While socially engaged Buddhists may not need much analysis or theory to oppose wars, help prevent further ecological damage, or respond to humanitarian issues and crises (all of which are crucial), helping to respond to major issues and build the framework of a more spiritually-grounded community and society will, I believe, require considerably more reflection, dialogue, and research.

4. A Need for Greater Communication and Networking

Although some of the major organizations have had important journals (some online), there remains a relative paucity of opportunities to connect with like-minded people outside of participation in particular programs (and relatively few journals and magazines dedicated to socially engaged Buddhism). Similarly, there are relatively few larger meetings and conferences.

Part of the need for communication is also in connecting with those who are socially engaged and spiritually-grounded either *from other spiritual traditions* or *from outside established traditions*. Increasingly, we are all responding to the *same* larger social issues, many of which are so challenging as to require to the collected resources and energies of a unified spiritual response. In this context, socially engaged Buddhists can contribute especially the sense of a socially engaged spiritual *path*, with *concrete contemplative practices* suitable for many aspects of an engaged life; such resources are generally more developed than in other traditions, and their relative universality makes them quite accessible to those from other traditions or no traditions.

5. A New Generation of Socially Engaged Contemplative Leaders

In many of the primary organizations linked with socially engaged Buddhism (and Buddhist practice in general), a new generation is poised to take on more leadership, as many of the long-time teachers, writers, and activists are in their sixties, seventies, and beyond. This new generation of leaders will also need to be much more ethnically diverse. Many socially engaged programs (as well as centers and communities) have made special efforts to develop new leadership with increased diversity of age and ethnicity.

6. The Challenges of Contemplation at a Time of Social and Ecological Crisis

The backdrop for our conference, which has not been named directly in the conference material, is the increasing number of signs of crisis. Perhaps the most ominous crisis is that of potentially devastating climate disruption, linked with the seeming inability of world leaders to respond adequately (witness the Copenhagen Conference last December). Such a crisis, as many have pointed out, makes problematic whether good conditions for contemplation will be possible in the long run (without confining contemplation to the enclaves of a few). A number of socially engaged Buddhists have recently responded to these issues.[29]

There are also, of course, many other major issues and concerns for those in the United States. Our leaders continue to wage major wars and occupy foreign countries, with probably one to two million dead in the last decade as a result, and with associated threats to security and democracy, both from our "enemies" and our government. A number of other forces are at work challenging the health of our society, democracy, economy, and ecologies. Globalization is increasing the gap between rich and poor; the sociologist Robert Bellah speaks of this gap as our most important contemporary ethical issue.[30]

It is a major challenge for socially engaged Buddhists to provide leadership in the context of these crises, such that the open hearts and minds of contemplatives become wonderful resources with which to respond (recognizing, as I mentioned above in terms of my own story, that there are cycles of withdraw-al and return in the engaged spiritual journey). Again, greater clarification of a socially engaged spiritual path and socially engaged analyses of the crises make possible responses which may make a great difference in the transition to a more sustainable and just world, with many more contemplatives!

Conclusion

Given the historical tendencies outlined above—to separate contemplation from action; to give a primarily subjective, inner interpretation of contem-plation; and to emphasize especially one part of traditional Buddhist train-ing, i.e., meditation (often with a considerably less emphasis on ethics and wisdom)—we need to be somewhat cautious when we find that "a larger contemplative movement is emerging in America," especially at a time of crisis. We need to ask *how* that movement is emerging and how it is being formed by social and historical conditions. To what extent is this contempla-tive movement linked with ethical sensitivity about, and responsibility for, the conditions of our world? Is contemplation practiced in a compartmen-talized way, so that it is not connected with the rest of one's life? I will ask this question in a somewhat more provocative way: To what extent is this contemplative movement taking place among an increasingly de-politicized, stressed-out, and anxious, but still privileged, middle class, giving them tools to find some degree of personal peace as many less fortunate persons are suf-fering, in part linked with the middle-class Western privileges?[31] (I ask this question of myself as well!)

We need, in other words, to ask not only how a contemplative movement can be nurtured, but also *what kind* of contemplative movement we will have. We need to be clear about how this contemplative movement is being struc-tured by social and historical forces at a key moment, with major decision points as to how contemplation develops in the society; if we don't reflect and see clearly our conditioning, we will tend to follow it. The developing set of resources of socially engaged Buddhism (as well as the resources of much of traditional Buddhism—and other contemplative traditions) offer an inten-tion to develop contemplatively, not by turning away from the suffering of others, but rather by linking contemplation to the intention to respond to suffering, both one's own and that of others. I believe that integrating many of these resources into any contemporary "contemplative movement" is, in other words, crucial for the very "soul" of such a movement, as it emerges in difficult times.

Notes

1   A manual for the program, written by Diana Winston and Donald Rothberg, is available on the BPF web site <www.bpf.org>, as *A Handbook for the Creation of the Buddhist Alliance for Social Engagement (BASE)* (1997; 2nd ed. 2000).

2   For a summary of the program, see my essay, "An Interfaith Training Program in Socially Engaged Spirituality," *Turning Wheel: The Journal of Socially Engaged Buddhism* (Summer 2006): pp. 36–37, 43.

3   Richard Woods, "Mysticism and Social Action: The Mystic's Calling, Development, and Social Activity," *Journal of Consciousness Studies* 3 (1996): pp. 158–171.

4   Elmer O'Brien, ed., *The Essential Plotinus*, 2d ed. (Indianapolis: Hackett Publishing Company, 1981), p. 167 (Enneads, III, 8: 30, 6).

5   O'Brien, p. 88 (Enneads VI, 9: 9, 11).

6   See Donald Rothberg, "The Crisis of Modernity and the Emergence of Socially Engaged Spirituality," *ReVision* 15 (1993): pp. 105 – 114; Hans Gerth and C. Wright Mills, eds., *From Max Weber* (New York: Oxford University Press, 1946); Jürgen Habermas, *The Theory of Communicative Action, Vol. 1: Reason and the Rationalization of Society*, Thomas McCarthy, trans. (Boston: Beacon Press, 1984).

7   Soren Kierkegaard, from *Concluding Unscientific Postscript*, in Robert Bretall, ed., *A Kierkegaard Anthology* (New York: Random House, 1946), p. 181.

8   Kierkegaard, "The Present Age," in Bretall, p. 265.

9   Max Weber, "Science as a Vocation," in Hans Gerth and C. Wright Mills, *From Max Weber: Essays in Sociology* (New York: Oxford University Press, 1946), p. 155.

10 See Donald Rothberg, "Responding to the Cries of the World: Socially Engaged Buddhism in North America," in Charles Prebish and Kenneth Tanaka, eds., *The Faces of Buddhism in America* (Berkeley: University of California Press, 1998), pp. 266 – 286, 334 – 341; I rely on Thich Minh Duc for this characterization of the three movements.

11 Thich Nhat Hanh, *Peace is Every Step* (New York: Bantam Books, 1991), p. 91. Emphasis added.

12 See Donald Rothberg, "Resources on Socially Engaged Buddhism," for a listing of English-language books, journals, organizations, and web sites, at www.bpf.org/html/resources_and_links/bibliography/bibliography.html.

13 Gary Snyder was one of the first to point out this tendency. See Catharine Ingram, Barbara Gates, and Wes Nisker, "Chan on Turtle Island: A Conversation with Gary Snyder," *Inquiring Mind* 4 (Winter 1988): pp. 1, 4–5, 25.

14 For an attempt to develop a kind of manual of socially engaged (Buddhist-based) practices, see my *The Engaged Spiritual Life: A Buddhist Approach to Transforming Ourselves and the World* (Boston: Beacon Press, 2006); see also the resource guide mentioned above and my "Responding to the Cries of the World: Socially Engaged Buddhism in North America," for a more detailed account of the socially engaged expansion of practice in terms of the traditional threefold training.

15 Bernie Glassman, *Bearing Witness: A Zen Master's Lessons in Making Peace* (New York: Bell Tower, 1998).

16 For a more extended discussion of connecting inner and outer attention, see *The Engaged Spiritual Life*, pp. 52–53.

17 I explore this interpenetration of inner and outer practices in much more depth in "Connecting Inner and Outer Transformation: Toward an Expanded Model of Buddhist Practice," Jorge Ferrer and Jacob Sherman, eds., *The Participatory Turn in Spirituality, Mysticism, and Religious Studies* (Albany, NY, 2008: State University of New York Press), pp. 349–370.

18 See *The Engaged Spiritual Life*, pp. 22–31, 45–49; Marshall Rosenberg, *Nonviolent Communication: A Language of Compassion* (Encinitas, CA: PuddleDancer Press, 2003, 2nd ed.).

19 Gregory Kramer, *Insight Dialogue: The Interpersonal Path to Freedom* (Boston: Shambhala, 2007).

20 See Jack Zimmerman and Virginia Coyle, *The Way of Council* (Putney, VT: Bramble Books, 2009, 2nd ed.).

21 See Joanna Macy and Molly Young Brown, *Coming Back to Life: Practices to Reconnect Our Lives, Our World* (Gabriola Island, British Columbia, Can.: New Society Publishers, 1998).

22 See, for example, Stephanize Kaza, *Mindfully Green: A Personal and Spiritual Guide to Whole Earth Thinking* (Redwing Book Company, 2008); Stephanie Kaza and Kenneth Kraft (eds.), *Dharma Rain: Sources of Buddhist Environmentalism* (Boston: Shambhala Publications, 1999).

23 See Winston and Rothberg, *A Handbook for the Creation of the Buddhist Alliance for Social Engagement (BASE)*; and Rothberg, *The Engaged Spiritual Life*, pp. 6–72.

24 See the work of Larry Yang, presented in Rothberg, *The Engaged Spiritual Life*, pp. 87–88.

25 See Sheridan Adams et al (eds.), *Making the Invisible Visible: Healing Racism in Our Buddhist Communities* (2nd ed., 2000, available online at <www.spiritrock.org/html/diversity_2invisible.html>); Hilda Gutiérrez Baldoquín, *Dharma, Color, and Culture* (Berkeley, CA: Parallax Press, 2004); Kate Dugan and Hilary Bogert, "Racial Diversity in Buddhism in the U.S."(Harvard University Pluralism Project, 2006, available online).

26 Thich Nhat Hanh, *Being Peace* (Berkeley, CA: Parallax Press, 1988); Glassman, *Bearing Witness*; Rothberg, *The Engaged Spiritual Life*.

27 See Taigen Dan Leighton, *Faces of Compassion: Classic Bodhisattva Archetypes and Their Modern Expression* (Boston: Wisdom Publications, 2003, rev. ed.).

28 See David Loy, *The Great Awakening: A Buddhist Social Theory* (Boston: Wisdom Publications, 2003); *Money, Sex, War, Karma: Notes for a Buddhist Revolution* (Boston: Wisdom Publications, 2008). There have been "Think Sangha" publications on consumerism and spirituality, modernity, and teachings (including social implications) related to karma. See my resource list mentioned above.

29 See John Stanley, David Loy, and Gyurme Dorje (eds.), *A Buddhist Response to the Climate Emergency* (Wisdom Publications, 2009) and the web site linked to this book, "Ecological Buddhism: A Buddhist Response to Global Warming" www.ecobuddhism.org.

30 Robert Bellah, "The Ethics of Polarization in the United States and the World," in David Batstone and Eduardo Mendieta (eds.), *The Good Citizen* (New York: Routledge, 1999), pp. 13–28.

31 There is a cautionary tale available when we study how psychoanalysis came to the United States in large part stripped of the social sensitivity characteristic of the second generation of analysts after Freud, who were working especially in Germany and Austria; the shift occurred in large part because of the pressures of U.S. social and political conditions. The result was arguably an approach to psychoanalysis, and more broadly psychotherapy, that focused on personal peace and did not raise issues about the relationship of social issues to psychological issues. See Russell Jacoby, *The Repression of Psychoanalysis: Otto Fenichel and the Political Freudians* (Chicago: University of Chicago Press, 1986). We can also look to the ways that yoga and the martial arts have lost their depth dimensions, as aspects of the traditions were taken out of their original contexts, or the ways that Zen practice became aligned to a significant extent with Japanese militarism in the 20th century, losing its ethical moorings in many cases.

THE GROWTH OF CONTEMPLATIVE PRACTICE IN CONTEMPORARY JEWISH LIFE

Rachel Cowan

> *Every moment is a potential meeting with God. If we are to be prepared, we will need to be mindful, to be awake and alert and engaged, to bring our whole being to every moment. Nothing can be excluded from our awareness... We will be more aware of how predispositions and habits of mind threaten to cloud our attentiveness. When we bring our full attention to the fullness of each moment, when we are fully present, we will then become aware of how we are to respond. In moments of clear vision, we see the truth of God's presence in everything that comes before us and we can discern how to respond—how we are to worship Adonai.*
>
> — Rabbi Jonathan Slater, *Mindful Jewish Living*

Meaning of "Contemplative Practice" in a Jewish Framework

Contemplative practices lie at the heart of Contemplative Judaism—a small but growing transformative movement that is renewing, reinterpreting and revitalizing the meditative stream that has always been present within Jewish tradition. "Contemplative Judaism" is used as the referent for a cluster of spiritual forms and practices that share to one degree or another, a series of related elements: silence, quieting the mind, concentration, attentiveness, inwardness, receptivity, reflectivity, cultivation of ethical/spiritual qualities, and disciplined practice. These are practices cultivated for the sake of transforming consciousness to diminish egocentricity and enable Jews to connect more deeply to the Divine, to recognize the needs of others and to access the inner resources we all possess to ease suffering and promote peace and justice. Traditional practices brachot (blessings), prayer, tzedakah (philanthropy), gemilut chasadim (deeds of lovingkindness), holidays, Shabbat CAN bring this about, but today's Jews need guidance to make the connection.

Jewish contemplatives are seeking to supplement and revive/revitalize these traditional Jewish practices through mindfulness meditation, yoga, spiritual direction, mussar, contemplative prayer—which develop and sustain the inner life—so that Jews are more connected to such inner qualities as compassion, lovingkindness, truthfulness, humility, patience and courage, and can see more clearly how they might be manifest through and supported by traditional Jewish prayer, study and action. The larger goal is to help people more readily express those inner qualities in all they do. To this end, contemplative practices are being taught to thousands of rabbis, cantors, educators, social justice activists, chaplains, leaders of organizations, seekers and learners of all ages and backgrounds. They are taught in the context of Jewish text study, liturgy, holidays and Shabbat—translating the insights of contemplative practice to a Jewish idiom and at the same time opening up traditional texts and practices to new meanings, and discovering and disseminating authentic texts that have not been part of mainstream learning.

The impact of the work so far is extensive. Contemplative practices open Jews to a new, more universalist theology that sees God as a force/consciousness/Presence known through experience and recognized through a wide range of practices including traditional liturgy and commandments, but also through meditation, experience in nature and art. Contemplative practice can foster a deep awareness of Unity and a commitment to justice for the planet and its living creatures. Hundreds of thousands of Jews now have access to a deep spiritual life, even when they don't know Hebrew or relate to traditional prayer services. Leaders have mindfulness skills that make them more effective and wise. In doing this work, the movement is also revitalizing American Judaism.

Development of Contemplative Practice in Jewish Life

Over the past twenty years, the teaching of contemplative practice in Jewish frameworks has evolved from awkward experimentation to profound integration as the understandings of the benefits, applications and resonance of contemplative practice have become manifest in the lives of thousands of Jews, and as the translation of insights from contemplative practice have been translated into the language of Jewish wisdom, and as new readings of Jewish texts and traditions have brought deep contemporary meaning to Judaism.

Jewish mystics have practiced meditation for thousands of years—the early rabbis would sit for an hour before praying. There are practices of meditating on the Hebrew letters, or the names of God, or chanting specific phrases. However, these techniques were not taught to the masses, or handed down in writings. Rather, intensive verbal, argumentative study of Talmud became the main methodology for passing on Jewish law and wisdom from generation to generation. In the 18th and 19th centuries, a religious revolution took place, as brilliant spiritual teachers developed a radical theology and practice of prayer. They taught that God is in everything, that there is nothing in this world that is not God. Spiritual practice of prayer, study and community enabled people to see through the illusion of separateness and to experience the central Mystery. The community of the Piazetsner Rav, Kalonymous Kalman Shapira, who became the rabbi of the Warsaw Ghetto, cultivated a meditative orientation. This brilliant and courageous leader wrote about his "Conscious Community" of practitioners in works that he buried in the ground of the Warsaw Ghetto before the Nazis killed him and nearly his entire community. These works were found after the war and published in Israel[1]. Several of them have been translated into English. His text, *B'nei Machshava Tova*, People of Good Consciousness (translated as *Conscious Community*), is one of the few indigenous Jewish texts describing what we today call mindfulness practice. One can only wonder what a bright light this profound lineage of contemplative practice would have been if it had been not been extinguished.

In the late 20th century a movement called neo-Hassidism was revitalized combining the wisdom of the early religious genius of the masters with a post-modern egalitarian, universalist consciousness and Eastern influences to create a contemplative stream of Judaism. Rabbi Zalman Schacter Shalomi was the pioneer in forming this new consciousness. His students and mentees have developed and broadened his teachings for a mainstream audience that hungers for a more meaningful Jewish spiritual life.

Some major influences and teachers emerging in the late 80's and early 90's:

- The visit of a group of rabbis—including Rabbi Schacter Shalomi—to meet with the Dalai Lama in 1990, which was chronicled in *The Jew and the Lotus* by Roger Kamenetz. This book showed thousands of Jews that a mystical, contemplative understanding of Judaism was possible.
- Rabbi Jonathan Omer-Man, a spiritual teacher in Jerusalem, was brought to Los Angeles in 1985 to find out why young Jews were joining "cults" and turning away from synagogues. He identified the absence of a meaningful spiritual life as the source of the problem. He then founded Metivta, a center for Jewish Spirituality in Los Angeles and taught Jewish meditation to hundreds of Jews.

- Rabbi Alan Lew (of blessed memory), while sitting in the Zen monastery at Tassajara, felt a call to return to Judaism. Ordained as a Conservative rabbi, he began a meditation center in his synagogue in San Francisco, and brought his close friend Norman Fischer—then roshi of the Zen Center and an educated Jew—to teach there as well. He wrote several influential books.

- Nan Fink and Avram Davis founded Chochmat Halev in Berkeley as a center for teaching and practice of Jewish mysticism and meditation.

- Rabbis Jeff Roth and Joanna Katz founded Elat Hayyim, a retreat center in upstate New York that housed and nurtured a remarkable range of programs on Jewish spirituality. David and Shoshana Cooper, Alan Lew, Sylvia Boorstein and Sheila Weinberg taught mindfulness retreats and teacher trainings.

- Rabbi Rami Shapiro founded a center in Miami and began to write and teach widely about the insights into Jewish spiritual wisdom he gained through contemplative practice and study of mysticism.

- Dr. Arthur Green, an academic, and Rabbi Lawrence Kushner from the more popular side taught and wrote about the wisdom of the classic hassidic masters, introducing important new ideas to rabbis and academics as well as seekers.

- A group of influential teachers (including Arthur Green, Sylvia Boorstein, Larry Kushner and Sheila Peltz Weinberg) formed the Spirituality Institute at Metivta in 1999 to bring contemplative practice to mainstream rabbis as a strategy for creating a deeper spiritual foundation for contemporary Jewish life. The Institute later became its own organization—the Institute for Jewish Spirituality.

- Alan Morinis brought a commitment to spiritual discipline cultivated in his work with the Seva Foundation into Jewish life through his teaching and writing about traditional mussar practice (the cultivation of such spiritual qualities as compassion, truthfulness, humility, loving-kindness, patience).

- Dr Alan Brill has been teaching mysticism and meditation in the orthodox world at Yeshiva University and on campuses.
- Yedidya and Lev Shomea were created to bring the practice of spiritual direction from the Christian world into Judaism. This practice involves deep listening, and is grounded in contemplative practice.

The field of Jewish contemplative practice grows constantly more sophisticated today, where none existed even fifteen years ago. The main evolution of the field has been from a few teachers to organizations that are beginning to thrive, from experimentation to confidence, from competition to cooperation, from a dearth of writings to dozens of books. Teachers are being trained, and venues for learning and contemplative community have been established in synagogues, community centers, summer camps, schools, college campuses, urban meditation centers and rural retreat centers. The existence of multiple formats, philosophies and programs has contributed to enriched dialogue, experimentation, and synergy among programs. Teachers from various philosophies now teach together. There is greater comfort with different approaches, more confidence in the field so less struggling for turf. The Jewish community more readily accepts that one can borrow practices from another tradition—acknowledging their source—and adapt them to the framework of Judaism without importing contradictory messages from another religion.

The number of people devoted to contemplative practice in a Jewish environment is still small—in the thousands—but many of them are community and thought leaders. Over the years thousands of people have come to experience or to trust that the practices of mindfulness, yoga and spiritual direction enhance Jewish life and thought. They have embraced Mussar as an authentic Jewish practice that can speak to modern Jews of all backgrounds. Community leaders have come to see that the interest in spirituality is a valid concern to which Jewish community institutions must respond. In the early 90's very few funders supported this emergent work (the Nathan Cummings Foundation was a notable exception—and played a central role in the development of the field). It was hard for organizations and teachers to find the resources to meet the growing interest in the work. Adequate funding is still a major challenge, but new supporters are being created every day as more people discover the wisdom in contemplative practice.

The main contemplative practices being taught are:

Mindfulness meditation: The founding teachers of meditation as Jewish spiritual practice come from both Eastern and Jewish traditions. Sylvia Boorstein, Jeff Roth, Sheila Weinberg, David Cooper were trained in Vipassana, Alan Lew and Norman Fischer. Alan Morinis comes from a background of studies of Hinduism. Jonathan Omerman and Alan Brill have taught meditation techniques they learned from Jewish sources in Israel and from the writings of Aryeh Kaplan. All of these teachers teach skills in concentration, paying attention, and use Jewish texts for their wisdom teachings on retreat.

Yoga: Yoga was traditionally a Hindu form of spiritual practice comprised in part of physical postures or asanas. Asana practice has become secularized and popularized successfully in America because working with the physical aspect of the self is such a powerful path to living a fully awakened life. Both the Torah Yoga teacher training program and the Institute for Jewish Spirituality teach physical poses culled from a vast array of yoga postures because they believe this practice offers a profound way to heal the mind-body divide that causes us all pain and for which traditional Judaism offers few direct remedies. They honor the tradition from which they come as they apply them to the growth of fully actualized Jews.

Spiritual direction: This practice involves deep listening. The Spiritual Director sits with the Directee in silence, holding the directee in the light of God's Presence, as they each understand it, and listens as the directee speaks, asking occasional questions that point to the places where the directee might or might not feel God in the experience being described. The process is often transformative, allowing the directee to access her/his inner teacher and find greater clarity on how to respond to the situation or life path choice in which she/he is at that moment.

Contemplative prayer: Contemplative practices are slowly making their way into the prayer life of congregation: periods of silence during the services, more reflective sermons, cultivation of personal prayer, and the awareness practice of daily blessings.

Mussar is a path of contemplative practices and exercises that have evolved over the past thousand years to help an individual soul to pinpoint and then to break through the barriers that surround and obstruct the flow of inner light in our lives. The roots of all of our thoughts and actions can be traced to the depths of the soul, beyond the reach of the light of consciousness, and so the methods Mussar provides include meditations, guided contemplations, exercises and chants that are all intended to penetrate down to the darkness of the subconscious, to bring about change right at the root of our nature.

Organizations that Support Jewish Contemplative Practice

The Institute for Jewish Spirituality: "seeks to transform Jewish life. We help clergy, leaders, and other Jews connect with their deepest inner resources, their communities, and the Divine through contemplative Jewish practices that integrate mind, body, heart and soul. We provide them with valuable skills to be effective leaders who can enrich everyday life with Jewish wisdom; link the search for inner wholeness with *tikkun olam*; and create a vibrant and enduring Judaism for the next generation." Since 2000, IJS has worked with over 300 rabbis, cantors and educators in intensive retreat-based programs that teach mindfulness meditation, yoga, Hasidic texts, contemplative prayer and spiritual direction. Sylvia Boorstein was a founding teacher; Rabbi Sheila Weinberg is the current lead teacher and is training 29 teachers of mindfulness as Jewish spiritual practice. These practices have enabled participants to serve as more thoughtful, reflective, compassionate and skillful leaders, more deeply aligning their "role with their soul," more sustained in their vocations, and bringing their more inspirational leadership to hundreds of thousands of congregants. IJS is now beginning to teach in rabbinical schools.

The Mussar Institute "exists to provide people with ideas and practical tools deriving from the Mussar tradition in Judaism that will help, guide and motivate them to develop and improve the qualities of their inner lives, in fulfillment of the potential of their souls as well as for the benefit of the world." The Institute trains teachers to lead mussar groups, and also creates web-based study groups. It is growing exponentially as more teachers are trained. Alan Morinis' books *Every Day Holiness* and *Climbing Jacob's Ladder* have generated students and spurred the popularity of the movement. This year close to 800 students will take yearlong classes.

Torah Yoga: Two skilled yoga teachers—Diane Bloomfield and Rabbi Myriam Klotz—have brought the teaching of asana poses from yoga into the Jewish community as a form of Jewish spiritual practice. They are now recruiting for their third cohort of students—all of them certified as yoga instructors – learning to become teachers of yoga as Jewish spiritual practice. Their trainees include rabbis, cantors, educators and yoginis who have not before connected their yoga practice with their Jewish spiritual lives. Hundreds of synagogues have now incorporated yoga into their congregational life—primarily as classes, sometimes even as a prayer experience.

Iyyun (meaning mindful examination, deep exploration, introspection) is a successful outreach organization of Chabad Lubavitch—a right-wing orthodox movement—dedicated to the study and experience of Jewish spirituality whose charismatic teacher Rabbi Dov Ber Pinson creates opportunities for people of all backgrounds to deeply examine and understand the intellectual, emotional and physical within themselves in the light of Chabad Jewish spiritual teachings and the wisdom of the Torah. His stated goal is to unify the disparate intellectual, emotional and physical dimensions of the human experience into a complete whole, empowering men and women to realize their full potential and together, build a global spiritual community. An unstated goal is to bring students into the fold of Chabad. Chabad—which is brilliantly attuned to the spiritual longings of young Jews—has begun to teach meditation in its centers on college campuses.

The Yedidya Center for Jewish Spiritual Direction and Lev Shomea are dedicated to the introduction and development of the emerging practice of spiritual direction in the North American Jewish community. Their work is a process of tikkun (repair, restoration) that brings Jews back to the spiritual dimensions of their tradition from which, for historical and cultural reasons, many have been alienated. Spiritual direction supports the deepening of Jewish identity and adult learning through the spiritual lens of deep listening. Yedidya's Moreh Derekh program has trained 3 cohorts of rabbis, cantors and psychologists in providing spiritual direction to Jewish seekers who want to deepen their relationship with God. Students in three of the leading rabbinic seminaries are now offered spiritual direction. Another program called Lev Shomea is also training Jewish spiritual directors. More than a hundred Jewish spiritual directors belong to Spiritual Directors International.

The Awakened Heart Project has an approach to Jewish meditation that comes out of a religious desire to cultivate an awareness of the Divine Presence along with the particular qualities of wisdom, compassion and kindness from a Jewish perspective. According to Rabbi Jeff Roth, its director, "The wisdom accessible through Jewish meditation supports the understanding that the Divine Presence is the ground of All Being, and the ground of All Being is part of a singular interconnected web of being. Jewish meditation also provides the wisdom to understand the nature of mind including those factors of mind that tend to obscure clear seeing. The practice teaches us how to direct our attention into the present moment of experience, which is the only place the Divine Presence can be experienced." Rabbis Roth and Joanna Katz and Norman Fischer have trained dozens of rabbis and others in developing their practice and forming small community groups for meditation. They regularly hold meditation retreats of three weeks or more.

The Elat Chayyim Center for Jewish Spirituality "offers transformational and cutting-edge retreat experiences. Our year-round programs promote practices that draw on the wisdom of Jewish tradition and reflect the values and consciousness of our evolving society. Experiential approaches to Jewish learning, ritual and prayer are designed to help us all on our search to cultivate awareness of the Divine presence in all aspects of life."

Unique retreat features such as alternative prayer services, sharing circles, silent breakfasts and evening programs invite guests to discover more about themselves and their Jewish lives.

Local meditation centers:

- **Makom** at the Jewish Community Center of Manhattan: This center was established in 2000, with a special oval room designed for the new building. It offers an array of courses including introductory meditation classes, meditation intensives and urban retreats, MBSR, self–healing and spiritual nourishing programming, spiritual Shabbat dinners, literary events and much more.
- **Makor Or** was founded in January 2000 in San Francisco by Rabbi Alan Lew. The work is now carried on by Rabbi Dorothy Richman and Norman Fischer. The meditation practice of Makor Or is Jewish meditation, but it draws its technique from basic Zen meditation practice. Makor Or offers occasional classes on Jewish topics and periodic Meditation It is currently a program of the San Francisco Jewish Community Center.
- **Nishmat Hayyim** was founded by Rabbi Moshe Waldoks in 2005 to cultivate and support Jewish meditation and contemplative practices in Greater Boston and New England. "Jewish meditations are contemplative practices developed through the ages to bring us closer to God, closer to our true self, and closer to the very nature of existence." Teachings and practices draw on the rich tradition of Jewish texts and traditions from the Torah, Talmud, and Hassidut, as well as contemporary meditation techniques, and the experience of daily life.
- **Jewish Meditation Center of Brooklyn** was founded in 2009 by two women in their 20s, responding to an articulated need for Jewish community, informed by their generation's desire for creative approaches to spirituality, social change, and leadership. The JMC is the only

Jewish contemplative practice community created and run by young Jews, a replicable and groundbreaking model, bridging awareness, compassion and Jewish wisdom.

Moving into the Mainstream

The first generation of contemplative practice programs are beginning to have an impact on rabbinical seminaries, synagogues, Jewish Community Centers, and other "mainstream" institutions. Hebrew Union College (the seminary of the Reform movement), Hebrew College—a dynamic transdenominational seminary, the Reconstructionist Rabbinical College and Jewish Renewal seminaries are offering retreats and classes on contemplative spiritual practices. Jewish Community Centers in New York and San Francisco have regular meditation programs and the national organization of JCC's is interested in bringing yoga as Jewish spiritual practice to other centers.

Demographics

It is very hard to know the numbers of people involved in these practices. The organizations providing services do not have funds for evaluation or impact studies. However there is strong anecdotal evidence for a significant growth in numbers and influence. The rabbis who have been introduced to, or trained in, contemplative practices number over 300, and they influence hundreds of thousands of congregants—directly and indirectly. Retreats for social justice activists–primarily in their 20's and 30's—have drawn several hundred who in turn bring this work back to their organizations. Local retreat centers each reach several hundred people on a regular basis. College students make periodic connections. The demand is growing exponentially, but the resources to meet all the demands do not yet exist.

A majority of those attracted to the offerings of Jewish spirituality are women over 50, but meditation programs attract a significantly higher portion of men and younger Jews. Recent studies have shown that the high numbers of young Jews choosing not to affiliate with synagogues are not actually defecting from Judaism. Instead, they've been looking for expanded, deeply authentic versions of spiritual practice in environments where their voices are represented. According to a 2009 report, young Jews are more spiritually inclined on every available measure than their elders. Jay Michaelson, an influential writer in his 30's with a deep meditation practice, has written *Everything is God*, and speaks and writes frequently about contemplative practice as a spiritual resource for younger Jews. Spiritually inclined Jews in their 30's do not ask the question that bothered the prior generations—is this practice

Jewish? They simply want to know how to practice and incorporate it. Hillel organizations on campus are now teaching yoga and meditation. The ethnic diversity is not wide, given that the teaching takes place within the American Jewish community, which is largely white, and Ashkenazi.

Key Trends, Opportunities and Challenges

The key trend is growth: in depth, sophistication and popularity. The opportunities are five-fold: 1) renewing Judaism itself—its theology, its worship and practice, its teachings; 2) providing mindfulness training to help leaders become more effective, compassionate, present, responsive rather than reactive, visionary and courageous–rabbis, cantors, educators, social justice activists, chaplains, organizational staff and volunteers, learners of all kinds; 3) teaching spiritual practices that can connect Jews of all ages and persuasions to Jewish wisdom even when they do not feel religious and find no meaning in mainstream Jewish communities; 4) strengthening the connection between the inner life and commitment to the well-being of all others; and 5) creating a basis for profound relationship with spiritual seekers from all faiths and backgrounds.

The challenges are many. A major task is to attract, train and sustain a new generation of teachers who can deepen and broaden Contemplative Judaism—reaching more Jews more profoundly, and connecting with teachers and seekers from other faiths who are engaged in the work of raising planetary consciousness. Training takes time and money, so students and their teachers must be subsidized.

Contemplative Jewish practices are not easy; they require practice. They cannot be "acquired" through anything but disciplined work. However, some benefit can be gained through only a small amount of practice. Thus, attracting new practitioners to contemplative Judaism presents unique challenges in terms of packaging programs, classes, and trainings that preserve and promote the integrity of rigorous practice as well as provide accessible opportunities from which everyone can benefit.

Contemplative Judaism is in need of a marketing makeover. There exist widespread misperceptions about who are contemplative practitioners and the nature of the practices. This image is beginning to change as more and more mainstream leaders bring their contemplative practice to bear on the life of their institutions, and as the findings of neuro-science become more widely understood. Nonetheless strategic exposure and intentional educational outreach are necessary.

Finally, to do this work of broadening the base, more funders will have to be engaged. That work requires attention to language, to communications and to marketing. It also requires evaluation of results—in itself a costly enterprise.

Nurturing the Growth and Development of a Contemplative Movement in America

From my perspective as the Director of the Institute for Jewish Spirituality and a board member of the Garrison Institute and a friend of the Center for Contemplative Mind in Society, I definitely see a growing demand for, and sophistication in, delivery of programs that bring contemplative practice to bear on a wide range of challenges we face in our social, political, religious and personal lives. I also see an amazing growth of relevant research—both basic and applied—that yield persuasive data on the effectiveness and importance of the field.

I think the main challenges are to the obvious ones: more research, more visibility, better messaging and marketing, more mainstream affirmation—all leading to greater funding and applications. There need to be networking and thought leadership gatherings. Organizations need to build strategic alliances to share and increase resources and outreach.

And I believe that the growth of this movement is hugely important, and on track!

Notes

1   Kalonymus Kalman Shapira, Andrea Cohen-Kiener, Trans. *Conscious Community: A Guide to Inner Work.* Jason Aronson Publishers.

Contemplative Practice and the Enrichment, Formation, and Training of Spiritual Directors

Liz Ellmann

Reflections and Intention

While writing this chapter, I learned that the government of Israel has immediately banned fishing on the Sea of Galilee for two years because of overfishing. This historic action invites deep reflection. In the Hebrew and Christian scriptures, fishing and fish are cited many times and given symbolic meaning. Jesus taught contemplative practices on the shores of the Sea of Galilee. Often he used parables or stories to teach, and frequently his parables involved fishing. In fact, the language he chose to commission disciples was, "I will make you fishers of [people]." When the Sea of Galilee suffers from pollution and overfishing such that there are no harvestable fish, what relevance do the traditional stories have for today? If these stories have connected people for thousands of years to their contemplative heritage, and fishing is banned, do we need new stories? Conversely, what might the contemplative traditions and sacred scripture teach us about the prophetic action needed in response to overfishing?

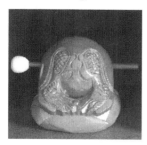

In the Buddhist tradition, the fish symbolizes wakefulness. A percussion instrument called a Mokugyo, or "wooden fish," is often used by monks and laity during rituals involving the recitation of sutras, mantras, or other Buddhist texts. The sound of the mallet striking the woodblock carved into the shape of a fish serves to keep rhythm during the contemplative practice of sutra chanting, reminding disciples to awaken.

All human institutions, programs and activities must now be judged primarily by the extent to which they inhibit, ignore or foster a mutually-enhancing human-earth relationship.

— Thomas Berry

My intention for participating in the Fetzer Institute contemplative project is to "foster a mutually-enhancing human-earth relationship." May our work together support the contemplative work of many institutions, programs, and activities. May contemplative practices continue to contribute to living in right relation with all beings. May it be so.

Prelude—What Is Spiritual Direction?

The ancient ministry and service of spiritual direction tends the spiritual aspect of being human by accompanying people on their sacred journey. The relationship between the spiritual director and directee involves listening with compassion for the ways that God-Beyond-All-Names or Ultimate Reality is truly guiding [for the purposes of this paper, I will use the word, God, to connote not only the theistic understanding of God, but also the non-theistic understanding of Ultimate Reality]. People generally meet monthly with a spiritual director either one-on-one or in group spiritual direction, and often spiritual directors teach contemplative practices as a way of accessing, enhancing, and tending their relationship with God. Drawing on the language of Saint Ignatius of Loyola, the fruit or hoped-for outcome of meeting regularly with a spiritual director is to find God in all things and constantly practice gaining freedom to cooperate with God's will (or way, orientation, direction).

In the Buddhist tradition, "spiritual direction is encompassed in the Buddhist student-teacher relationship; the connection between director and directee is most reminiscent of the 'spiritual friend' relationship—known in ancient Pali as *kalyanamitta*. This sacred friendship is one in which there is a depth of connection and commitment—a joining together through empathy and wisdom. In Buddhist spiritual direction, the director, in mindful presence, shares in a heartfelt way, the feelings expressed by the directee—meeting the directee's inherent goodness—the sacred still place within. Through empathy and wisdom, the director skillfully leads the directee to know his or her inherent goodness, inspiring the directee to envision and meet his or her true potential. Mindfulness practices are often introduced as tools to enhance clear seeing and ease of well-being." (Karin J. Miles, Spiritual Directors International website, www.sdiworld.org)

Invitation to Contemplative Practice

In a spirit of sharing a contemplative practice from spiritual direction, I invite the reader to pause for a moment of silence before continuing to read. Ponder these questions:

➢ What is your intention as you begin reading about contemplative practice and spiritual direction?

➢ What are you curious about?

➢ How will reading connect you with your spiritual heritage?

➢ How will reading contribute to serving your community, world, and all beings?

➢ What is your experience of God, a Higher Power, Ultimate-Reality-Beyond-Names in the present moment as you prepare to read?

➢ Scan your body, your thoughts, your feelings, your spirit.

➢ Simply notice, without judgment.

➢ Smile.

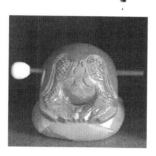

At random intervals through this chapter, you will discover a wooden fish of contemplation. The wooden fish is an invitation to pause and simply notice. Breathe. Spiritual directors often encourage repetition of contemplative practices. Perhaps reflect on the questions again. Scan your body, your thoughts, your feelings, your spirit. Simply notice. Smile. Begin reading anew. Awake.

I. Spiritual directors have historically played an important role in teaching traditional contemplative practices as well as experimenting with and introducing new contemplative practices. Recent educational events of Spiritual Directors International illustrate changes in the educational emphases of spiritual direction formation during the past twenty years.

Spiritual Directors International celebrated its twentieth anniversary in April 2010 with educational events that attracted more than six hundred people from six continents. SDI was founded at Mercy Center, a Catholic Christian context, in Burlingame, California. It has grown into a multifaith global learning community of more than 7,000 people in over fifty countries with its home office located in Seattle, Washington. Spiritual Directors International is a multifaith, independent, educational non-profit, supporting the global learning community of seekers and spiritual directors with publications and educational programs.

Comparing the recent Spiritual Directors International educational events with two prior events provides a micro view of the macro changes that are occurring in the education of spiritual directors around the world and across traditions. The diversity of spiritual directors as well as the variety of plenary presentations, workshop topics, and the communities' growing desire to go deeper together in silence represent significant changes from twenty years ago.

Twenty years ago, the location for the annual educational events was a Catholic retreat center in suburban California on acres of beautiful land dotted with oak trees. The plenary presentation by Jesuit priests Brian McDermott and Robert Egan was titled, "Contemplative Experience in Spiritual Direction." Educational workshop topics included how to train spiritual directors in non-Roman Catholic settings and how to teach contemplative practices to people struggling with addictions. Most of the presenters and faculty were clergy or religious women. They generously shared their Christian heritage of spiritual direction and contemplative practices with religious and lay Christian participants called to offer contemplative practices through spiritual direction.

Flash forward to 2004, in a Miami, Florida hotel. The SDI educational events included Richard Rohr, OFM as the plenary speaker. The theme was "Everything Belongs." During the educational events, a Jewish professor from a rabbinical college publicly thanked the Roman Catholic religious sisters for carrying mystical and contemplative traditions into the twenty-first century. The professor explained that because of the Holocaust, the Jewish mystical traditions were all but lost, and many Jews no longer believe in God. Ever since she had begun meeting with a Roman Catholic spiritual director and working with contemplative practices at the rabbinical college, she felt a renewed commitment to reclaiming the mystical Jewish tradition as a way to participate in *tikkun olam,* or "repairing the world."

Fast forward to 2010. The venue for the Spiritual Directors International educational events was a high-rise hotel in the heart of urban San Francisco, and the theme was "Gratefulness: the Heart of Spiritual Care." During the opening contemplative ritual that included dance, chants, sacred images, and silence, we told the evolving story of spiritual direction (also known as spiritual guidance, spiritual companionship, spiritual accompaniment, spiritual teaching, *mashpiah* in Hebrew, *sheikh* in Arabic, *anam cara* in Gaelic). With gratefulness, we celebrated that for thousands of years, in many spiritual traditions, including indigenous spiritualities, Hinduism, Taoism, Buddhism, Judaism, Christianity, and Islam, spiritual directors have been important carriers of contemplative practices and spirituality. We honored the contemplative elders in the global learning community of Spiritual Directors International, many of whom are clergy (rabbis, priests, pastors, imams) or live in vowed religious communities. We welcomed the younger new generation of contemplative spiritual directors, many of whom are lay people: hospice caregivers, doctors, nurses, lawyers, government and non-profit sector workers, social workers, high tech professionals, musicians, artists, teachers, writers, and lay leaders in spiritual communities.

We acknowledged a shift happening in our lifetime. The educational topics for plenary sessions and workshops reflect the shift. They included contemplative practice and cosmology, neuroscience, creativity, Sufi mysticism, and Jewish practices of gratefulness through the ages. Workshop presenters were clergy and laity, from many spiritual traditions. Harrison Owen's Open Space Technology, which has been incorporated into the educational events for many years, allowed participants to spontaneously create their own specific

educational experiences to serve their unique needs. Spontaneous topics included spiritual direction in the workplace and spiritual direction with gay, lesbian, and transgendered people.

Keynoter Brian Swimme, PhD, a cosmologist, passionately put in plain words, "The task of spiritual direction is to deconstruct the maladaptive story that humans are living out of. The central task of spiritual direction is to create a culture that amplifies life's hum … to learn that Earth is not a collection of resources but a community of life that the human is invited to join."

According to keynoter Rev. Jane Vennard, "Our task here is to continually attend to the experience of Oneness, realizing again and again that nothing truly separates us from God, from each other, and from all creation. I am not only to love my neighbor, I am my neighbor. I am not only to care for this created world, I am the created world. All is one and All is holy."

Keynoter Brother David Steindl-Rast, OSB, explained that etymologically, *Spiritus* means "life breath." "Spirituality is about aliveness, and the role of the spiritual director is to bring forth aliveness." He invited spiritual directors to remember times when we were given what we needed. We learned that life can be trusted. "Because life is trustworthy, we must say yes to belonging together with one another in order for our actions, not just our speech, to convey love."

Keynoter Alexander Shaia offered spiritual directors a framework or great pattern of four spiritual movements he calls *Quadratos*, which describe the recurring spiritual tasks:

❖ facing change
❖ moving through the suffering change evokes
❖ receiving joy in a way that opens us to our essential oneness in communion with all
❖ maturing in service as we move into community and the world with a deepening perspective.

Notice how all the 2010 plenary messages taught spiritual directors to utilize contemplative practices to engage inwardly in the service of acting outwardly, to "move into community and the world with a deepening perspective." To "amplify life's hum" spiritual directors need to trust life and its mysterious source and teach spiritual practices that encourage trusting life. Contemplative practices enable people to notice where and when our human potential for destruction overwhelms our human capacity to amplify life's hum, and make a conscious and sometimes painstaking choice to choose life. Courageously, we practice leaning into thousands of years of spiritual tradition, and choose life.

II. What is Contemplative Practice?

When I teach the value of the ancient practice of spiritual direction re-appropriated for today, I often use the image of three chairs. The image makes spiritual direction available for everyone, not the pious few. In one chair sits the seeker, looking for meaning and orientation in the chaotic world we live in. In the second chair sits the spiritual director, a trustworthy companion listening with compassion and offering contemplative practices that for thousands of years have helped people find their way through existential angst to truth and joy. In the third chair sits God, (Christ, Buddha, Krishna, Muhammad, Pachamama, Ein Sof) always present and offering guidance. Contemplative practices are the activities and reflective in-activities that open our hearts, minds, and souls to God's movement in our lives. Contemplative practices help us notice God in all things and encourage us to engage in the life-giving direction where God is guiding. Throughout human history, contemplative practices have nurtured the sacred aspect of being human and cultivated the courage to be God's friend, as well as God's prophetic servant[1], in service of all beings, especially the poor and outcast. The act of meeting regularly with a spiritual director to reflect on the spiritual direction, course, or orientation of one's life is itself a contemplative practice.

Three chairs of spiritual direction:
Seeker, Spiritual Companion, God/Ultimate Reality

To gain perspective on teaching spiritual directors in enrichment, formation, and training programs[2], I interviewed spiritual directors and spiritual teachers who have been involved in spiritual director formation for more than twenty years. I am deeply grateful for their wisdom, and it is an honor and privilege to include their outlook. In their teaching settings, here is how they answer the question, "What is contemplative practice?"

> **Wilkie Au, PhD** - Professor of Theological Studies at Loyola Marymount University, California, "Contemplation, in brief, is pausing to notice; tending the holy by paying attention to the

presence of God and all of our reality. So within us and in nature, in our interactions, in our daydreams, and night dreams, basically, whatever we do to pay attention to the mystery that is God, that is spirit."

> **Rev. Tilden Edwards** - Founder of the Shalem Institute, Bethesda, Maryland, "Contemplative practices are ways of claiming the desire in me for communion with God and guidance in God, and ways of assisting openness to that communion and guidance."

> **Michelle and Joel Levey, PhD** - Founders of The International Center for Corporate Culture and Organizational Health at InnerWork Technologies, Inc., Seattle, Washington, "Contemplative practices are a set of liberating techniques for cultivating greater wisdom and compassion" (Michelle). "There are two main categories or approaches to contemplative practice that are commonly engaged. One are the contemplative practices that in a sense help us clear the rubble from our true nature to reveal the essence of who we are—that we can abide in that more fully ... There's a "finding our way home" aspect of practice so that we can abide in that state of being. And there are also the contemplative practices that affirm that we have never left home. That our divinity is nothing that can be reclaimed or has never been lost; it's something to affirm and to awaken to" (Joel).

> **Sandra Lommasson** - Founder and co-executive director of Bread of Life, Sacramento, California, "Contemplative practices include looking with eyes of compassion ... Growing the depths of my own understanding that my story had been pervaded by spirit, mystery, holy – waking up to that, struggling to believe that... [Then] moving contemplative dialogue to the structural arena."

> **Janet Ruffing, RSM, PhD** - Professor of the Practice of Spirituality and Ministerial Leadership at Yale Divinity School, New Haven, Connecticut, "Contemplation is the experience of God, an organic growth in discipline of prayer that moves through stages of development until God is the primary actor."

> **Mary Ann Scofield, RSM, PhD** - Emerita Faculty Mercy Center Spiritual Direction Institute, Burlingame, California, "Contemplation is a gift God gives. You can always ask for the gift … You can do all the practices to dispose yourself for the gift, but only God can give it. I can't give it to myself."

> **Rabbi Jacob Staub, PhD** - Chair, Department of Medieval Jewish Civilization; Professor of Jewish Philosophy and Spirituality; Director, Jewish Spiritual Direction Program at Reconstructionist Rabbinical College, Wyncote, Pennsylvania, "Much of Jewish meditation practice is contemplative practice, because it is a practice of noticing. Of listening and noticing what arises, which then is a skill or orientation of a position one carries into all aspects of life and into the practice of listening … It's a new practice in the Jewish community."

III. How have the contemplative practices evolved over the past twenty-five years?

"Twenty five years ago, my understanding of contemplative practice was quite personal," said Sandra Lommasson. Learning and teaching contemplative practices involved "a sequence and a methodology for examining one's own life and growing in a relationship with God … [Later] the practices and wisdom for looking at my life, at patterns of life in family systems, began growing out into [the] structural arena, because I was getting a new pair of eyes and ears. And that's another way I think of contemplative practice."

Lommasson uses the "Ladder of Inference[3]" to teach individuals how contemplative practices may be used not only for personal learning but also for organizational learning. If God is everywhere always, then contemplative practices are not only for use during weekly spiritual gatherings or a monthly

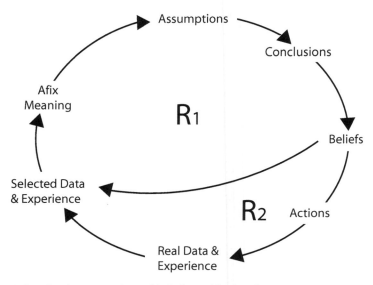

Cultural, religious, and social beliefs can blind us from compassionate action

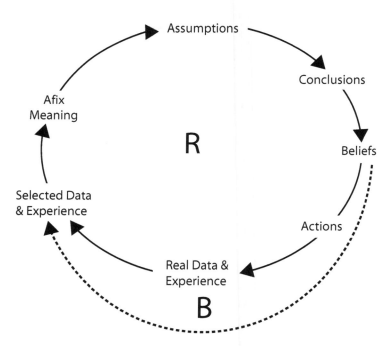

Spiritual direction offers contemplative practices that balance and open eyes to new compassionate possibilities for action

meeting with a spiritual director, but also contemplative practices may be helpful to notice God in everyday life: in workplaces, communities, family, and congregational life.

A circular rendering of the "ladder of inference" process, created by organizational developer, Gene Bellinger, illustrates how our beliefs and habitual thinking patterns can tend to short circuit the raw data we select and experience. Contemplative practices are reflective tools that help individuals as well as organizations concretely name the reality they experience. Contemplative practices empower individuals and organizations to become aware of whether their beliefs are short-circuiting Ultimate Reality, which includes ever-expanding sets of raw data.

In the diagram, "R" stands for reality. Notice how the upper process, R1, bypasses real data and experience, because the person or organization chooses only information that supports their beliefs (cultural, religious, social patterns). Contemplative practices assist individuals, organizations, and society to awaken to the interdependent and interconnected reality that includes and incorporates more and more real data and experience. Contemplative practices build tolerance to the uncertainty and disorientation that real data and experience may induce.

In the second diagram, "B" for balancing illustrates the expansive and balancing quality that arises when spiritual directors learn contemplative practices and teach contemplative practices in their communities. When individuals, organizations, and society learn contemplative practices, a counter-balancing of the tendency to turn away from real data and experience occurs. As the inner spiritual life of spiritual directors becomes strengthened, the capacity to choose compassionate action increases. Teaching contemplative practices to spiritual directors allows individuals to be present to the ever-evolving and emergent reality with resilience and a grateful heart, learning that life is trustworthy and that the right next action will emerge.

Several people I interviewed mentioned the essay by Walter Burghardt, SJ, *Contemplation: a Long Loving Look at the Real* as helpful for teaching contemplative practice to spiritual directors. Mary Ann Scofield, RSM, commented that teaching the *long loving look* has not changed, yet the Real has changed significantly in the past twenty-five years. "We've grown in our understanding, for example of the universe, conscious evolution, the poor and the marginalized—I don't think they were fully in our awareness. They should have been, but they weren't, not long ago—other cultures, globalization… so what we're looking at, the reality that we see before us has expanded so much more." Janet Ruffing, RSM, reflected, "if contemplation is fully opened to what is, it also leads us to social justice, it leads us to see evil operating in the world, it leads us to see suffering without flinching and in the company of God."

Rabbi Jacob Staub said, "I don't think anybody would have taken even a minute of silence before we started a program in 1987... Most non-Orthodox Jews didn't believe in God, didn't pray twenty years ago; didn't know how, but yet wanted some sanctification of their lives. Part of the general culture they wanted was some mystery. Contemplative practice offers that to them without requiring a crash course in Hebrew or revision in theological beliefs. It allows them to be discerning, to notice blessings, to live in mystery without knowing more than they know... The first time I taught contemplative readings of Jewish text was 1999 or 2000; it was a new and groundbreaking moment. I opened the first class and said, 'unlike all of your other courses you're not interested in the historical background, the grammatical constructions, you are reading the text and seeing what happens when you read them. You can use the methods and practices of scholarship to enhance your reading, but you may not use them to discount a reading...' It was unlike anything they had ever done in a classroom."

Wilkie Au talked about teaching busy people *crabgrass contemplation*, which will grow in the tiny cracks between e-mail, text messages, and tweets. "Twenty-five years ago, I was mainly teaching Jesuit novices and going through traditional modes of praying. In my first book, *By Way of the Heart*, I break it down to apophatic and cataphatic ways, using the way of images and the way of no images... But, these days I don't do that as much. I go for a generic form of contemplation, which could be integrated into their religious practice. If you can acquire this kind of attentiveness, or sensitivity, it can help you spot God, not only in nature and relationships, but also if you're attending liturgy. It focuses your awareness, so it's a generic posture of being open to the mystery of God."

Teaching contemplative practices in spiritual direction
includes befriending God in the world.

Teaching contemplative practices in spiritual direction has evolved during the past twenty-five years increasingly into the prophetic realm, which is not to say that the prophetic aspect of contemplative practice has not always been present. Mary Ann Scofield, RSM quoted Hebrew scripture during the Leadership Institute educational events several years ago, "…in every generation, she [Wisdom] passes into holy souls, and makes of them friends of God, and prophets." [Wisdom 7:27.] The three chairs illustrating spiritual direction no longer float abstractly in a clean, white vacuum, exploring only the interior spiritual world and the personal relationship with God. The spiritual direction relationship is now engaged in befriending God in the world, and living into the prophetic call God's friendship invites.

IV. What organizations have developed to support teaching contemplative practice to spiritual directors?

The Spiritual Directors International website lists nearly 300 enrichment, formation, and training programs on six continents that teach contemplative practices to spiritual directors. A spectrum exists from academic programs in seminaries and rabbinical colleges, to programs hosted in retreat centers with or without graduate credit, to a handful of distance learning and Web-based programs. The SDI website[4] helps people locate educational programs on a Google map.

Publications such as *Presence: An International Journal of Spiritual Direction,*[5] *Listen: A Seeker's Resource for Spiritual Direction,*[6] *SDI* blog,[7] and many books listed in the Web library, including ten books in the imprint series of Spiritual Directors International, support the teaching of contemplative practices among spiritual directors. Certainly many other retreats, publications, and online resources, as well as a multitude of educational events assist in the ongoing formation of contemplative practices in spiritual directors.

V. Demographics

The people called to share contemplative practices through the ministry and service of spiritual direction are changing. Contemplative practices are being transmitted to a broader sector of society, from ordained and vowed religious people to laity. Vowed religious and clergy have been the historical carriers of contemplative practices, and they are diminishing in numbers in North America, while the lay people in many spiritual communities and in secular realms are stepping into the role of carrying and transmitting contemplative practices. Networks are emerging to support spiritual direction with people of color, GLBTs, as well as people of only a specific faith (Jewish network, Methodist network). Young people are finding their way through the arts and music, offering classes online, for example, in photography as contemplative practice.

In the 2010 PBS television program about spiritual directors, *Religion and Ethics*,[8] Lucky Severson reported how "An increasing number of Americans say they are searching for spirituality. And many inside and outside of church are finding it with the help of a spiritual director, someone to listen and offer guidance in the quest for the experience of God's presence. Sometimes it's in groups, like this retreat. Most often it's one on one and deeply personal." Mainstream Americans are looking for the contemplative practices that have helped saints and mystics deepen the experience of God's presence.

Moreover, the contemplative practices traditionally taught in spiritual direction are not only being offered as a way to deepen one's experience of God, but also to alleviate suffering, reduce stress, and increase the capacity for compassion in communities. People with little or no spiritual background show up to learn a contemplative practice to manage pain, and then discover they are really seeking a spiritual community to explore the deeper meaning of life, death, and living with integrity and joy, even in the presence of pain.

At Group Health, where Joel Levey once worked as a clinician in stress management, he noticed, "a big caseload of patients who weren't getting much help from other departments that were sending them to the stress clinic or the pain center for help. Many of them, though they had significant psychophysical problems, were really suffering from various dimensions of existential stresses.... [Later] I started a weekly meditation group, essentially a kind of dialogue and deep reflection, a kind of spiritual direction group for leaders and clinicians at the hospital that had an appropriate designator to it that people could justify the time to show up. It was actually a profound moving force that gave rise to many significant initiatives within Group Health over the years... It was from there that Group Health started sending me out to do corporate programs to see if we could build healthier organizations."

Other changes in demographics include people with little or no theological background discerning the call to offer spiritual direction. Some programs invite a first-year of study in adult spiritual formation before engaging in spiritual direction formation. Gradually people from all walks of life are discerning the call to spiritual direction. Upon completion of spiritual director formation programs, spiritual directors are offering spiritual direction in more than the traditional spiritual community setting. A wide variety of settings for spiritual direction now include: in prisons, with the homeless, in health care and hospice, in community buildings and art studios, outdoors on wilderness retreats, in corporate conference rooms, with lawyers and in mediation, through e-mail and Skype.

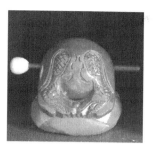

Trends, Movements, and Investments

1. Yes, a contemplative movement in America (and worldwide) continues to emerge. According to Tilden Edwards, "I increasingly feel like a contemplative evangelist. I am aware that this is not something you just have a little private group doing and then just expect it all to blossom. There are connections that are needed, and there are implications of what's going on inside for every dimension, of not only your life but of the whole society and world's life. And therefore there's a sociopolitical dimension, there's contemplation in action in the fullest sense of the term." The investment challenges and opportunities to support the contemplative movement are enormous. For thousands of years, spiritual communities, monasteries, congregations, churches, vowed religious and a priestly class have been the carriers of the contemplative traditions. Funding by institutional religion created relative stability over time. What is the emerging funding model to educate and foster spiritual directors and future carriers of contemplative practices?

2. Contemplative practices in spiritual direction need financial support to be present on the margins, for healing communities, and learning about God's transformative way in urban life. From Sandra Lommasson, "We intentionally relocated Bread of Life several years ago. Originally located in an upper middle-class church building, in a highly educated university community, we moved into one of the most challenged neighborhoods of Sacramento. It's mostly asphalt, with noise, sirens, and helicopters overhead, generations of drug abuse, and where people's bodies look thirty years older than they look at the same age in Davis [California] because they've lived such a hard life in poverty. The call was to pray the city, to be a place of contemplation, peace, and sanctuary in a church building, but of a dying congregation that had very few people left. People can come in from that very urban, fractured life and pray with their hands at a free open art studio space... We have between 500 and 600 visits a month right now. It's every ethnicity, it's men and women, it's families, it's people who are disabled with caregivers, it's elderly it's 2-year-olds with moms, it's everybody." Funding is difficult for inner city spirituality centers as well as the traditional rural and suburban retreat centers that have provided refuge for many generations of contemplatives to learn and to grow spiritually. What is the future business model for spirituality centers? How might the diverse contemplative community experiment with and share information among inner city spirituality centers so that healthy growth and new models emerge? What publications and educational events (Web and in person) would foster resilient models for contemplative living and retreat centers?

3. Contemplative practices in spiritual direction will continue moving into the mainstream. Traditionally, spiritual directors spent years in spiritual formation and lived in community as God honed their gifts of offering spiritual direction. The founding members of Spiritual Directors International were clergy and vowed religious, supported by their religious communities. As spiritual direction evolves into the world, there will be pressure to fund spiritual direction and programs through non-traditional means:

> ➢ exclusivity (only people who can pay-to-view publications, or pay-for-the-service will be offered spiritual direction enrichment, formation, training, or contemplative support);

> ➢ commercialization, i.e., auto insurance ads on Beliefnet.com and real estate brokerage on Findthedivine.com; spirituality is popular, so it attracts advertising sometimes antithetical to traditional spirituality;

> ➢ incomplete or false advertising, i.e., people call themselves spiritual directors with little or no formation or training, and they are not supported by a spiritual community. The potential for psycho-spiritual harm exists.

How might we plan for the future with media campaigns to educate the public about the value of contemplative practices and spiritual direction, informing the public what to seek and what to avoid?

4. **Spiritual director enrichment, formation and training programs offer an opportunity for growth in the next decade. Programs need to keep up with evolving brain science, technology, and adapt language to suit multiple environments where spiritual direction will be offered in the future.** As more Americans search for spirituality, and simultaneously the vowed religious communities that traditionally supported spirituality shrink, the demand for spiritual support will surpass the supply of clergy and vowed religious. Lay people need psychic, spiritual, financial, and social support to pursue the ministry and service of spiritual care. Technology can expand opportunities for education (see Spiritual Directors International YouTube educational videos,[9] SDI-Facebook,[10] and website[11]), yet one-on-one and group spiritual direction will remain as carriers of contemplative practices. What can we do to support lay people and to support enrichment, formation, and training programs that will need to evolve to meet the demands? For example, how might we help build bridges between spiritual director formation programs and in-services for health care providers, educating health care about the value of contemplative practices and health care?

5. **How is the spiritual heritage of contemplation around the world and across traditions inviting conscious change in the way humanity is evolving?** What changes are needed in enrichment, formation, and training programs of spiritual directors so the ancient contemplative practices remain relevant for today? When traditional stories no longer have meaning, or are destructive, how do we teach new stories? What does spiritual direction offer "to deconstruct the maladaptive story that humans are living out of" (Brian Swimme). Return again to the opening concern about the fish in the Sea of Galilee: how do we ensure that the prophetic edge in the contemplative traditions remains resilient and supports prophets?

6. **Lastly, how do we approach these questions in a contemplative manner, not as problems to be fixed, but instead as a communal contemplative practice?** Without becoming too analytical by using Western science and systems-thinking as models, how do we let God guide us in and through the wildly diverse, contemplative field, allowing our *head knowledge filled with words* to empty into the non-knowing, empty-fullness of the cosmos? William McNamara, a Carmelite, wrote, "You can study things, but unless you enter into this intuitive communion with them you can only know about them, you don't know them. To take a long loving look at something—a child, a work of art, a beautiful meal—is to enter into a natural act of contem-

plation, of loving admiration." What would it be like to patiently, reverently take a long loving look at the real and wait together to be infused through our body and heart's intuitive knowing of the emergent next action or inaction?

The prophetic call in spiritual direction requires listening to each other and the Universe with a contemplative heart and responding with compassion for all of creation.

Notes

1   Scofield, Mary Ann, "Friends of God and Prophets," chapter in *Sacred is the Call*, Suzanne M. Buckley, ed., The Crossroad Publishing Company 2005.

2   Historically, in the Abrahamic spiritual traditions, spiritual directors responded to a call by God to serve as a spiritual guide. The language used to communicate the cultivation of the "charism" or "gift from God" varies among spiritual traditions: enrichment, formation, and training are most commonly used. Several spiritual director formation programs are offended by or concerned about the language of "training" because training suggests a trade like any other skill. Training might infer disassociation from God and a spiritual community.

3   The "Ladder of Inference," was initially developed by Chris Argyris and subsequently made popular in Peter Senge's book, *The Fifth Discipline: The Art and Practice of the Learning Organization*. In brief, people tend to live in worlds of self-generating beliefs, which remain largely untested and unexamined. We adopt beliefs because they represent patterns based on conclusions, which are inferred from what we observe, including past experience.

4 http://www.sdiworld.org/programs-locator.html.

5 http://www.sdiworld.org/presence_journal.html.

6 http://www.sdiworld.org/publications/listen.html.

7 http://info.sdiworld.org/.

8 http://to.pbs.org/SDIworld.

9 http://www.youtube.com/watch?v=qxcovadPz2Q.

10 http://bit.ly/SDIforspiritualcare.

11 http://www.sdiworld.org/.

Contemplative Practice and Online Communities

Mary Ann Brussat

In December 2000, the Pew Internet and American Life Project[1] released the first extensive quantitative effort to discover how churches and synagogues in the United States use the Internet. In a report titled "Wired Churches, Wired Temples: Taking Congregations and Missions into Cyberspace[2]," they found that 21% of Internet users (about 19 million people) reported using the Internet to seek spiritual and religious information; more than 2 million sought such information daily.

By 2001, when the Pew Project released "CyberFaith: How Americans Pursue Religion Online[3]," 25% of Internet users were getting religious or spiritual information online; more than 3 million were doing so daily. In 2004, the Pew Project's "Faith Online[4]" report found that 64% of the nation's 128 million Internet users (about 82 million) had done things online that relate to religious or spiritual matters. Internet access had grown dramatically in just four years, and the percentage using it for spiritual or religious reasons had tripled. The Pew Project has not released another study since 2004, but we can reasonably assume that use of the Internet for spiritual and religious reasons has continued to grow.

This paper will look at what's happening on the Internet in the areas of religion and spirituality in general and what's happening in terms of Internet-facilitated contemplative practices in particular.

Contemplative Practices

I am using "contemplative practices" here as synonymous with "spiritual practices." I see them as activities that engage, enhance, and expand our connections with the sacred dimension of life. At Spirituality & Practice, we have not found it helpful or necessary to distinguish between "inner" and "outer" work, or to separate practices into those that are primarily for self-observation, focusing, and quieting the mind and those that are primarily devotional in nature or action-oriented.

We include three types of spiritual practices in our coverage: (1) Those that connect you to God, making you aware of and inviting the Sacred

Presence into your life; (2) Those that connect you with your neighbors and the Creation. (3) Those that connect you to your true self, helping to remove veils, confusions, and issues that get in the way of your knowledge of your inner core and the Divine in the depth of your being. The three types of practices usually overlap and point to the essential Oneness of reality and the interconnection of all things. They are also transformative in that they open the heart and enable you to "see with God's eyes, hear with God's ears" (Joan Chittister).

We have organized the Spirituality & Practice website around 37 essential spiritual practices of the world religions and so my understanding of what qualifies as a practice is quite broad. We do begin with Attention and Being Present (mindfulness, concentration) but we also include Compassion, Justice, Reverence, Unity, and Wonder. I will comment later on about how these contemplative practices are supported by online experiences.

History of Online Religious/Spiritual Communities

Church people have been creating community online since the earliest days of the Internet. The first organized denominational experiments with telecommunications began in 1983 - 1986 when the United Methodists, the United Church of Christ, the Presbyterians, the Lutherans, and the Disciples of Christ began using various systems to share information. These connections eventually birthed Ecunet, a network of mainline denominations with clergy and lay members.

Two events cemented early relationships within the network. One was a meeting set up online where news and reports from an ecumenical conference were shared. The other was an online memorial service held in response to the tragedy of the crash of the space shuttle Challenger on January 28, 1986. The service was led by four pastors of different denominations. Most of the service consisted of read-only notes but people were also invited to post their own prayers and thoughts during the service. Afterwards, a "coffee hour" was held in a chat section of the system, where people could express their sadness about the explosion and their thanks to those who created the memorial service. This was one of the first examples of shared contemplative practice online.

Ecunet functioned like a listserv except that multiple topics could be created and comments were better organized through one system. Members joined meetings where they could send notes and receive batches of notes posted to their meetings back via email. Connection costs were still quite high in those early days and people preferred to do their writing offline. This had the welcome effect of creating more thoughtful conversations. Eventually, a web interface was added but the email format continued to be the way most people interacted. One of the earliest meetings was "Sermonshop" where clergy shared sermon ideas and interpretations of the weekly texts. The other was "Prayer Chapel" where people posted prayer concerns and celebrations and responses to those requests. Both meetings are still going today.

Ecunet's early content reflects two trends of online activity by religious and spiritual people that have continued to this date: searching for information/news and prayer. As the 2000 Pew Report noted, most congregations use their websites primarily for one-way communications: basic information on the church, directions, mission statement, staff bios, photographs of congregational activities, sermons, and links to denominational sites. Clergy use the Internet to get information for sermons, worship services, devotional resources, and theological statements, etc. Some congregations do collect prayer requests from their websites, and some offer educational materials, especially Bible study.

The most popular online activities, according to Pew's 2001 study, are solitary ones. Seekers use the Internet as a library, seeking information on their own faith (67%) and other faiths (50%). The Internet seems to be especially helpful to those not part of mainstream religious groups; and 27% attributed to the Internet "at least some improvement in their faith lives."

This study also showed that email and the Internet are influencing the prayer lives of Americans. 38% said they used email to send prayer requests. Nearly half (44%) said that the Internet provides easier access to prayer and other devotional materials than they could find offline.

Pew's 2004 report focused again on what people were doing online. It described the "online faithful" as using the Internet for personal spiritual matters more than for traditional religious functions. Among the most popular activities:

- 38% have sent and received email with spiritual content.
- 35% have sent or received online greeting cards related to religious holidays.
- 32% have gone online to read news accounts of religious events and affairs.
- 21% have sought information about how to celebrate religious holidays.
- 17% have looked for information about where they could attend religious services.

Many of these users were devout (including evangelicals as the most fervent users). They were more likely to be women (55%), white (83%), college-educated (49%), and well-to-do (31% in households earning more than $75,000). The survey asked them to describe their relationship to religion and spirituality.

- 54% of the online faithful described themselves as religious and spiritual.
- 33% described themselves as spiritual but not religious.
- 6% described themselves as religious but not spiritual.
- 4% described themselves as not religious and not spiritual.

Although it's easy to assume that the spiritual but not religious group, who often are not involved with a local religious community, would be the most likely to seek one online, the study actually showed that the religious and spiritual group were the most active online.

Religious and Spiritual Information on the Internet

It's not surprising that religious and spiritual people turn to the Internet primarily for information. There is an enormous amount of religious/spiritual information online! Those wanting to learn about the beliefs and practices of the religious and spiritual traditions can easily find overviews of each religion, columns and blogs by respected teachers, and theological papers. There are numerous sites run by denominations and religious groups providing in-depth content. Sites such as Beliefnet.com and Patheos.com feature portals to content on all the major traditions. Esoteric, New Age, and sites targeted to "Spiritual But Not Religious" people further expand the information field.

You can find almost anything about religion and spirituality--from ancient times to the present—on the Internet these days. You can read and search sacred texts from all the world's religions in multiple translations. You can listen to podcasts by spiritual teachers and tune in to webcasts. For those seeking degrees, many seminaries are now offering distance learning through the web.

This content has moved a long way from the days of congregational "brochure" websites. Now Oprah.com can host a series of 10 professionally produced webcasts with Ekhart Tolle and attract more than 30 million viewers worldwide. In its first season, "Global Spirit," a spirituality series that broadcasts both through cable channels and on the Internet through Link TV, reached 45 million viewers weekly; in addition, streams of the series available online were viewed more than 50,000 times in an eight-month period. A live chat with Deepak Chopra following one Global Spirit episode this spring attracted an audience of 44,000 viewers.

Contemplative Practice on the Internet

The Internet is a great resource for those seeking background on and even instructions in contemplative practices. But what opportunities are provided to actually do practices online?

Beliefnet has a section of the site devoted to audio programs of meditations from different traditions. Visitors can be led through a Lovingkindness meditation by Buddhist Sharon Saltzberg, hear prayers and chants in English and Arabic from the Mevlevi Sufi prayer book, listen to Hindu mantra meditations, and instructions for doing Christian Centering Prayer.

At ExploreFaith.org, visitors are encouraged to try different forms of meditation, including meditating on art (using an online gallery), music (with audio downloads of contemplative music), poetry, and sacred texts. Another section on prayer invites visitors to put in their zip code and get the prayers for the present time from the Divine Office.

Many sites have collections of prayers from all traditions; some are recorded so you can listen to them sung or chanted as you pray. SacredSpace.ie, a very popular site run by Irish Jesuits, offers an online prayer experience, moving the visitor through a set of prayers, scripture selections, and reflection questions for the day. Intent.com invites visitors to set an intention for each day and to indicate your support for others' intentions. Muslims can download a program from Islamicfinder.org to have the call to prayer come through their computers five times a day.

Several types of contemplative practices are available at Gratefulness.org. There is an online labyrinth that visitors can navigate through accompanied by images or text. A program introduces the Angels of the Hours with music and short meditations. The most popular feature is the online candle. The visitor is invited to take a deep breath and quiet his/her thoughts, to click on a candle so it lights up, to reflect upon the reason for lighting it, then to add a dedication and initial the candle so it can be identified on a page of candles. People can associate their candles with a group (such as for Haiti or peace) and can also email notice of their candle lighting. To date, 9.5 million candles have been lit from 242 countries.

At SpiritualityandPractice.com, we have homepages devoted to 37 essential practices which provide many perspectives on each practice through quotes;

book, audio, and film reviews; book excerpts (often containing detailed practice instructions); and specific ways to practice in daily life. The Compassion pages, for example, include instructions on the Buddhist practice of tonglen, an imagery exercise based on the Parable of the Good Samaritan in the Bible, and a compassion cue, reminder, vow, blessing, mantra, and prayers. Music and art that evoke compassion are recommended for meditation. Journal exercises, household and community projects, and questions for group discussion are also suggested.

These sites provide a good sampling of contemplative practices available on the Internet. Although some have community building elements—such as the ability to email notice of a candle, check support for an intention, or participate in a discussion—most are consistent with the research finding that most online spiritual activity is solitary.

Online Communities for Contemplative Practice

At SpiritualityandPractice.com, we have been creating opportunities for people to join intentional communities for contemplative practice. We offer e-courses and online retreats that people subscribe to for a fee. The e-courses consist of emails, each containing a short passage from a spiritual book and a suggestion for how that thought can be practiced during the day. The online retreats use emails, short audio programs, video clips, and teleconferences to teach contemplative practices. Retreats have covered Lectio Divina, the Contemplative Prayer of Forgiveness, The Monastic Hours for Prayer, Lovingkindness Meditation, and Intercessory Prayer. We have also offered retreats on sacred texts—the poetry of Rumi, the Qur'an, the Prophets, and InterSpiritual Wisdom (texts from five traditions).

Many websites have public forums and discussion groups. Because these are open to the whole world, we find that posts in those forums are either quite ego-centered or superficial; they are more like what you would comfortably say to strangers than thoughtful engagement around a subject or a practice with a group of spiritual companions. Some websites—Zaatz/Gaiam (now closed)—have been able to create forums with threads of regular participants, but they are not typical.

Further, the programming used for many forums encourage people to create their own threads, which can result in very fragmented conversations. Some forums on spiritual sites are dominated by religious conservatives or evangelicals, which are still the largest groups online. Their exclusivity discourages many seekers. Finally, throughout the Internet today, sites are making it possible for people to "comment" on posts, blogs, articles, etc. Unfortunately, some individuals use comments to vent their anger, frustration, or hostility. There is a noticeable lack of courtesy in many comments, and this discourages open and transparent sharing, especially on spiritual/religious issues.

At Spirituality & Practice, we have set up private "Practice Circles" for participants in our e-courses and online retreats. Only paid subscribers can login. This turns the forum into an intentional community where everybody knows that everybody else has gathered because of an interest in the same subject and with the same intention. Discussion guidelines reinforce the understanding that these are communities of trust where respect and courtesy are expected. Like a 12-Step program, we discourage people from trying to "fix" others with unsolicited advice. Also like a 12-step program, participants have the option of anonymity; they choose their own screen name and avatar (photo), and we do not display email addresses.

As a result of the privacy and guidelines, we find that people are amazingly transparent in their Practice Circle posts. And this is important when we are asking them to share their experiences with spiritual practices. Contemplative practices need to be tested out in the context of life experience. Instructions for a practice can be delivered in nuggets of Internet information, but then it needs to be tried. We can tell someone how to meditate or do lectio divina with a sacred text, but they won't appreciate the value or feel the impact until they do it.

It's also important that people have a way to get further guidance in the practice and support for sustaining it. This happens when they can talk about and process their own experience with someone who has also used the practice. Such conversations go on during group sharing in face-to-face retreats or in a personal conference with a spiritual teacher or mentor. Online, it happens in a Practice Circle. Through these Circles we are creating and holding a safe but open container in which people can explore, experience, and share contemplative practices.

Online communities for contemplative practice have other distinguishing characteristics that make them different from face-to-face communities. Participants encounter people from all over the world and from different traditions from their own. The Circle is available to people who may not have the extra time or extra money to attend a face-to-face retreat. Because these are forums where you post, not live chats, they are flexible for very busy people who can participate when they have a moment any time of the day.

The Practice Circles are godsends to shut-ins, people with disabilities, and parents with young children. In the "Introductions" thread for the Circles, people mention that they are "isolated" and need to "connect with like-minded people." One woman in North Dakota said she takes our courses because she is "completely surrounded by conservatives"! Another from South Georgia said her area was just "not a hub of spiritual adventures." Participants in e-courses on Buddhist practices often mention that they do not have a sangha in their community.

In some cases, these online circles are replacing local study groups that have become unfeasible. People are leading increasingly "wired" lives; they appreciate being able to get spiritual nourishment through their technology. Ministers tell us that their congregants are so busy that they can't get them out to a week-night study program at the church. To address this situation, some churches have taken advantage of our "custom e-course" service; they choose a course and recruit a group to receive it, and we give them their own Practice Circle. After a Lenten program done this way, the minister reported that one member of her congregation said that she appreciated having more "face-time" with her. Actually, all her encounters were through the minister's posts in the Practice Circle.

The teachers of our online retreats have expressed deep satisfaction with this way of teaching and interacting with retreatants. One described teaching an online course with a Practice Circle as being in the middle between a face-to-face retreat and writing a book. She gets instant feedback to her ideas along with the time to reflect upon questions before needing to answer. Reading posts gives her a deeper sense of where people are and enables her to refine her teachings. Many of the teachers have noted that people are often more forthcoming in the online Practice Circles than they are in person, when all kinds of things influence participation.

Survey of Participants

We surveyed more than 8,400 recent participants in our e-courses and online retreats. 87% are women; 13% are men. The largest age group are 55-64 (40%), followed by 45-54 (26.6%), 55 - 64 (21.5%), 35 - 44 (6.7%), and over 75 (3 %). This means that almost 2/3rds of the subscribers are over 55. We predict this percentage will increase as more Baby Boomers and WWII generation people are coming online[5] to use social media sites such as Facebook and Twitter.

Echoing the description of the "online faithful" in the 2004 report from the Pew Internet and American Life Project, the largest groups of our e-course subscribers are "religious and spiritual." 37.6% describe themselves as

Christian Anglican/Protestant, and 29.3 percent are Christian Catholic. The third largest group, at 14.2%, are "Spiritual but not Religious." Other significant groups are Jews (7%), Buddhists (13.4%), Sufis (6.2%), New Thought (5.4%), Unitarian Universalist (5.4%), and 12-Step Spirituality (5.1%). Other traditions were under 3%. 7.3% self-described as No Affiliation.

Other questions revealed that 41.7 live in cities, 22% in suburbs, 19.6% in towns, and 16.7% in rural areas. For highest education level, 53% have a graduate degree; 11% have a seminary degree; 24.7% have a college degree; 6.2% have some college; 3% have a high school degree; and 1.3% have a technical school degree.

Employment status was interesting to us as we have long thought from reading the Introductions threads in the Practice Circles that the ones with time to fully participate in an online community are retired or working part-time. The survey confirmed this. Only 40.3% are employed full-time. 30.1% are retired, 19.4% are employed part-time, 4.6 are homemakers or unpaid caretakers of children and parents, 3.5% are disabled, and 2.2% are unemployed.

The reasons given on the survey for taking an e-course or online retreat confirm our prior assumptions based on reading posts in the Introductions thread and individual course evaluations. People were asked to check as many as applied to them:

- Interest in the subject of the e-course or retreat 88.4%
- To renew/deepen my spiritual practice 67.5%
- For regular spiritual nourishment 59.4%
- Desire to learn about or from a particular teacher 50.3%
- To get support on my journey 34.9%
- To learn a new spiritual practice 30.4%
- To connect with other like-minded people 25.0%

Although the subject and the teacher are obvious draws, the desire for a regular practice and support from others also are important influences on participation. In the Practice Circle threads, subscribers have cited other reasons for doing a program, including seeking inner peace, deeper awareness, less fear, living more in the present moment, mindfulness, letting go more, more balance, and making friends with themselves. They said they wanted help with dealing with change, navigating transitions, developing consistency with their practices, and integrating new spiritual concepts. These openly expressed needs bode well for the continued growth of the contemplative movement online.

Challenges and Opportunities for Online Communities

When we read between the lines in many posts in our Practice Circles, we see that people want to do contemplative practices, have good feelings about the benefits of practices, and have specific needs for them. But they have not been able to carve out the time to do them. People's lack of time to practice is a challenge facing the contemplative movement as a whole. Because they are flexible and can be accessed at any time, online communities are one way for time-starved practitioners to get motivation and support for their practice.

Online groups also can service groups that may not be reached in other ways—elders, shut-ins, people with disabilities, and those physically isolated from like-minded people. The Internet is a lifeline to these people, and as the technology continues to advance and become more friendly, so will their participation.

Another challenge facing online contemplative communities is habitual behavior in this medium. People tend to have short attention spans while online, and they are always looking for the latest content. Contemplative practice, however, deepens over time and through repetition. The Internet makes finding practices easy, but it also makes it easy to click away to something else when the user encounters a difficult teaching and experiences ego resistance. Yet contemplative practices are often based upon hard teachings, such "Forgive those who have hurt you," "Embrace your fear," or "The most difficult people in your life may be your best teachers." Teachers and group leaders presenting these kinds of practices need to be aware of the user impatience on this medium.

At the same time, the Internet opens the door to new contemplative experiences. Already, we've seen how it is used to expand prayer forms. Online photo galleries at news sites can be used to evoke compassion and as prompts for compassion practices. Photographs of space at the NASA site or galleries of nature scenes and animals create experiences of wonder. There are websites where you can listen to the sounds of the Amazon rainforest or birds singing in the woods; these are opportunities to practice deep listening and reverence, two of our 37 essential practices from the world's religions. Flying around using Google Earth reinforces feelings of unity and connections. Online petitions and sites collecting donations enable people to act justly and show mercy. These are all ways to expand our repertoire of practices, made possible by our being connected through the Internet.

Finally, people today are living pressured and time-starved lives, juggling many responsibilities, and facing more possibilities than ever were available to them before. Sometimes stumbling upon a simple practice reminder can be transformative. This one appears at Thich Nhat Hanh's Plum Village website[6]:

Notes

1 Pew Internet and American Life Project, http://www.pewinternet. org/topics/Religion.aspx.

2 http://www.pewinternet.org/Reports/2000/Wired-Churches-Wired-Temples.aspx.

3 http://www.pewinternet.org/Reports/2001/CyberFaith-How-Americans-Pursue-Religion-Online.aspx.

4 http://www.pewinternet.org/Reports/2004/Faith-Online.aspx.

5 http://www.chron.com/disp/story.mpl/life/main/6553113.html.

6 http://www.plumvillage.org/.

THE ROLE OF CONTEMPLATIVE PRACTICE IN TRANSFORMING CONFLICT

Dena Merriam

When I began organizational work in the inter-religious field in the late 1990s I recognized two glaring omissions, which I felt seriously impeded the work being done in this area: the absence of women and the lack of participation on the part of contemplative spiritual figures. As the work of the Global Peace Initiative of Women has grown and developed, we have sought to address both of these shortcomings. In the following pages I will address why it is essential to bring contemplative practice to efforts to transform conflict and create a more balanced world with mechanisms to deal with differences and conflicting interests.

The first inter-religious summit that I helped to organize was the Millennium World Peace Summit of Religious and Spiritual Leaders held at United Nations headquarters in New York in 2000. Because the United Nations was involved, the invitation list included almost exclusively high level religious officials—few of whom were women and almost none of whom were contemplatives. There were a few exceptions. Rev. Joan Brown Campbell, who was then General Secretary of the National Council of Churches, was one of the few women in a high enough official position to warrant her being invited to address the General Assembly of the United Nations on the opening day of the Summit. Acutely aware of the poor representation of women, she was one of the first to call for a follow up summit of women religious leaders, which I subsequently was able to organize at the Palais des Nations in Geneva, and this led to the founding of the Global Peace Initiative of Women, with Rev. Campbell as the Chair.

The lack of a contemplative presence at the Summit left the space empty of any neutralizing or integrative force and opened the way for contentious debate on key religious themes as well as a competitive vying for the few speaking opportunities in the General Assembly Hall. The Peace Summit showed that there was no peace among the religions. There were however exceptions and a few of the religious figures were also contemplatives. One example was the great Buddhist master and Patriarch of Cambodia, the Venerable Maha Ghosananda, who had lead peace walks through that country and helped in the healing from the Khmer Rouge terror. Maha Ghosananda sat in meditation through most of the Summit, one of the few oases of silence and peace. His presence taught me the power of contemplative practice in the public space, and I later wondered what the Summit would have been had even ten percent of the participants been contemplative practitioners! This led to a commitment to create contemplative spaces in which to hold peace dialogues.

My first attempt at this was the summit of women religious leaders in Geneva in 2002—called the Global Peace Initiative of Women Religious and Spiritual Leaders. Since few women held senior positions in the religious institutions we were not obliged to abide by the hierarchies. I was a long time practitioner of yoga meditation with close ties to the Buddhist world, and thus we looked for contemplatives in the East and found wonderful Buddhist nuns and Hindu swaminis, along with Catholic nuns and a scattering of rabbis and Islamic scholars. We decided to be bold and begin the Summit with one full day of spiritual practice—a mix of meditation, chanting and readings from various traditions. By many accounts it was the highlight of the gathering and set the tone for the discussions to follow. Although we had women from an array of religious traditions and over 45 countries, including a number of conflict regions, there was not one complaint about the shared spiritual practice, which at that time was unheard of at inter-religious gatherings. This became the model for all our future dialogues, although most often due to time pressures we have had to limit the contemplative opening period to a few hours.

What I found from this was that the experienced meditators were able to enter a deep enough space so that something could be transmitted. They were able to bring along the newcomers, enabling them to experience some taste of the interior world. We also found that just the exposure to deep silence helped to calm the emotions, soften long-held views, and gave people perspective and some distance from the conflicts in which they lived. We saw many instances of changed perspectives. The interaction of Afghan women with Tibetan Buddhist nuns, for example, revealed many shared values and demonstrated possibilities neither group had dreamed of.

Contemplative Practice and Middle East Peace Dialogues

During the Summit in Geneva, we were called by a group of Palestinian and Israeli women to help them convene a peace dialogue. This was in 2002 at the height of the second intifada. We immediately began preparing to bring a group of Palestinian and Israeli women from the sectors of religion, government and business to meet at the Nobel Peace Institute in Oslo, Norway.

Moderating the dialogue was a group of women religious leaders, including several contemplative Buddhist nuns. This was the first of many peace dialogues we organized between Israelis and Palestinians, and for each successive dialogue we brought more contemplatives to create a safe space for interaction, and later to teach mindfulness and the awakening of compassion. As we began to work in the region, we discovered that contemplative practice was spreading in Israel and that yoga meditation centers and Dharma center were sprouting throughout the country. We also discovered that a few world renowned Buddhist leaders were quietly teaching and having a significant impact. Yet, these new contemplatives were never invited to inter-religious dialogues, which was reserved for the rabbis, imams and Christian clergy. These contemplatives were lay people but there was a growing community of serious practitioners. Thich Nhat Hanh, in particular, was active in the region, leading regular combined meditation retreats for Israelis and Palestinians. Among the Americans teachers, Bernie Glassman and Jack Kornfield were also active. Among the groups teaching yoga meditation were the Brahma Kumaris and the Shivananda Ashram. While contemplative practice has been spreading in Israel over the last decade, it has come more recently to Palestine. There is now a Buddhist Center in Bethlehem where a significant number of Palestinians come weekly for meditation practice. What impact is this having?

Initially, we saw that bringing contemplatives from outside the region to peace dialogues helped to create a certain safe, neutral space for dialogue. It helped each community connect to the other, moving out of their own suffering to perceive the pain of the other. As we began to include contemplatives from the local community, we saw a different scenario unfold. They were part of the conflict and yet there was some level of removal. They were clearly working on the historical and personal memories that prevented the cycle from breaking. Some of them were doing deep inner healing work— for example, the Palestinian head of the Buddhist Center in Bethlehem goes regularly with a small meditation group to meditate by the gas ovens of Auschwitz, becoming part of the healing of the trauma experienced by the Jewish people, no longer identifying solely with the Palestinian pain.

These practitioners were much less attached to the historical narrative of the region, their sense of identity had changed. They had become part of a larger, global contemplative community, an identity of equal importance as their birth identity. Priorities shifted. Compassion was more predominant. They understood the meaning of interconnection and knew that the suffering of the other was in some way their own suffering. They could no longer ignore the well being of the other. They were undergoing transformation, a consciousness change.

In the process we came to realize that the way to neutralize the historic karmic patterns that keep a community enmeshed in a cycle of conflict is to work at consciousness change. Political solutions are not enough. Dialogue with official religious leaders is not enough. The thinking must change. A new sense of identity must unfold. This comes from the inner work born of contemplative practice.

We had a similar experience in our work with Iraqis. In March, 2008 we brought a group of 40 young community leaders from Iraq to Dharamsala, India for dialogue. We organized this gathering in partnership with the US Institute of Peace (USIP), and it was our second convening of Iraqis. We had invited a group of Buddhist nuns to hold the contemplative space for the dialogue and had also planned sessions with Tibetan spiritual leaders. We arrived in Dharamsala just as the Tibetans began protesting the holding of the Olympic in China. When the group of Iraqis arrived, after a patience-testing two-day journey from Bagdad, they were met by hundreds of Tibetan monks walking in a silent, candlelight procession. Their pain was evident as was their peaceful inner state. This made a great impression on the Iraqis. They knew nothing about Tibet but in the space of a few days they came to understand the Tibetan view of compassion. This was our first collaboration with the US Institute of Peace, and we were concerned about organizing sessions on meditation, and so we only asked the Buddhist nuns to lead one session on mindfulness. This took place toward the end of the gathering. Early sessions on listening and dialogue skills had been led by USIP trainers. A noticeable shift took place as the group moved from listening and communicating, to learning about extracting themselves from anger and grief and being mindful of the emotions that come and go, without losing their sense of center. We had penetrated the surface so that it was no longer about communicating what they were feeling but about working through the emotions. The surface could only be scratched in one session but it was a beginning. At the end of the dialogue, our colleagues from USIP recommended that in the future we make mindfulness training a more prominent part of the dialogue. They felt that the presence of the Buddhist nuns had contributed a great deal to the transformation the Iraqis experienced.

We had an opportunity to experiment further when in 2009 we brought a group of Afghan community leaders, including some clergy, to Dharamsala. For this gathering we were able to bring contemplative practice to the center of the dialogue, led by strong teachers from the Chan Buddhist, Jesuit and yogic traditions. The Afghans did not hesitate to ask for training is ways to cope with fear. Anger had been predominant among the Iraqis, but for the Afghans it was fear. They lived with it day and night, and some of the younger people said they had known nothing but war and violence for their whole life. A few had learned simple meditation practices from NGOs working in their community and they were eager for more techniques. Even the imams were fully engaged in these sessions. They didn't see any contradiction between the practice of meditation and their religious beliefs. On the last day they had a long session with His Holiness Karmapa Orgyen Trinley Dorje. They had learned much about Tibet from their stay in Dharamsala. They asked the Karmapa why he didn't have anger toward the Chinese as a result of the suffering of his people. He spoke beautifully about the interconnection of all beings, and he said that whatever we seek or hope for ourselves cannot be at the expense of others. We must consider the wellbeing of one billion Chinese people, he explained. More than any words could convey, it was the experience of being in Dharamsala with hundreds of practicing Tibetan monks and nuns that left an impression. Both the Iraqis and Afghans expressed how powerful the experience had been. But it was just a beginning.

What the Iraqis and Afghans realized in Dharamsala was that one could be at peace in the middle of conflict, that peace was an inner state. Some participants in both groups have stayed in touch with us and have requested further mindfulness training. Much remains to be done in this region, and it will be most effective when training in contemplative practices can arise organically from those within the region who themselves have been trained.

Contemplative Practice and Dialogues in Africa

In 2007, GPIW organized a dialogue with 40 young community leaders from throughout Sudan, including a delegation of 7 from the Darfur region. We brought them to Kenya where they could speak more freely. To help create a contemplative space for this dialogue, we invited 7 Buddhist monastics. The Sudanese were initially uncomfortable with their presence, in part because some of the monastics were Taiwanese and the Sudanese mistook them for coming from mainland China. The growing influence and presence of China in their country made them feel as if they could not speak or act freely. So we asked the monastics not to lead any sessions but just to hold the meditative space. They sat at a distance in meditation while the Sudanese, from north and south, east and west, came for the first time to know others from different parts of their country. It was a very emotional experience for them. By the end they were inviting the monastics into the circle, asking questions about meditation and the contemplative life. We have since brought our coordinator from Darfur to a gathering of American contemplative leaders, where he was able to meet Father Thomas Keating as well as contemplative leaders from other faiths, and he is now in the US for our first retreat for young contemplatives. Hopefully he will receive training that he can bring back home.

Contemplative Practice and Climate Change Action

As the work of GPIW has expanded we have moved beyond the organization of dialogues in conflict regions to bringing a contemplative presence to the venues where major global decisions are being made. One example of this was the United Nations Climate Change Conference (COP15) held in Copenhagen, Denmark in December 2009. Realizing the political challenges posed by the conference, we organized a delegation of about 30 contemplative leaders from around the world to come to Copenhagen both to bring a contemplative presence and to express the spiritual dimensions of the climate change issue. Several hours of the first day of this gathering was spent in shared contemplative practice. The following days were spent participating in the UN meetings and speaking to the many NGOs present on the inner shifts needed to adapt to the unfolding climate scenario. The contemplative leaders offered an oasis of peace and stability amid the collapsing political discussions and the frustrations of the NGO community. The group committed to continuing this effort to bring the wisdom and compassion born of deep contemplative practice to help generate a significant response to climate change.

Building a Contemplative Movement

Research shows that contemplative practice has come of age in America. No matter what religious tradition one has been born into, Americans now have access to a range of contemplative practices and an array of teachers. Meditation is no longer viewed as a fringe activity. It has become mainstream. Considering the many challenges facing the nation, it is clear that we must undergo a significant shift in our understanding and priorities if we are to evolve a more balanced, peaceful and sustainable society. Contemplative practice plays a great role in helping to develop the inner resources that can aid this shift. Thus, GPIW has organized two gatherings of contemplative leaders in this country and is planning a third meeting for October, 2010. The purpose is to bring together the disparate groups and individuals who are engaged in serious contemplative practice and are also dedicated not just to personal growth but to bringing benefit to the collective.

In the early stages of contemplative life, one seeks to advance one's own understanding and to improve one's nature—to become a better person, a more peaceful and loving presence. But as the contemplative life deepens, the desire grows to offer the benefit of one's practice to the greater society. So the question arises: how can our collective contemplative practice aid in the awakening of consciousness in our society? How can it become a unifying force, enabling more and more Americans to see the common thread among the religious? How can it bring back the sacred into everyday life so that we once again see the sacredness of the natural world and no longer abuse the forests, waters, air, etc.? How can it help foster a culture of non-greed and help us redefine prosperity so we can re-prioritize and adjust our values to be more in keeping with what the earth can sustain? These are the challenges facing America and the world. We will, with or without contemplative practice, have to address them. What contemplative practice has to offer is access to a stream of wisdom that has flowed continually through the ages, across all traditions, waiting to be tapped by turning within. It also awakens the deep compassion that leads to right action, and it helps to redefine identity, attuning us to the wellbeing of the whole, not just to our individual self and family. This movement from the individual to the greater whole is essential now if we are to avoid future battles over water and other finite resources.

More than any other country, America over the last decade or so has experienced an integration of religious traditions and a joining together of various contemplative practices. In our international work, we have found the world hungry for this integration and expansion of personal spiritual opportunity. It is what we have to offer now. It is a journey many of us in have undergone in our own spiritual search. It is a defining aspect of American spiritual life today and it could be of enormous benefit to those communities still struggling with identity, history and long-held traditions.

The growth of the contemplative movement is one of the most hopeful signs in the world today. This movement, now that it is coming of age, needs to evolve a distinctive voice and a more noticeable presence in American society so that it can help nurture the changes we need to undergo as a nation, so that it can help us restructure our society and our lives to be more in keeping with the spiritual principles that ultimately leads to greater wellbeing and happiness.

Contemplative Practice in a Frantic World

Michele Gossman

I have the nagging feeling that I am not doing what I'm meant to be doing. It often wakes me up at night.

I want to think that there is more to life than this, but I haven't been in situations where I felt comfortable talking about it.

I want to find more balance. I'm tired of trying to please people all of the time. I just want off the treadmill.

I find myself blowing up over things that seem pretty minor later, and then I'm completely ashamed.

Since 1994, the Transformations Spirituality Center (TSC) has been a place where people have been encouraged to come to ask questions and express deep feelings as they look at themselves in relationship to self, others, God and all of creation. A sponsored ministry of the Congregation of St Joseph, a women's Catholic religious order, guests with varied religious and spiritual backgrounds seem to intuit that this is a place where they, their ponderings and their questions are valued.

TSC arose from the charism—the spiritual gift—of the Congregation of St Joseph which is to "live and work that all people may be united with God and with one another." This passion for unity and reconciliation has led us to design and offer programming that encourages people in their spiritual growth. Spiritually grounded people are more inclined to be at peace within themselves and to bring a sense of peace to those around them.

Our goal is to provide support for those who seek a greater awareness of the presence of God. Realizing that the spiritual journey is seldom neat and linear, our work and our joy is reaching people where they are, in hopes that they will become aware of something more. To paraphrase a line from the movie *Junebug*[1], "God loves you just the way you are, but too much to let you stay there!" We interact with those from established faith traditions, those who are distanced from a tradition, as well as those who have never participated in any particular tradition. In this way we are able to exercise "love and service to the dear neighbor without distinction." [2]

Our strategy in providing opportunities to grow in contemplative spiritual practice has been to stretch to meet those we serve. We stretch in providing work that will appeal to people at different places in their life journeys. We stretch in demystifying some of the language that makes these experiences seem too exotic or distant. We stretch to outreach in the community and demonstrate that these practices are available to very ordinary people living in the world and not just to Saints of old tucked away behind monastery walls. We stretch to share practices and wisdom that are very different from what most people experience daily.

This is a challenging task at this time, in this culture. First there is the matter of attention. Barbara Brown Taylor, in a talk entitled "Personal Narrative in the Age of Twitter,"[3] observed that we live in time of "fractured consciousness," when the multiple demands on our attention leave us without reflection, introspection or contemplation. We multitask and find ourselves with scant ability to do anything well.[4] Next there is the issue of money. In these unstable economic times, people are reluctant to devote time and/or money to things not considered necessities. It often takes much suffering for distracted, fearful people to even admit to a holy longing. It takes longer to become aware that addressing the longing is a necessity. This suffering is the cracked seed of transformation, the shoot that pushes through the dark toward the light. Mary Oliver captured this moment of awareness beautifully in her poem *The Journey* which opens with these words, "One day you finally knew what you had to do, and began..."[5]

Who are those who come? We don't collect detailed demographic information on those who come to TSC, but we have noted general trends and verified our experience with some of our sister centers in the Midwestern United States. Approximately 75% of our guests are female. Most, perhaps 85%, have been involved with formal religious practice at some time, but may no longer be active participants. Nearly 50% are not Roman Catholic. A small percentage, perhaps 5%, are not Christian. We don't ask people's educational attainment levels, but interact with them enough to know that they are intelligent and thoughtful people —sometimes—just like most of us!

One noticeable trend in the past three years is that more men are coming. We have intentionally included male presenters who have name recognition in religious circles, and this has helped. Our Advisory Board, which was once overwhelmingly female, is now one third male. The programming that we have offered on contemplative practices, such as Centering Prayer, has inspired more men to come. Men make up about one third of our spiritual direction clients, and this tends to be a group that is very sincere about the spiritual journey.

Another more recent trend is the appeal of programming that is focused on contemplative practice such as Centering Prayer. An insightful, local pastor sent nearly 60 parishioners to learn the "how's and why's" of Centering Prayer and to have some initial experience of this practice. They have formed a core group to continue this prayer communally at the parish. We drew people from a 160 mile radius to be part of a full day of Centering Prayer. Our book study of Cynthia Bourgeault's *Centering Prayer and Inner Awakening* drew well, as did Richard Rohr's *Everything Belongs: The Gift of Contemplative Prayer*. Both spawned book studies at other locations around town.

Trends in society and in the church give us hope that the time is right for contemplation to re-emerge as a key Christian practice. We see much suffering, and recognize this as the deep groaning of a world ready for transformation. Dualism's tendency to separate into "us and them" has ramped up the violence in our world. We can start to heal the violence within ourselves—and then beyond—through contemplation. Our minds are scattered and distracted and we are losing the thread of personal narrative that defines us individually and collectively as part of something larger than ourselves. Contemplative practice helps us set aside the "dangerous master"[6] of the ego-driven "self" so that we may live more fully from the larger "Self" to whom we are called in God. Faith communities that can model the fearless living that made early Christian communities so potently attractive will reconnect with the soul of Christianity and know how to coexist in a world of diversity.

Predicting the shape of the world over the next 10 years is dicey at best. Ten years ago, few could have predicted the timeline or impact from events such as banking deregulation, the creation of the internet, or the decoding of the human genome sequence. We live in a world which changes very rapidly. We realize that the prognosis for our continued survival as a species is not good—our "doomsday clock" now stands at 6 minutes to midnight.[7] We lack time for evolution to repair this. "We can't evolve quickly enough to heed the call before we destroy ourselves. We cannot comprehend the world we have created. We need a way to replace our old minds quickly—a new kind of education—an evolution of consciousness–and become literate in completely new disciplines. One of these disciplines is contemplative interiority."[8]

The challenge and the greatest opportunity will be to truly "go viral"—to reach the tipping point defined as "that moment in an epidemic when a virus reaches critical mass".[9] When enough people are seasoned in contemplative practice so that they can embody lives of balance between interiority and everyday life, others will notice. When people reclaim a sense of the sacred and live with a sense of meaning, wisdom and new vision, others will

notice. When people respond from a place of centeredness rather than re-
act—regardless of the circumstances—others will notice. At some point,
when enough people practice, and enough people notice, and enough hearts
are transformed this will no longer be considered something esoteric and
beyond reach. It will be normative.

So, where do we begin? Sr. Constance Fitzgerald asks...

- What if there were schools of contemplation or interiority all
  over the country?
- What it we taught the art of reflection and listening, the art
  of prayer, the art of accessing our authentic selves?
- What if we answered the cry of God for union?[10]

Some other questions to live with might be...

- What if religious leaders began to see the transformative power of these practices and encourage parishioners /
  congregants in this effort?
- What impact would result in business and industry?
- What if these practices bore fruit in reduced violence in a
  quantifiable demonstration projects?
- What if more people participated in spiritual direction with
  trained, compassionate listeners?

These would seem good places to start in nurturing growth and development of a contemplative movement in America. The conditions seem right.
The baby boomers are entering the age when people have traditionally been
most devoted to the spiritual search. Religious traditions that have held these
practices in safe-keeping exist and are longing to share. The pain of the world
will force drastic change. We tire of the endless cycle of violence and yearn for
more wholesome ways of being. We know the truth in Einstein's statement,
"We cannot solve our problems with the same thinking we used when we
created them."[11]

We accept the paradox that we don't have to "do" anything except "be"
open to God's healing presence. We don't so much actively seek God, as allow ourselves to "be still and know"[12] God. We reach a point of resting in
God, by quieting our own restless egos.

In the words of poet David White in "Enough:"[13]

Enough. These few words are enough.
If not these words, this breath.
If not this breath, this sitting here.

This opening to the life
we have refused
again and again
until now.

Until now
　　　　　— David Whyte

It is simple, but it isn't easy. The point at which we consent to grace is where the real work of being real becomes embodied.

Notes

1　*Junebug*. Dir. Phil Morrison. Sony Pictures, 2005.

2　Fr Jean-Pierre Medaille, SJ, Maxims of the Little Institute, Founding Documents of the Sisters of St Joseph.

3　Taylor, Barbara Brown. "The Role of Narrative in the Age of Twitter" 27th Annual United Church of Christ Synod, Grand Rapids, MI; 27 Jun. 2009.

4　Kuchinskas, Susan. "Why Multitasking Isn't Efficient" *WebMD the Magazine* 12 Aug 2008. http://www.webmd.com/mental-health/features/why-multitasking-isnt-efficient.

5　Oliver, Mary. "The Journey" *New and Selected Poems: Volume 1*. Boston: Beacon Press, 2004, p. 114.

6　Bourgeault, Cynthia. *Centering Prayer and Inner Awakening*. Lanham, MD: Cowley Publications, 2004, p. 82.

7   "It is 6 minutes to midnight" *Bulletin of the Atomic Scientists.*
     14 Jan. 2010. http://thebulletin.org/content/media-center/
     announcements/2010/01/14/it-6-minutes-to-midnight.

8   Fitzgerald OCD, Constance. "The Desire for God and the Trans-
     formative Power of Contemplation" *Light Burdens, Heavy Blessings:
     Challenges of Church and Culture in the Post Vatican II Era: Essays
     in Honor of Margaret R. Brennan.* Ed. Mary Ellen Sheehan, Mary
     Heather MacKinnon, and Moni McIntyre. Quincy, IL: Franciscan
     Press, 2000.

9   Gladwell, Malcom. *The Tipping Point: How Little Things Can Make
     a Big Difference.* Boston: Little Brown and Company, 2000.

10   Fitzgerald OCD, Constance. "The Desire for God and the Trans-
     formative Power of Contemplation" *Light Burdens, Heavy Blessings:
     Challenges of Church and Culture in the Post Vatican II Era: Essays
     in Honor of Margaret R. Brennan.* Ed. Mary Ellen Sheehan, Mary
     Heather MacKinnon, and Moni McIntyre. Quincy, IL: Franciscan
     Press, 2000.

11   "Albert Einstein." *BrainyQuote.com.* Xplore Inc, 2010. 9 May 2010.
     http://www.brainyquote.com/quotes/quotes/a/alberteins121993.
     html.

12   Psalms 46:10, New International Version Bible.

13   Whyte, David. "Enough" *River Flow New & Selected Poems 1984-
     2007.* Langley, WA: Many Rivers Press, 2007.

Naming, Connecting, Nourishing, Illuminating: How the Shambhala Sun Foundation is serving the Contemplative Movement

Barry Boyce

"It's not what you say about yourself. It's how you work in the kitchen." I learned this principle from the Tibetan meditation master Chögyam Trungpa, Rinpoche, on one of the first meditation retreats I attended in the early 1970's, and it expresses an understanding of the contemplative I carry with me to this day. He was saying that when we meditate we often have a lot to say about our experience, but the way to tell whether something is taking root is to watch how we work in the kitchen. In the early years of learning meditation—and also learning how to teach and tell others about meditation—my fellow students and I came to know meditation not as something that made one into a greater, bigger, and better being, but as something that resided, as Trungpa Rinpoche liked to say, in "kitchen sink reality."[1] Meditation is not a verb; it's a noun. It's not something you do; it's something you are. It expresses a way of being.[2]

That way of being is *nonconceptual*. It is not fixated on an idea, which requires a definition, which itself requires a further definition, and so on in an unending discursive chain. It is *unconditional*. It is not the result of something else. Like our "original face before we were born," as Zen would have it, it "just is." It is a way of *knowing*. But it is, as Tobin Hart, author of *The Spiritual Life of Children*, said, "a third way of knowing beyond the rational and the sensory."[3]

Whether we find the contemplative in centering prayer, in the zone we enter on a swift downhill ski run, in resting our mind on a sacred image, in mindfulness meditation, or while making art or doing carpentry, the experience—or non-experience, if you like—is the same: there is a moment outside of time, a suspension of any attempt to make permanent and solid what is dynamic and everchanging. For a moment there is a gap. Presto. We are mindful. As educator and activist Parker Palmer wrote, "Contemplation happens any time that we catch the magician deceiving us and we get a glimpse of the truth behind the trick."[4] A glimpse is all we need, because we can glimpse it again, and again, and again, without ever having to hold on to it as a personal possession.

It can take a lot of words to try to describe the moment of non-thought, and yet no words will ever pin it down. It's not a *word* thing. But one of the main areas I want to address is precisely that: talking about and reporting on people and organizations who are engaging this world beyond words and helping people to learn how they can live mindfully. I suppose that's what a contemplative journalist does: uses words to talk about what is beyond words.

What does "contemplative" mean?

Finding a word to define this area of endeavor is itself a great challenge. *Contemplative*—the most widely chosen term of art—is slippery. Its etymology is encouraging for our purposes, containing within it the Latin *templum*, which derives from the idea of "a place reserved or cut out."[5] That works nicely with the idea of meditation as a "cutting of discursive thought." It also contains the idea of sacred space. We get further encouragement if we go to the Oxford English Dictionary, where we find that the first recorded usage of the verb *contemplate* is from Francis Bacon, in 1605, who wrote about the seventh day of creation, when God took rest to "contemplate his works." Surely, when God contemplates, it is beyond discursive thought.

However, when we turn to contemporary usage, as evidenced for example by the entry below from the Visual Thesaurus,[6] we see that the glosses for contemplative—even those branching off from meditate—have a lot to do with thinking, brooding, mulling, ruminating, and the like. These words do not suggest glimpsing, nor Tobin Hart's third way of knowing. That said,

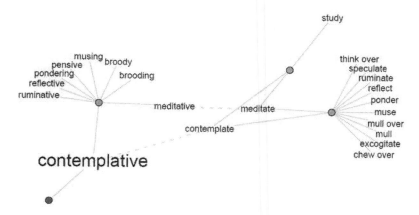

there is an element here of sustained attention, which gets very close to what is usually meant by mindfulness.[7]

And if we consider the red dot in the diagram, which is code to indicate the noun form of "contemplative"—meaning not one who contemplates but rather one who undertakes the spiritual life—we have a clue as to why we speak today of endeavors such as contemplative education, contemplative architecture, and contemplative photography. St. Augustine, writing in the *City of God* in the early fifth century CE, made the distinction between the *contemplative* life of the religious ascetic and the *active* life of the man in the street, following earlier philosophers such as Seneca and Aristotle. That way of thinking, common in both East and West, places a rather bright line between the life of the mind and spirit in repose and the life of the body acting out in the world.

Today, it would seem, in so many areas of life, we are trying to bring those two together. It's not a new idea, mind you. Bacon spoke of bringing together the contemplative and the active back in the seventeenth century. The mandarins of Confucian China were expected to be both scholars (contemplating deep meaning in their study and beauty in their garden) and people of action (serving as ministers of government). The newness of the idea is not what is significant, though. What so motivates so many of us today is the apparent consequences of splitting our life out in the world from the meditative, reflective life. Our life in the world has brought us stressed-out bodies, stressed-out families, stressed-out institutions, and a stressed-out planet. It is time we bring the contemplative into the street. It's time to make mindfulness manifest vividly in everyday life.

As I mentioned above, the aspect of this movement that I would like to talk about is reporting on the movement itself; what the organization I represent, the Shambhala Sun Foundation, has been doing in that regard; how we think about it; what our plans are for the future; and where we see this movement going. In order to do that, I want to first give some background on the Shambhala Sun Foundation and how it finds itself reporting on the mindfulness and contemplative disciplines movement.

From a Community Newspaper to a Newsstand Magazine

The *Shambhala Sun* magazine began life in 1978 as the community newspaper for Vajradhatu, a group of meditation centers established by Chögyam Trungpa, Rinpoche, who fled Tibet in 1959 in the wake of the Chinese invasion and came to America in 1969. He envisioned the *Vajradhatu Sun* as a paper that would not only cover the events of the spreading Vajradhatu community but also of the Buddhist world at large, as the teachings and practices began to be introduced more widely in the Western world. The starting of the newspaper also coincided with the beginning of an effort to teach meditation in a more secular context, which was becoming a goal for members of other Buddhist communities as well. Within Vajradhatu, the effort was inspired by the Asian legend of the kingdom of Shambhala, whose subjects lived a meditative, but not monastic, way of life. In 1992, following this inspiration, the *Vajradhatu Sun* became the *Shambhala Sun*, which soon became a bi-monthly glossy magazine directed toward anyone interested in a meditative way of life. It was now under the editorship of Melvin McLeod, a professional journalist who had been a television reporter for the Canadian Broadcasting Corporation.

The *Shambhala Sun* rode the crest of a wave of interest in dharma that followed the Dalai Lama's receiving the Nobel Peace Prize in 1989 and saw three major motion pictures and a *Time* magazine cover devoted to the topic. The Shambhala Sun proved to be increasingly popular on the newsstand, which allowed us to keep improving its quality. Over the course of our first decade or so, as our readership and range of offerings expanded, the transition from reaching an audience of Buddhists to reaching an audience inspired by Buddhism was complete. For some time, we had also begun to pay attention to a cluster of phenomena that signaled that a shift might be taking place in the perception of meditation and contemplative disciplines in the public mind: patients were learning meditation in hospitals and being advised to meditate by their doctors; researchers were studying meditators to seek neuroscientific proof of the benefits of contemplative living; the pioneer Daniel Goleman was popularizing new ways of looking at intelligence and changing how we think about the dimensions of the mind in the West—to name just a few. Another turning point awaited the *Shambhala Sun* and the scope of our coverage and our connections.

The opportunity presented itself in 2005 when Jon Kabat-Zinn, the founder of Mindfulness-Based Stress Reduction, accepted Melvin McLeod's request to be profiled for a cover story on the occasion of the release of his new book *Coming to Our Senses*. I interviewed Jon in his home and wandered about the nearby fields in Lexington, Massachusetts, spending about half a day with him in splendid conversation. The resulting piece would prove to be a watershed for us. It was very well received, but more than that, it led to Jon visiting with key people at the Sun's offices. The visit sparked a friendship with Jon and a number of his colleagues that continues to grow. What Jon and others were accomplishing confirmed for us that this movement went far beyond mere popularizing: the practices were genuine, they were based on a profound understanding of the implications of paying attention quietly in a sustained way to the workings of your own mind, and they were reaching people where they lived. It was time for us to begin to serve all the people who were interested in the benefits of secular mindfulness and to report more widely on how mindfulness and other contemplative practices were insinuating themselves into more and more areas of life. This new thing from the outskirts was appearing in the public square in more and more places.

This led us to the next stage in our evolution: the launching of a new mindfulness and contemplative practice initiative directed by publisher Jim Gimian, editor-in-chief Melvin McLeod, and me. We created a new department in the magazine, directed by me, called the Mindful Society. My mandate was to meet and learn from as many people as possible who were bringing contemplative disciplines into the wider society.

The hallmark of this emerging area is that the practices and disciplines are presented as secular methodologies that reflect basic human capabilities of mind, with practical benefits emphasized, and objective evidence presented of their efficacy rather than simply authority or self-report. The methodologies do not depend on ideology or allegiance. We had been reporting on meditation and offering profound and helpful dharma teachings from many traditions since 1978, so we found ourselves in a unique position to take part in the big conversation about how meditation and its offshoots would be viewed now in America—and who one could learn it from and where and how. By launching the Mindful Society initiative we would find out firsthand whether the shifts we detected represented a passing event or a trend of long-term significance—and our readership would accompany us on the journey.

Around the same time, in 2007, the magazine's ownership shifted to the independent and newly created non-profit, the Shambhala Sun Foundation. This move allowed us to be free of affiliation with any particular tradition of Buddhism, so that we could report on, share the teachings of, and support the aspirations of all Buddhist traditions. In addition, as a secular non-profit, we could advance the cause of dharma, meditation, and contemplative life as an independent force for good and a partner with many kinds of organizations.

The Mindful Society

When we launched the Mindful Society initiative, before too long publisher Jim Gimian found himself at dinner with the psychologist Paul Ekman, neurosurgeon James Doty, and neuroscience researcher Philippe Goldin, among others, and at lunch with Chade-Meng Tan of Google—connections that had been made for him by Mirabai Bush, a long-time leader in the contemplative movement, former director of the Center for Contemplative Mind in Society, and now a "fellow"—an epithet she loves, I might add. In the wake of Jim's meetings, I found myself doing a story on how mindfulness and emotional intelligence was being taught at the most famous corporation in the digital world. My research for the Google story led me to talk to Mirabai at length, and we haven't stopped talking to each other since. (She's also inspired me to become a mindful e-mailer, by the way, and the results are astounding.)

With the connections we were making through the Center for Mindfulness in Health Care, Medicine, and Society, the Center for Contemplative Mind in Society, the Garrison Institute, the Mind and Life Institute, and others, the floodgates were opening. I had more stories than I knew what to do with. Traditionally, journalists are supposed to maintain a crusty cynicism that prevents the wool from being pulled over your eyes by the demagogues, charlatans, and snake oil salesmen who are trying to drag the world down. And, I'm not without that. But the people I report on in my world make me cry. And I mean that in a good way.

Broadly speaking, there is objective journalism of the kind that we all rely on from the mainstream media—the fourth estate—and mission-driven journalism, which is the kind we do. Our role is to report on and advocate for the beneficial work people like you are doing. We strive to do this while adhering to high journalistic standards for accuracy, fairness, and taste. But we are not on the outside looking in. Because we know this world from the inside out, we can help the movement communicate to itself, serving as a connector and cross-pollinator within the movement. And we can provide ways for the movement to speak to the wider world of interested people, in a way that does not compromise the integrity of the contemplative practices themselves.

If we started the Mindful Society initiative as a proof of concept, then the number of people I have met in the last year alone who are bringing mindfulness and contemplative practices to the broader society has amply demonstrated the profound implications of this movement. The proof of the pudding has been in the tasting, and the results are very, very good. Let me share with you a sampling of the people and projects I've encountered to give an idea of the picture of society starting to emerge from my work.

Elana Rosenbaum, one of the first teachers—along with Jon Kabat-Zinn and Larry Rosenberg—at the Stress Reduction Clinic at UMass, twice survived cancer and now teaches patients and health-care practitioners how to face illness with courage and equanimity. This is mindfulness in the face of death, which is also the specialty of Frank Ostaseski, founder of Zen Hospice and the Metta Institute, which is working to bring contemplative discipline and participatory medicine to mainstream health care practitioners throughout America. I learned that mindfulness begins at birth from Nancy Bardacke, a midwife with decades of experience who created Mindfulness based Childbirth and Parenting in 1998. With MBCP, Nancy says, three generations can be affected by mindfulness being brought to bear on what can be one of the most stressful—and most joyful—periods of the adult life cycle.

One of the most moving days of my last year was the day I went into the Alameda County Juvenile Hall near Oakland with instructors Jon Oda and Amani Carey-Simms of the Mind Body Awareness project, along with their executive director, Chris McKenna. They amazed me with the skill they showed in communicating about meditation with 14-year-old gang members, some of whom were already fathers. Later, at the Center for Mindfulness annual scientific conference, I met Angela Marie West, a young woman who is working on the research that hopes to prove the efficacy of MBA's methods. Angela works as a psychologist in a prison in central California.

Through Angela, I met Gina Biegel. Gina had a difficult life growing up and started living on her own when she was 14. Now, in her mid-thirties, she is a therapist in the Child and Adolescent Psychiatry Department and author of the Stress Reduction Workbook for Teens, and is under contract for two more books on mindfulness for adolescents and teenagers.

Through the Center for Contemplative Mind in Society, I met Doug Chermak, who under Charlie Halpern's direction is spearheading the Contemplative Law Program. The very same week, I met Judge Michelle Lowrance, who uses mindfulness to diffuse the tension in her family court in downtown Chicago by "being a judge who's not judgmental." A lawyer who attended one of the law program's annual retreats, Robert Chender, told me about how he teaches mindfulness to lawyers through the City Bar of New York, which gives continuing legal education credits for the course. Ten percent of the L1 class at the University of Miami Law School completed Scott Rogers' course in contemplative practice for lawyers last year. Rogers' program turns legal language on its head and uses it to express contemplative principles.

I've had long talks with many people in universities doing work spearheaded by the Center for Contemplative Mind in Society. The leading light in that campaign is Arthur Zajonc, who told me in an interview, "Knowledge, from the point of view of any contemplative tradition, is not primarily object-oriented. It is epiphany- or insight-oriented. It's not good enough to know *about* reality; you need to change how you see reality. Real education is transformation."[8]

Because the university is a mirror of society as a whole—all the disciplines for creating and managing our world reside there—it can be a very powerful seedbed for bringing contemplative approaches to society at large. Historically, the universities were also places that were themselves dedicated to the contemplative life. I had a long and fruitful phone conversation with Hal Roth, whose Contemplative Studies Initiative at Brown University "brings together traditional academic third-person inquiry and the first-person inquiry of the great contemplative traditions." His students take part in meditation labs that emphasize the "scientific and exploratory nature of contemplative practice."

I went to the weekly sitting at Brooklyn College of the City University of New York Contemplative Network with Geri DeLuca and David Forbes. David, who teaches social work, is the author of Boyz 2 Buddhas, a chronicle of teaching contemplative disciplines to high school football players. He put me on to Stan Koehler, who teaches meditation and martial arts to youth in Spanish Harlem through his organization Peace in the Street.

From Norman Fisher—dubbed the Abbot of Google for his work teaching meditation in Silicon Valley—I learned about Teah Strozer, who teaches meditation and ethics as the chaplain of the Bay School, a high school in the Presidio in San Francisco. I found out that Teah also has meditation students in Brooklyn. One of them, Adam Bernstein, a music educator, invited me to come by and sit with his Jazz Mindfulness students and hear them play. The sounds these teenagers made blew me away. They had achieved what meditation teacher Joan Sutherland calls "improvi-satori." I made sure to connect him up with Ed Sarath, who created the Bachelor of Fine Arts in Jazz and Contemplative Studies at the University of Michigan.

Madeline Bruser, a pianist and piano teacher, developed a wonderful four-part method for helping performers use contemplation to overcome stage fright. Her husband, Parlan McGaw, collaborates with traditional acting teachers to help their students use mindfulness to clear away the mental clutter that gets in the way of a genuine performance. Based on reading what I'd written about Scott Roger's adaptation of legal language to mindfulness instruction, Parlan has decided to do the same thing for the language of acting. To conclude our interview, he regaled me with something he'd worked on in a contemplative acting class: a stirring version of the opening speech from *Henry V.* "O for a muse of fire…"

I cannot hope to list all the people doing great work in contemplative education, but a few cannot go unmentioned. There's Linda Lantieri, America's most inspiring education activist. A Fulbright Scholar, Linda has been an educator in New York City for forty years. After 9/11, Linda established a program in twelve schools in and around Ground Zero, to help strengthen the inner resilience of students, teachers, and families dealing with the trauma. She is spearheading an effort to build on the successes of the Social and Emotional Learning movement and add a dimension of deep inner resiliency, or "spirit," as she likes to say. Currently she serves as the Founding Director of The Inner Resilience Program (IRP) whose mission is to cultivate the inner lives of students, teachers and schools by integrating social and emotional learning with contemplative practice. Linda prefers to think and talk in terms of "nurturing young people's inner lives, which includes activities that we might call 'contemplative' and 'mindful,' but it can include a lot more." One of the challenges of this developing field, she says, "is building common ground and finding a common lexicon for discussing students' and teachers' ultimate questions about meaning and purpose, the spiritual dimension of learning, and the connectedness we have that goes beyond our own mind and emotions." This work includes, she says, "what we might call 'contemplative' techniques for quieting the mind, but also the arts, storytelling, and spending time in nature, and I've certainly noticed that it is not at all difficult to get children excited about this kind of work."

Tish Jennings, who is here at the conference, is breaking new educational ground. Tish is the director of the Garrison Institute's Initiative on Contemplation and Education and a research associate in the Prevention Research Center at Pennsylvania State University. Tish can speak for herself, but I want to celebrate the great work of Garrison's professional development program for teachers, Cultivating Awareness and Resiliency in Education (CARE), which combines exercises for recognizing emotional patterns—one's own and others'—with contemplative practices such as mindfulness meditation. Last year, the program received a grant of over $900,000 from the US Department of Education's Institute for Education Sciences (IES) for further development and evaluation of the CARE program in two rural schools in Central Pennsylvania, including measuring the effects of the CARE program on students.

At a Mind and Life Institute event in Atlanta with His Holiness the Dalai Lama, I first encountered Thubten Jinpa. In addition to being His Holiness' principal translator, Jinpa is an esteemed scholar who is one of the driving forces of Stanford University's Center for Compassion and Altruism Research and Education (CCARE). Jinpa developed an eight-week course for cultivating loving-kindness and compassion that is being piloted at Google and several other locations. It includes exercises for what Jinpa calls "moistening the heart." CCARE and Mind and Life are both committed to demonstrating through neuroscience and other branches of science the efficacy of contemplative practices and the important place of the inner life. Amazingly, studying the effects of contemplative practice has become a hot new discipline.

There are also dangers that most of us are all well aware of and continue to be on the lookout for. As many contemplative teachers have pointed out to me, there are ethical implications to the mindful life—being more attentive in the pursuit of harmful aims is not the way of the contemplative. Mindfulness can't just be about producing attention-focusing superstars. And some will always try to find easy ways and low roads. How many books just paste *mindful* in the title as little more than a marketing ploy, creating the risk that the term will become so generic as to lose all meaning. Some people are taking MBSR courses so they can turn right around and declare themselves teachers, whether they have any bona fides or not. An ad in my local alternative paper offers a 150-hour personnel and professional development program that entitles you to call yourself a life coach. It is led by a person who advertises herself as a "Neuroscientist, Life Coach, and Yoga Teacher." The complete package.

In spite of the dangers, the overall picture is very promising, and organizations are responding to the challenges. Finding reliable, well-trained teachers is the watchword of the day. The first generation of teachers has come from Buddhist training programs. Where will the next generations come from? The Center for Mindfulness has a well-respected institute for mindfulness-based professional education and innovation already, and we have heard of plans to develop rigorous certification programs for mindfulness teachers at UCLA's Mindful Awareness Research Center, Stanford's CCARE, and the California Institute of Integral Studies Center. I'm sure there are more.

Frontiers

When I attended my first meditation retreat in my bright orange cotton pants from India, I never would have dreamed that mindfulness would be turning up in grade school and law schools, not to mention hospitals and laboratories. Yet now I've started to think of these as the obvious places. As I've ventured further, I've begun to find glimpses of the contemplative in some not so obvious places.

At Jim Saveland's session at the Center for Mindfulness' annual meeting, he didn't have a fancy powerpoint presentation. He had only one slide, which showed smoke jumpers rappelling from a helicopter into the heart of a raging forest fire. Jim is the program manager for Human Factors and Risk Management at the Rocky Mountain Research Station of the US Forest Service in Fort Collins, Colorado. His crews also wear bright orange clothing, but it's more Kevlar than cotton. He teaches "mindfulness-based situational awareness" and he uses Jon Kabat-Zinn's definition of mindfulness as "paying attention, on purpose, in the present moment, as if your life depended on it, nonjudgmentally." And in the case of the smoke jumpers, their life does depend on it. One member of a crew recently fell to his death from a helicopter when a safety check missed a faulty fastener. Jim taught us a type of meditation he uses in his program that I had never done before. With your eyes open, you place all of your attention on the periphery, and when your mind tries to come to a central focus, you go back out to the periphery. It is not intended as a condition to aspire to, but it is rather a practice that confounds our tendency to tunnel vision when we are faced with threat.

Elizabeth Stanley represents the ninth generation of her family to serve the United States as a member of the Army. In the late nineties, Liz left service at the rank of Captain following a tour of duty as part of the UN Peacekeeping Mission in the Balkans. Following her military service, she earned an MBA from MIT's Sloan School of Management and a PhD in government from Harvard, and is now assistant professor of security studies in Georgetown's school of foreign service.

She began practicing yoga, and after a while a friend in her yoga class suggested they attend a nine-day retreat at IMS taught by Sharon Salzberg. For the first few days, Stanley found the experience of sitting meditation almost unbearably difficult, despite having experienced the rigors of combat. Things began to turn around, though, when she gave herself permission to leave if she felt it was just too difficult to continue. She stayed, and the rest of the retreat became her initiation into mindfulness, a path that has become a central feature of her life. She has returned to IMS for a number of intensive retreats, including several three-month retreats, and also took temporary ordination and trained in Burma for six months. When she put on her robes, she said, the people began to regard her just in the same way they had when she received her commission as an officer. The uniform brought instant respect and expectations. She regards the military, at its best, as a form of selfless service, just as the way of the monk is a form of selfless service.

She completed teacher training in Mindfulness-Based Stress Reduction and co-taught with Jon Kabat-Zinn in 2009. She then designed a program that would adapt MBSR for use with soldiers and others in high-stress environments: Mindfulness-Based Mind Fitness Training (MMFT). For MMFT to gain acceptance, Stanley felt, it must be validated through scientific research in the same way as MBSR. Stanley teamed up with Dr. Amishi Jha, a neuroscientist at the University of Pennsylvania to begin to conduct studies on MMFT. In 2008, the research team conducted a pilot study of MMFT to test its cognitive, psychological and behavioral effects among US Marines before their deployment to Iraq. In 2009, Stanley founded the Mind Fitness Training Institute. In 2010, in collaboration with Jha's lab, the institute began a large, federally funded, multi-year, randomized control study for the US Army, to evaluate different versions of MMFT taught to soldiers before deployment.

Stanley invited Jim Gimian and me to give a talk at Georgetown on the books we've written on Sun Tzu's Art of War as a contemplative strategic discipline. In the front row sat Tim Ryan, fourth-term democratic congressman from the Youngstown-Akron area of Ohio. When he took in office in 1993, at age 29, he was the youngest representative in Congress. Ryan is a member of the 30 Something Working Group, which includes House democrats who have not yet reached the age of 40. It was organized by the House Speaker Nancy Pelosi to engage younger people in politics by focusing on issues important to them. Among the "issues" that Ryan thinks are important for young people is mindfulness and health. A few years ago, he became a yoga practitioner. Long interested in meditation, he also attended a retreat for leaders led by Jon Kabat-Zinn. Since that time, he has become a zealous advocate for contemplative practices being supported in government-funded programs in health and social services. Several schools in Tim's district are now receiving funding to implement Linda Lantieri's Inner Resiliency Program.

As the featured speaker at a gala event celebrating the Center for Mindfulness' entering its fourth decade of work, Ryan emphasized the cost-saving that could come from mindfulness-based interventions in health care. He also asked for the attendees' support in helping put mindfulness on the health care agenda in Washington. "Contact your representative or senator," he said, "and let them know about the work you are doing and who it is helping. Let me know what you are doing. I need your help."

When I asked Tim if he ever got any blowback for being a publicly declared meditator, he said, "What can I say? I exhaled and I paid attention to it. Shoot me."

Mindful Living

Shambhala Sun publisher Jim Gimian helped us to understand that whatever we would end up doing in this area would be a co-creation of the experienced journalists, designers, and publishing professionals in our house *together with* a growing network of people bringing mindfulness and contemplative practice to whatever area of life you can think of. He was inspired by the insights coming out of chaos and complexity theory and the understanding of emergence, which tells you, in the nicest way, that it is not all about *you*. If you want to make something happen, as our good friend the Zen teacher John Tarrant says, "You just need to show up." When the ingredients come together, the right mix just seems to emerge.

Earlier I talked about our initiative to "report" on the mindful society, but that verb is a little too limiting for how we see our work in this world. It's a little more like a four-stage process that Margaret Wheatley talks about in *Finding Our Way: Leadership for an Uncertain Time*:

- You *name* something important.
- You *connect* people together who have a shared interest in bringing about change.
- You *nourish* those who are doing the work.
- And you *illuminate* it, so others can see how valuable it is and be drawn to it.[9]

Having become convinced that something really was changing with respect to the role of the contemplative, reflective, and mindful in American life, we considered what the next step in the evolution of this initiative ought to be. We'd been telling our readers what leaders in the mindfulness and contemplative practice movement were doing, but it was clear now that what our readers—and many would-be readers—needed was to hear about how to bring mindfulness and contemplation into their daily lives: in the kitchen, the office, the garden, the school, the gym—wherever life is lived.

We decided to do a special issue devoted to Mindful Living in March of this year, which to our delight became our largest-selling issue ever. It is still being passed around, months later, and many of its pieces have a second life on the internet. In that issue, we also announced that the Shambhala Sun Foundation would expand on our commitment to support the work of mindfulness teachers, researchers, and practitioners. I'd like to share with you some of the statement of commitment that we made at that time and then close by sharing a little of what our plans are for the coming year and what we see in the future.

The Shambhala Sun Foundation will happily serve as a cross-pollinator and incubator of contemplative ideas and methods. We want to support the great work done by this movement's pioneers and help develop the means for mindfulness to become an everyday thing. Mindfulness is what the Buddha practiced, but it is not the property of any one tradition. We're taking a big-tent attitude. Inviting in all those with a good heart and an intention to discover a way of living less caught up with self and more about just being—finding relaxation and awareness to be our natural state.

The big tent we're erecting in mainstream America includes both mindful living and what we've been calling "mindful society"—two aspects of the same fundamental quality. In promoting mindful living, we report on its personal aspect: how to practice mindfulness, how to approach life mindfully, and how to plumb greater depths of the practice. In promoting mindful society, we report on its community aspect: who is doing what in health, law, business, defense, activism, athletics, the arts, and so on. Authentic mindfulness is never stingy and self-confirming; it seeks to rediscover itself in the works of others. As a result, concern for the greater community also means having under our tent disciplines that exhibit mindfulness but don't necessarily carry the label, including, for example, social and emotional learning, the slow food movement, contemplative arts and education, alternative dispute resolution, innovative models of strategic thinking, and many others.

There are several key elements to genuine mindfulness. The foundation of all mindfulness is instruction in the nonconceptual practice of just being here. Out of that develops approaches for working with obstacles (such as wandering thoughts and laziness) and negativity (such as frightening or aggressive states of mind). But mindfulness is not only about what to reject; it's about what to embrace and how to let awareness unfold choicelessly, so there's lots for seasoned practitioners to say about how daily living can become a path, a feedback system, and something to savor and celebrate.

Finally, as mindfulness flowers into a rich blend of mindfulness–awareness that ties the whole room together, we recognize interdependence: our connectedness to others and to all the world's processes. The way the world works is the way we work. *We* are not mindful. Mindfulness just is, timelessly, and there is no emerging decade of mindfulness to make a big deal about. And yet there is.[10]

We are a non-profit, mission-driven organization, and the Mindful Society and Mindful Living are the next phase in the evolution of our mission. We will continue to serve those we have served in our existing publications for over three decades, while expanding to reach out to more people who are waiting to experience the benefits of bringing a larger contemplative element to their lives. We will serve this movement through a variety of media, including magazines, websites, books, digital publications and conferences.

In the fall, we will offer a free 32-page publication, *Your Guide to Mindful Living*, which will feature short, practical pieces from leading writers with experience and expertise in the mindfulness field. At the same time, we will launch a Mindful Living website that will be free-standing and separate from our existing sites. Next year, we will expand our coverage of the Mindful Society in the Shambhala Sun. In the spring of 2011, *The Mindfulness Revolution*, an anthology edited by us, will be published by Shambhala Publications in Boston.

Having participated and partnered with so many other great people and organizations (most of them represented at this conference) in the work of naming, connecting, nourishing, and illuminating the mindfulness and contemplative discipline movement, we look forward to the next glimpse of the truth coming our way. One project we're dipping our toe into may give us some clues of the shape of things to come. We're collaborating with the Garrison Institute to revive a project they started to map the contemplative and mindfulness worlds. As we take the first tentative steps in building this map, we are seeing a very big world of interconnections, which if exploited well can enhance and multiply the power of the work that each of us is doing. The extent to which we can all learn to cultivate those interconnections—and form new alliances, friendships, playmates, and partnerships—may well dictate just how much influence mindfulness and contemplative discipline can have on the world of our children, grandchildren, our great-grandchildren, and beyond.

Notes

1 Chögyam Trungpa, "Glimpses of Abhidharma," *The Collected Works of Chögyam Trungpa*, Vol. 2, Carolyn Gimian, ed.: p. 250.

2 Chögyam Trungpa, "The Path is the Goal: a Basic Handbook of Buddhist Meditation," Sherab Chödzin Kohn, ed. *The Collected Works of Chögyam Trungpa*, Vol. 2, Carolyn Gimian, ed.: p. 11.

3   Tobin Hart, "Opening the Contemplative Mind in the Classroom," *Journal of Transformative Education* Vol. 2 No. 1, January 2004: p. 28.

4   Parker J. Palmer, *The Active Life: A Spirituality of Work, Creativity, and Caring* (New York: Wiley, 1990): p. 17.

5   *The American Heritage Dictionary of the English Language* (Boston: Houghton Mifflin, 2000.): p. 2,050.

6   www.visualthesaurus.com.

7   Notably, the respected Harvard psychologist Ellen Langer, published a best-selling book in 1989 called *Mindfulness*, which presented a meaning of that term that did not involve meditation practice of any kind. Langer says that "many qualities of the Eastern concepts of mindfulness and of the one being described in this book are strikingly similar," but there are clear differences. To oversimplify, Langer's focus is on mindfulness as the opposite of mindlessness—a human performance measure—while mindfulness as used in contemplative contexts is a means to deeper awareness and self- (or non-self-) knowledge. On a side note, a Langer experiment from the mid-1970's, chronicled in her 2009 book *Counterclockwise*, showed very positive results from having nursing home residents exercise more choice in their day-to-day living, allowing them to be, in Langer's terms, more mindful (not on auto-pilot following the staff's routines). In an upcoming movie based on the book, Langer will be played by Jennifer Aniston. This definition of mindfulness may get even more play in the public mind.

8   Barry Boyce, "Please Help Me Learn Who I Am," *Shambhala Sun*, January 2007: p. 73.

9   Margaret Wheatley, *Finding Our Way: Leadership for an Uncertain Time* (San Francisco: Berrett-Koehler, 2005): pp. 174–175.

10 Barry Boyce, "Editorial: Why We Are Taking Mindfulness to Heart," *Shambhala Sun*, March 2010: p. 11.

Contemplative Practice In America: Retreat Center Trends

Michael Craft

Introduction / Background

This is a brief overview of the state of the field of contemplative practice in the context of "broad-spectrum" (public, multidisciplinary, nondenominational) retreat centers in America, especially the not-for-profit Omega Institute in Rhinebeck, New York. Omega itself was founded in the late 1970s by Stephan Rechtschaffen, M.D., and Elizabeth Lesser, both students of the late Sufi spiritual teacher, Pir Vilayat Inayat Khan. (The name, "Omega," was suggested by Pir Vilayat in reference to the "Omega Point" of the Jesuit scientist and philosopher Pierre Teilhard de Chardin,[1] posited as a transcendent experience of shared unity and interdependent, higher order complexity that is the goal of the evolutionary process.) Omega has grown over the years since its founding and is now one of the largest, and (like Esalen Institute in California) longest-running, centers of its kind.

Regarding "Contemplative Practice"

As the term is currently employed at most nondenominational retreat centers, "contemplative practice," refers to a broad spectrum of techniques, practices and modalities oriented around self awareness and interior experience. This may include: basic mindfulness meditation and stress-reduction meditation; nondual meditation systems such as Advaita or Dzogchen; meditative movement forms including Taijiquan; meditative journaling; any of a multitude of contemplative arts including Zen flower arranging or Chinese watercolor; or simple sensory awareness practices in the mode of the late Human Potential educator Charlotte Selver. In general, at American retreat centers (including Omega Institute, one of the largest wide spectrum centers in the US), the term "contemplative practice" has long been used as a catch-all definition for "meditation" and "meditative experience."

While Omega itself has always supported contemplative study and practice from the beginning and over the course of its 34 years of operation, the language used to describe this topic has changed significantly as has the popularity of different schools of practice. In its early years, Omega participants (students) were clearly interested in exploring as many different systems of practice as possible. Vipassana, Zen, Tibetan Buddhism, Sufism, Kabbalah, Christian contemplation and many new approaches such as quantum physics and consciousness studies were equally popular. (This writer recalls a study group in which friends met to debate the now long-forgotten insights of Franklin Merrell-Wolff [2] and where his work fit within the Perennial Tradition, or even if it did.)

This early openness to new disciplines was accompanied by a spirit of inquiry and a willingness to engage in intellectual study to support experiential practices, such as the exploration of quantum physics, Abhidharma or Goethean phenomenology (to mention three examples) as an adjunct to a meditation practice. However, as the outside culture has shifted in the last decade and a half, this commitment to intellectual rigor in our sector has been eclipsed by an interest in emotional experience and content.

Demographics in This Sector and How They Have Changed Over the Past 25 Years

In its early years, one would have been hard pressed to enter the dining hall at Omega and identify who were guests and who was a staff person. Similarly, one might have a difficult time determining who was American and who was a foreign student. In those formative years Omega's practice community (including both staff persons and guests) was composed of all ages and all walks of life, with a high number of foreign citizens attending. This changed profoundly in the early 1990s, partly in response to diminishing attendance at workshops and retreats.

Currently Omega's chief demographic (65%–75%) is composed of women in the 35- to 55-years of age group, mainly Caucasian, with most earning over 160–180K per year. A high percentage of these are professionals, including many educators and therapists. While there are certainly many males, young people, African Americans, Asians, Latins and foreign citizens also attending Omega events, until very recently Omega's demographic has been overwhelmingly composed of Caucasian, female Baby Boomers. (The past 2 years especially have seen a pronounced shift in this area; see below.)

The demographic shift toward a middle-aged female audience followed an internal decision to "go mainstream," (as it was called then) by consciously choosing to pursue best-selling authors, leading teachers and avoiding non-esoteric teachings whenever possible. All phases of the organization, from curriculum development to marketing materials, were realigned to match the new vision. This realignment paralleled the rising popularity of the Oprah Winfrey Show (launched in 1986) which featured many of the leading presenters in Omega's faculty lineup such as Caroline Myss, Gary Zukav and Deepak Chopra, and also the growth of "Self Help" as a major publishing category around the same time.

While the shift proved highly profitable and contributed to Omega's longevity in a field where most not-for-profit retreat centers do not survive more than a decade, it also highlighted a temporary movement away from intellectual dimensions of learning in favor of more formulaic, emotional healing approaches better suited for a mass audience. The enormous growth of "Self Help" as a publishing category, with subsets of "Psychic" and "Inspirational," became the bellwether for Omega's curriculum development for the late 1990s and into the early part of the 21st century.

It is interesting to note that at various times, different genders appear to gravitate toward or away from specific contemplative practices. It used to be a standing joke that, "If you want to meet men, you should attend a zen *sesshin,* but if you want to meet women, you should attend a vipassana retreat." (Of course the joke was on whoever attended one of these retreats hoping to meet someone socially!) However, there does appear to be a pronounced gender preference for different forms of contemplative practice, which in the case of the workshop/retreat sector at large, generally favors trainings popular with women, especially over the past decade.

This 15-20 year transition period served as Omega's great "Occam's razor," shaving many practices down to the most simple or essential basics and establishing it as a premier center for beginners on the path. Currently, over the past three or four years only, there has been signs of a swing back towards earlier themes and approaches, with a growing change in audience demographics to include more youth and greater ethnic diversity partly due to the continuing strength of yoga programs with its younger, more diverse audience. This has been accompanied by a recent, and major, repositioning of Omega by its core leadership to realign its non-for-profit identity towards a more environmentally- and socially-focused curriculum, and towards a greater role for privately underwritten programs as opposed to past market-driven programming.

Despite the pendulum shift away from intellectually-based learning over the time period described above, interest in personal contemplative experience has always remained strong at Omega and at its sister retreat centers. It is believed that this is chiefly due to the essential human need for interior experience and validation, and as such is generally independent of changing societal trends. There is also ample evidence that people of all times and cultures instinctively reach out for contemplative practice upon reaching a certain age or level of personal experience. In other words, at certain times in their lives, people tend to seek out contemplative experience because it is human nature to do so.

It is apparently also human nature to seek to profit from, or to commercialize, all human activities and contemplative practice has not been exempt from this. For example, Omega Institute receives more than three thousand unsolicited course proposals each year and a high number of these are related to contemplative practice. Quite of few of these come from people with apparently little or no serious practice experience, but each year the number of obviously-experienced practitioners grows.

Descriptors of Contemplative Topics and Their Evolution

This one center's experience reflects the larger realities of the growing interest of independent and mainstream publishers in the same topic. Each year the lineup of books in the contemplative publishing category grows larger, and many of these works possess a long shelf life. Most of the current books appear to break down into roughly three main categories: mindfulness; nondualism; and consciousness studies.

For the first term, the following definition culled from the U-MASS website seems as good as any: "Mindfulness is described as a calm awareness of one's body functions, feelings, content of consciousness, or consciousness itself. Mindfulness practice, inherited from the Buddhist tradition, is increasingly being employed in Western psychology to alleviate a variety of mental and physical conditions, including obsessive-compulsive disorder and anxiety and in the prevention of relapse in depression and drug addiction."

While mindfulness in essence simply means, "self awareness," *mindfulness practice* is a description of a technique and not an end result in itself. The technique is applicable to an extremely wide spectrum of situations and modalities and is currently experiencing a tremendous expansion in professional circles ranging from psychotherapy to pain management to education.

Many popular writers, teachers and researchers in this area have been offering retreats at Omega since its founding, including writers like Sharon Salzberg, psychologists Jack Kornfield and Tara Brach, and a small host of Zen masters and Tibetan Lamas. Some of the credit for the current interest in mindfulness is certainly due to the pioneering efforts of biologist and stress-reduction expert Jon Kabat-Zinn,[3] Professor of Medicine Emeritus and founding director of the Stress Reduction Clinic and the Center for Mindfulness in Medicine, Health Care, and Society at the University of Massachusetts Medical School. Alongside his U-MASS colleague Saki Santorelli, Kabat-Zinn for years championed the stress reducing qualities associated with the practice of meditation. Seeking to avoid the spiritual and religious overtones associated with the word "meditation," practitioners attempting to work with professional communities had qualified it during the 1970s by describing a secular version, "stress-reduction meditation," shortly followed by the more neutral-sounding (but actually Buddhist term) "mindfulness." Since 1979 Kabat-Zinn has taught Mindfulness Based Stress Reduction MBSR) at the Stress Reduction Clinic. Offered at many locations including Omega Institute each year, MBSR has since found an enthusiastic audience among health care professionals, especially physicians, nurses, social workers, psychologists and psychotherapists, and has spawned a host of spinoff trainings, such as "MBSR for Depression." Other widely recognized investigators in this field include psychologist Shauna L. Shapiro,[4] author of "The Art and Science of Mindfulness: Integrating Mindfulness into Psychology and the Helping Professions," and psychiatrist Daniel Siegel, MD,[5] author of several books including the recent "Mindsight: The New Science of Transformation" and "The Mindful Therapist: A Clinician's Guide to Mindsight and Neural Integration." Omega is now hosting its third annual retreat on Mindfulness and Education, designed for professional educators, so far without outside funding. Even so, in three years the number of attendees has risen from 65 to nearly 300; interest is clearly growing.

That mindfulness has become an increasingly recognizable word in the American lexicon is also due to the writings and public teachings of many spiritual teachers, including Vietnamese Zen Master and peace activist Ven. Thich Nhat Hanh,[6] who has offered many public retreats in North America over the past 20 years. Known for his extremely simple and quiet style of approaching complex insights, his best-selling books including "The Miracle of Mindfulness" have familiarized many tens of thousands of readers with the term.

Unlike mindfulness, the term, "non duality" (or a host of similar phrases suggesting oneness or "not two-ness"), is indicative of a state of being, perception or experience, and not merely a technique. While Omega has attracted teachers in this area for many years, including luminaries such as Ram Dass, Jean Klein and Gangaji, this was once largely an esoteric concept in America remote from the concerns of most beginning meditators. Its popularity has grown in recent years most probably resulting from a convergence of several factors.

The multimillion-dollar American yoga movement is beginning to develop additional depth and openness to the ideas of classical yogic thought, including the philosophical tradition of Advaita Vedanta (the nondual school of the Vedas). This has created fertile ground in the popular imagination for the teachings of Indian gurus (already long embraced by a smaller spiritual elite of Westerners). Similarly, a second (and third) generation of Buddhists in America, including Tibetan Buddhists, is coming of age and once rarified nondual teachings such as Dzogchen (the Great Perfection of the Nyingma School) and Mahamudra (the Great Seal of the Kagyu and Gelug Schools) are now far more common. These have traditions, simply doing their own inner work for the students over the past few decades, have along with the various mindfulness schools perhaps inadvertently built a wider, general audience for a new generation of maverick teachers.

In our busy, breakneck-speed society, I imagine few people have stopped to ponder what a unique time it is when hundreds of thousands of Americans (and others around the world) drop whatever they are doing to watch someone like Eckhart Tolle[7] explore the nondual state on Oprah. In fact, the third of these "webinar" sessions with Oprah attracted over 11 million viewers! Tolle's written works have become international bestsellers and is a testament to the growing societal openness to nondual or presence-based spiritual practice.

Tolle has since been called by Time magazine "the leading spiritual teacher in America." His teachings, if they can be called such, follow a classical model in the tradition of past teachers like Ramana Maharshi, in that he simply rests in the state of natural awareness and speaks from that state in response to whatever question or situation has arisen. Dialogues with students tend to follow the timeless and unstructured "satsang" model.

While he continues to write and to teach publicly, Tolle has chosen to avoid the construction of a school with formal trainings, disciples, etc.. However, this has not stopped the appearance of a large number of similar teachings and teachers influenced by him, many of whom do attempt to formalize a teacher-student relationship. In its work as a leading conference and retreat center, Omega sees more than its fair share of such teachers and a high number appear to be sincerely and purely motivated to genuinely help people achieve a level of freedom from fear and suffering, something to be thankful for in these times.

One of the most interesting and uniquely-modern venues for the ongoing exploration of the nondual state is the internet, now the home of numerous online forums exploring this topic. Many new seekers and practitioners are now contacting their teachers, or their communities of fellow travelers, on the web. While not yet attaining financially sustainability, this "nonlocal" venue for the sharing of teachings seems to be one of the most promising new developments in this field in terms of communication.

Regarding the issue of financial sustainability, one of the most common discussions in the field at present is the challenge of "monetizing" online content, including spiritual content. The current consensus among most marketing experts is that, outside of a few specific "star teachers" with enormous followings, extracting financial profit from online content is simply not possible. Most people online have grown accustomed to receiving such material at no cost, and many attempts as launching subscriber-based web sites have failed. (Whether or not this is in fact a healthy thing is another discussion.)

The final of the three publishing categories mentioned above is the so-called, "consciousness studies." This is a perennial category that has waxed and waned many time over the past four decades, and is currently experiencing a tremendous resurgence. Neither a specific practice like mindfulness, or a state of being like nonduality, consciousness studies refer to a generally scientific exploration of the working of the human mind. Many of these studies and their authors are in fact nonspiritual and frankly materialistic, but there is now a growing body of recent work in the "meditative neurosciences" that is taking its place alongside of other scientific approaches to consciousness such as certain streams of physics. Some of these are a deeper investigation of mindfulness studies as now practiced at the hospital and university level.

Economic Realities and Challenges

It is no coincidence that this exploration of trends in the retreat center field as experienced by Omega Institute and similar centers has wandered into a discussion of trends in the publishing industry. The two separate fields are in fact deeply interconnected (at least among those centers relying on public ticket sales for income). This has presented both financial opportunities and serious limitations. For example, Omega Institute, widely known as one of the more successful centers of this types, hosts between 250 and 350 teachers per year at its Rhinebeck, New York campus. Out of these, perhaps 40 teachers traditionally account for more than 50% of all program income. As one would expect, these are the presenters that have appeared on Oprah or Larry King Live, or are household names, or have written bestselling (and often beginner-level) books. Often the presence of these top-drawing presenters is seen as not just valuable in themselves, but also providing essential support for the organization to host less popular but still important (or mission-driven) programs and teachers.

While there is nothing unethical about such a situation, and Omega is always proud to host such well-known and widely respected faculty, in fact the annual quest to negotiate future contracts with top-drawing teachers has become an extremely competitive, essential aspect of the business, without which it is not currently sustainable. In our New York-New England region, for example, each retreat center whose target is a general audience, including Kripalu, Wainright House, Rowe, the New York Open Center, Hay House (book publishers who also produce events), Omega, and even Canyon Ranch are all competing for the same small pool of bestselling presenters. This competition tends to increase faculty fees and expenses and the list of competitors includes the presenters themselves, as many of them find it more profitable to cut out the "middlemen" and produce their own events in-house.

The situation is further exacerbated by the fact that despite the increasing mainstream popularity of contemplative practice, the actual audience that can afford to attend these increasingly expensive retreats is comparatively small and increasingly linked to the same publishers, web sites and television shows. In other words, all these centers, and the presenters who produce their own events, are all marketing to the same limited pool of students.

Also, as expenses and faculty fees have risen over recent years, the overall economy has also suffered and fewer people have the "disposable income" to enjoy many such retreats. In terms of the "business" of producing large retreats dependent on "celebrity" or best-selling faculty, the current situation does not seem sustainable in the long term for most retreat centers. Again, this is not a criticism of the quality of such popular teachers but rather a reflection on economic realities of the centers sponsoring their events.

Some New Directions

Different centers are responding to this economic situation in different ways. One major center is in the process of repositioning itself as a luxury spa catering to a higher-end audience while still attempting to retain some of its yogic and meditative roots. For its part, Omega Institute itself has reaffirmed its not-for-profit identity and mission. For years a center that did not fund raise at all, instead relying solely on public event sales and housing rentals for its income, Omega now possesses an entire staff department of fund raising professionals developing a community of active donors. While much past focus was directed towards capital development, such as the construction of Omega's new "eco machine" waste water facility that employs revolutionary, ecologically-sustainable technology to process waste in a glassed-in classroom setting open to tours by schools, architects and environmental groups, a substantial amount of energy and effort is currently being redirected toward curriculum development that furthers its evolving mission goals.

Omega is now in the final stages of launching two (of a planned three or four) internal institutes or centers that are funded in large part by public grants and private donations, the Omega Center for Sustainable Living (OCSL), and the Omega Women's leadership Center (WLC). The work of both of these new internal departments include the development of invitational conferences for creative peer review and think tanks; large-scale, public events with high-profile presenters; scholarship funds for students; research projects; and residential internships for young scholars and activists. This work is being supported by the new technologies (new to the retreat center field, that is) including video recording for online learning, live streaming, and social networking sites on selected topics of interest.

Socio-political Ramifications of Contemplative Practice

The above two examples at Omega (the Omega Center for Sustainable Living and Women's Leadership Center) might seem at first glance to exist totally in the realm of political or environmental activism. Yet internally, Omega's staff and many of its guests understand these developing institutions to be the fruits of years of contemplative practice. Despite popular myth, the experience of contemplative practice does not necessarily result in inward-looking individuals living in isolated retreat from the activities of the busy world. The Omega leadership has become convinced that the sincere practice of contemplation in these times fosters an abiding awareness that is separable from a holistic, life-affirming understanding of sociopolitical realities.

For example, one would be hard pressed to develop any significant level of calm, penetrating insight through a (any) meditative practice without simultaneously achieving some understanding of interdependence. The truth of interdependence is realized through insight. Yet while existential at its root, the understanding of interdependence is also ecological and relational in its application. The contemplative experience is not necessarily linear and one can proceed towards inner transformation through outward contemplation of nature. Current and future retreats on sustainability and the environment at Omega incorporate strong contemplative practice highlighting the inseparability of individual humanity and the wider web of life. We now believe that the internal experience of interdependence cannot be separated from environmental awareness.

A related subject area that is well-known in environmental and engineering circles is the category of biomimicry [8] and natural design theory (strongly influenced by general systems theory). Focused on the application of holistic natural processes to architectural, medical and environmental design (among others), the concept is grounded in personal and direct observation and perception of nature. The Omega Center for Sustainable Living is now hosting annual conferences exploring the meeting of contemplative practice and environmental design, with substantial grants available for student scholarships. The intention is to support a new generation of architects, engineers and environmental activists having a strong contemplative practice as a continuing source of guidance, inspiration and community.

A common feature of the state of contemplative practice throughout most American retreat centers (and publishers) is to rely on Buddhist and Asian traditions, yet there is also ample material found in many European and Western tradition. For example, one continuing inspiration in the area of nature-based, contemplative practice is the phenomenological legacy of the German poet Goethe.[9] His approach to meditative observation of nature has great relevance to the subject of biomimicry and design theory and there is a real need to link practice communities and teachers in this field with the larger mainstream of Buddhist influenced, nature-based contemplation, especially in the field of green architecture and permaculture.

Similarly, the Women's Leadership Center at Omega sees the cultivation of compassion and the awareness of interconnected humanity as essential dimensions of a curriculum building future women's leadership. Many of the past eight years of conferences and retreats supporting this goal have included a strong contemplative component. Such trainings have invariably resulted in a growing support of natural human rights and in the acceptance of multicultural justice and gender equality. Just as the experience of contemplative practice fosters awareness of interdependence (including ecological interdependence), it also supports the human values of compassion and caring for all life.

Quite clearly we all live in the same precarious situation, now facing tipping points in the global economy and society and across the natural world on a number of discouraging fronts. Yet while this dire situation is understood by most people in varying degrees, people are far from agreement about what to do in the face if these multiple crises. American society, and the world at large, are more divided and polarized than ever before.

This same division also arises in relation to Omega's public communications (including marketing and PR) when discussing the above topic areas. Many people have a historical tendency to view contemplative practice as nonpolitical and irrelevant to social issues, on some occasions even taking offense at suggestions to the contrary. There is also a definite need for practices and places devoted to deep retreat and to be effective such environments must be kept free of distractions.

While there remains an abiding commitment at Omega to preserving the practice of personal and group retreat, there is also a perception that in these unprecedented times, contemplative experience by its very nature possesses political, social and environmental dimensions that now must be addressed openly rather than merely acknowledged. The challenge for Omega, a not-for-profit intended to be in service to all, lies in doing so without falling into partisanship or dogmatic certainty about particular political solutions.

Other Key Trends, Challenges, and Opportunities Facing Contemplative Practice

People today live in an age of constant distraction, with multiple sources clamoring for ever shorter and shorter moments of ones attention. "Reality television;" videogames; "nature deficit disorder;" shocking current events displaying the ongoing disintegration of social institutions; and the constantly accelerating speed of business and society; all contribute to the existential crisis. Yet this dire situation also highlights the growing need for avenues to renew one's connection with essential nature, inside and outside. While most people remain distracted and disconnected from themselves and each other, we are also seeing that more and more people require contemplative experience and the renewal and wisdom it provides. This is an opportunity requiring the proper application of new resources.

This growing need does not exist only to be served by an elite pool of isolated retreat centers. Many of the diverse venues for contemplative work mentioned above are seeing the work of decades of past work by contemplative practitioners beginning to reach ever larger audiences. It does appear that a larger contemplative movement is now emerging in America, and in other parts of the planet and there are many resources available. There is an acute need for many separate individuals and organizations to now reach out and create stronger connectivity with one another.

Among the many challenges of our time is the increasing division between religions, and the corresponding rise in religious fundamentalism. One of the strongest beacons of hope in this area are the many dedicated organizations working with interfaith dialogue, often in the forms of common contemplative practices shared together in spiritual retreat. This is another area that represents both positive possibility and an acute need for the application of more resources.

There are additional trends more specific to the American retreat center field. One of these is the growing yoga movement in America, mentioned above. Many years of working closely with leading yoga instructors of all schools shows the great hunger to lead this hitherto-physical exercise oriented movement into a direction focused on contemplative practice. Interest in this dimension of yoga practice is currently expending among students. The field is wide open for more programs focusing exclusively on contemplative practice in yoga, including current professional trainings in yoga therapy and yoga psychology.

Another area of great interest at Omega is the expansion of program focused on devotional contemplative practices, as opposed to purely mindfulness-oriented practices. We have always understood that there are many pathways to awakening and to experiencing the Divine. While decades later few of Omega's original staff remain with any personal experience of Sufism, it is interesting to note that among Omega's participants interest in Sufism and Sufi-inspired literature is at an all time high. Some of this is due to the popular annual retreats of Sufi teacher Llewellyn Vaughn Lee[10], though the ongoing popularity of the work of Rumi among Omega's audience is also a factor. Perhaps a larger background factor is the growth of Islam in America, leading many people of conscience to wish to understand more about a belief system regularly demonized in the mainstream media and by successive government administrations. There is now strong interest at Omega in developing more Sufi-oriented contemplative retreats, and hopefully and annual conference featuring multiple presenters.

Another devotional-contemplative area currently showing immense popularity are the retreats devoted to the practice of *kirtan,* or vedic devotional chanting. These include the "Ecstatic Chant" three-night retreats held twice a season at Omega, generally to sold-out crowds. Though yoga is only minimally a part of these programs, these all-night affairs draw a high number of enthusiastic yoga practitioners of all ages (according to market research and participant feedback).

Moving away from devotional practice, another area of great interest at Omega is the application of contemplative practice in business leadership. The work of Peter Senge and Otto Schwarmer[11] on the subject of presence-based leadership, for one example among many, has attracted great enthusiasm. This topic has many crossover links with the categories of creativity, women's leadership, human rights, and environmental sustainability.

Finally, one other area of contemplative practice is of growing interest among Omega's audience, the subject of death and dying. America's reluctance to face death at individual and societal levels is enormous and outside the scope of this paper, but the importance of contemplative practice in this area is beyond dispute. There currently exists a small but continuing audience drawn to this work. Much as the desire to experience contemplative practice seems to dawn on many people at certain points in their lives, so there is a significant portion of the population who look to such practices as a resource when facing death, whether personal or that of a loved one, in hospice settings or outside of them. While not yet a "popular" field that shows high public demand for retreats, this area is seen as extremely important and that awareness of contemplative practice as a resource for those facing death and dying is projected to grow as the field as a whole finds wider recognition in the mainstream.

Intentions and Goals

There are currently very many outstanding authors, teachers, schools, retreat centers, yoga studios, academic institutions, professional trainings, websites and magazines throughout America all offering one or another form of contemplative practice. So why is there a need for additional such institutions? Rather than resort to profit-oriented discussions of publishing trends, in which authors and publishers produce more product to take advantage of a growing market, a better answer is to refer to the precarious state of life on this planet. We live in a time when individuals and societies alike require the benefits of contemplative practices of all stripes. We also live in a time when nearly all other life forms on earth require humans to develop the wisdom, understanding and restraint associated with contemplative practice!

Each of the above-mentioned individuals and institutions will meet this need in its own way. Currently Omega is exploring the steps needed to develop a Mindfulness Center at Omega as a way of better providing:

- deep personal retreat for individuals
- professional conferences for business leaders, activists, scientists, educators and healthcare professionals
- interfaith dialogue and retreats
- support for scholarships and internships

- research projects and educational materials
- dedicated social networking

Another way Omega is carrying this work forward is to no longer focus solely on its upstate New York retreat center. Omega has a 30 year history of large scale conferences held in Manhattan and elsewhere, and there is a growing interest in adding smaller events to these larger annual conferences. There are many people who, while deeply interested in learning more about contemplative practice, will not venture out to a rural retreat center without first gaining more confidence. Economic realities are also a factor and many people view the concept of a personal retreat as a luxury item dependent on disposable income. It is to reach these large numbers of interested or uncommitted people that Omega sees the importance of producing more urban events.

One interested in contemplative practice in urban centers already has a rich environment and many resources to draw upon. Part of Omega's successfully implementing this intention is to partner with existing centers to ensure greater success. A recent day and-a-half workshop in Manhattan for psychologists, therapists and social workers, led by psychologists Jack Kornfield, Tara Brach and Mark Epstein, drew an attendance of nearly one thousand people, in part due to the co-marketing of sister organizations like New York Insight. There are many such large scale, contemplative events and trainings now occurring regularly and this represents one of the more hopeful trends in American society.

Notes

1 De Chardin, P. T. (1955) *The Phenomenon of Man*, Harper Perennial Modern Classics (reprinted 2008).

2 Merrell-Wolff, F. (1973) *Philosophy of Consciousness Without An Object: Reflections on the Nature of Transcendental Consciousness*, Julian Press.

3 Kabat-Zinn, J. (2006) *Coming to Our Senses: Healing Ourselves and the World Through Mindfulness*, Hyperion.

4 Shapiro, S., & Carlson, L. (2009) *The Art and Science of Mindfulness: Integrating Mindfulness into Psychology and the Helping Professions*, American Psychological Association (APA).

5 Seigel, D. (2010) *Mindsight: The New Science of Personal Transformation,* Bantam.

6 Hanh, T.N. (1999) *The Miracle of Mindfulness,* Beacon Press.

7 Tolle, E. (2004) *The Power of Now: A Guide to Spiritual Enlightenment,* New World Library.

8 Benyus, J. (2002) *Biomimicry: Innovation Inspired by Nature,* Harper Perennial.

9 Bortoft, H. (1996) *The Wholeness of Nature : Goethe's Way Toward a Science of Conscious Participation in Nature,* Lindesfarne Books.

10 Vaughn-Lee, L. http://www.goldensufi.org/.

11 Senge, P. & Scharmer, C.O. et al (2005) *Presence: An Exploration of Profound Change in People, Organizations, and Society,* Broadway Business.

CONTEMPLATIVE HIGHER EDUCATION IN CONTEMPORARY LIFE

Mirabai Bush

Introduction

> *The fruit of education, whether in the university or in the monastery [is] the activation of that innermost center, that apex or spark which is a freedom beyond freedom, an identity beyond essence, a self beyond ego, a being beyond the created realm, and a consciousness that transcends all division, all separation.*
> — Thomas Merton, *Learning to Live*

Imagine an architecture professor saying this: "I ask my students to sit in silence and then draw a simple map of their childhood, a map of the built environment where they grew up, with their house or apartment, school, playground, city block, friend's house, corner store, grandmother's house, whatever they remember that mattered to them, and they see how the structures of a community fit together and create meaning." Bradford Grant, Contemplative Practice Fellow in Architecture at Hampton University (now Professor and Director, School of Architecture and Design at Howard), shared this practice with us at the conference on Uncovering the Heart of Higher Education. In his course, "Urban and Community Design and Contemplative Environmental Design Practice," he uses contemplative practices to help students get to a deeper and more connected understanding of what it means to build, to create, to live a meaningful life inside a structure.

Fellow David Haskell, Associate Professor of Biology at the University of the South, teaches a course called "Food and Hunger: Contemplation and Action." As part of this course, students not only learn the biology of hunger but also work with local hunger-relief organizations and learn the contemplative practices that motivate and sustain many of those who work with the hungry. With increased awareness of their own minds and emotions, David reports, students are better able to process the disturbing subject matter. Without some self-knowledge of one's center, it is very hard to receive the bad news about hunger and even harder to discern what one's own response might be.

When University of Connecticut poet and professor Marilyn Nelson was offered a Contemplative Practice Fellowship and an invitation to teach at West Point during the same semester, she combined the two invitations and taught poetry and meditation to cadets who were later deployed to Iraq. They emailed back to her about how meditation and poetry were helping them through difficult times. One said that both he and his wife (both are Black Hawk helicopter pilots) had continued to meditate during their deployments. He said that, although military culture is in some ways the antithesis of the contemplative life, they had both found it an invaluable tool to use in a crisis, especially as officers who must show composure before their soldiers, as, for instance, when one of their soldiers was killed or wounded. He said he camouflaged his meditating by sitting on his cot wearing headphones: everyone thought he was listening to music, which is cool. But his headphones were silent. He was being in the moment, thinking "here, now, here, now."

Brad, David, and Marilyn are just three of the 158 Contemplative Practice Fellows, a program of the Center for Contemplative Mind in Society funded by The Fetzer Institute. At more than 100 colleges and universities in virtually every discipline, they have been teaching courses that incorporate a range of practices, including mindfulness, *lectio divina*, yoga, tai chi, and others that emerge from the disciplines. Together they are designing pedagogical methods and building a body of knowledge that is formulating a new way of teaching—and of learning and knowing—that complements critical thinking and the scientific method. They are demonstrating how contemplative development opens the mind to new possibilities, cultivates wisdom though deepening one's relationship to the world, and encourages compassion and empathy through an understanding of the interconnection of all life. And, at the same time, scientific research is confirming that contemplation/mindfulness develops such cross-disciplinary cognitive capacities as decision making, attention, intuitive understanding, and memory as well as emotional capacities such as self-awareness, self-management, and empathy.

Contemplative practices, a vital part of all major religious and spiritual traditions, have long had a place in intellectual inquiry. The predecessors of our colleges and universities in the West, of course, were established as *alternatives* to monastic schools, where contemplative practices had been central to learning. These new institutions were committed to the pursuit of rational knowledge and later to the scientific method. But, as Brian Stock (Professor, Centre for Comparative Literature, University of Toronto) explained in an address to the Symposium on Contemplative Education at Amherst College in 2003, there are important examples in Western intellectual history of the use of contemplative practices, which he defines as based on "a spirituality that does not depend for its validity on pre-existing metaphysical assumptions or associations, that is, a secular spirituality." He names Montaigne, whose writing practice was a form of contemplative reflection, and whose interest in the nature of attention and the nature of the self is shared by contemporary contemplatives. Seneca gave such Zen-sounding advice as "To be everywhere is to be nowhere." Augustine and Seneca both used a literary device, the soliloquy, as a form of self-inquiry through oral dialog. And Augustine was the first to use autobiography as contemplative practice; the *Confessions* is an inquiry into his life and the nature of all life.

These courses have been introduced at an interesting time in academic history. They both complement and challenge the postmodern campus culture. Contemplative practice focuses on moment-to-moment nonjudgmental awareness, the rising and passing away of momentary phenomena, which in some way confirms the idea of the fragmentary nature of reality that postmodernists posit when they claim that there is no metanarrative, no unifying story. No defining story, true contemplatives would agree, but unified nevertheless, in that all phenomena are interconnected, share an "interbeing," are part of a, some would say, divine wholeness.

The question of contemplative epistemology is only beginning to be explored, but the contemplative approach is one of inquiry into the nature of things, a scientific suspension of disbelief (and belief) in an attempt to "know" reality through direct observation by being fully present in the moment. Chogyam Trungpa, educated in both Lhasa and at Oxford, said wisdom is "immediate and nonconceptual insight which provides the basic inspiration for intellectual study." Having seen clearly one's own mind, one has a natural desire to see how others experience reality.

The challenge to the other great foundation of all contemporary institutions, modernity (from the Enlightenment onward), is probably greater. Buddhist contemplatives would say there is no stable self, certainly not one that is dependent on thinking (as in Descartes), and no contemplative from any tradition would agree that it is reason alone that leads to ultimate truth. Although the contemplative investigation is in some sense scientific, and although some scientists (notably Amherst physicist Arthur Zajonc) say that a nonrational leap happens in the moment of scientific insight, contemplatives look to an intuitive, nonconceptual, direct, experiential "knowing" as the path to wisdom. The practical legacy of the modernist tradition has also been a compartmentalized, fragmented way of learning and teaching, a dualistic alienation of body from mind, emotion from intellect, humans from nature, and art from science, whereas the basis of contemplative understanding is wholeness, unity, integration.

So what is the role of contemplative practice in the classroom? Just as introducing computers into students' lives didn't just affect the amount of research they could do or the length of their papers but also the way that they think (PowerPoint! Wikipedia!), the way they relate to other students and their teachers, their health, and so on, contemplative practices have had an extraordinary range of effects on the teachers, the students, the classroom, and on learning, teaching, research, and personal relationships. These include increased concentration, greater capacity for synthetic thinking, conceptual flexibility, and an appreciation for a different type of intellectual process, distinct from the linear, analytical and product oriented processes so often valued in contemporary education. For example, Robin Hunt at the University of Washington worked with contemplative practice to develop balance in a theatre piece: "I conceived of a play in which actors have to deal with all the literal meanings of balance while playing scenes dealing with the figurative meanings of the word.... Using the practice of *slow tempo*, the physical requirements of balancing demand that one find a calm and clear mental state in the moment."

The definitions of contemplative learning and teaching are in process. Ellen Langer, part of the Williams James legacy at the Psychology Department at Harvard (described below), addressed "the power of mindful learning" in 1997. She described it as having three characteristics: the continuous creation of new categories, openness to new information, and an implicit awareness of more than one perspective. She states that the essence of mindfulness is flexible thinking. Dan Siegel, in *The Mindful Brain*, identifies the essential dimensions of mindful learning as openness to novelty, alertness to distinction, context sensitivity, multiple perspectives, and present orientation. He calls reflection the fourth "R" of education, the skill that embeds self-knowing and empathy in the curriculum. Fellow Mary Rose O'Reilly, in *Radical Presence: Teaching as a Contemplative Practice*, says that it has to do with being awake, being there, being present, listening, creating a space for learning and for developing an inner life by your very attention to the moment. Tobin Hart says that the contemplative teacher doesn't add to the curriculum but invites students to the *inside* of the subject matter. And Arthur Zajonc says that in teaching college physics, he looks for experiments and experiences over which he can linger with his students so they and he can live more fully into them. He uses quantum paradoxes as koans to challenge their thinking.

Education systems reflect society's values; therefore, most of current American education pays little attention to the potential contributions of contemplative values and perspective, including compassion and loving kindness. But society is changing, and education can either support the status quo or prepare students for the emerging new directions. By encouraging contemplative ways of knowing in higher education in diverse disciplines, we can encourage a new form of inquiry and imaginative thinking to complement critical thinking, and we will educate active citizens who will support a more just and compassionate direction for society. At a Center conference at Columbia, Jon Kabat Zinn, founder of the Center for Mindfulness in Medicine, Health Care, and Society, urged us to *come to our senses*, to break through to the knowing that is based on direct experience, to see with eyes of wholeness, to practice awareness of the mind as if our lives depended on it—because, he said, "in virtually every way that has any meaning, literal or metaphorical, they surely do."

Contemplative education is becoming a field. At this meeting, Susan Burggraf will report on Naropa University, an early leader and an important center for this work. I'll report in this paper on some developments in the rest of the field, which I hope will suggest the extraordinary work emerging across the country.

History and Growth

I'd like to begin with a "Cliff Notes" history of American contemplative education:

1890: William James publishes *Principles of Psychology*, in which he describes four methods, including introspection, or his study of his own state of mind and concludes with this quote which is included in every Power Point and website on contemplative education: "The faculty of voluntarily bringing back a wandering attention, over and over again, is the very root of judgment, character, and will.... An education which should improve this faculty would be *the* education *par excellence*. But it is easier to define this ideal than to give practical directions for bringing it about."

1970's, William James Hall, Harvard: After Tim Leary and Richard Alpert leave the department that was inspired by William James and is housed in William James Hall, interest in expanded consciousness continues, encouraged in part by David McClelland, former Chair of the Social Relations Department whose students then—Dan Goleman (*Emotional Intelligence*), Richie Davidson (U Wisconsin, Laboratory for Functional Brain Imaging and Behavior and the Laboratory for Affective Neuroscience), Cliff Saran (Shamatha

Project, UC Davis), and Mark Epstein (*Thoughts Without a Thinker*)—later become important research and thought leaders of the new contemplative movement in this country. Outside the classroom, David and his artist wife Mary, both Quakers with an interest in Thomas Merton and Eastern religions, host an ongoing conversation in their home about meditative practices and consciousness. A lifelong teacher, David wants to know, How can contemplative practices affect knowing and learning as well as healing, social relationships, and motivation? Among the diverse voices that join David's students and other of us who lived in the McClelland's big Cambridge house were Mexican poet Octavio Paz, *Secular City* author Harvey Cox, Insight Meditation teachers Joseph Goldstein, Jack Kornfield, and Sharon Salzberg, Zen master Seung Sahn, Tibetan teacher Kalu Rinpoche, and, eventually, Allen Ginsberg and Chogyam Trungpa Rinpoche. Richard Alpert, now Ram Dass, is also part of David's circle.

1974: Chogyam Trungpa founds the Naropa Institute, based on Buddhist principles of contemplative education, with a summer session in Boulder. He hopes to create an institution, where learning is "infused with the experience of awareness, insight and compassion for oneself and others, honed through the practice of sitting meditation and other contemplative disciplines." Not well known in the United States at that time, Chogyam Trungpa asks Ram Dass, who has a huge following after publishing *Be Here Now* in 1971, to teach at Naropa in order to attract students. The organizers expect between three hundred and five hundred people to show up to take courses at the Institute. Instead, more than 1,300 students flock to Boulder.

> Almost overnight, Boulder has become a magnet of learning and excitement and promise... The student body is made up of an astonishing assortment of college students, dropouts, scholars, scientists, artists, therapists, dancers, heads of departments, musicians, housewives, and on and on. The whole first week seems to be filled with a sort of joyous incredulity that Naropa is really happening.
> —*East-West Journal*, September 1974

Fast Forward to 1995: Charles Halpern, president of Nathan Cummings Foundation, and Rob Lehman, president of the Fetzer Institute, initiate the Working Group on Contemplative Mind in Society and invite scholars to explore contemplative education in white papers (http://www.contemplative-mind.org/resources/publications.html).

Robert Thurman, Columbia: "Contemplation fits in the traditional inner science curriculum at the highest level of the cultivation of wisdom: first learning wisdom, then reflective wisdom, then contemplative wisdom. Therefore, it is virtually indispensable if wisdom is to become fully transformative. The question then for academic, especially liberal arts, institutions, is not a question of adding a desirable frill to their vast smorgasbord of offerings. It is a matter of their effectively fulfilling their duty to provide a liberal, i.e., a liberating and empowering, education.

He suggests:

1. "Encouraging the establishment of contemplative centers on campuses such as that proposed but not yet implemented at Middlebury by Steven Rockefeller. Harvard's Center for the Study of World Religions was set up by its donors with such a purpose in mind, though, significantly, its meditation room was eventually turned into a library. Colgate's Chapel House was set up by the same donors, and has provided some contemplative relief in its undergraduate center over the years. At Columbia we would have the opportunity to set up such a center at Earl Hall in the University's pluralistic religious group meeting spaces I have had the opportunity for some time, but I simply have not had the time or resources to accomplish it successfully. I'm sure every liberal arts college and university has the seeds of the kind of center and process we would like to see available for the students and faculty already there within it.

2. Encouraging departments to introduce contemplative experience and expertise in whatever tradition as a recognized and rewarded accomplishment in the professor and the student.

3. Encouraging individual scholars in the natural and social sciences to expand their researches into physiological effects of various meditative disciplines, into institutions affected by the centrality of meditative experiences, and so forth.

4. Encouraging scholars in religious studies to research, translate, and publish more of the contemplative literature, technical as well as evocative, born of the contemplative disciplines, from all traditions, but especially the Indian traditions.

5. Encouraging media productions that inform about and instruct in the practice of contemplation, thereby reaching a wide audience, demystifying contemplation, and creating greater public acceptance of contemplation in the educational arena."

Brian Stock, University of Toronto: "We have to teach students what contemplative activity is all about. Among other things, they have to be instructed in reading meditative literature, not as they would read modern poems, plays, or novels, but as contemplatives read them, using texts as a means to an end and not considering them, as is the fashion in contemporary literary practice, as ends in themselves. They would also have to explore types of meditation that are unlike the Judeo-Christian tradition in not requiring the presence of texts, images, or other sensory supports. Beyond that, teachers of the humanities would have to use the renewed interest in the contemplative life to begin an exploration of what we mean by 'the modern identity,' that is, as a means of tracing the various strands of what it means to be a human agent, a person, or a self. This implies broadening the discussion of ethics beyond the traditionally narrow confines of academic speculation and taking up a number of cultural connections: religious history, gender orientation, ecological considerations, etc."

Steven Rockefeller, Middlebury College: "Meditation can improve the quality of life of those who choose to practice it under the guidance of competent teachers. When pursued seriously as a discipline, it can add a unique depth to democratic and ecological living. It can help people become free and fully human. By itself meditation does not impel human beings to social action, and it needs to be counterbalanced by a concern with social reconstruction and personal relationship. However, in a democratic ecological society that affirms life in the world and values social action and community, the practice of meditation can help to shape the direction of social action, contributing to an integration of the ethical and the political, the spiritual and the practical. The undergraduate college is one place where these issues should be thoughtfully explored.

"That undergraduate education should emphasize the experimental method of knowledge and the arts of critical reflection is not to be questioned. A question can be raised about whether the education of the undergraduate college in America today fails to put science and discursive reason in proper perspective and whether it tends to encourage a character orientation that is too head-centered as distinct from heart-centered, more interested in information than appreciation, more concerned about the knowledge which is power than wisdom and ethical values, more oriented toward I-it than I-thou, more skilled at striving for future ends than living a fulfilling life in the present. It is a question of balance."

He recommends the following:

1. The truth about meditation should be carefully researched and studied.

2. New research is needed on the effects of meditation on human growth and mental illness.

3. Students can also be introduced to meditation by health care and counseling professionals on campus and through a extracurricular college program.

4. An academic department or a chaplain's office could establish a program of visiting speakers and teachers in the field of meditation.

5. Administration policy could allow staff time for meditation during the work day and creation of a space where people are working.

1997: The Center for Contemplative Mind in Society is incorporated and partners with the American Council of Learned Societies to offer fellowships to academics who are interested in developing courses with a contemplative component. Advisors to the project include Carolyn Brown from the Library of Congress, Robert Thurman, Sharon Daloz Parks (Kennedy School of Government at Harvard), Francisco Varela (who introduced into neuroscience the concept of "first person science," in which observers examine their own conscious experience using scientifically verifiable methods, later key to the research on meditation) and members of the original Cambridge group: Dan Goleman, Deborah Salter-Klimburg (Director of the Institute for Tibetan Art History at the University of Vienna), Joseph Goldstein, and David Mc-Clelland. Although the Selection Committee is unsure that they will receive any proposals at all, 136 are submitted. The committee finds many of them extraordinary, creative, and rigorous, and they award the first 16 Contemplative Practice Fellowships to "create curriculum in diverse disciplines that encompass and encourage the study of contemplation." By 2010, there are 158 Fellows in more than 100 colleges and universities.

1999: Mindfulness and Education Conference, the first of its kind, at University of Massachusetts under the direction of Chancellor David Scott.

Joseph Goldstein and Mirabai Bush are keynoters. It is followed by a larger conference in 2000: Going Public with Spirituality in Work and Higher Education. Peter Senge declares that, in higher education, "Contemplative practice is a survival skill for the 21rst Century."

2000: Humane Creativity and the Contemplative Mind project at Harvard (Howard Gardner), Stanford (Bill Damon) and Claremont (Mike Csikzentmihaly) does research on creativity and contemplative practice.

2000: University of Michigan offers the first contemplative BA: Bachelor of Fine Arts in Jazz and Contemplative Studies. Highly interdisciplinary program combines a solid grounding in jazz and improvised music study with courses that involve meditative practices and other areas related to creative development.

2003: The Center hosts the Symposium on Contemplative Practice and Higher Education at Amherst College, followed in subsequent years by conferences at Columbia and University of Michigan.

2004: Arthur Zajonc, Professor of Physics at Amherst College, becomes the Director of the Center's Academic Program and begins to articulate the nature of contemplative epistemology:

> ... knowing itself remains partial and deformed if we do not develop and practice an epistemology of love instead of an epistemology of separation. Harvard's motto is *Veritas* or Truth. Knowing is, in this view, the central project of higher education. I maintain, however, that truth itself— *veritas* itself—eludes us if we bring to the world and to each other an epistemology of separation only. Our conventional epistemology hands us a dangerous counterfeit in truth's place, one that may pass for truth, but in fact is partial and impoverished.

> ...Surely, science has brought enormous advances, but we cannot turn away from the central fact that the modern emphasis on objectification predisposes us to an instrumental and manipulative way of being in the world. While I am emphatically *not* calling for a roll-back of science, I am calling for resituating it within a greater vision of what knowing and living are really all about. That re-imagination of knowing will have deep consequences for education, consequences that give a prominent place to contemplative

pedagogies. Indeed, I hope to convince you that contemplative practice can become contemplative inquiry, which *is* the practice of an epistemology of love. Such contemplative inquiry not only yields insight (*veritas*) but also transforms the knower through his or her intimate (one could say loving) participation in the subject of one's contemplative attention. Contemplative education is transformative education.

2004: Columbia Teachers College Bulletin publishes a special issue on Contemplative Education, edited by Fellow Christopher Hill.

2005: Hal Roth, with a Contemplative Practice Program Fellowship grant, forms The Brown University Contemplative Studies Initiative, a group of Brown faculty with diverse academic specializations who are united around a common interest in the study of contemplative states of mind, including the underlying philosophy, psychology, and phenomenology of human contemplative experience. At the Brown Alpert Medical School students may now pursue a concentration in contemplative studies as part of their medical education curriculum.

2005: First Summer Session on Contemplative Curriculum Development, hosted by the Center at Smith College.

2007: Uncovering the Heart of Higher Education: Integrative Learning for Compassionate Action in an Interconnected World, San Francisco, CA, a conference of more than 600 faculty members, administrators, student-life professionals, and chaplains from the broad spectrum of American colleges and universities, co-sponsored by the Fetzer Institute and California Institute of Integral Studies (CIIS).

2008: Toward the Integration of Meditation into Higher Education: A Review of Research. Prepared for the Center by Shauna L. Shapiro, Kirk Warren Brown, and John A. Astin.

By this point, the field expands so much that there too many activities to catalog. On the basis of evidence from surveys and conferences, a community of teachers now exists at all levels of higher education, from community colleges to research universities, who are using a wide range of contemplative practices as part of their classroom pedagogy.

In 2008, the Center forms the Association for Contemplative Mind in Higher Education to promote the emergence of a broad culture of contemplation in the academy by connecting a network of leading institutions and academics committed to the recovery and development of the contemplative dimension of teaching, learning and knowing. There are now more than 500 members from across North America, and some from other countries. In 2010, at the second annual conference, 65 professors from a wide range of disciplines presented their work. Examples:

- Borges, Buddhism and Cognitive Science: A New Approach to Applied Cognitive Science and Intuitive Knowing through Contemplative Practice (UC Berkeley)
- Education of Peacemakers: Challenges and Opportunities in Interreligious Dialogue in Undergraduate Education (Mt. St. Mary's)
- We Teach Who We Are: Contemplative Pedagogy in Teacher Education (Bowdoin)
- The Contemplative Moment: an artistic presentation (Dartmouth)
- Neurobiology of Meditation (Harvard)
- Contemplating Time: Contemplative Approaches in Earth Science (Vassar)

Professional schools developing contemplative programs and courses include the Brown Medical School (mentioned above), University of Massachusetts Medical School (where Saki Santorelli of MBSR has taught Medical Practice and Contemplative Practice for many years), UC Berkeley Boalt Hall School of Law (Charlie Halpern teaches a meditation course for law students). Courses are also taught in many other law schools (see white paper by Rhonda Magee). Harvard Law School hosted a symposium on Mindfulness and Alternative Dispute Resolution. At the Peter Drucker Graduate School of Management at Claremont, Jeremy Hunter teaches The Practice of Self-Management, a curriculum that cultivates human capital by developing mindfulness skills.

Other current notable events and centers that take contemplative education beyond the classroom include:

- Smith College School of Social Work, Contemplative Clinical Practice: An Advanced Certificate Program in Spirituality and Social Work Practice. A paradigm-shifting initiative in American social work education, the program considers the clinical relationship as a potential locus of the sacred. Deepens the clinician's awareness of the sacred dimension of his/her work by exploring his/her own religious histories and spiritual practices, the clients' spiritual beliefs and practices, and the clinical relationship itself. Provides a framework for assessing religious and spiritual development and exploring issues of ethics and social justice as they relate to spirituality.

- Emory-Tibet Partnership. The Emory-Tibet Partnership has made Emory University a center for the study of Tibetan philosophy and religion in the West. They are conducting research in Tibetan medicine and meditation, as well as educational initiatives for teaching modern science to Tibetan monks and nuns. His Holiness the Dalai Lama was appointed Presidential Distinguished Professor, which gives students unique access to him, his teachings, and his insights both on campus and in India. Through a National Institutes of Health grant, the Partnership is also leading research in the use of compassion meditation to treat depression and stress.

- The Center for Compassion and Altruism Research and Education (Project Compassion), Stanford University. Project Compassion will host a visit by His Holiness the Dalai Lama in October 2010, during which he will give a public lecture entitled, "The Centrality of Compassion in Human Life and Society." Following the public lecture there will be a scientific symposium entitled, "Scientific Explorations of Compassion and Altruism." Project Compassion is also developing a compassion curriculum, to be taught in diverse settings, including higher education.

- CUNY Contemplatives in New York City. An informal association of CUNY professors dedicated to the use of contemplative practices in academia, has sponsored several one-day events on contemplative education, with guest speakers.

- Mind and Life Institute: Educating World Citizens for the 21st Century. A 2009 Conference with the Dalai Lama asking how our educational system can evolve to meet the challenges of the 21st century? How will we educate people to be compassionate, competent, ethical, and engaged citizens in an increasingly complex and interconnected world?

- The 2010 Mind & Life Summer Research Institute: Education, Developmental Neuroscience and Contemplative Practices. Focus on linking the work in contemplative science and practice with the work in the developmental sciences, including developmental neuroscience, to provide a scientific foundation from which we can investigate the feasibility, effectiveness and potential challenges of attempting to introduce secularized versions of contemplative practices into public educational settings.
- Mindfulness in Education Network 2010 Conference: Mindfulness: Foundation for Teaching and Learning
- UC Davis Extension, Commitment to a Mindful Organization. Includes workshops, guidelines, guest speakers.

Opportunities and Challenges in the Coming Decade

The groundwork described above has prepared a real opportunity for the growth of contemplative education within the academy, especially in light of the emerging research on meditation and the brain. Scientists interested in the neural pathways associated with attention, empathy, compassion, memory, and other capacities are leading us toward more understanding of the ed uca tiona lues ofcont   em pla tivep ract ice si ned uca tion.

The discovery of neuroplasticity, the ability of the brain to change throughout life and the stimuli that cause it to change, has fundamentally altered our view of the human potential. Early results show that meditation throughout life stages increases attention, resilience, internal attunement, empathy, memory, and ability to form ideas into a coherent whole. This should require us to re-think our fundamental ideas of education, including the value of first-person learning (investigating one's own mind/body) as well as the traditional third-person data of objective science.

The changing religious/cultural national and world maps are also driving educational reform. In 2005, Daniel Yankelovich identified "public support for other ways of knowing" as one of five most important trends to radically transform higher education by 2015 (see "Ferment and Change: Higher Education in 2015," *The Chronicle Review*, Nov 25, 2005) And as contemplative practices become more accepted in society at large through the popularization of the research results, which are showing up in *Time*, *Newsweek*, and the Huffington Post and in Oprah's magazine (*Time* reported on the value of meditation for becoming "smarter, one breath at a time" in "How to

Sharpen Your Mind," January 16, 2006), and through their use by people searching for relief of pain and stress, there should be an urgent call from within the university for the integration of practices that can complement critical thinking and help students live in a more-complex world with clarity and commitment.

Support for the following initiatives (and others I have not thought of) will take us to the next level:

- publications that expand both the breath and depth of our understanding of contemplative education;
- conferences and meetings that build the network;
- exploration of distance-learning and enhanced digital contemplative methods;
- models of contemplative educational institutions; high profile programs like one that Hal Roth is now proposing at Brown; scholarships for students to majoring contemplative studies;
- fellowships for doctoral students and professors to expand the contemplative curriculum; and
- research on mediation's effects on the cognitive and social factors of higher education.

And a few words would help from our contemplative president about the importance in a 21rst century democracy of flexible, adaptive, coherent, compassionate, energized, engaged, and stable, that is, contemplative, citizens if we are to sustain and care for this country and this fragile planet.

Notes

Epstein, M. 2004. *Thoughts without a Thinker,* New York: Basic Books.

Goleman, D. 1995. *Emotional Intelligence*, New York: Bantam Books.

Hart, Tobin. 2001. *From Information to Transformation: Education for the Evolution of Consciousness*, New York: Peter Lang.

Hill, Christopher, ed. "Contemplative Practices and Education," *Teachers College Record*, Vol. 108, No. 9, September 2009.

James, William. 1890/2007. *Principles of Psychology*, New York: Cosimo Classics.

Langer, E. 1997. *The Power of Mindful Learning*, Cambridge, MA: Da Capo Press.

O'Reilly, M. 1998. *Radical Presence: Teaching as a Contemplative Practice*, Portsmouth, NH: Boynton/Cook.

Palmer, P., and Zajonc, A. 2010. *The Heart of Higher Education*, San Francisco: Jossey-Bass.

Scott, David K., et al. 2006. *Integrative Learning and Action: A Call to Wholeness*, New York: Peter Lang.

Siegel, D. 2007. *The Mindful Brain*, New York: Norton.

Trungpa, Chogyam. 2003. *Training the Mind and Cultivating Loving-Kindness*, Boston: Shambhala.

Varela, F., Thompson, E., Rosch, E. 1993. *Embodied Mind*, Cambridge, MA: MIT Press.

Zajonc, A. 2010. *Meditation as Contemplative Inquiry*, Great Barrington, MA: Lindisfarne Books.

CONTEMPLATIVE HIGHER EDUCATION: A CASE STUDY OF NAROPA UNIVERSITY

Susan Burggraf

Background

> Naropa University was founded in 1974 by Chögyam
> Trungpa, Rinpoche, a Tibetan Buddhist meditation mas-
> ter, scholar, and artist... With the founding of Naropa,
> [he] realized his vision of creating a university with a Bud-
> dhist heritage that would combine contemplative studies
> with traditional Western scholarly and artistic disciplines.
> (Naropa University Self Study 2009–2010)

Naropa was accredited in 1984 with three masters programs in Buddhist
Studies, Contemplative Psychotherapy, and Dance Therapy in addition to six
upper division undergraduate degree completion majors. The full four-year
undergraduate curriculum began in 1999.

In Fall 2009, Naropa enrolled 592 graduate students in MA (Somatic Psychology, Contemplative Psychotherapy, Environmental Leadership, Contemplative Education, Religious Studies and others), MFA (in Contemporary
Theater and Writing and Poetics), and MDIv programs. The largest department is Transpersonal Counseling Psychology with concentrations in Counseling, Wilderness Therapy and Art Therapy. There are 464 undergraduate
students in eleven majors (including Contemplative Psychology, Interdisciplinary Studies, Peace Studies, Early Childhood Education, Environmental
Studies, Music, Performance, Visual Arts, Writing and Literature, Traditional
Eastern Arts and Religious Studies).

Contemplative inquiry is central to Naropa's identity as a university both
in terms of curricula and in terms of the community life among students,
staff and faculty. Naropa has always recruited its members from diverse contemplative traditions while rooted in the Shambhala tradition, which was
also founded by Chögyam Trungpa, Rinpoche, as a secularized integration of
many of the practices of the Kagyu and Nyingma lineages of Tibetan Buddhism as well as the indigenous Bön tradition of Tibet with forms also drawn
from Japanese, British, and American traditions. The founder intended that

Naropa University be deeply respectful of the plurality of wisdom lineages found in the world's cultures and religions. These sensibilities are reflected in the university's mission statement:

> Inspired by the rich intellectual and experiential traditions of East and West, Naropa University is North America's leading institution of contemplative education.
>
> Naropa recognizes the inherent goodness and wisdom of each human being. It educates the whole person, cultivating academic excellence and contemplative insight in order to infuse knowledge with wisdom. The university nurtures in its students a lifelong joy in learning, a critical intellect, the sense of purpose that accompanies compassionate service to the world, and the openness and equanimity that arise from authentic insight and self-understanding. Ultimately, Naropa students explore the inner resources needed to engage courageously with a complex and challenging world, to help transform that world through skill and compassion, and to attain deeper levels of happiness and meaning in their lives.
>
> Drawing on the vital insights of the world's wisdom traditions, the university is simultaneously Buddhist-inspired, ecumenical and nonsectarian. Naropa values ethnic and cultural differences for their essential role in education. It embraces the richness of human diversity with the aim of fostering a more just and equitable society and an expanded awareness of our common humanity.
>
> A Naropa education—reflecting the interplay of discipline and delight—prepares its graduates both to meet the world as it is and to change it for the better.

In keeping with this meeting's theme of Contemplative Practice in America, I will give an overview of the many ways that contemplative practice permeates Naropa's activities and a glimpse of the faculty's diverse definitions and methods of contemplative education.

Guiding Questions

Describe the demographics of those who participate in contemplative practice in this sector. Please include, where available, information on the number of practitioners as well as their age, gender, education, and ethnicity. Have the demographics changed over the past twenty-five years? Please provide citations if references are available.

Naropa's community of faculty, staff and students include practitioners of many contemplative wisdom traditions including (but not limited to) various Buddhist traditions (e.g., Insight Meditation, various lineages of Zen and Tibetan Buddhism, among others)—with many practitioners from the founding tradition of Shambhala. There are many Jewish, Christian (e.g., Roman Catholic, Quaker, Unity Church etc.), Hindu, and Pagan practitioners and practice opportunities from various practice groups within these traditions as well as an increasing presence of Muslim contemplative practitioners. The Religious Studies department offers courses in many of these contemplative traditions.

Naropa's current students come from more than 45 of states and several countries. A large majority is white, and reflecting national trends, more than half are female. Recruiting students, faculty and staff from diverse racial and ethnic groups is a high priority at Naropa and slow progress is evident. The CIRP inventory indicates that for the vast majority of Naropa undergraduate students, the university is more than 500 miles from their permanent home, they graduated from a public high school, and Naropa was their first choice college. The number of Naropa students eligible for Pell grants is greater than the national average. A 2008 survey indicates that approximately 11% identified as Buddhist, 22 % Jewish, 22% Christian, and 33% as having no religious affiliation.

Describe how you define or use the term, "contemplative practice."

While there are many manifestations of contemplative practice in Naropa's complex pluralistic community, the common ground is found in the cultivation of active attention, mindfulness, embodied awareness, and the ongoing experiential distinction among perception, thought and emotion. Discerning the basic difference between the immediacy and aliveness of non-conceptual direct experience and the mental verbal mediation that usually accompanies it is crucial for contemplative inquiry. As Robert Spellman, a faculty member in Visual Arts is fond of saying, "It's the difference between reading the menu and eating the meal." Another important element of contemplative practice at Naropa is cultivation of a mind that is both precise and vast, which is reflected in the phrase in the university mission statement "the interplay of discipline and delight." You might say that these are practices until they become habitual qualities of a mind that is flexible, self aware and spacious. Equally, the cultivation of compassion and a continuous ongoing appreciation of the interdependence of all beings are highlighted in the many practices in which the Naropa community engages. Compassion is one of the ways that the precision mentioned above manifests.

Contemplative practice and insight are the cornerstones of Naropa's curricula at all levels. There is a required undergraduate Contemplative Learning Seminar that introduces the many ways that contemplative inquiry is used in academic inquiry. Between 2006 and 2009, I conducted a study of definitions and methods of contemplative education among Naropa faculty using interviews from which I extracted a list of themes that focus groups of faculty participants organized into a taxonomy. The results revealed three broad levels of definitions and practices. Initially, we labeled these: outer, inner, and innermost (or inspirational). Specific pedagogical methods rooted in contemplative inquiry were identified in the following areas: perceptual, embodied, intellectual, emotional, social and community. As we worked with the interview themes and continued to discuss them, we realized that the terms "inner" and "outer" were insufficient because they seem like opposites and because they imply direction (similar to a geographical sense of "here" and "there"). My research group has now replaced them with the terms *doing, becoming,* and *being,* which in their mature form operate simultaneously. The *doing* aspect includes techniques (e.g., contemplative academic inquiry of holding paradox, kinesthetic awareness practices, critical thinking, examining assumptions, valuing ambiguity, deep listening, willingness to have ones view disturbed while maintaining curiosity, etc.); *becoming* captures the inner transformation of values and motivation, engagement on the level of identity, and how oneself and ones relationships are changed by engaging in contemplative inquiry; and *being* is the self-existing sense of goodness, mystery, the spaciousness of mind that comes from relaxation into the inevitability of the moment, the sense of aliveness, sacredness, and the existential ground of aliveness. When they are integrated, these three—*doing, becoming,* and *being*—constitute a holistic education that rests on the foundation of contemplative inquiry. Through the course of their journey at Naropa, students become increasingly fluent in simultaneously integrating and distinguishing these three aspects of experience.

"...[T]he relationships between and among ...contemplative education, contemplative practice, and contemplative pedagogy (and in the case of staff, contemplative administration)..." are the focus of lively inquiry at Naropa:

> It is our contention that meditation practice can strengthen ones capacities for open-minded, creative and critical examination of premises, evidence, and experience; deepen listening skills that are at the heart of learning; increase capacities to embody openness to new perspectives; and transform the relationship between the student and the world. Admittedly, these connections between practice and the classroom can sometimes be superficial or tenuous, none of which is our view of contemplative education. For example, a class that begins with a few minutes of silent sitting and then does not connect this experience to the subsequent lecture and discussion is not, in our view, contemplative pedagogy. To the extent that contemplative practice contributes to, and is integrated with, academic content or disciplinary methods and bodies of knowledge, the University's mission is served (Naropa University Self Study 2009–2010).

What specific contemplative practices are most commonly used in this sector?

Contemplative practices that are popular in the Naropa community include sitting meditation (with many variations of technique), the compassion practice of exchanging self and other (tonglen), lovingkindness, walking meditation, tai chi, yoga, aikido, dharma arts (e.g., ikebana), "aimless wandering," mudra space awareness practices, maitri meditation (working with the various energies embedded in human nature), mindfulness of sound and other sensation, the contemplative inquiry practices of Madhyamika logic, contemplative dance and movement practices, and many others.

Each semester there is a Community Practice Day at Naropa when no classes are held and offices are closed so that all faculty, staff and students can come together to do contemplative practices (there's a menu of many different practices in different locations) and then share a meal. In addition, there are some common practices that punctuate the life of the university including a pause and bow to each other at the beginning and end of meetings and classes, mindfulness bell, the construction of a community spontaneous poem (using the principle of "first thought best thought") at Convocation, among others.

Contemplative practice at Naropa could also be described as turning values into verbs that can be practiced in the course of daily life; this is common among many faculty, students and staff. For example, the value of nonviolence can become a practice where one might view ones inner life with kindness. Or the intention to be of benefit to others might be practiced while walking across the parking lot at the end of the day and mentally 'dedicating the merit' of the day to all who are suffering. Some practices may be difficult to explain such as the practice of "no hope, no fear" or easy to explain but difficult to do such as maintaining continuous mindfulness of the body and opening the heart in difficult moments. Naropa's community is graced by several long term practitioners (with decades of deep practice in retreat and daily life) who convey a quality of openness and equanimity that is palpable and contagious even in the tightest of circumstances. As someone who is fairly new to Naropa (since 2005), I am continually inspired by encounters with this quality of mind that is so open it's ambient.

Describe the development of contemplative practice in this sector over the past twenty-five years. How have these evolved or been adapted over the past twenty-five years?

Over the past twenty-five years, the Naropa community has become increasingly more diverse in terms of religious and spiritual traditions among faculty, staff and students and we have met the opportunities and challenges that arise from diversity with varying moments of openness, curiosity, overwhelm, compassionate engagement, mutual learning and misunderstanding. The Naropa community frequently explores diversity issues both inside the classroom and in Town Halls and other community-wide forums with a focus on our need to meet our growing diversity with increasing fluency and understanding. The paradox of becoming both simpler as contemplative practices mature us and more complex in our capacity to meet a complex and changing world is alive in ones daily experience at Naropa.

Within particular academic disciplines, contemplative methods are emerging and adapting to meet the growing curricular needs. For example, the field of somatic psychology, which includes dance and movement therapies, engages embodied inquiry into psychological problems such as trauma, eating disorders, depression and many other challenging psychological conditions in ways that incorporate new knowledge in the field of somatic intelligence and neuroscience. The new undergraduate major in peace studies includes learning outcomes of proficiency in several practices of conflict resolution and compassionate engagement with community and individual challenges that arise from inter-group conflict. The environmental studies department's curricula on both the graduate and undergraduate levels include working with environmental degradation and environmental racism by adapting traditional compassion practices to include ecosystems, cultivating a view of sacred world, a sense of place and pilgrimage.

In the area of assessment, Naropa is beginning to develop methods to evaluate students' progress and overall program success in contemplative learning goals such as compassionate engagement, self awareness, and many others. This is an area of rapid development for the Naropa faculty as we build on the success with assessment that was recently acknowledged in our reaccreditation site visit. One well-established assessment technique that has been part of Naropa's pedagogy since the beginning is the Warrior Exam, a group oral exam where students take turns asking and answering questions from the perspective of having practiced and eventually embodied the answers. Over the years the faculty has developed and continuously improved on grading rubrics that make this practice rigorous and transparent to students.

What organizations have developed to support contemplative practice in this sector?

The Center for Contemplative Mind in Society
International Association of Buddhist Universities (iabu.org)
The University of Michigan Contemplative Jazz program
Brown's Contemplative Studies Initiative
California Institute for Integral Studies
Naropa University
Khyentse Foundation
The Lenz Foundation
Contact Program at SIT (Paula Green)
Nitartha Institute
And others

What are the key trends, opportunities and challenges facing contemplative practice in this sector in the coming decades? To what extent do you agree with the notion that a larger contemplative movement is emerging in America? What does contemplative practice in your setting contribute to such a movement? What in your opinion would be needed to nurture the ground and development of a contemplative movement in America?

While we have begun to make progress, it is important that we continue to develop techniques and instruments to assess the contemplative learning outcomes of Naropa's graduate and undergraduate curricula so that we can better communicate with mainstream academic disciplines and institutions. In order for the power of contemplative inquiry to be understood by faculty and administrators in higher education, we need to demonstrate its effectiveness both in enhancing learning within the disciplines and by adding depth and engagement in areas such as gaining insight into the big questions, embodied understanding, capacity for compassionate engagement and deep listening, self awareness, and many others. In a similar vein, it is crucial at Naropa that we make more rapid progress in moving beyond anecdotal understanding of contemplative developmental paths to systematic research.

As contemplative higher education is now well established, it is important to share experience and insight across institutions on best practices. The annual conferences of the Center for Contemplative Mind in Society are providing such opportunities. Now that the field of contemplative higher education in North America has a few decades of experience, many faculty are examining the relationship between on the one hand their contemplative work (in teaching, writing, and their own deepening contemplative practice) and on the other, their work within their academic discipline. For some fields (e.g., the creative arts, transpersonal psychology, etc.) the contemplative and the academic work are quite compatible. In terms of my field of developmental psychology, the fit is awkward and I increasingly realize that contemplative inquiry challenges the field's assumptions (e.g., about human nature). For many of us, we developed within our academic field and our contemplative practice community separately; it is generative to see what becomes of each (and what has become of us) as we bring those two streams of inquiry together. I am grateful for the opportunity to explore these issues with my Naropa faculty colleagues, with colleagues from the Center for Contemplative Mind in Society, and from Mount Holyoke and Bowdoin Colleges where I got my start. A journal of contemplative studies is needed to broaden these explorations beyond the interpersonal both as a way to create a formal enduring meeting ground and to invite other voices and views.

One challenge in the field of contemplative higher education is that of remaining connected to the deep well of spirituality found in the various wisdom traditions while making contemplative practice available in secular settings. Secularization enables us to learn from many traditions, develop a shared language, prevent marginalization of contemplative inquiry, make it accessible to people without invoking religious beliefs or membership, and acknowledge the basically human function of cultivating mindfulness. But just as with religious pluralism generally, it is crucial to many of us to both be rooted within a tradition that provides methods, language and community in order to deepen understanding while also practicing openness, deep curiosity, engagement and not knowing when exploring other traditions. A related challenge is to continue to examine the varying roles and purposes of spiritual teachers and college professors. This is something that the Naropa faculty has explored for over thirty years, and can offer insight and broader exploration to the higher education community. Also, as contemplative inquiry becomes more well established in higher education, will college professors increasingly develop the capacity to teach contemplative techniques in the classroom? What are the faculty development opportunities that are needed to support students in their contemplative practice? This training is available to Naropa faculty through the Mindfulness Instructor Training program with its system of Mindfulness Instructors who are widely available for consultation. This is a contribution that experienced Naropa faculty can make to the higher education community.

An ongoing opportunity is found in the inherent juxtaposition of on the one hand the simplicity or oneness that is found through contemplative practice and on the other, meeting the increasing complexity of our organizations and communities—both local and global. Contemplative higher education needs to express the insights and techniques that come from the encounter between the academic disciplines and contemplative practices because these new hybrids can offer insight into living in a complex and diverse world. In other words, contemplative higher education can offer public intellectuals and artists who offer discovered methods and insights into living simple and complex in ways where neither diminishes the other.

ENVISIONING THE FUTURE OF K – 12 CONTEMPLATIVE EDUCATION

Patricia Jennings and David I. Rome

The Vision

> NOW is the moment . . . there's a growing recognition that contemplative education addresses a missing dimension in the lives of children who are increasingly stressed out by schools narrowly driven by test results. This burgeoning movement needs leadership. The Garrison Institute could provide support for pioneers in the field, act as a catalyst for high quality programs, and help jump-start a growing movement that can bring some balance and resilience to the lives of children.
>
> Dr. Jerome Murphy
> Harvard Graduate School of Education

The Garrison Institute envisions a future in which contemplative approaches are widely used in mainstream educational settings and provide a foundation for building inner strengths and skills—such as attention, awareness, self-regulation, reflection, and the ability to transcend narrow self-interest—that help children become resilient, capable, engaged and compassionate adults.

As Daniel Siegel describes in his book *The Mindful Brain*, recent science validates the positive effects of contemplative activity in strengthening key functions associated with the prefrontal cortex: regulating body systems, balancing emotions, attuning to others, modulating fear, responding flexibly, and insight, empathy, intuition and morality. All children possess these abilities as innate potentialities. Just as physical exercise builds strength, flexibility and endurance, contemplative practice builds inner strength, resilience, a sense of purpose, and the capacity for continuous learning in the face of all kinds of life challenges and changes.

The Need

> So much of school experience focuses on acquisition of important skills and knowledge regarding the outer world. We learn to read, to write, to calculate numbers. Perhaps this approach stems from our educational system's emphasis on a curriculum of content rather than one that focuses on the process of cultivating the mind itself. Wouldn't it make sense to teach children about the mind itself and make reflection become a fundamental part of basic education? If teachers became aware that attuning to the self, being mindful, can alter the brain's ability to create flexibility and self-observation, empathy and morality, wouldn't it be worth the time to teach such reflective skills, first to teachers and then in age appropriate ways to the students themselves?
>
> Daniel Siegel, *The Mindful Brain*

In the last 40 or 50 years, schooling has become central to American society in a way that it never was before. For many Americans, school is the only socializing institution that can impart the kind of long-term values and goals that family, church and community once did.

Even as the expectation and demand that out schools to perform socialization functions are increasing, their ability to do so is getting undermined by a severe attrition problem and lack of resources. Far too many children—40 to 50 percent in most urban districts—do not graduate from high school. Teachers suffer from dropout rates almost as high. For those who stay, teachers' confidence level is under assault.

While Social-Emotional Learning (SEL) is now an accepted and widely used term, the larger goal has yet to be attained: bringing the deeper parts of the inner lives of children, teachers, and parents into K-12 education. Achieving this requires an approach which is not threatening or alienating, but rather helps sustain teachers, students and families, drawing them closer together in caring communities of learning.

Our experience suggests that contemplative practices can help. They heighten awareness that people are interrelated, help bridge differences, and lead naturally to a sense of togetherness and compassion that facilitates and sustains community.

The State of the Field

There are three major dimensions of contemplative life. The one that most people think of is contemplative practice—the consistent performance of meditation, prayer, mindful walking, etc. But for a practice to be meaningful, it must arise from a contemplative mindset, philosophy or meaning context. To live that mindset, to apply contemplation in practical ways to one's daily life, it helps to be part of a community of practitioners, supporting one another and sharing a sense of connectedness and interdependence.

All three of these dimensions—practice, context and community—are discernible parts of the emerging field of Contemplative Education. For example on a macro level, advocates may bring educators, policy experts and stakeholders together to actually experience contemplative practices themselves, as one way to encourage education policy reforms. On a micro level, researchers address the meaning context for contemplation—for example, how can contemplative methods be applied in educational settings in developmentally appropriate ways that respect the needs and abilities of children? Teachers work at the "transactional" level at which the macro policy ideas and micro methodological questions must be combined into daily practice. This requires what could be called a community of contemplative education practice—teachers, principals, researchers, advocates, contemplative practitioners and others.

On each of these levels, Contemplative Education remains an emerging field. Surveying its topology one finds more unexplored areas than explored ones. Research is in its infancy. Model programs exist but are not yet connected to the elements that normally comprise a recognizable field: shared identity and knowledge base, leadership, resources, infrastructure for collaboration and systemic support.

While these elements remain under construction, there is some question whether Contemplative Education can be called a field per se. There are also questions concerning how it relates to existing fields and trends in education and culture, such as the Social Emotional Learning (SEL) movement, or various efforts to integrate spirituality into mainstream education without running afoul of church-state issues.

There are also many strategic questions. Where can Contemplative Education gain leverage in the existing educational landscape? Should it attempt to fly above or below the radar? Should it focus on constituencies that are already inclined in its direction or take on the educational system as a whole?

Questions of framing and language are critical areas for further work. Public health and wellness may be an effective—and fundable—policy framework for introducing contemplative activities into schools. Linking Contemplative Education to academic achievement has obvious political advantages, however as yet there is little hard evidence to support that hypothesis.

Among leaders in the field, there is an ongoing debate between those who feel that any reference to spirituality, either explicit or implied, should be avoided and those who feel a strong need to find ways to discuss inner life and meaning outside the context of religious belief. Maria Montessori and Rudolf Steiner have been cited as examples of the latter. When writing or talking about Contemplative Education, there is a delicate balance to be struck between avoiding words that risk transgressing boundaries or offending sensibilities on the one hand, and finding apt words that convey what the field is, and is not.

It is not the same as Social Emotional Learning, though experts agree that Contemplative Education adds value to SEL. At a Garrison Institute meeting of field leaders, Mark Greenberg of Penn State put forward a two-part framework that differentiates Contemplative Education from SEL as conventionally understood. The first part relates to *orientation*. As distinct from SEL, Contemplative Education is oriented towards:

1. A greater focus on adults and on the embodiment of an already implicit ethical framework;
2. A worldview based on interdependence;
3. A view of "basic humanness" that elicits compassion for all people regardless of differences.

A second factor that differentiates Contemplative Education from SEL is the acquisition of specific contemplative *skills,* such as:

1. Attention—the ability to voluntarily shift and sustain one's focus of attention. As William James said, "The faculty of voluntarily bringing back a wandering attention over and over again is the very root of judgment, character and will. An education which should improve this faculty would be the education par excellence."
2. Meta-cognition—the ability to reflect on cognition and have awareness vs. automaticity of thought. This awareness encompasses emotions and an understanding that emotions are something to be aware of but are impermanent and insubstantial, like thoughts.

3. Positive affect—viewing the attainment of wisdom as an antidote to suffering, cultivating positive affect through consistent practice. As the Dalai Lama often points out, the mind is like a muscle—the more it lies in certain states, the more it will seek them.

Nurturing a New Movement

Since its founding in 2003, the Garrison Institute has designated education as one of three priority social change fields that could benefit from contemplative-based approaches, and through which contemplative practices and ideas could be further disseminated into the wider culture. The Institute's role is not to lead a Contemplative Education movement, but rather to nurture it by supporting the leaders, providing a network and a collaborative hub for those pursuing high-quality, evidence-based work in the field.

To that end, the Institute's Initiative on Contemplation and Education (ICE) promotes cross-fertilization of ideas, initiating and/or participating in research partnerships among scientists and other experts in education, psychology, human development and neuroscience. These partnerships explore developmentally appropriate ways to integrate contemplative methods into classroom curricula from pre-school through high school. Through convening, dissemination and advocacy, ICE promotes the introduction, use and institutionalization of contemplative methods for teachers and children, in school settings and within the broader educational and scientific communities.

ICE has made significant contributions to the emergence of Contemplative Education as a field of study and practice. In 2005, we published the first mapping survey of the field, providing an overview of emerging practices and science, and offering a preliminary theoretical framework. We then convened many of the leaders the report identified for the first Contemplation and Education Symposium. The report and symposium essentially launched Contemplative Education as a discrete field. A series of six more cross-disciplinary forums followed, each assembling leading researchers and practitioners around specific themes, written up and disseminated more widely in reports. In 2008 we held our first public symposium on "Developmental Issues in Contemplative Education," attended by 93 researchers, education leaders and classroom teachers from North America and Europe.

ICE also works to introduce Contemplative Education in mainstream educational and psychological settings. Our CARE (Cultivating Awareness and Resilience in Education) teacher training curriculum has been piloted in several school districts across the U.S. and is currently being refined and tested under a multi-year federal grant from the Institute of Educational Sciences. We present ICE's work frequently in published articles and at universities and major international conferences including AERA, APA, SRCD, and SPR. Our collaboration with CASEL, Dr. Jennings' participation in the SEL Special Interest Group at AERA, and a peer-reviewed article by Dr. Jennings and Mark Greenburg on "The Pro-Social Classroom" helped frame Contemplative Education in the context of Social and Emotional Learning. The attached fact sheet contains a current list of ICE articles and presentations.

We are actively fostering the development of a community of Contemplative Education practitioners and researchers aligned with a common purpose and set of core values. In order to bring the new field to a state of coherence, credibility, visibility and widespread practice, the Institute and the ICE Leadership Council have identified six necessary building blocks or "field elements" that must be put in place. They serve as a template and a set of milestones for ICE's long-term (10–20 year) strategy:

1. Building the knowledge base
2. Developing infrastructure for collaboration and information exchange
3. Codifying standards of practice
4. Generating resources (funding, etc.)
5. Strengthening the workforce and leadership
6. Cultivating the grassroots and policy climate

These six elements are both sequential and overlapping. The art of field-building is in orchestrating all of them in an organic and balanced way. The Garrison Institute provides a central hub for coordinated planning, knowledge sharing, reflection and reporting for leaders involved in all aspects of developing the field. We are encouraged by the fact that so many of the most respected practitioners have accepted our invitations to partner and share in this venture.

Field Leaders

ICE's core visioning and coordinating team is the ICE Leadership Council, chaired by Mark Greenberg, director of the Prevention Research Center at Pennsylvania State University. Last fall the Council was restructured and enlarged to include a broad spectrum of contemplative education pioneers and organizational leaders, including Linda Lantieri (Inner Resilience Program),

Arthur Zajonc (Amherst College and the Center for Contemplative Mind in Society), Pamela Seigle (Courage and Renewal), Susan Kaiser-Greenland (Innerkids), Trish Broderick (Learning to BREATHE program), Dave Sluyter (Fetzer Institute), Peggy McCardle (NIH/National Institute on Child Health and Development), Mark Wilding (PassageWorks), and Jerome Murphy (Harvard Graduate School of Education). They join a distinguished group of founding Council members including Mark Greenberg, Adele Diamond (University of British Columbia), Richard Brown (Naropa University), and Liz Robertson (NIH/National Institute on Drug Abuse). Biographies of council members are posted online[1].

The ICE Senior Advisory Board is a group of distinguished leaders who endorse our work and are available for high-level guidance. These include Daniel Siegel, Paul Ekman, Peter Senge, Clancy Blair and Alan Wallace.

Next Steps

Today we are witnessing rapid growth in contemplative education programs and in basic and applied research to study their efficacy. The Institute works to insure that new research findings are disseminated to educators and policy-makers, that they inform the development of evidence-based standards of practice, and that gaps in the scientific literature are identified and addressed.

During the next two years we plan to update and extensively revise the 2005 field mapping study and to conduct a new mapping study of research. Taken together, the two surveys will give essential guidance to educators, administrators and policy-makers to begin developing evidence-based standards of practice. They will also help target new areas for further research.

As the field grows and the work becomes scientifically validated and more widely known, we anticipate that schools and other institutions will come to the table with resources to further develop the field in their own settings. As more contemplative education programs receive certification through CASEL, they will also increasingly qualify for federal funding of public school programs.

In the long term, field leaders agree that moving the field forward will require further development in the following four basic areas:

Networking People, Refining Ideas

More exchange is needed between researchers, practitioners and others to further define the scope and context of Contemplative Education. Does it include movement practices like yoga and chi gong, art-making and art ap-preciation, nature observation, etc.? Or is it more a question of the qualities of *intention* and *attention* brought to activities of all sorts? Should contemplative practices be presented as autonomous mind-training methods or should they be introduced within an explicit philosophy, worldview and/or ethical framework?

Further, more inclusive dialogue will help evolve answers to such key questions. There is a continued need for expert forums and public symposia which include a broader range of presenters, particularly classroom teachers, contemplatives, and younger stakeholders. These gatherings should showcase evidence-based practices and foster networks that connect researchers with the people doing the work at the transactional level, building face-to-face relationships that can be extended virtually. The Garrison Institute is currently upgrading its IT capacity and creating a web-based hub for a Contemplative Education learning community, offering interactive communications and document sharing.

A Broad Research Agenda

CASEL (Collaborative for Academic, Social and Emotional Learning) has relied on science-based evidence when advocating SEL-oriented policy changes. But there is currently a paucity of scientific research on Contemplative Education. Effective advocacy for it will require systematic study of a range of specific contemplative applications for teachers, children and parents, distinct from SEL interventions. When possible, sub-components should be isolated and measured to determine which aspects of contemplative training are most effective in achieving desired outcomes. Research should also address the developmental needs of children in relation to different methodologies, as well as the personal and professional needs of teachers, administrators and parents.

Deeper Inquiry into Context

There is a need to develop a framework for the deeper study of specific contemplative practices within the K-12 educational context.

Adult contemplative practices are rarely applied to children in the cultures where they originate. They cannot be applied wholesale to children, in fact they may not be appropriate for children at all. It is especially problematic to assume that secularized contemplative programs designed for adult clinical populations can be directly applied to youth in educational settings.

On the other hand, contemplative interventions have shown promise in early education. Things as simple as having children pause before giving a response can help build self-regulatory capacity. Developmentally appropriate contemplative practices have been used in alternative educational settings with great success (Montessori, Waldorf, Friends, etc.). Many of these employ sensory modalities and movement including art, dance, music, etc. Before a section studying fish, for example, children might gather around an aquarium or fishbowl and observe in silence, attending with all of their senses alert. Some alternative educational systems also enhance attention and learning by incorporating contemplation into the way teachers teach.

Such practices deserve further study, taking into account the developmental stage of the child and the nature of the classroom context.

Messaging

There is a need for a general statement articulating what Contemplative Education is and what it is not. The field also needs an informal "elevator speech" that can quickly convey its essence to non-initiates. Finding the right language might entail holding focus groups with administrators, teachers, parents, business leaders, congressional aides, etc. This might be an area in which the Contemplative Education and Social Emotional Learning fields can share costs since they have overlapping concerns. Language used in the new field of "positive psychology" may be relevant.

In communications the key question is, "who is the audience?" In the search for effective ways to communicate about Contemplative Education, the key question is "Where are the leverage points for building this field and how do we address them?" Different constituencies, for example teachers vs. health practitioners, may respond differently to the same language. We may need different language to convey the same message to the general public, school boards, specific opinion leaders or "early adopters." We also need to develop a vocabulary that is welcoming to different faith traditions, as well as age-appropriate ways of talking to children and adolescents.

Conclusion

This is an exciting, formative time in the field of Contemplative Education. There are growing numbers of teachers introducing contemplative methods to support their students' learning. At the same time, there are still many more questions than answers, and not much evidence to form a basis for this work—yet. But the field is ripe for discovery and development.

GARRISON INSTITUTE

Fact Sheet: Field Development in Contemplative Education

The Garrison Institute Initiative on Contemplation and Education
June 2010

Goal:

To promote the widespread use of contemplative approaches in mainstream educational settings for the purpose of developing children's inner strength and skills, including attention, awareness, self-regulation, reflection, and the ability to transcend narrow self-interest.

Objectives:

a. Promote cross-fertilization of ideas and initiate and/or participate in research partnerships
b. Engage in dissemination and advocacy activities

Programs, Presentations and Publications:

- Contemplation and Education Symposium (April, 2005)
- Attention and Behavior (April, 2006)
- Awareness, Concentration and Social-Emotional Learning (November, 2006)
- Awareness and Concentration in Teacher Professional Development (January, 2007)
- Assessment for Social, Emotional, and Academic Learning with Preschool and Elementary School Children (October, 2007)
- Developmental Issues in Contemplative Education Symposium (April, 2008)

- Envisioning the Future of Contemplative Education (October, 2008)
- Exploring Methodological Issues in Contemplative Education Research: A Focus on Teachers (February, 2009)
- Mindful Parenting "Science Meeting" (September, 2010)

Initiative Director Tish Jennings recently presented papers at
- Society for Research in Child Development (SRCD)
- American Psychological Association (APA)
- American Education Research Association (AERA)
- Society for Prevention Research
- Third International Conference of PATHS (Promoting Alternative Thinking Strategies) (keynote address)

Articles published focusing on contemplative education:
- Article about contemplative education featuring an interview with Tish Jennings in the *Shambhala Sun* ("Please Help me Learn Who I Am," January 2007)
- Article about contemplative education featuring an interview with Tish Jennings in *Greater Good* magazine ("Mindful Kids, Peaceful Schools," Summer 2007)
- Article about CARE featuring an interview with Tish Jennings in *Buddhadharma* ("Teaching the Teachers," Spring 2008)
- Article by Tish Jennings on contemplative education in a special issue of *New Directions for Youth Development* ("Contemplative Education and Youth Development," July 2008)
- An extensive peer-reviewed article authored by Tish and Mark Greenberg published in the professional journal *Review of Educational Research* ("The Prosocial Classroom: Teacher Social and Emotional Competence in Relation to Child and Classroom Outcomes," Winter 2009)
- Article by Tish Jennings on contemplative education in *Mandala* ("Sitting at School: The Case for Contemplative Education," October-December, 2008)

- Article about CARE published in the *Shambhala Sun* ("The Mindful Society: Teach Our Children Well," September 2009)
- Article about CARE published in *Edutopia* ("CARE Program Teaches Educators to Manage Their Emotions," December 2009)
- Article about Garrison Institute published in *Business Education Forum* ("The Garrison Institute: Bringing Mindfulness to Education," April 2010)
- Article by Tish Jennings in *Greater Good* ("Mindful Education," May 2010)

For more field resources see our website: http://www.garrisoninstitute.org/index.php?option=com_content&view=article&id=229&Itemid=195.

Notes

1   http://www.garrisoninstitute.org/index.php?option=com_content&view=category&id=87:leadership-council&layout=blog&Itemid=80.

CONTEMPLATIVE PRACTICE AND HEALING TRAUMA

Deborah Rozelle

Introduction

This paper surveys the potentials and challenges of using contemplative practices to help heal and transform the debilitating effects of psychological trauma. It represents work at the Garrison Institute's Initiative for Transforming Trauma (ITT), and is built on a representative sample of prominent contemplative methods, models and programs currently being used to address trauma. This paper is the first published fruit of an extensive mapping survey of the intersection of contemplative practices and psychological trauma under way since 2008, and it references work presented at a private professional forum on the use of contemplative practices in the trauma field held at the Garrison Institute in June 2009.

We begin by explaining key concepts of psychological trauma, followed by a working definition of contemplative practices to support analysis of their application to trauma. Next we present example methods, models, and programs that represent some of the most prominent current uses of contemplative practice in healing trauma. We conclude with reflections stimulated by the examples and by the broader field, and a preliminary summary matrix to capture some of the most important features of the various methods, models, and programs.

What Is Trauma?

Psychological trauma, also known as Post-Traumatic Stress Disorder (PTSD) is a worldwide pandemic. On a global scale natural cataclysms, manmade disasters, wars, civil unrest, genocide, economic disasters, oppression and exploitation leave countless living victims in their wake, not only physically injured but psychically damaged by the trauma of violence, poverty, displacement and so on. On a personal level, apart from everyday accidents, disease, loss and separation and other personal problems, more than 2,000,000 cases of domestic abuse are reported in the U.S. each year (American Bar Association 2010) and over 750,000 children are maltreated (US Department of Health and Human Services 2008). A substantial fraction of all people—estimates range from 50 to 90%—will experience traumatic events in their life and 8% of those will get PTSD (Kessler RC 1995; Breslau 1998; Breslau 2009). Over 5 million Americans have PTSD at a given time (NIMH). And many will experience repeated trauma throughout a substantial part of their life, for example a child who is abused or neglected every day or a victim of genocide who lives in constant fear for their life.

What is a traumatic event? In brief, when a person *perceives* an event as *potentially or actually threatening the life or physical or psychic integrity of themselves or someone else*, that event is a trauma. What happens to people who experience a trauma or series of them? The answer depends on the person, the actual events and innumerable other variables, many of which are not well understood. But basically two things can happen. In one, the victim experiences the violence, pain, deprivation or abuse, it ends, they more or less get over it and go on with their life. In the other, they don't get over the trauma, even long after the perceived threat has ended, and it continues to profoundly affect their life. They have *psychological trauma*, *PTSD* (and related disorders). That's an estimated 8% of people who experience a traumatic event (Breslau 1998), substantially more for wars and other extremely violent environments.

Symptoms of Psychological Trauma

What is it like to have psychological trauma, to *not* get over a trauma? It varies, of course, but PTSD potentially affects every domain of a sufferer's life: psychological, emotional, interpersonal, social, occupational, physiological and spiritual/existential. Specific symptoms can include frequent involuntary flashbacks or re-experiencing of the traumatic event, persistent physiological arousal such as increased heart rate, avoidance of stimuli that remind the victim of the trauma, hypervigilance and exaggerated startle response, and many others. More general effects can include loss of interest in former activities, emotional numbing, irritability, difficulty concentrating, loss of core beliefs, self-destructive and impulsive behavior, somatic complaints, guilt, shame, despair, social withdrawal and even dissociation. PTSD sufferers can lose their sense of safety, trust, control and choice. They are more prone to obsessive-compulsive disorder, panic disorder, phobias, depression, substance-abuse and addiction. They are more likely to have interpersonal, marital and occupational problems. In the case of children, psychological trauma can disrupt, distort, or delay the natural developmental trajectory, creating cumulative negative effects.

Not without reason has having PTSD been called hell on earth. The costs of trauma to society are immense, and the resources available to identify and treat its victims are nowhere near adequate. PTSD is difficult to treat. Conventional psychiatric, therapeutic, and psychosocial interventions often fall short. Also, mental health personnel who work with trauma sufferers are significantly prone to develop symptoms of psychological trauma themselves, by their empathic connection with those they serve. This is called *vicarious trauma* (VT), and though it is typically less severe than primary trauma, it can be subtle, easily go undiagnosed, and have far reaching effects. VT extracts a significant and often unrecognized cost on institutions working with trauma victims, not only affecting the personal well-being of workers, but also impairing their effectiveness in helping their clients (Pearlman 1995).

Trauma symptoms are divided into three basic clusters: *hyperarousal, re-experiencing* and *hypoarousal.* Hyperarousal is exaggerated or heightened reactions such as physiological turbulence and reactivity, hypervigilance and exaggerated startle response. Re-experiencing means repetitive replay of the original trauma in literal form, and includes intrusive imagery, nightmares and behavioral reenactment. Technically, re-experiencing is a form of hyperarousal, but because it is so intense and frequent, it is considered a third symptom cluster. Hypoarousal includes two main reactions: numbing and avoidance. Numbing is not being able to feel feelings or the body, or a range of dissociation symptoms from simple disconnection to fragmented identity. Avoidance includes social withdrawal, avoiding external stimuli and internal cues associated with the trauma.

Another way of categorizing trauma symptoms is by the natural defensive responses to life threat: *flee, fight, freeze* or *fold* (usually called "submit and collapse"). *Flee* and *fight* are forms of hyperarousal; *fold* is hypoarousal; *freeze* has elements of both. These defensive postures are adaptive at the time of an actual threat, but are maladaptive when the threat is gone.

In PTSD both hypoarousal and hyperarousal are always present to one extent or another, and re-experiencing always occurs. A trauma sufferer is thus said to have a *window of tolerance* between hypoarousal and hyperarousal, which, if exceeded, leads to significant distressful symptoms and maladaptive behavior. The sufferer has *triggers* regarding this window of tolerance—situations, images, thoughts, feelings and sensations associated with the sufferer's trauma history that elicit the unprocessed traumatic memories and push the sufferer outside their window in one direction or the other. Of course, all people have something like a window of tolerance, but in psychological trauma the window is very much narrowed, the triggers more readily tripped, the reaction much more dramatic, the ensuing suffering much more intense, and the effects on their lives much more debilitating.

Treatment of Psychological Trauma

PTSD is by nature self-perpetuating. Traumatic memories get "stuck" and not eventually placed in their natural, non-threatening context like ordinary memories (Stickgold 2002). Also, because a sufferer is constantly re-experiencing their trauma through dysfunctional episodic memories of the event, they are, in effect, getting re-traumatized, maintaining their symptomology.

Our current understanding of recovery from PTSD is that it requires the sufferer to directly reprocess the maladaptive memories in one way or another, placing them in adaptive context. But if they cannot approach their memories without re-traumatization, how can they heal them?

This conundrum leads to a phase-oriented approach to treating PTSD in which actually confronting traumatic memories is postponed to a second phase. In phase one, called *safety and stabilization*, sufferers first learn skills to reduce both poles of symptoms. They learn to reduce hyperarousal symptoms, for example, with a mental and/or physical *safe place* where they can feel secure from threats in the present. On the hypoarousal side, they might need to bring themselves out of a numbed and/or avoidant state by cultivating tolerance for the pain of re-experiencing the trauma and the ability to know when to stop because the pain is too great.

With phase one skills in hand and symptoms sufficiently reduced, but without having approached the traumatic memories yet, the sufferer and the therapist can begin phase two, *trauma reprocessing*. In this phase, the client faces, reprocesses and if successful depotentiates the traumatic memories so they no longer induce distress. When this has been accomplished, the client can enter the third phase, integration, where they focus on engaging in life.

For PTSD sufferers, therapists, and researchers alike, there is a relatively recent and growing sentiment that the mere absence of symptomology, though welcome, is an insufficient goal. Instead, the former sufferer, having literally come through hell and back to the world, is in an excellent position to strive for formerly unthinkable levels of post-traumatic growth, resilience, well being and flourishing.

Contemplative Practice: A Definition

Integral to a definition of *contemplative practice*, in our view, is its *goal*, which we understand to be the realization of the interconnectedness, oneness or unity of all phenomena, inner and outer, and the concomitant impetus to cherish and care for all beings. Together, these realizations are often spoken of as transcending the individual self. Contemplative practice in simplest terms, then, is any method that promotes that realization of interconnectedness and the impetus to cherish and care for all and work to relieve their suffering.

This is, of course, a lofty goal, one which very few people would readily adopt in full. But any significant attainment in that direction is also an aspiration that defines contemplative practice. In particular, for those of us struggling with everyday life, a worthy goal and prerequisite to higher attainment is wholeness and unity within ourselves along with genuine self-compassion.

Those who suffer from psychological trauma are particularly damaged by the loss of those states. Their inner experience has thorny, intractable islands of constant suffering, sometimes so many that their entire experience is fragmented; their traumatic memories of past danger are cut off from the truth of present safety; they are fearful, shamed, unworthy, powerless and hopeless. Especially for trauma sufferers, therefore, a personal version of the ultimate goal of contemplative practice is the compelling and necessary step.

This definition of contemplative practice at all levels is both personal and, we hope, resonates with the diverse range of contemplative practice across many if not all cultures and ages. It is also informed by the nature of psychological trauma and the challenge of healing from it. The statement of the goal is inspired by the notions of wisdom and compassion in Mahayana Buddhism. We believe, however, that it also connects with theistic traditions in which the godhead represents omniscience, omnipotence and infinite love, and the goal may therefore be expressed in relationship to that godhead.

The fundamental method of contemplative practice at any level is *sustained, focused attention*, motivated by *intention* toward the goal, applied with *skill and help,* to direct and train the energy of mind and/or body. *Focused* attention means that the force of directed energy is strong, not diffuse. *Sustained* attention means placing and holding attention on an object or field for a length of time, not intermittently or momentarily. Together, focusing and sustaining attention provide the power needed to dissolve deeply entrenched patterns of mind and body that block the goal and which cannot be simply willed or reasoned away. Focused, sustained attention also forms new patterns that promote the goal. *Skill and help* in practice means using methods known to be effective, benefiting from experienced helpers, applying the methods conscientiously, observing their effects within oneself, and adjusting as necessary.

There are many ways to direct mental attention and energy by sustained focus on an object or aspect of experience consistent with the goal. Suitable objects of attention span an enormous range across traditions and systems of contemplative practice. This range includes inner experiences such as thoughts and feelings; abstractions such as space, time and impermanence; strong positive wishes, prayers and entreaties; open acceptance of experience; aspects of physical experience such as breath and body; external objects such as sacred images and mandalas; natural objects and scenes and corresponding inner visualizations; sounds such as mantra, chant and song; words such as scriptures, prayers and the verbal objects of Centering Prayer; paradoxical images or concepts such as koans; the nature of consciousness itself, or of the subjective "I"; or even the whole of ones experience. Concentrating on a benefactor, teacher, helper or other admired figure, to connect with, be inspired by and even incorporate their positive qualities, is a class of contemplative practice that appears in most traditions in various forms. Rituals and ceremonies can involve contemplative attention to the extent that the individual participates actively.

We use *attention* metaphorically for the body as well as the mind, meaning a sustained or repetitive, active body activity such as a posture, movement or dance that promotes focused attention of the mind. Methods which direct the body's "attention" include yoga, meditative martial arts such as tai chi, and certain kinds of dance and movement. Some contemplative techniques involve the body and mind together, such as walking meditation and meditation on the breath. But in a larger sense, many contemplative practices address the body and mind as a unitary whole.

In fact, a particularly powerful class of contemplative objects are visualizations of a *mental body* (or *subtle body*), comprising three-dimensional visualized images superimposed on the practitioner's own or another's body that represent the structure and energy of the body-mind complex. Chakras (Sanskrit for wheels) are perhaps the most well-known components of subtle body meditation, but there are other aspects as well. Mental body contemplation is often combined with other objects such as analytical sequences, mantras, mandalas, ideal states and so on. Many Hindu, Buddhist and indigenous traditions contain a fully articulated subtle body system, or psycho-spiritual anatomy, as it were. As we shall discuss, the notion of mental body, or the energy and psychic structure of the body-mind complex, is particularly useful in addressing contemplative methods for healing trauma.

An important class of targets for contemplative attention, less well known but of great value, are sequences of linked ideas. An important feature of Tibetan Buddhism, this is called analytical meditation, and can be used to address both aspects of the goal. An example in the affect realm is developing compassion for others through a sequence of thoughts about the similarity and relationship of self and others. An example of a conceptual analytical meditation is a carefully reasoned, step-by-step exploration of the nature of phenomena to cultivate realization of interdependence. Contemplative practices may also combine objects simultaneously as well as sequentially, like the well-known *tong-len* practice which develops love and compassion by joining attention on the breath with images that represent relieving the suffering of others and giving them joy.

Tong-len also exemplifies another very important class of contemplative object, namely an ideal future state, in this case oneself having the power to bestow joy on others. Imagining or visualizing an ideal future state is particularly exemplified by the Vajrayana Buddhist practice of visualizing oneself as a realized being in an idealized environment, but it can be effective at many levels.

The class of practices known as *mindfulness* are the most widely used and thoroughly studied contemplative practices in psychology, primarily in the form of Mindfulness-Based Stress Reduction (MBSR). Germer and others define *mindfulness* as moment-by-moment awareness, and psychotherapy based on mindfulness adds an element of non-judgementality: "by not judging our experience, we are more likely to see it as it is" (Germer, Siegel et al. 2005). Mindfulness connects with our proposed goal of contemplative practice, as indicated by this quote from John Kabat-Zinn, founder of MBSR: "woven into (mindfulness) is an orientation towards…seeing deeply into the nature of things, which in some way implies, or at least invites, one to see the interconnectedness between the seer and the seen, the object and the subject" (Cullen 2010).

As should be apparent, the variety of objects and methods of contemplative practice defies characterization. It ranges from abstract to concrete, from silence to sound, from no thought to active conceptualization, from inner to outer, from past to present to future, from entreaty to acceptance, across all the senses, from single-pointed to broadly focused, from content-less to complex, and so on.

We believe, therefore, that the essence of contemplative systems and practice lies not in their specific methods and objects, but in the quality of *attention* or directed mental energy. And this quality of directed mental energy is crucial for applying contemplative practices to healing psychological trauma. (van der Kolk 2002).

Example Programs

In the next sections we discuss several example programs using contemplative practices to address psychological trauma. First we treat Yoga and mindfulness, the two explicitly contemplative practices in the body and mind realms, respectively, most used for this purpose today. Next, we take a look at EMDR, a highly successful psychotherapeutic methodology for trauma which, although secular in origin and emphasis, is actually rooted in a number of techniques which are implicitly but firmly contemplative in nature. Finally, we consider multi-modal programs, with emphasis on the Garrison Institute's Wellness Project, which integrates a variety of contemplative practices with secular and educational components to address vicarious trauma in human service workers.

This is not meant to be a comprehensive survey of the field, which though nascent and developing, is already quite extensive. Instead, we hope these representative and important examples of practices, models and programs exemplify the major themes and challenges of applying contemplative practices to trauma treatment as well as the range: modern secular paradigms and methods from ancient contemplative traditions adapted to modern use, explicit vs. implicit use of contemplation, mind vs. body practices, different trauma treatment modalities, and the many ways that contemplative practices intersect the complexities of trauma and its healing.

Yoga

Many contemplative traditions and secular models with contemplative features address mental health by working primarily through the body, movement and sensation. Also, the plethora of current neurobiological work on physiological function provides possible support for exploring "bottom-up" (body-based) mental health treatment models (van der Kolk 2002).

Given the intense body involvement represented in PTSD symptoms, body-based models of intervention are potentially effective models for trauma treatment. Various forms of Yoga are among the body-based systems most used and studied for PTSD to date. For this paper, we consider programs and studies that address PTSD using the active physical components of Yoga, the physical postures and breathing practices, rather than mantra and mindfulness, because the former are the most used and studied for trauma treatment.

The general therapeutic potential for physical yoga are that it can: 1) reduce arousal; 2) facilitate body and breath awareness; 3) facilitate other contemplative practices; 4) provide physical release of subconscious patterns; and 5) offer opportunities for physical mastery, competency, and self regulation (Khalsa 2009). Yoga practices can be very targeted in their effects. For example, poses can have specific positive effects on mood (Shapiro 2004).

The general positive effects of Yoga on stress, depression and anxiety are supported by considerable anecdotal evidence that goes beyond mere physical exercise – everybody seems to know (or be) someone who believes Yoga makes them calmer, less anxious, more productive (Ray 2006). There are also many formal outcome studies documenting these benefits, but also scientific controversy about the quality and standardization of the research on the benefits of Yoga (and of meditation in general). Yet, one of the most critical of such reports (Ospina 2007) did conclude, by meta-analysis of hundreds of studies, that research validated the value of Yoga in reducing stress and anxiety.

The Yoga Program at the Trauma Center at Justice Research Institute (JRI)

The Trauma Center at JRI is a program that provides services to traumatized individuals, offers post-graduate training, consultation, and educational programming in trauma, and conducts studies on trauma's effects and treatment. The founder and director is Dr. Bessel van der Kolk, an internationally recognized leader in the field of psychological trauma.

The Trauma Center is active in studying the application of Yoga to trauma treatment (van der Kolk 2006; Emerson 2009) and developed a gentle, trauma-informed Hatha Yoga protocol for women diagnosed with PTSD, using principles and practices specifically designed for trauma survivors. These include: creating a safe, non-competitive environment; positive teacher qualities; a policy about verbal and physical assists; the building of community through gentleness and the offering of choice; a non-religious approach and the mindful use of language, and others. Yoga practices include diaphragmatic breathing, awareness of sensations and easy movements without forcing through pain or strain.

A pilot study of the model showed that Yoga significantly improved PTSD symptoms across the board as compared to a Dialectical Behavioral Therapy (DBT) group. Though small sample size made the study statistically inconclusive, the promising results justified a larger, randomized, controlled study on women with treatment-resistant PTSD now in progress (Emerson 2009).

Yogic Breathing

Breathing and breath awareness techniques from Yoga (pranayama) and other traditions have been used in the treatment of trauma as well as other mental problems (Franzblau, Echevarria et al. 2008). One of the best documented and researched is Sudarshan Kriya Yogic (SKY) breathing (Brown 2005; Gerbarg 2008; Descilo T. 2009): "Yogic breathing is a unique method for balancing the autonomic nervous system and influencing psychological and stress-related disorders.... Although more clinical studies are needed to document the benefits of programs that combine pranayama (yogic breathing) asanas (yoga postures), and meditation, there is sufficient evidence to consider Sudarshan Kriya Yoga (SKY) to be a beneficial, low-risk, low-cost adjunct to the treatment of stress, anxiety, post-traumatic stress disorder (PTSD), depression, stress-related medical illnesses, substance abuse, and rehabilitation of criminal offenders. SKY has been used as a public health intervention to alleviate PTSD in survivors of mass disasters." Gerbarg (2008) details a long psychotherapeutic case study of a man suffering from numerous disorders and debilities based in extensive childhood trauma, for whom SKY was a significant part of his ultimately successful recovery and flourishing.

From the traditional SKY practices Drs. Brown and Gerbarg developed a yoga breath program including slow resistance breathing, bellows breath, chanting "om," and cyclical breathing. In one study with Australian veterans of the Vietnam War who had PTSD, pranayama and meditation significantly reduced PTSD symptoms, including sleep disturbance, flashbacks, and anger outbursts (Brown 2005; Gerbarg 2008; Carter 2009).

Yoga: Conclusion

Yoga can reduce overt symptoms of trauma, calm the mind as well as body, and improve overall functioning. This is extremely valuable for trauma sufferers whose lives are often disrupted by those symptoms. There seems to be little or no evidence, however, that purely physical Yoga addresses the root of trauma itself, the "stuck" traumatic memories, in anything like the way that state-of-the art psychologically-based treatments can (e.g. EMDR, exposure therapy). In short, physical Yoga appears to address primarily phase one of trauma treatment, the establishment of safety and stabilization. Interestingly, however, the work on yogic breathing suggests a possible path toward body-based practices for trauma memory reprocessing, the crucial second phase of trauma treatment. We hypothesize that this is because the breath is the body process most closely associated with mental energy.

Mindfulness

Mindfulness, as a secular adaptation of the Buddhist Theravada tradition, is certainly the most widely adopted and researched contemplative practice in psychotherapy today. The major models in this vein are: Mindfulness-based Stress Reduction (MBSR), Acceptance and Commitment Therapy (ACT); Mindfulness-Based Cognitive Therapy (MBCT), and Dialectical Behavior Therapy (DBT), which though it has roots in Zen actually uses a meditation style more akin to mindfulness.

Adapted Theravada mindfulness has been widely used in therapy to address stress, depression, chronic pain, anxiety, borderline personality and other disorders (Baer 2006). Despite the prevalence of psychological trauma, however, and the many applications of mindfulness to stress and other psychological problems, mindfulness has been applied far less to PTSD. Until the last three or four years, there were essentially no studies. There are several likely reasons for this. First, PTSD has until relatively recently been considered all but intractable to treat, almost in a class with psychosis, and thus out of the range of the mostly group and adjunctive methods represented by mindfulness.

More significantly, however, there are potential specific challenges using mindfulness with PTSD sufferers. Intrusive imagery, hypervigilance and other hyperarousal symptoms may be so pronounced that a trauma sufferer cannot even begin to quiet their mind, and may therefore become frustrated with meditation when attempts to exercise detachment and non-judgment fail. In some cases, hypervigilance and mood changes can be triggered when a trauma sufferer involuntarily mistakes relaxation for inattention. On the hypoarousal side, attempts by a PTSD sufferer to slow and relax the mind and body, may, if they succeed, overshoot into numbing and even dissociation. Worse, the client can misinterpret the resulting numbed state as calm and peaceful, believing they have succeeded at the meditation exercise, when in fact their PTSD symptoms are now more active, and they are impeded from reprocessing or even further symptom reduction.

Therefore, a mindfulness protocol needs thoughtful adaptation to work with PTSD patients. This has been done, to our knowledge, for only a few recent projects (Robinson 2008; Kearney 2009; Kimbrough and al 2009; OHSU 2009; Smith 2009; Bremner 2010).

In this paper, we discuss MBSR in general and one particular adaptation of MBSR for trauma from the University of Maryland.

Mindfulness-based Stress Reduction (MBSR)

The MBSR training program includes a standard eight week sequence of 2–3 hour group sessions with one full day of mostly silent meditation in week six. Patients are trained in directed, stable attention and non-judgmental awareness of specific objects and experiences. The targets are both body-based—eating, walking, breath, and body scan—and open awareness of experiences that naturally arise or appear—sensations and feelings about them, environmental sounds, thoughts, emotions, urges and so on. Later meditations may include images and concepts such as stability, strength and stillness, with some comparative analysis aimed at the notions of change and impermanence. Patients are asked to commit to meditating on their own for 45 minutes a day. There are also some didactic psycho-education presentations on stress (Baer 2006).

The general MBSR model was originally developed for use in a behavioral medicine setting, and for patients with chronic pain and stress-related conditions (Kabat-Zinn, Lipworth et al. 1985; Kabat-Zinn, Massion et al. 1992). Since then, MBSR has been used for a variety of physical, psychosomatic and psychiatric disorders, including depression and anxiety, and validated for a range of mental and physical health-related benefits, including: enhanced emotional processing and coping; improved self-efficacy and control; and more differentiated and nuanced understanding of wellness. A recent meta-analysis of MBSR (Grossman, Niemann et al. 2004) validated short-term benefits of MBSR, but concluded that long-term effects, while promising, need further research. That analysis also noted several methodological flaws across MBSR studies they reviewed, particularly that the construct of mindfulness itself has not been sufficiently operationalized or evaluated.

MBSR for Child Abuse Survivors, University of Maryland

A significant program applying an adapted MBSR protocol to PTSD is the training project on mindfulness intervention for child abuse survivors at The Center for Integrative Medicine (CIM) at the University of Maryland (Kimbrough and al 2009; Kimbrough 2010).

The extensive adaptations to trauma include use of active compassion throughout, with specific sessions on loving kindness meditation, "Power of Yes," and other techniques. At the level of process and skill building, the program attends to safety in room layout and teacher demeanor; gives patients choice and control over pacing; stays explicitly within the patient's window of tolerance for arousal. In addition, it carefully orchestrates the body scan exercise in a number of ways to accommodate trauma sufferers, for example helping find a "home base" within the body to serve as a safe place; acknowledging specific body experiences that might occur with PTSD, such as numbing; instructing on how to manage self-loathing; using a resource of loving presence; teaching self regulatory behaviors; and many others. It also uses a smaller group than is usual for MBSR; keeps the class structure predictable uses closing rituals that emphasize connection to body, breath, other group members, and earth; increases process and discussion time; practices how to stay in the body; and cultivates positive states of being such as gratitude, inner wisdom, and dedication.

The CIM MBSR program also attempts to address deeper problems related to traumatic content. For example, it targets re-experiencing symptoms with the mindfulness non-reactivity skill to stay present and work with intrusive memories and their triggers. Avoidance symptoms are addressed with training how to move toward what is happening even in the face of dislike. Hyperarousal symptoms are countered by calming the nervous system with mindfulness, and noticing the safety available in the present moment.

The outcome study for the CIM project showed statistically significant effects on all symptom clusters and secondary symptoms such as depression and anxiety. Effects were particularly strong on hypoarousal symptoms and effects, a result in keeping with the strength of mindfulness meditation in raising awareness of thoughts, feelings and emotions, which would counter especially the avoidance aspects of hypoarousal. It is not clear, however, if adaptations for countering numbing and dissociation were measured and successful. On the whole, the CIM MBSR study, as a group model, appeared to work successfully in a phase one mode, not directly addressing traumatic memories.

Mindfulness: Conclusion

Mindfulness, like Yoga, appears to be best suited for phase one trauma treatment. It provides a rich array of resources that can be adapted to facilitate safety and stabilization and reduce overt symptoms. Mindfulness's emphasis on active attention can be particularly helpful in countering a hypoaroused state, as long as it is not too pronounced or severe.

However, despite a promising fit with the general dynamics of PTSD (Goldstein 2010), mindfulness remains largely unexplored as a tool for reprocessing actual traumatic memories in phase two treatment, and there are reasons to question its current suitability. Besides the issues with hyperarousal and hypoarousal discussed above, mindfulness as used today in therapy has no mechanism for reprocessing or integrating trauma memory content beyond treating those memories like any other phenomena to be attended to non-judgmentally. But traumatic memories are so easily triggered in a sufferer and so intense when they are, that they require special processing. Additionally, group-based, adjunctive models that integrate mindfulness cannot provide the highly individualized reprocessing guidance and feedback to the client that phase two usually requires. Adapting mindfulness to *one-on-one* phase two intervention, or hybrid models where individual re-processing is augmented by group mindfulness training might be feasible, but if any trauma therapists are trying such models, we are currently not aware of them.

Eye Movement Desensitization and Reprocessing (EMDR)

EMDR is a comprehensive, robust secular treatment model and protocol for healing trauma and milder subjective distress. Created by clinical psychologist Francine Shapiro, PhD beginning in 1989 and continuously refined since (Shapiro 2002). EMDR is practiced worldwide by over 9,000 therapists trained in its use. (EMDR-Europe; EMDRIA)

EMDR is a rich therapeutic approach that integrates, in structured protocols, elements of many psychological and contemplative systems, including psychodynamic, cognitive behavioral, experiential, physiological, and relational therapies, as well as non-judgmental mindfulness, metacognition, visualization, future ideal state, free association, and imagery of the traumatic event itself (http://www.emdr.com/q&a.htm#q11). EMDR aligns very well with the phase-oriented trauma treatment paradigm. It addresses all phases of the paradigm, but is especially strong in phase two.

Validation of EMDR

According to the EMDR Institute (http://www.emdr.com/), which oversees training and certification for EMDR therapists, "EMDR is the most researched psychotherapeutic treatment for PTSD" (http://www.emdr.com/q&a.htm#q4). It has undergone rigorous formal treatment outcome studies (see http://www.emdr.com/studies.htm#meta for a comprehensive listing), which suggest that EMDR is an effective treatment in reducing the range of post-traumatic symptoms, intrusive imagery and hyperarousal and hypoarousal symptoms, with particularly robust effects on reducing intrusive imagery. Outcome studies show that initial symptom relief and transformation from EMDR actually continue to grow in strength beyond the treatment period.

EMDR is recognized by the International Society for the Study of Traumatic Stress (Foa 2008); the Veterans Administration (Department of Veterans Affairs and Defense 2004), and numerous other official bodies as an efficacious treatment for post-traumatic stress (http://www.emdr.com/studies.htm#meta). And, with the obvious cautions regarding anecdotal evidence, it should be noted that there is a steady, ongoing stream of reports from a wide spectrum of professional, licensed therapists about EMDR treatment rapidly and fully resolving many cases of PTSD that had resisted treatment by other methods for years, even decades.

The EMDR Process

The unique and distinctive feature of EMDR is the use of bilateral stimulation, usually eye movements, to induce *dual attention*, the process in which the client attends to both external and internal stimuli (Shapiro 1995). We will use "dual attention" in this paper for the *combined* inner/outer *and* bilateral nature of the stimulus and resulting attention. Dual attention facilitates both phase one and phase two work, but especially phase two reprocessing of actual traumatic memories (http://www.emdr.com/q&a.htm#q13). This was Shapiro's initial observation that led her to develop EMDR, and it has remained at the center of EMDR ever since. Though there is some controversy, the preponderance of evidence confirms the importance of eye movements to the efficacy of EMDR, particularly its apparent crucial role in dissipating distressing emotions associated with trauma (http://www.emdr.com/q&a.htm#q15). Again, this is supported by considerable anecdotal evidence from therapists who frequently report dramatic breakthroughs as a result of the eye movements and dual attention, as well as remarkable efficacy in building experiences and skills for safety and security in phase one. Though there have been no formal studies on them, other forms of dual attention stimulation, such as rapid, repetitive tapping, touch, and tones are also used in EMDR. It seems justifiable, therefore, to say that the common factor is the dual attention induced by a variety of sensory stimulation techniques.

The established descriptive model of EMDR's action, Shapiro's "Accelerated Information Processing" model (Shapiro 1995) hypothesizes that traumatic memories are "stuck" and not fully processed, and resist resolution by reasoning and observation of current, non-threatening reality. Trauma victims *know* they should feel safe now but they don't. In this model, treatment by EMDR helps the sufferer reprocess and digest those memories by bringing them into effective contact with more adaptive internal and external information. Guided by the therapist, the client juxtaposes an ideal state to which they aspire, free of the distress of a traumatic memory with thoughts of the subjective mental and physiological objects associated with trauma memories in the form of images, thoughts, feelings, emotions and sensations. The therapist then presents bilateral stimulation, the client turns inward for a few moments, and catalyzed by the resulting dual attention, the traumatic memory becomes depotentiated. The illusion which besets PTSD survivors—that the traumatic events of the past still threaten them today—finally merges with knowledge and experience of safety in the present moment, which quickly and permanently dissolves the distress of the traumatic memory.

As effective as EMDR is, and however plausible this information processing model may be in light of actual therapeutic experience, the model remains essentially theoretical. And the situation is equally undeveloped for neurobiology that might elucidate *how* dual attention facilitates rapid, complete reprocessing of traumatic memories (Gunter 2009). There are several such proposed mechanisms, such as similarity to the orienting response (Shapiro 2002) and REM sleep, (Stickgold 2002) but only suggestive or indirect scientific results. Of course EMDR is hardly unique in this regard. Essentially all psychotherapy protocols for complex disorders, and even many psychopharmacological treatments, lack both models and neurobiological correlates with sufficient scientific evidence to say that they are explained in any functional sense. In this light, we must take the accelerated information processing model of EMDR simply as a descriptive metaphor, albeit one that can be useful in therapy to "explain" to the client how it might work.

EMDR As a Contemplative Practice

How EMDR actually works is thus a mystery, and perhaps more than most psychological treatment models because of its reliance on bilateral stimulation and dual attention, features entirely outside the usual array of techniques and tools in modern clinical psychology. In fact, some neurobiology researchers concede that information storage and processing accounts of mental processes are at best metaphorical (Stickgold 2002). That leaves open the possibility of other models and metaphors. Interestingly, Pierre Janet, the founder of current theories for understanding the maladaptive psychological effects of trauma, coined the term "psychic energy" to describe the latent and manifest psychological force that helps us attend to the present moment as well as other functions (Van der Hart 1989).

I would like to suggest that EMDR's action might be related to the notion of subtle or mental energy, which exists in many contemplative systems such as esoteric Buddhism and Hinduism, Eastern movement and martial arts disciplines, shamanistic traditions as well as modern adaptations of such traditional systems. In fact, the present use of the words "information" and "mental energy" may be viewed as terms for the same or related phenomena. The gist of these systems, which are remarkably consistent across many traditions, is that subtle or mental energy (known as prana, chi, wind and others depending on the particular tradition) flows in a structured "anatomy," parallel to physical anatomy. These energies can become blocked, disturbed and dysfunctional, leading to pathology. Contemplative practices such as visualizations in and around the body, as well as body movement, mantra and focused attention such as yoga and other body practices, alter these energy flows, unblocking, smoothing and balancing them. This can not only relieve the pathologies of mind and body, but also promote the focused attention which lies at the heart of contemplative practice. The dual attention techniques of EMDR may well constitute such a mental energy meditation, and in that role works to relieve blocked energy that constitutes unprocessed trauma memories. The mental energy metaphor also resonates with Shapiro's notion of unblocking the unprocessed information of traumatic memories and balancing the information processing system.

While dual attention is the defining technique of EMDR, it is by no means the only contemplative component. The EMDR protocol builds a strong witness perspective, the metacognitive capacity to observe and rework one's subjective experience, a technique that resonates with Buddhist, Hindu and other traditional meditation practices. Also, EMDR has at its heart the supposition that everyone has an innate capacity to heal, which aligns with spiritual notions and practices such as Buddha Nature and the Divine within. EMDR makes this supposition operational, asking the client to imagine their own future healed state as immediate preparation for depotentiating the distressing traumatic memories.

Many other elements of EMDR are implicitly but powerfully contemplative. These include: the safe place or sanctuary exercises, though these are common in other PTSD therapies; imagining a healing light entering you from above; merging with an admired person, real or fictional; and visualizations of symbols and metaphors to promote positive experiences, feelings and states. For all these, the therapist often uses dual attention stimulation to facilitate and deepen the effect.

For these reasons we may reasonably regard EMDR as a contemplative system of trauma treatment, whose orientation is secular and whose contemplative nature is implicit rather than overt.

EMDR: Phase Three and Beyond

In phase three of trauma treatment, a client healed of traumatic reactions reintegrates their newfound healthy functionality back into their life. Beyond that, successful healing of PTSD with EMDR may empower a trauma victim to flourish and grow even beyond their pre-trauma state. Dr. Shapiro recognized this potential (Brown and Shapiro 2006), and urged the EMDR community to embrace it as a higher goal. It is addressed in EMDR by processes based on earlier phases that build further positive, even transformative inner resources and templates for future action (Korn 2002). Nevertheless, there is relatively little literature or outcome research in this area, and the potential for EMDR to help create ideal future states and true flourishing remains strong but underdeveloped.

EMDR: Conclusion

EMDR offers an effective method and protocol for addressing PTSD, one of the most difficult mental disorders to treat. It does this within a secularized treatment protocol by integrating dual attention with an eclectic but well-developed system of other contemplative practices and techniques from clinical psychology. EMDR thus constitutes a salient and successful combination of contemplative practices and modern psychology, one which has been scientifically validated and officially recognized by professional bodies.

Multi-modal Programs

In this section we treat multi-modal programs to address trauma. We mainly discuss the Garrison Institute's Wellness Project (WP) to ameliorate and prevent vicarious trauma among health care workers, but also mention James Gordon's series of mind-body skills programs applied to victims of violence. (I have served as a consultant to WP since 2007.)

The Garrison Institute's Wellness Project

The Garrison Institute's Wellness Project (Garrison Institute 2009) is "a pilot model for integrating contemplative methods into a training to prevent and ameliorate vicarious trauma (VT) among domestic violence workers." WP operated from 2004 to 2009, and was delivered to 400 staff in 40 domestic violence agencies in the New York City area. The Wellness Project provides an innovative model ready for possible adaptation in the human services sector generally and is currently being considered for use in other venues.

The three main goals of WP are: inform trainees about VT through psycho-education; build skills for prevention and amelioration of VT primarily through worker self-care; and build an engaged community and workplace culture that support the other goals. All three are essential and are interwoven and balanced. The skills and community aspects of WP use a broad spectrum of contemplative methods and other practices to build awareness of vicarious trauma, provide trainees with skills for its prevention and alleviation, reduce burnout rates, enhance worker effectiveness and promote wellness principles and practices in workplace culture.

The mind-heart-spirit component of WP includes basic mindfulness in the Buddhist Theravada and MBSR style, including breath, walking and eating mediation, as well as body scan and loving-kindness practice. A notable feature of WP not often found in less integrated programs is the use of group visualization, ritual and ceremony to help develop participants' inner and outer safety, including one to develop a personal safe place and another to deepen the sense of connection with themselves, the earth and each other.

Hatha Yoga is the primary body-based technique in WP, with adjunctive use of Alexander Technique. Recognizing that many domestic violence workers are themselves victims of trauma, not always acknowledged, WP adapts Yoga for trauma victims with emphasis on gentle, restorative poses plus a few to develop strength, and avoids poses that are potentially problematic for trauma survivors.

A notable feature of WP is the use of culturally resonant creative expression such as art-making, dance, voice work and journaling as vehicles for recognizing negative effects of VT and exploring options for positive change. These are arguably methods with contemplative characteristics in this context, and while not unique for this purpose, WP's integration of creative expression into a broad program for trauma-sensitive wellness appears to be particularly effective.

Building connection and community and fostering a culture of wellness are a special dimension of WP, which is specifically designed for existing workplace communities that train together. Trauma, including VT, can lead to profound disconnection from others, and studies show that a supportive professional community can help minimize the risk for VT in formalized settings (Way, VanDeusen et al. 2004). WP helps build this supportive community by weaving group awareness into all activities contemplative and otherwise. The entire program is highly interactive, with participants meeting frequently in dyads and small groups. The faculty continually model and promote teamwork and group process. In addition, the creative expression activities and group rituals create a powerful sense of community as participants share their inner worlds in a mutually supportive atmosphere.

Conclusions about WP

WP is unique in a number of respects. It is multi-modal, employing a variety of methods in an integrated curriculum, many adopted later in the project in a spirit of experimentation and creative eclecticism. Loving-kindness meditation from the Buddhist Theravada tradition was an original element of the mix and remained important throughout. The significant emphasis on community is a crucial element for vicarious trauma training. WP also strives explicitly for cultural sensitivity in its choice of faculty and activities.

Though no formal outcome study of WP has been done yet, strong anecdotal evidence and participant feedback indicated that the project was successful in helping participants to "recognize trauma patterns in themselves earlier and address them more quickly and efficaciously," as well as feeling overall more hopeful and resilient.

The Center for Mind-Body Medicine

The Center for Mind-Body Medicine (CMBM), (Gordon 2010) does global trauma relief, professional training in mind-body methods for PTSD and a variety of physical conditions, and research in these subjects. Relevant for this paper are CMBM's trauma relief programs which use a variety of group contemplative techniques to provide trauma symptom relief in areas beset by war and disaster. CMBM has delivered programs in Gaza, Kosovo, Haiti, Louisiana and other area as well as a for the US Military. CMBM's contemplative techniques include meditation, self-hypnosis, and creative expression through words, drawings, and movement. Body-based methods include relaxation, breathing exercises, physical exercise and diet. Though group support is listed as one of CMBM's methods, it is unclear whether they address building of community as a source of post-training support for trauma survivors.

Two studies with schoolchildren have validated the benefits of CMBM's programs for reducing PTSD symptoms for significant groups of victims (Gordon, Staples et al. 2004; Gordon, Staples et al. 2008). As a group model the CMBM program seems to comprise mostly phase one healing. CMBM appears to be well-organized, keeps its methods simple, effectively trains local teachers to deliver the programs, and therefore reaches large numbers of people with beneficial results.

Reflections

We end with a number of observations and hypotheses that emerge from this sample of applying contemplative practices to the healing of trauma as well as from the larger universe of such applications.

Overall Application to Trauma Healing

Based on an overview of the current state of the field, nascent though it is, we believe that contemplative methods are generally very well-suited to healing trauma at all levels and in all phases of treatment, perhaps more than for any other serious psychological disorder. However, the case is nuanced and specific to the goals and phases of treatment and to the types of contemplative practice. Below are some reflections on this theme.

Phase One

As we have seen throughout our examples, contemplative practices, properly adapted with trauma-awareness, are excellent tools for phase one trauma treatment. Both mind and body practices help clients calm and ground themselves, improve their sense of safety in the present, and reduce and better control their traumatic symptoms. Contemplative practices enhance attention skills in both perceptual and action aspects, making clients more aware of and sensitive to their internal states and better able to control those states, directing and modulating attention toward safety in the present and away from the distress of both hypoarousal and hyperarousal, thus widening their window of tolerance. All this fits well with the crucial goals of phase one treatment.

Two further aspects of contemplative practices have special advantages for phase one, even lifting them above the majority of non-contemplative methods. First, the unified mind-body character of many contemplative practices is ideally suited for the complex psycho-physiological clusters of symptoms that sufferers face in the wake of trauma.

Second, contemplative practices can provide well-founded hope in those suffering from a malady often marked by hopelessness. This hope is more than just motivational. Many contemplative practices emphasize an ideal future state to promote unblocking and shifting mental energy toward healing, which in turn actually facilitates healing. The motivational aspect is the most important for phase one, and shifting mental energy for phase two, but both work in both phases.

There is a paradox in motivation, however. Those guiding trauma sufferers in phase one methods must at once provide hope for the huge improvements in quality of life that will follow from phase one and celebrate improvements when they occur. At the same time, the therapist must acknowledge the limits of symptom reduction so as to motivate the sufferer for phase two, where they can dissolve the traumatic distress altogether.

Phase Two

True trauma resolution, in current understanding, requires conscious, active work on the traumatic memories themselves, something that both psychotherapy and contemplative practices should conscientiously postpone to phase two. It is here that the demands sharpen considerably for all healing methods, both contemplative and otherwise, because of the sensitivity of actual traumatic memories and their power to destabilize and re-traumatize the client. Only two systems of psychotherapy, EMDR and Cognitive Behavioral Exposure Therapy, have so far attained enough evidence through outcome studies to be recognized effective by several professional bodies for actually resolving psychological trauma, though there are certainly other effective methods without that imprimatur.

EMDR is, by many accounts, among the most rapid and effective approaches for actually healing traumatic memories. We hypothesize that this power of EMDR is due in no small part to the conscientious, systematic and intimate integration of dual attention, modern psychological methods, and other contemplative practices. In this regard, EMDR, and a handful of other promising secular treatment models or techniques (for example: Internal Family Systems; Focusing) may represent viable templates for integration of contemplative practices and modern psychological systems.

Furthermore, contemplative methods that do work for trauma reprocessing may be uncommonly effective. We hypothesize that this subset uses the processing, flow and blockages of "information," or in traditional terms, "mental energy." The dual attention of EMDR is the most salient such practice in wide use, but Yoga approaches it with various breathing exercises. In fact, it feels like this potential is far from fully realized today. There are likely techniques that are little explored or even undiscovered for trauma and other disorders that capitalize on the information/mental energy concept. If so, a fruitful place to look might well be the traditional systems that have, over the centuries, developed powerful contemplative methods around the "mental body" and three-dimensional psychic landscapes.

Observations on Current Outcome Studies

Hypoarousal — avoidance vs. numbing. Many PTSD outcome studies treat the entire hypoarousal symptom cluster as avoidance. In fact hypoarousal has two subdivisions with very different mechanisms and implications for treatment. One is indeed active avoidance, the *flee* reaction, internally or externally moving away from the triggering stimulus. The other is numbing, the *fold* reaction, which is marked by anhedonia, physical anesthesia and/or dissociation.

Mindfulness seems like a good antidote to avoidance, and it can work if avoidance is indeed the only hyperarousal reaction. But if numbing is an issue, then mindfulness and other meditation techniques can inadvertently induce exactly that. If an outcome study does not distinguish numbing from inner avoidance, that becomes a confounding variable and treatment efficacy will be underestimated. A possible solution is tools like the Mindful Attention Awareness Scale (MAAS), which measures disposition to be aware of and attend to events in the present, and also seems able to distinguish numbing from avoidance (Brown 2003; Baer, Smith et al. 2006).

General well-being vs. the effects of contemplative practice. There is evidence that contemplative practices lead to reduction in symptoms of PTSD *indirectly*, by improving overall functioning rather than through any inherent contemplative characteristics. The simple good exercise of Yoga or the general calming effect of mindfulness might be as or even more important in reducing symptoms than any contemplative effect such as improved attention to and control over inner states. For example, Smith (Smith 2009) found that a scale that measures "orientation to life" correlated better with PTSD symptom improvement after mindfulness training than did the MAAS, which was not even statistically significant.

If some contemplative practices work indirectly, for instance through general well-being or the relaxation response, that is obviously not a bad thing for trauma sufferers. But it does suggest that some therapy practice, theorizing and further research need rethinking.

Phase one vs. phase two—symptom reduction vs dissolution of traumatic distress. All outcome studies that we know of on contemplative methods for

PTSD measure success exclusively by overall, pre-to-post-treatment symptom reduction, aggregated over all subjects. If there is phase two work going on, such studies do not distinguish the total (and in the case of EMDR, sometimes rapid) dissolution of traumatic distress that successful reprocessing achieves; that just gets aggregated and averaged with partial symptom reduction in subjects who did not enter and complete phase two. Addressing this important distinction may be difficult. It probably involves both more complex research design and new tools to differentiate and measure the dissolution effect of successful phase two treatment, which seems so striking to the client and therapist when it happens, but may be slippery to capture.

Love and Compassion

The impetus toward love and compassion as well as methods for developing those faculties are an integral part of most, if not all systems of contemplative practice. Compassion plays a prominent role in Christianity, Islam, Hinduism and many other traditions, and is actually one of the two foundational principles of Mahayana Buddhism.

The role of compassion in trauma treatment, however, is relatively undeveloped. The major problem is that trauma sufferers' ability to relate to others is often so severely damaged, particularly for interpersonal trauma, that restoring a capability for empathy seems a distant goal, to be addressed, if at all, only toward then end of treatment. Even when trauma treatment methods address relational functioning, they do not explicitly target compassion. In my own experience as a trauma therapist, however, I have found that aspects of compassion are not only attainable throughout treatment, but can serve as an actual means toward healing of trauma across all phases. In this endeavor, I draw both strategy and tactics from various source, particularly Buddhism and modern attachment theory.

Phase one trauma treatment emphasizes developing skills of self-compassion, to manage and cope with symptoms. This includes contemplative practices such as mindfulness and mind-body techniques discussed above. When applied in this early stage of treatment, such self-soothing practices—as acts of kindness toward oneself—are perhaps the sufferer's first felt experience of any form of compassion since their trauma. Such experience is also a necessary precursor for recovering or developing compassion for others. It also helps heal the trauma survivor's often resistant negative self-image by demonstrating to them their capacity for giving and receiving.

While phase one involves mainly soothing and grounding, which has an inherent motivation for the client, in phase two the sufferer moves *toward* the pain, and that activates a natural avoidance which can impede or prevent further healing. Phase two therefore requires considerable determination by the client, and this is where a compassionate motivation to heal oneself for the sake of others can be a valuable force.

When a trauma sufferer sees, however tenuously, that their affliction affects others as well as themselves, their natural concern for others can motivate them to undertake the difficult work of confronting painful memories, without reinforcing the dysfunctional narrative of self-loathing and deserved suffering. It can be a simple as "I'm doing this for my kids, and that's good!" This is analogous, at a psychological level, to the fundamental role of compassion in Mahayana Buddhism as motivation to develop oneself in order to become a skillful instrument for helping others. The trauma client can use contemplative practices and techniques to develop and intensify this motivation, for example cultivating the determination to heal for the benefit of their loved ones, while visualizing or gazing on a photograph of them.

The role of compassion in trauma treatment has been embraced in a number of models used in trauma treatment. Attachment theory addresses the biological, psychological and social importance of love and compassion from parent to child and how to repair the relational damage when childhood abuse and neglect prevailed instead (Schore 2001). In EMDR, the resource development protocol (Korn 2002) names and strengthens positive relationship experiences in preparation for the reprocessing of trauma memories. Gilbert and his colleagues (Gilbert 2005) have compiled an impressive range of other examples applicable to trauma sufferers such as Lee's work on developing an internal "perfect nurturer" (Lee 2005). In a similar vein, Makransky (2007) describes the value of and methods for building an internal "benefactor" based on the Buddhist understanding of the student-teacher relationship. Briere (Briere, to appear) addresses the value of the therapist's compassion for treating trauma. Neuroscientists are also exploring the therapeutic effects of love and compassion (Davidson and Sutton 1995; Pace, Negi et al. 2009).

All these observations, techniques and examples point to a crucial, often unappreciated role for love and compassion in healing trauma and suggest significant contributions from the realm of contemplative practice worthy of further exploration.

Phase Three

Having succeeded at phase two, having reprocessed and depotentiated the traumatic memories, the former PTSD sufferer is still left with many residues and scars of their—possibly long and from childhood—period of dysfunction and maladaptations. They probably have habits and patterns that they employed to cope with their suffering, patterns they no longer need but do not simply recede on their own. For example, they might have avoided intimate contact, and never developed or lost the capacity for forming love relationships. They can now take on such a task.

At this point, the whole palette of both contemplative and non-contemplative methods and practices for enriching ones life, for personal growth are once again, or for the first time, available to the former trauma sufferer, including but not limited to methods they used to heal. They can, if they choose, sit in meditation without triggering either hyperarousal or hypoarousal. They can practice self-compassion without evoking intense guilt, shame and hopelessness. They can begin to practice compassion toward others, compassion that was impossible in the face of pervasive fear and anger toward so many others. They can engage fully in the joys and sorrows of life without the threat of intractable suffering erupting at any moment.

It's more than just release from suffering, however. The former PTSD sufferer has been to hell and back. They know deeply, non-conceptually, the possibility and power of transformation, of seeing through an illusion that once gripped their lives. In short, they are ripe for the full depth of contemplative practice, to seek the next level of attainment toward that lofty goal.

They can also just putter in the garden.

Contemplative Trauma Treatment Matrix

Following is a summary matrix of the contemplative methods covered in this paper, describing both their applicability to treating trauma under three broad categories and their relevant contemplative characteristics.

Each row represents a method or example project discussed in the text, with Yoga divided into two rows. Each column represents a summary characteristic. In cells with diamonds, the number of diamonds represents a 5-point scale (0 to 4) rating the applicability of each method (row) to the particular characteristic (column) or the extent to which the method addresses or implements the concept for the column.

Please note that this is a preliminary version of a larger and more articulated matrix, in these ways:

Contemplative Trauma Treatment Matrix (Preliminary, June 2010)

EMDR	TGI ITT[5] Wellness Project	MBSR (UM CIM[4] adapted)	Yogic Breathing (SKY[2])	Yoga Postures (TC JRI[1] adapted)		
◇◇/◇◇	◇/◇◇	◇/◇◇	◇/◇◇	◇◇/◇◇	Phase 1: Safety & Stability	Trauma Treatment Phases Addressed
◇◇/◇◇	◇	◇	◇◇/◇◇	?	Phase 2: Trauma Reprocessing	
◇/◇◇	◇◇/◇	◇◇/◇	?	?	Phase 3: Reintegration	
◇/◇◇	◇/◇◇	◇◇/◇	◇/◇◇	◇/◇◇	Hypoarousal	Trauma Symptoms Addressed
◇/◇◇	◇/◇◇	◇	◇/◇◇	◇/◇◇	Hyperarousal	
◇◇/◇◇	◇	◇	?	◇	Intrusive Re-experiencing	
Pri.	Adj.	Adj.	Adj.	Adj.	Primary vs. Adjunctive	Trauma Treatment Modalities
Indiv.	Group	Group	Group	Group	Individual vs. Group (Typical)	
—	◇/◇◇	◇	◇	◇	Community & Relational	
Imp.	Exp.	Exp.	Exp.	Exp.	Implicit vs. Explicit Contemplative	Contemplative Characteristics
◇/◇	◇/◇◇	◇◇/◇◇	◇◇/◇	◇	Uses Attention	
Secular	Adapted Tradi-tional	Adapted Tradi-tional	Tradi-tional	Adapted Tradi-tional	Secular vs. Traditional	
Mind-Body[6]	Mind-Body[6]	Mind-Body[6]	Body-Mind[3]	Body	Mind & Body	

[1] The Trauma Center at JRI
[2] Sundarshan Kriya Yoga breath methods, as discussed by Gerbarg, et. al.
[3] Body-Mind = Body-mind complex with body emphasis ("bottom-up")
[4] University of Maryland, Center for Integrative Medicine
[5] The Garrison Institute, Initiative for Transforming Trauma
[6] Mind-Body = Body-mind complex with mind emphasis ("top-down")

- We have not thoroughly validated and operationalzed the ratings represented in each cell, which are summations of complex, multi-fold issues, and therefore somewhat arbitrary and one-dimensional.
- In the full and better-developed matrix, there will be many more columns, arranged hierarchically, to address the complexity of each summary characteristic represented here.
- In the more-developed matrix there will be more rows, representing many more methods, models and programs, since the set treated in this paper is only a small, though representative sample.

Acknowledgements

I wish first and especially to thank Diana Rose, co-founder of The Garrison Institute, for supporting me in my work as Senior Fellow. Her compassion for the suffering of others and commitment to doing something about it are an inspiration.

This paper is a product of Garrison's Initiative for Transforming Trauma (ITT), specifically the mapping survey project, which aims to delineate and support the growing field of contemplative practices for healing psychological trauma. Direct contributors to the mapping survey have included Dr. Anthony King, Dr. Jim Hopper, Madhur Kulkani, Dr. David Lewis, and especially Stephanie Bosco-Ruggiero, who built the extensive reference database on which the survey relies.

I also wish to thank the people who conceived and implemented ITT's Wellness Project, beginning with its first director Marie O'Neil, its second DaRa Williams, Sharon Salzburg, co-founder of the program and lead meditation teacher, along with the other amazing women on the Wellness faculty. Their diverse and collective example is a compelling demonstration of how to tap the wellspring of hope and help from the world's contemplative traditions for transforming trauma.

I thank Diana Rose and David Rome for their insightful feedback on the content and presentation of this paper.

I am grateful to my husband, Dr. David Lewis, who was a valuable editor on this paper, took the lead on the working definition of contemplation and the matrix of practices, and served as my interlocutor to help refine and sharpen the ideas.

Above all, I am grateful to Gehlek Rimpoche for spurring me to integrate what I have learned about contemplative practice into my work as a traumatologist.

May our collective efforts bear positive fruit for the benefit of all those who suffer from trauma.

References

American Bar Association, C. o. D. V. (2010). "Survey of Recent Statistics," from http://new.abanet.org/domesticviolence/Pages/Statistics. aspx#prevalence.

Baer, R. A. (2006). *Mindfulness-based Treatment Approaches: Clinician's Guide to Evidence Base and Applications.* San Diego, CA, US, Elsevier Academic Press.

Baer, R. A., G. T. Smith, et al. (2006). "Using Self-Report Assessment Methods to Explore Facets of Mindfulness." *Assessment* 13(1): 27–45.

Bremner, D. (2010). "Neural correlates of PTSD prevention with mindfulness-based stress reduction (MBSR) in Iraqi veterans." from http://clinicaltrials.gov/ct2/show/NCT01058031.

Breslau, N. (2009). "The epidemiology of trauma, PTSD, and other posttrauma disorders." *Trauma Violence Abuse* 10(3): 198–210.

Breslau, N., et. al. (1998). "Trauma and posttraumatic stress disorder in the community." *Arch Gen Psychiatry* 55.

Briere, J. (to appear). "Compassion and mindfulness in trauma treatment." *Compassion and Wisdom in Psychotherapy.* C. K. G. a. R. D. Siegel, Guilford.

Brown, K. W. R., Richard M. (2003). "The benefits of being present: Mindfulness and its role in psychological well-being." *Journal of Personality and Social Psychology* 84(4): 822–848.

Brown, R. P., Gerbarg, P. L. (2005). "Sudarshan Kriya Yogic breathing in the treatment of stress, anxiety, and depression. Part II--clinical applications and guidelines." *Journal of Alternative and Complementary Medicine* 11(4): 711–717.

Brown, S. and F. Shapiro (2006). "EMDR in the treatment of borderline personality disorder." *Clinical Case Studies* 5(5): 403.

Carter, J. (2009). "Multi-component yoga breath program for Vietnam veteran posttraumatic stress disorder: Randomized controlled trial." *International Journal of Yoga Therapy.*

Cullen, M. (2010). "Contemplative practice in healthcare MBSR: Mindfulness-based interventions," Fetzer Institute.

Davidson, R. J. and S. K. Sutton (1995). "Affective neuroscience: the emergence of a discipline." *Current Opinion in Neurobiology* 5: 217–224.

Department of Veterans Affairs and D. o. Defense (2004). VA/DOD Clinical Practice Guideline for the Management of Post-Traumatic Stress.

Descilo T, V. A., Gerbarg PL, Nagaraja D, Gangadhar BN, Damodaran B, Adelson B, Braslow LH, Marcus S, Brown RP. (2009). "Effects of a yoga breath intervention alone and in combination with an exposure therapy for post-traumatic stress disorder and depression in survivors of the 2004 South-East Asia tsunami." *Acta Psychiatrica Scandinavica*(4): 289–300.

EMDR-Europe. from http://www.emdr-europe.org/.

EMDRIA. from http://www.emdria.org/.

Emerson, D. S., Ritu; Chaudhry, Serena; Turner, Jenn (2009). "Yoga therapy in practice.Trauma-sensitive yoga: Principles, practice, and research." *International Journal of Yoga Therapy* 19: 123–128.

Foa, E. (2008). *Effective Treatments for PTSD: Practice Guidelines from the International Society for Traumatic Stress Studies*, The Guilford Press.

Franzblau, S. H., S. Echevarria, et al. (2008). "A preliminary investigation of the effects of giving testimony and learning yogic breathing techniques on battered women's feelings of depression." *J Interpers Violence* 23(12): 1,800–1,808.

Garrison Institute (2009). The Garrison Institute's Wellness Project, 2004–2009.

Gerbarg, P. L. (2008). Yoga and Neuro-psychoanalysis. *Bodies in Treatment: The Unspoken Dimension.* F. S. Anderson: 127–150.

Germer, C., R. Siegel, et al. (2005). *Mindfulness and Psychotherapy.* New York, Guilford Press.

Gilbert, P. (2005). *Compassion: Conceptualisations, Research and Use in Psychotherapy.* Routledge

Goldstein, E. (2010). Mindfulness and Trauma: An Interview with John Briere, Ph.D.

Gordon, J. (2010). "The Center for Mind-Body Medicine." from http://www.cmbm.org/.

Gordon, J. S., J. Staples, et al. (2004). "Treatment of posttraumatic stress disorder in postwar Kosovo high school students using mind-body skills groups: a pilot study." *Journal of Traumatic Stress* 17(2): 143–147.

Gordon, J. S., J. K. Staples, et al. (2008). "Treatment of posttraumatic stress disorder in postwar Kosovar adolescents using mind-body skills groups: a randomized controlled trial." *J Clin Psychiatry* 69(9): 1,469–1,476.

Grossman, P., L. Niemann, et al. (2004). "Mindfulness-based stress reduction and health benefits: A meta-analysis." *Journal of Psychosomatic Research* 57(1): 35–43.

Gunter, R. B., Glenn E (2009). "EMDR Works...But How? Recent Progress in the Search for Treatment Mechanisms." *Journal of EMDR Practice and Research* 3(3): 8.

Kabat-Zinn, J., L. Lipworth, et al. (1985). "The clinical use of mindfulness meditation for the self-regulation of chronic pain." *J Behav Med* 8(2): 163–190.

Kabat-Zinn, J., A. O. Massion, et al. (1992). "Effectiveness of a meditation-based stress reduction program in the treatment of anxiety disorders." *American Journal of Psychiatry* 149(7): 936–943.

Kearney, D. J. S., Tracy. (2009). "Mindfulness Based Stress Reduction for Posttraumatic Stress Disorder: A Pilot Study." from http://clinicaltrials.gov/ct2/show/NCT00880152.

Kessler RC, S. A., Bromet E, Hughes M, Nelson CB (1995). "Posttraumatic stress disorder in the National Comorbidity Survey." *Arch Gen Psychiatry* 52(12): 1,048–1,060.

Khalsa, S. B. S. (2009). Path I: Healing the Body. *Garrison Institute Transforming Trauma Forum*, Garrison Institute.

Kimbrough, E. M., Trish (2010). Mindfulness Intervention for Childhood Abuse Survivors.

Kimbrough, E. M., Trish; Langenberg P.; Chesney M.; Berman B.; and e. al (2009). "Mindfulness Intervention for Child Abuse Survivors."

Korn, D. L. L., Andrew M. (2002). "Preliminary evidence of efficacy for EMDR resource development and installation in the stabilization phase of treatment of complex posttraumatic stress disorder." *Journal of Clinical Psychology* 58(12): 1,465–1,487.

Lee, D. A. (2005). The perfect nurturer: A model to develop a compassionate mind within the context fo cognitive therapy. *Compassion: Conceptualisations, Research and Use in Psychotherapy.* P. Gilbert, Routledge 326–351.

Makransky, J. (2007). *Awakening Through Love: Unveiling Your Deepest Goodness*, Wisdom Publications.

NIMH. "The Numbers Count: Mental Disorders in America." from http://www.nimh.nih.gov/health/publications/the-numbers-count-mental-disorders-in-america/index.shtml#PTSD.

OHSU. (2009). "PTSD MBSR Study." from http://www.emindful.com/article.php?item=9.

Ospina, M. B., K; Karkhaneh, M; Tjosvold, L; Vandermeer, B; Liang, Y; Bialy, L; Hooton, N; Buscemi, N; Dryden, DM; Klassen, TP (2007). Meditation practices for health: state of the research.

Pace, T. W., L. T. Negi, et al. (2009). "Effect of compassion meditation on neuroendocrine, innate immune and behavioral responses to psychosocial stress." *Psychoneuroendocrinology* 34(1): 87–98.

Pearlman, L. A. S., Karen W. (1995). *Trauma and the Therapist.* New York, Norton, W. W.

Ray, S. L. (2006). "Embodiment and embodied engagement: central concerns for the nursing care of contemporary peacekeepers suffering from psychological trauma." *Perspectives in Psychiatric Care* 42(2): 106–113.

Robinson, E. K., Tony (2008). A pilot dtudy of a mindfulness-based hroup therapy for combat veterans with post-traumatic stress disorder. *6th Annual Mindfulness-based Stress Reduction (MBSR) Research Conference.*

Schore, A. N. (2001). "The effects of early relational trauma on right brain development, affect regulation, and infant mental health." *Infant Mental Health Journal* 22(1-2): 201–269.

Shapiro, D. C., Karen (2004). "Mood changes associated with Iyengar Yoga practices: A pilot study." *International Journal of Yogatherapy* 14: 35–44.

Shapiro, F. (1995). *Eye Movement Desensitization and Reprocessing, Basic Principles Protocols and Procedures.* New York, The Guilford Press.

Shapiro, F. (2002). *EMDR As an Integrative Psychotherapy Approach: Experts of Diverse Orientations Explore the Paradigm Prism,* American Psychological Association Washington, DC.

Smith, J. D. (2009). Mindfulness-based stress reduction (MBSR) for women with PTSD surviving domestic violence, Fielding Graduate University Ph.D.

Stickgold, R. (2002). "EMDR: A putative neurobiological mechanism of action." *Journal of Clinical Psychology* 58: 61–75.

US Department of Health and Human Services, A. f. C. a. F. (2008). Child Maltreatment 2008, Chapter 3.

Van der Hart, O. F., Barbara (1989). "A reader's guide to Pierre Janet: neglected intellectual heritage." *Dissociation* 2(1): 3–16.

van der Kolk, B. (2002). "Posttraumatic therapy in the age of neuroscience." *Psychoanalytic Dialogues* 12(3): 381–392.

van der Kolk, B. A. (2006). "Clinical implications of neuroscience research in PTSD." *Annals of the New York Academy of Sciences* 1071: 277–293.

Way, I., K. M. VanDeusen, et al. (2004). "Vicarious trauma: a comparison of clinicians who treat survivors of sexual abuse and sexual offenders." *J Interpers Violence* 19(1): 49–71.

MINDFULNESS-BASED INTERVENTIONS: AN EMERGING PHENOMENON

Margaret Cullen

Abstract

This paper offers an overview of the rapidly growing field of mindfulness-based interventions (MBI's). A working definition of mindfulness in this context includes the brahma viharas, sampajanna and appamada and suggests a very particular mental state which is both wholesome and capable of clear and penetrating insight into the nature of reality. The practices in MBSR which apply mindfulness to the four foundations are outlined, along with the history of the program and the original intentions of the founder, Jon Kabat-Zinn. The growth and scope of these interventions is detailed with demographics provided by the Center for Mindfulness, an overview of salient research studies and a listing of the varied MBI's which have grown out of MBSR. The question of ethics is explored, and other challenges are raised including teacher qualification and clarifying the "outer limits," or minimum requirements, of what constitutes an MBI. Current trends are explored, including the increasing number of cohort-specific interventions as well as the publication of books, articles and workbooks by a new generation of MBI teachers. Together, these form an emerging picture of MBI's as their own new "lineage" which look to MBSR as their inspiration and original source. The potential to bring benefit to new fields, such as government and the military, represent exciting opportunities for MBI's, along with the real potential to transform health care. Sufficient experience in the delivery of MBI's has been garnered to offer the greater contemplative community valuable resources such as secular language, best practices, and extensive research.

Keywords: mindfulness, overview, potential, Buddhism, MBSR, MBI.

Introduction

"In the One Dharma of emerging Western Buddhism, *the method is mindfulness, the expression is compassion, the essence is wisdom*" (Goldstein, 2002, p. 13).

The interest in mindfulness-based interventions (MBI's) has grown exponentially in recent years. Programs are being written and taught by professionals from all walks of life: psychologists, scientists, athletes, lawyers, professors and more. This emergent phenomenon is both promising and perilous as it is increasingly difficult to gauge, not only the quality and integrity of the program, but whether or not the content has anything to do with mindfulness, let alone which definition of mindfulness is operationally applied in and philosophically guiding the curriculum. This paper outlines the contemplative practices which are integral to Mindfulness-Based Stress Reduction (MBSR), explains the various practices which are taught and examines how they have developed over the past thirty years. Particular attention is paid to the use and meaning of the term, "mindfulness." Estimates are made as to the numbers of graduates and programs, support organizations and scope of MBSR both in health care and beyond, including the variety of MBI's which have been spawned by MBSR. Trends, opportunities and challenges facing MBI's in the coming decade are explored, along with the role that MBI's play within the emergence of a larger contemplative movement in America.

What Is Mindfulness?

As the founder of MBSR, Jon Kabat-Zinn's (1994) definition of mindfulness is that which is commonly used: "paying attention in a particular way: on purpose, in the present moment, and non-judgmentally" (p. 4). Kabat-Zinn frequently describes mindfulness as a "way of being", choosing to think of the work as a dynamical process, embedded within all of life, both *intra-* and *inter*-personal, rather than a static technique, practiced only "on the cushion" and thereby compartmentalized to "x" minutes per day.

There are two main branches of Buddhism: Theravada and Mahayana. Though technically a part of Mahayana, Vajrayana or Tibetan Buddhism, functions as a third branch insofar as its practices differ significantly from Zen Buddhism, the other principal Mahayana school (Smith, Novak, 2003). Their historic differences are complex, subtle and beyond the purview of both this paper and most contemporary practitioners. Yet these historical differences, though still debatable, shape the practices that are taught in meditation centers in the west. Most western vipassana centers are rooted in the Theravada branch of Buddhism. Vipassana, or "seeing clearly", also known as the practice of insight, is comprised of meditation practices based primarily on the Satipattana Sutta, usually translated as the Four Foundations of Mindfulness. In this context, the practice of mindfulness has the potential to liberate the mind from greed, hatred and delusion as in the following excerpt from the Satipattana Sutta:

> This is the sole way, monks, for the purification of beings, for the overcoming of sorrow and lamentation, for the destroying of pain and grief, for reaching the right path, for the realization of Nibbana, namely, the Four Foundations of Mindfulness (Thera, 1965, p. 139).

For some Mahayana schools of Buddhism, mindfulness also plays a central role. Thich Nhat Hanh, world-renowned Vietnamese Zen master, poet and peace activist, defines mindfulness as "the *miracle* which can call back in a flash our dispersed mind and restore it to wholeness so that we can live each minute of life" (Hanh, 1975, p. 14). However, according to Buddhist scholar, B. Alan Wallace, in Vajrayana Buddhism mindfulness has the more narrow function of remembering to bring the mind back to the chosen object of meditation and as such functions as the foundation for shamatha. Conversely, vipassana practice considers samadhi (shamatha) as the foundation for vipassana (Cullen, 2006).

In the Theravadan Abhidhamma (Buddhist psychology), *sati* is precisely defined as one of nineteen "beautiful" mental factors whose function is the absence of confusion or non-forgetfulness. In the context of the Nikaya (Buddha's Discourse) *sati* is referred to as a "kind of attentiveness that . . . is good, skilful or right" (Thera, 1965, p. 9). However, in the Tibetan Abhidharma, mindfulness is considered a neutral factor. For example, a sniper could be mindful while carefully taking aim at his target (Cullen, 2006).

Many contemporary Buddhist teachers use the term mindfulness in a more comprehensive way than simply "remembering" or lacking confusion. According to John Dunne, Buddhist scholar at Emory University, the components of mindfulness as it is more broadly construed might include not only *sati*, but also *sampajanna* (meaning clear comprehension) and *appamada*, (meaning heedfulness). Clear comprehension includes both the ability to perceive phenomena unclouded by distorting mental states (such as moods and emotions) and the meta-cognitive capacity to monitor the quality of attention. Heedfulness in this context can be understood as bringing to bear during meditation what has been learned in the past about which thoughts, choices and actions lead to happiness and which lead to suffering (Cullen, 2008)

This broader use of mindfulness could be widened even further to include the four *brahma viharas* which are alternately called the immeasurables or sublime states and include: lovingkindness, compassion, sympathetic joy and equanimity. As the first three are all aspects of unselfish care or friendliness, they can be seen as different expressions of the same quality of heart which is often referred to as "basic goodness." They differ more in terms of context than content or affective tone and can be distinguished by their proximal causes: compassion arises in the face of suffering and carries with it the impulse to act to relieve the suffering of another; lovingkindness arises when we witness qualities or actions which are lovely or loveable; sympathetic joy arises in the face of others' good fortune. Equanimity is distinct from the other three insofar as it is not associated with the same affective tone and tends to provide the "leavening" quality of even-handedness, providing the insight and/or perspective necessary to meet experience with skill and open-heartedness and appreciate our equality with all living beings. Kabat-Zinn (Cullen, 2006) describes mindfulness as "affectionate" attention in which an orientation of non-harming is inherent. Joseph Goldstein, prominent Vipassana teacher and writer described mindfulness:

> . . . mindfulness is *always* a wholesome factor . . . in a true moment of mindfulness there is freedom from greed, hatred and delusion. . . . through the practice of mindfulness, all of the other factors of enlightenment (mindfulness, investigation, energy, rapture, calm, concentration and equanimity) are automatically cultivated. Mindfulness does have that function of drawing the other factors of enlightenment together (Cullen, 2006, p. 5).

Andrew Olendzki, Executive Director of the Barre Center for Buddhist Studies, explained how this was detailed in the Abhidhamma (the Pali compendium of Buddhist psychology):

> One of the more astonishing insights of the Abhidhamma is that mindfulness always co-arises with eighteen other wholesome mental factors. We are used to thinking of these factors as very different things, but the fact that they all arise together suggests they can be viewed as facets of the same jewel, as states that mutually define one another. By reviewing the range of wholesome factors that co-arise with it, we can get a much closer look at the phenomenology of mindfulness. First, there is equanimity (*tatra-majjhattata*, 34). . .

It is therefore also characterized by non-greed (*alobho*, 32) and non-hatred (*adoso*, 33). This is the generic Abhidhamma way of referring to generosity or non-attachment on the one hand and loving-kindness on the other (Olendzki, 2008).

What Is MBSR?

MBSR began in 1979 in the basement of the University of Massachusetts Medical Center. As a student of zen, vipassana and yoga, Jon Kabat-Zinn included a range of both formal and informal practices for the cultivation of mindfulness. Due to its focus on specific and detailed instructions for directing, sustaining and deepening attention, Vipassana lent itself beautifully to application in a mainstream setting. Other Buddhist traditions tend to be more culturally influenced and to rely more heavily on ritual, Buddhist philosophy, and the teacher–student relationship, making them harder to export to conventional institutions in a country constitutionally bound to the separation of church and state, and reflexively suspicious of even the word meditation. The formal practices in MBSR are: mindful movement (gentle hatha yoga with an emphasis on mindful awareness of the body); the body scan (similar to the sweeping method employed by S.N. Goenka and designed to systematically, region by region, cultivate awareness of the body—the first foundation of mindfulness—without the tensing and relaxing of muscle groups associated with "progressive relaxation"); and sitting meditation (usually taught as western vipassana: awareness of the breath and systematic widening the field of awareness to include all four foundations of mindfulness: awareness of the body, feeling tone, mental states and mental contents). As such, the intention of MBSR is much greater than simple stress reduction. Through systematic instruction in the four foundations and applications in daily life, as well through daily meditation practice over an eight week period, many participants taste moments of freedom which profoundly impact their lives. All of life serves as the ground for the informal cultivation of mindfulness, but each week new themes invite participants to explore mindfulness through different aspects of daily life (e.g. food, perception, relationships, work, stress, etc.). This principle is captured beautifully in Kabat-Zinn's second book: *Wherever You Go, There You Are.* Even the title underscores the essential principle of bringing mindfulness into all aspects of daily life.

In 2000, Saki Santorelli became the Executive Director of the CFM. With an MA in psychology and an EdD in Education, 35 years of practice in the Sufi tradition and almost 30 years in the Vipassana tradition, this choice of leadership would not only serve to assert the core intention of mindfulness as an expression of "universal *dharma*," but set a course that would result in a multi-dimensional organization firmly embedded in a major academic health care center with an annual international scientific conference, an institute for professional education and training, and a multi-tiered training and certification program in MBSR, as well as community programs, international trainings, academic curricula and research studies.

Demographics and Research

As discussed earlier, no data exists as to exact, or even approximate numbers of MBI's worldwide and, if it did, it would be inexact before reaching publication. However, the CFM provided the following numbers:

- Over 18,000 graduates of the eight-week MBSR program at UMass (since 1979)
- Over 9,000 graduates of Oasis—the Center for Mindfulness' institute for professional training (individuals from 35 countries have attended)
- Professional Training offered since early 80's, formalized into Oasis in 2005
- Over 500 "clinics" around the world (from 1)
- 8 years of the Annual International Scientific Conference, and international meeting of clinicians, researchers and educators (R. Theberge, personal communication, April, 2010)

There are hundreds of research papers on the effects of MBI's on physical and mental conditions including, but not limited to depression (Jain, et al., 2002) and relapse prevention (Segal et al., 2010; Teasdale, et al., 2002), anxiety (Baer, 2003), substance abuse (Bowen, et al., 2006), eating disorders, binge eating (Baer, 2006), insomnia (Kreitzer, Gross, Ye, Russas, Treesak, 2005), chronic pain (Morone, Greco, Weiner, 2008), psoriasis (Kabat-Zinn, wheeler, Light, 1998), type 2 diabetes (Rosensweig, et al., 2007), fibromyalgia (Grossman, Tiefenthaler-Gilmer, Raysz, Kesper, 2007), rheumatoid arthritis (Pradhan, et al., 2007), attention-deficit/ hyperactivity disorder (Zylowska, et al., 2007), HIV (Creswell, Myers, Cole, Irwin, 2009), cancer (Carlson, Speca, Patel, Goodey, 2003 and Witek-Janusek et al., 2003), and heart disease (Sullivan, et al., 2009). A comprehensive literature review of four of the largest health science databases (EBSCO, CINAHL, PSYCHLINE and

MEDLINE) found that "MBSR is an effective treatment for reducing the stress and anxiety that accompanies daily life and chronic illness" (Praissman, 2008).

Growth/Scope

In 2002, Zindel Segal, Mark Williams and John Teasedale published *Mindfulness-Based Cognitive Therapy for Depression: A New Approach to Preventing Relapse.* The rigorous and robust research on this novel intervention compelled both clinicians and academics to explore the potentiating power of marrying mindfulness with the more traditional approach of cognitive behavioral therapy. There is now a graduate program in Mindfulness-Based Cognitive Therapy (MBCT) at Oxford University and the British National Health Service pays for the cost of the program. Another prominent mindfulness center in the United Kingdom is the Centre for Mindfulness Research and Practice at Bangor University. Numerous other MBI's have been spawned from MBSR including: Mindfulness-Based Childbirth and Parenting (MBCP), SMART in Education/ Mindfulness-Based Emotional Balance (MBEB), Cool Minds™ (for adolescents), A Still Quiet Place (children of all ages), Mindfulness-Based Eating (MBEat), Mindfulness-Based Relapse Prevention (MBRP), Mindfulness-Based Elder Care (MBEC), Mindfulness-Based Mental Fitness Training (MBMFT), Mindfulness-Based Art Therapy for Cancer Patients(MBAT), Mindful Leadership™, Mindful Schools, Mindfulness without Borders, Trauma Sensitive MBSR for women with PTSD, along with many other programs designed for specific age groups from preschool through higher education. Norway, Sweden, Holland, France, Ireland, Germany, South Africa, Switzerland and Italy are among many countries that have institutes and national associations of mindfulness teachers and trainings.

The organic "grass-roots" growth of MBI's worldwide can be explained several ways. The sense that mindfulness is the medicine (or food) which many in the developed world are starving for is a sentiment frequently expressed at meetings of MBSR teachers. It is an antidote to the *dis*-ease of 21st century life and its attendant and ever increasing pull toward multi-tasking and 24/7 connectivity. The costs to our mental and physical well-being are many and may include depression, anxiety and a variety of stress-related health concerns. From the perspective of Buddhist philosophy, in which intention determines the ultimate fruits of our actions, perhaps we could extrapolate that the original intentions of Jon Kabat-Zinn play a key role in deciphering the phenomenon of MBSR. In the foreword to *Teaching Mindfulness*, Kabat-Zinn wrote:

> The early years of MBSR and the development of other mindfulness-based clinical Interventions were the province of a small group of people who gave themselves over to practicing and teaching mindfulness basically out of love, out of passion for the practice, knowingly and happily putting their careers and economic well-being at risk because of that love, usually stemming from deep first-person encounters with the dharma and its meditative practices, often through the mediation of Buddhist teachers and acknowledged masters within a number of well-defined traditions and lineages (McCown, Reibel, Micozzi, 2010, p. xii).

In 1990, at a Mind and Life meeting in Dharamsala, Jon Kabat-Zinn was to present his work in MBSR to His Holiness the Dalai Lama. There had been heated debate among some meeting participants as to whether or not MBSR was genuine "buddha dharma" and might undermine Buddhism itself. Kabat-Zinn reports that he spent that entire night meditating and reflecting on what he would do should His Holiness espouse such a view. In the end, he came to the conclusion, before giving his presentation the following morning, that his experience with the positive effects of MBSR on the thousands of patients who had gone through the program in the prior eleven years would have to take precedence over even the Dalai Lama's disapproval. Fortunately, His Holiness readily saw the value of such a program as a skillful means for catalyzing freedom from suffering in many people. At a public Mind and Life meeting years later, Kabat-Zinn asked His Holiness if there was any difference between Buddha dharma and universal dharma. The answer was "no."

The value and benefits of these mindfulness-based programs are undeniable. However, there has been debate over the years as to what place MBSR and its ensuing "lineage" should assume in relationship to the various Buddhist schools and traditions. There has been concern, particularly among Buddhist scholars and some monastics, that MBI's might foreshadow the dilution or "dumbing down" of the rich, vast and deep teachings of the Buddha. Perhaps it is important to reiterate here that MBSR is informed by and grounded in the application of the four foundations of mindfulness and the view, argued above, that mindfulness, as taught in this program, has elements of all of the *brahma viharas* seamlessly integrated into it. More importantly, the most salient distinction between MBI's and Buddhism is that the former are secular and the latter is religious. Secular is not equivalent to shallow, nor is religious necessarily equivalent to deep.

There has also been concern about the absence of emphasis on *sila* or ethics. Most Buddhist traditions require vows of ethical behavior prior to meditation training. Although this formality is extremely helpful in providing a structure of safety for retreatants and monastics and useful in purifying the mind for deeper practice, it is equally possible to integrate a foundation of ethical behavior into the practice of mindfulness itself. The emphasis in MBSR is on learning through first-hand experience and insight. This is very much in keeping with the original teachings of the Buddha who exhorted his students to find out for themselves if his teachings were useful and not to believe anything because he said so. When ethics are understood through direct insight into the relationship between skilful behavior and personal flourishing, it is possible to obviate the psychological resistance that frequently arises in response to "shoulds" and external mandates to behave in a particular way. Unlike a cloistered retreat setting, most MBI's are taught over an eight week period and there is an explicit emphasis on using all of one's inner and outer life as a laboratory to empirically explore which behaviors lead to suffering and which lead to happiness. Like the moral inventory in the 12 step programs, this can be the ground for profound insight into the direct link between unethical behavior and personal suffering (often the fuel for addictive behaviors). These insights, arising from first hand experience, can be easier to integrate than externally imposed edicts from parents, church and society. It is also of critical importance in most mainstream settings (particularly in education) that a single set of ethics is not imposed, as this can both create conflict with different faith traditions and bring an association of religion into a setting where this is inappropriate and threatening. Interestingly, many participants in MBI's report a deeper connection to their own faith tradition, and its attendant moral code, after completing the program.

It could be argued that ethics and mindfulness have a bi-directional potential for supporting each other. While the practice of ethics makes it much easier to cultivate mindfulness, the cultivation of mindfulness necessitates a wholesome relationship to experience:

> Although the brain science has yet to discover why, this tradition nonetheless declares, based entirely on its phenomenological investigations, that when the mind is engaged in an act of harming it is not capable of mindfulness. There can be heightened attention, concentration, and energy when a sniper takes a bead on his target, for example, but as long as the intention is situated in a context of taking life, it will

always be under the sway of hatred, delusion, wrong view (*ditthi*, 19), or some other of the unwholesome factors. Just as a tree removed from the forest is no longer a tree but a piece of lumber, so also the caring attentiveness of mindfulness, extracted from its matrix of wholesome co-arising factors, degenerates into mere attention (Olendzki, 2008).

Also, the insights that arise for MBI participants, just like the insights for yogis on intensive retreat, arise within the scaffolding created by the teacher and the curriculum. It is the job of the skillful teacher to engage directly with the students, challenging beliefs, inviting deeper exploration, suggesting where and how to pay attention, all within the framework of a secular articulation of the four foundations of mindfulness.

As tiresome as debates among scholars can be, there is much utility in preserving both the culture and teachings of the great religions. These debates contribute to the general good by continuing to clarify and enliven ancient teachings for modern audiences, refining translations and unearthing new clues to ancient wisdom traditions. Further, the vast and deep teachings of Buddhism, beginning with the Buddha himself, and then developed by enlightened beings over many centuries, in many countries, must never be lost as they contain, not only detailed descriptions of mental life and phenomena, but highly refined and systematic instructions for achieving enlightenment. These debates, however, have little relevance to the patients with chronic pain conditions and a host of other medical disorders and stress-related problems who enroll in MBSR classes. However one may feel about it, a "lineage" of mindfulness-based interventions is already here. Not only is it impossible to stop, its scope and future potential can barely be grasped.

There is both excitement and fear that MBI's might herald the emergence of a new, American Dharma: democratic, non-hierarchical, organic, non-devotional, embodied, eclectic, non-dogmatic, pragmatic, utilitarian, non-discriminatory (race, age, gender, SES), creative, emergent and widely accessible. Given the global interconnectivity of the 21st century, contemporary Buddhism may not emerge and evolve according to geographic locale as it did in the first few centuries as it wound its way through Asia. It may be that we don't yet have the language to describe the affinity group that is co-creating this new emerging dharma but, whatever their physical location, they share a love of the liberating potential of the *dharma*, a conviction that it can play an important role in the treatment of 21st century *dukkha* (suffering), and an interest in the cultivation of a universal idiom accessible to those in need, whatever their backgrounds or belief systems. By offering access to insight and deep levels of mind *without* religion, a growing group of post-modern, post-partisan, intellectually skeptical, and scientifically grounded people are able to experience these practices without having to believe in something on faith alone.

Trends

One of the many currently unfolding trends of the MBI's is to offer interventions tailored to increasingly narrow cohort groups such as people with depression, the military, cancer patients, overweight women, medical students and the like. The advantages of teaching a homogeneous cohort include unique opportunities for bonding, empathy and support as well as enhanced social relationships. In these cohort-specific trainings, modules can be added that address more directly the diagnoses or difficulties faced by that particular group. However, something is also lost. As is often expressed in the first MBSR class, "You are more than your diagnosis. There is more right with you than wrong with you. We are here to gain access to that part of us which is never broken." The beauty of a diverse class is the possibility of connecting with people who are very different from oneself and seeing that we share the same mind, the same wish to be happy and many of the same challenges.

Another trend as indicated elsewhere in this paper is the increasing number of books published by the second generation of MBI professionals (Kabat-Zinn and Santorelli are the first generation). These include not only popular books for the general public (Carlson and Speca, 2010, Flowers, 2009, Rosenbaum, 2005), but academic texts (Shapiro, Carlson, 2009), (Baer, 2006), (Hick, 2009), (McCown, et al, 2010), and educational tools (Stahl, Goldstein, 2010), (Biegel, 2009). Those books footnoted here are not only an incomplete representation of the field, there will likely be more published by the time this paper reaches the hands of the reader. These books could be understood as the fruition of the original co-emergent philosophy of MBSR. Each of these authors has seen a new potential through their own unique prism of contemplative training, professional experience and the secular application of mindfulness.

A recent and potentially far-reaching trend has been the advocacy of MBI's on Capitol Hill. Tim Ryan, Congressman from Ohio, proposed MBSR to HHS Secretary Kathleen Sebelius as a key intervention in preventative health. Speaking at a recent event for the Center for Mindfulness, Ryan declared his intention to propose the integration of mindfulness into every government program. He has walked his talk in his home district by allocating funds for social and emotional learning programs in the schools.

Yet more remarkable, and more controversial to some, has been the introduction of mindfulness interventions to the military. Two prominent researchers, Elizabeth Stanley and Amisha Jha, studied the protective effects of mindfulness training on working memory capacity and affective experience in military service members preparing for deployment. They found that those participants who practiced meditation at home increased their working memories, exhibited lower levels of negative affect and higher levels of positive affect (Stanley, Jha, 2010).

Opportunities

One of the greatest opportunities facing MBSR and MBI's is the potential to revolutionize the understanding and delivery of healthcare. In "The Role of Mindfulness in Healthcare Reform: A Policy Paper," a very strong case is made for mindfulness interventions reducing the cost of health care at a time when the annual cost of $2 trillion is under great scrutiny as key national health indicators lag and budget deficits soar. The authors concluded:

> Regardless of who pays for healthcare in the United States, the cost must come down. Without a reduction in health-care expenditures, no system will be sustainable for long. Applying what we know about the potential for (MBI's) to prevent disease, promote health, treat chronic conditions and improve the quality of care may well turn out to be a cornerstone of a more humane, equitable and effective approach to health and healthcare that can actually reduce costs in a meaningful way. Leveraging the body's innate capacity to heal itself may be the key to creating a sustainable healthcare system for the 21st century (Ruff, Mackenzie, 2009, p. 320).

Consider the costs of delivering an MBI: instructor hourly fee plus overhead for room space, materials and registration. With zero diagnostic or technology costs, this averages out at approximately $3 per contact hour per patient. Furthermore, Roth and Stanley (2004) report that an eight-week MBSR program at a community health center (N=73) resulted in a significant decrease in chronic care office visits after the MBSR program was completed.

On a parallel track, Santorelli has been revolutionizing medicine from the inside by teaching mindfulness courses targeted specifically within medical school from undergraduate to graduate, to residency and beyond and, as well, conducting mindfulness programs and retreats for attending physicians and medical school faculty.

Moreover, Santorelli, Kabat-Zinn and MBSR have played key roles in the evolution of our very understanding of healthcare from: 1) alternative medicine to 2) complementary medicine to 3) integrative medicine to 4) comprehensive medicine. These stages were outlined in a keynote by David Eisenberg, MD, and director of the Harvard Medical School Osher Research Center, presented at the 2010 CFM Scientific Conference. With each new level came a more equal role for complementary therapies within the practice of medicine itself. Importantly, from its earliest beginnings, Kabat-Zinn and Santorelli have described MBSR as a public health initiative—a highly accessible research-proven form of what is termed participatory medicine. Kabat-Zinn has won a number of awards which attest to the role MBSR has played in the evolution of integrative medicine including the 2007 Bravewell Philanthropic Collaborative award as a Pioneer in Integrative Medicine, and the 2008 Mind and Brain Prize from the Center for Cognitive Science, University of Turin. He is also the founding convener of the Consortium of Academic Health Centers for Integrative Medicine, a network of deans, chancellors and faculty at major US medical schools engaged at the creative edges of mind/body and integrative medicine.

Challenges

One of many challenges facing all MBI's as programs mature and graduates proliferate is the offering of ongoing support for the deepening and continuation of practices begun in the secular setting of a mindfulness class. Most people benefit dramatically from these programs and want to continue. Group support is often key in providing scaffolding for the learning and accountability for the practice. Although "graduate" programs exist (at the CFM they have been in place for thirty years), they can sometimes be an afterthought and not always successful in retaining students and providing an ongoing sense of community. MBI graduates are sometimes encouraged to support their practice by attending local contemplative centers, primarily Buddhist. However, not everyone is comfortable relating to the language and iconography of a religious center. If MBI is indeed emerging as an important stream in the new "American *Dharma*," it will need to find a way to address the question of how to cultivate and support a lifelong secular practice, an idiom and a community (*sangha*).

This challenge is also expressed in the increasing need for talented and highly experienced teachers. The exponential growth in MBSR and its many derivatives has created a universe of programs too big for either coordination or quality control by the CFM. At the 2010 MBSR conference, a meeting was held to begin to address the needs of centers around the world which offer training for MBI instructors, and the role the CFM could play in either endorsing or overseeing these programs. Although there is a certification program for MBSR instructors, after ten years the program has certified only about 100 teachers worldwide, making it untenable at this point in time for research projects or health care institutions to demand certification as a standard for hiring new instructors.

A more subtle aspect of the same challenge is the need for the instructor to continuously deepen his or her own practice sufficiently to teach mindfulness at the introductory level of MBSR and beyond. Although number of years practicing meditation is certainly a factor, it is not the only variable in measuring this competency. How do you measure the understanding and embodiment of the *Dharma*? It is no wonder the CFM was loathe to take on this issue in the first place and, if *they* struggle with it, how can a medical center or school district begin to establish and require the necessary qualifications and standards of competency and excellence?

One answer that has emerged in only the past year takes the novel form of intensive meditation retreats for MBI professionals. Taught by Kabat-Zinn, Christina Feldman (Vipassana teacher) and John Teasedale (co-creator of MBCT), these nine day retreats may herald the emergence of MBSR as a "lineage." First, they filled up immediately, validating the thirst for MBI instructors to deepen their practice within this unique framework. Second, both Spirit Rock and the Insight Meditation Society hosted these retreats, which served not only to endorse them but foster their growth and situate them squarely within the broadly defined Buddhist "pantheon." Third, and perhaps most important, they are similar to, but also clearly distinct from other retreats at these centers. They share the same reliance on the original teachings of the Buddha, and *Dharma* talks are offered to illuminate essential components of Buddhist philosophy. Sitting and walking practice are taught much as they would be at any other vipassana retreat. Though Buddhist retreats increasingly offer different forms of mindful movement, rarely are they offered by the meditation teachers themselves, at 6:00 a.m. every morning as Kabat-Zinn does. A hallmark of MBSR is embodiment: both literally and figuratively. Instructors are called upon to embody mindfulness as the primary vehicle for teaching it. There is also the invitation to re-inhabit the body as, not only the first foundation of mindfulness, but the doorway to the present moment. Another remarkable expression of this embodiment is the participation of the teachers in all of the practices. It was surprising to see Kabat-Zinn doing the walking meditation every day and the teachers clearly choosing to engage as much as possible with the schedule. Kabat-Zinn and Teasedale also chose whenever possible to eat their meals in silence, with the yogis in the dining hall, which served as a powerful expression of the democratic and non-hierarchical spirit of MBSR. Unlike other retreats at these centers, Americans were in the minority, suggesting a unique pull to draw participants from all corners of the globe. In their book, *Teaching Mindfulness,* McCown, Riebel and Micozzi explained the MBI phenomenon this way:

> It is here, now, in this emerging moment, with a democratic and ethical view of spiritual teacher-student relations, a secular spirituality of life, and a drive for the paradoxical fluidity and stability of spiritual practice that the mindfulness-based interventions are growing and evolving (McCown et al., 2010, p. 58).

Another larger challenge facing all MBI's at this moment in time is the question of what constitutes an MBI? Terms like mindfulness, concentration, awareness and contemplation are often used interchangeably. Though the operational definition of mindfulness expressed in this paper may already be considered too broad for some, is there a clear outside limit to what may reasonably be called a mindfulness-based intervention? One important, distinguishing feature of mindfulness practice is the systematic application of a particular type of awareness to a variety of phenomena (i.e. the four foundations of mindfulness). In mindfulness practice, though it is common to begin with breath awareness, it is essential to bring awareness to other aspects of experience, such as thoughts and mental states in order to promote insights into no-self, impermanence and the reality of suffering. After the practitioner develops sufficient clarity and stability of mind, awareness can be directed not only towards more subtle aspects of experience, but towards the fleeting and ephemeral nature of experience itself.

Conclusion

In the past thirty years, MBSR has grown organically and exponentially, reaching people young and old, around the globe and from many walks of life. Through the exponential growth of rigorous research studies published in the professional literature, MBSR can provide evidence-based rationales for the implementation of contemplative programs in mainstream settings such as hospitals, schools, prisons, and businesses. MBSR provides a highly refined yet accessible language for sharing contemplative practice and values in a universal, non-religious, and non-dogmatic way. Along with this, a pedagogy has emerged which emphasizes the role of embodiment and mindful engagement of the instructor as the primary vehicle for teaching mindfulness.

The success of the research and the inherent value of the program have, in turn, spawned off-shoots of MBSR, for which a new acronym has been coined: MBI. As new books outlining MBI's continue to be published (MCown et al., 2010), (Stahl, et al., 2010), other contemplative programs can avail themselves of these methods. Though they target different groups, MBI's ideally share the organizing principle of mindfulness, not simply as the ability to stay focused, but as the "miracle" which can liberate the mind through insight and which inherently cultivates wholesome mental states. MBI's share core curricular components which invite participants to explore the four foundations of mindfulness with the intention of creating the grounds for this particular, heightened mental factor of mindfulness to arise. Without a clear understanding of mindfulness, secular interventions using the name "mindfulness" can easily degenerate into mere stress reduction.

Through decades of teaching and thousands of courses delivered, a knowledge base has been established which can share experience with the greater emerging contemplative community, particularly in the areas of secularity, evidence-based research, best practices, accessibility, teacher training, contemporary idioms, cohort-specific applications and learning mindfulness within the dynamic and interactive setting of group process. This rapid expansion also raises questions as to what constitutes an MBI. What is the operational definition of mindfulness? What is the background and training of the instructor? How is their understanding embodied as they teach? Do ten minutes of breath awareness constitute a mindfulness-based intervention? Do the curriculum writers, instructors and researchers of an MBI share a similar understanding of and training in mindfulness? In other words, even given the broadest definition of the term mindfulness, along with the broader acronym of MBI, what are the outer limits of what constitutes a mindfulness-based intervention?

There is tremendous potential for practitioners from all the contemplative traditions to bring programs which can relieve suffering to the society at large. Ideally, as programs proliferate, scientists strive to measure and identify active ingredients, and scholars debate meaning, they will each add to our collective understanding and create only more opportunities for creative and diverse interventions designed to bring compassion and wisdom to our afflicted world.

Kabat-Zinn concluded:

> In the emerging of new and compelling fields of inquiry and understanding, in this case the various potential applications of mindfulness in mainstream society, there are usually many different streams of thought and effort that arise more or less simultaneously, sometimes running in parallel, sometimes taking very different directions, but all issuing into the one ocean of what is. All can be said to add value in one way or another to the overall vector of the work because their experience and findings, particularly if the individual efforts have integrity, expand our understanding of what works well under what circumstances, and what doesn't. But, sooner or later, the different streams tend to recognize each other, take stock of each other's virtues and limitations, and finally come together in the emergence of a new and inclusive synthesis, one that does indeed add value to what has come before (McCown, et al., 2010, p. x).

Acknowledgments

Sincere thanks to the Fetzer Institute for soliciting and supporting this paper and to Jon Kabat-Zinn and Saki Santorelli, for their encouragement, generosity and invaluable input.

References

Baer, R.A. (2003). Mindfulness training as clinical intervention: A conceptual and empirical review. *Clinical Psychology (New York)*; 10: 125–143

Baer R.A., ed. (2006). *Mindfulness-Based Treatment Approaches. Clinician's Guide to Evidence Base and Applications*. San Diego, CA.: Academic Press.

Biegel, G.(2009). *The Stress Reduction Workbook for Teens: Mindfulness Skills to Help You Deal With Stress.* Oakland, CA: New Harbinger Publications, Inc.

Bowen, S. Witkiewitz, K., Dillworth, T.M., Chawla, N., Simpson, T.L., Ostafin, B. . . G. Alan Marlatt, G.A. (2006). "Mindfulness meditation and substance use in an incarcerated population." *Psychology of Addictive Behaviors*; 20: 343–347.

Carlson, L.E., Speca, M, Patel, K., Goodey, E. (2003) "Mindfulness-based stress-reduction in relation to quality of life, mood, symptoms of stress, and immune parameters in breast and prostate cancer outpatients." *Psychosomatic Medicine*; 65(4): 571–581.

Carlson, L.E., Speca, M. (2010) *Mindfulness-based Cancer Recovery.* Oakland, CA: Harbinger.

Creswell, J.D, Myers H.F., Cole S.W., Irwin, M.R. (2009). "Mindfulness meditation effects on CD4 + T lymphocytes in HIV-1 infected adults: A small, randomized controlled trial." *Brain Behavior and Immunity*; 23: 184–188.

Cullen, M., Gates, B., Nisker, W. (2006) "Mindfulness: The heart of Buddhist meditation." *Inquiring Mind*; 22(2).

Cullen, M. (2008) On Mindfulness. In Ekman, P., His Holiness the Dalai Lama, *Emotional Awareness.* New York: Henry Holt.

Flowers, S. (2009). *The Mindful Path Through Shyness: How Mindfulness & Compassion Can Help Free You from Social Anxiety, Fear, & Avoidance.* Oakland, CA: Harbinger.

Goldstein, J. (2002). *One Dharma.* New York: Harper Collins.

Grossman, P., Tiefenthaler-Gilmer, U., Raysz, A., Kesper, U. (2007). "Mindfulness training as an intervention for fibromyalgia: Evidence of post intervention and three year follow-up benefits in well-being." *Psychotherapy and Psychosomatics*; 76: 226–233.

Hanh, T. N., (1975). *The Miracle of Mindfulness.* Boston: Beacon Press.

Hick, S. (2009). *Mindfulness and Social Work.* Chicago: Lyceum.

Jain, S., Shapiro, S.L., Swanick, S., Roesch, S.C., Mills, P.J., Bell, I.,

Schwartz, G.E. (2007). "A randomized controlled trial of mindfulness meditation versus relaxation training: effects on distress, positive states of mind, rumination, and distraction." *Ann Behav Med.*, 33 (1): 11–21.

Kabat-Zinn, J. (2005). *Coming to Our Senses.* New York: Hyperion.

Kabat-Zinn, J., Wheeler, E., & Light, T (1998). "Influence of MBSR intervention on rate of skin clearing in patients with moderate to severe psoriasis undergoing phototherapy (UVB) and photochemotherapy (PUVA)." *Psychosomatic Medicine.*; 60: 625–632.

Kabat-Zinn, J. (1994). *Wherever You Go, There You Are.* New York: Hyperion

Kreitzer, M.J., Gross CR, Ye X, Russas V, Treesak C. (2005). "Longitudinal impact of mindfulness meditation on illness burden in solid-organ transplant recipients." *Prog Transplant.* 2005; 15: 166–172.

McCown D., Reibel D., Micozzi M., (2010). *Teaching Mindfulness,* New York: Springer.

Miller, D.I. (2005, November 28). "Finding My Religion," *San Francisco Chronicle.*

Morone, N.E., Greco, C. M., & Weiner, D. (2008) "'I felt like a new person'–The effects of mindfulness meditation on older adults with chronic pain: Qualitative narrative analysis of diary entries." *Journal of Pain.*; 9: 841–848.

Olendzki, A. (2008). The real practice of mindfulness. *Buddhadharma: The Practitioner's Quarterly;* http://www.thebuddhadharma.com/issues/2008/fall/mindfulness.

Pradhan E.K., Baumgarten M., Langenberg P., Handwerger B., Gilpin A.K., Magyari T., Berman, B.M. (2007). "Effect of MBSR in rheumatoid arthritis patients." *Arthritis and Rheumatology.*; 57: 1,134–1,142.

Praissman, S. (2008). "MBSR: A literature review and clinician's guide." *Journal American Academy Nurse Practitioners.* 20: 212–216.

Rosenbaum, E. (2005). *Here For Now: Living Well With Cancer Through Mindfulness.* Hardwick, MA: Satya House.

Rosenszweig, S., Reibel, D.K., Greeson, J.M., Edman J.S., Jasser, S.A., McMerty, K.D., Goldstein, B.J. (2007). "MBSR is associated with improved glycemic control in type 2 diabetes mellitus: A pilot study." *Altern Ther Health Med.*; 13: 36–38

Roth, B., Stanley, T.W. (2002) "Mindfulness-based stress reduction and healthcare utilization in the inner city: Preliminary findings." *Altern Ther Health Med.* 8: 60–62, 64–66.

Ruff, K., Mackenzie, E. "The role of mindfulness in healthcare reform: A policy paper, *Explore*, November/December, Vol. 5, No. 6, p. 320, 2009.

Santorelli, S. (1999). *Heal Thy Self.* New York: Random House.

Segal, Z.V., Bieling, P., Young, T., MacQueen, G., Cooke, R., Martin, L., . . . Levitan, R. (2010) "Antidepressant monotherapy vs sequential pharmacotherapy and mindfulness-based cognitive therapy, or placebo, for relapse prophylaxis in recurrent depression." *Archives of General Psychiatry*; 67 (12): 1,256–1,264.

Shapiro, S., Carlson, L. (2009) *The Art and Science of Mindfulness: Integrating Mindfulness into Psychology and the Helping Professions*, APA

Smith, H., Novak, P. (2003) *Buddhism*. San Francisco, CA: Harper-Colllins Stahl, B., Goldstein, E. (2010) *A Stress Reduction Workbook*. Oakland, CA: New Harbinger.

Stanley, E., Jha, A. "Examining the protective effects of mindfulness training on working memory capacity and affective experience. *Emotion;* 10 (1): 54–64.

Sullivan, M.J., Wood, L., Terry, J., Brantley, J., Charles, A., McGee, V., Cuffe, M. (2009) "The support, education and research in chronic heart failure study: A mindfulness-based psychoeducational intervention improves depression and clinical symptoms in patients with chronic heart failure." *American Heart Journal.*;157: 84–90.

Teasdale J.D., Moore, R. G., Hayhurst, H., Pope, M., Williams, S., & Segal, Z. V. (2002) "Metacognitive awareness and prevention of relapse in depression: Empirical evidence." *Journal of Consulting and Clinical Psychology*; 70 (2): 275–287.

Thera, N. (1965). *The Heart of Buddhist Meditation*. York Beach, ME: Weiser Books.

Witek-Janusek, L., Albuquerque, K., Chroniak, K. R., Chroniak, C., Durazo-Arvizu, R., Mathews, H. L. (2008) "Effect of MBSR on immune function, quality of life, and coping in women newly diagnosed with early stage breast cancer." *Brain Behav Immun.*; 22: 969–981.

Zylowska, L., Ackerman, D. L., Yang, M. H., Futrell, J. L., Horton, N. L., Hale, T. S. (2008) "Mindfulness meditation training in adults and adolescents with ADHD: A feasibility study." *Journal Atten Disord.*; 11: 737–774.

Contemplative Practice and End-of-Life Care: A Preliminary Discussion

Judy Lief

Defining "Contemplative Practice"

Contemplative practice takes many forms, but at its core it is a way of training the mind-heart with the goal of developing greater awareness, kindness, and openness. It begins with the deliberate cultivation of positive mental states by means of formal practice and continues by joining the results of such practice with the demands and activities of daily living. Contemplative practice is a deeply personal experience. It is transformative in a way that simply theorizing about it is not. The term *contemplative practice*, in reference to end-of-life care (EOL) includes both meditative training and contemplative disciplines (see below).

Contemplative practice can be related to in at many levels. Like any other practice, it assumes that the student engage in regular and repeated training sessions. That is, you work with the same technique over and over again, in the same way that a musician practices scales or an athlete works out. It is by working with it in that way that contemplative practice can be understood.

There are stillness forms of practice, such as sitting meditation, and movement forms such as walking meditation. Such practices are not only mental exercises, but they include the feelings or emotions and the body, as well. They are holistic, and designed to synchronize the body, emotions, and mind and bring them into harmony.

Meditation / Formless Practices

In the Buddhist tradition the term *meditation* usually refers to formless practices, based on repeatedly bringing one's attention back to the object of the meditation, which is usually the breath. Such practices are simple and nonconceptual. The foundation is taming the mind or mindfulness practice (Sanskrit: *shamatha*). It is developing the ability to rest the mind in a state of relaxed alertness, free from distractions. Equally important is the development of awareness or insight (Sanskrit.: *vipashyana*). This natural outgrowth of mindfulness practice is a continual expanding of one's mental horizon beyond fixating on the self. It is a way of overcoming self-absorption or self-centeredness. With mindfulness-awareness, you are joining a quality of stability with a quality of expansiveness. You are joining presence and openness.

Contemplation / Practices with Form

Compassion practices such as *tonglen*, or sending and taking, are called *contemplative* practices. In contemplative practice you reflect on a topic or a quality such as kindness in order to understand it and to nurture it in yourself. Tonglen is a form of prayer in which you breathe out healing energy and breath in any pain and suffering. You engage in a continual exchange, taking in what you would normally avoid and giving out what you would normally hold onto. The insight and spaciousness cultivated in mindfulness-awareness provides the context that prevents such a challenging practice as tonglen from becoming heavy-handed or moralistic. In the process of exchange, nothing is held, but everything is let go.

Accepting Vulnerability

Contemplative practice is a means of integration that requires the courage to take a clear-eyed look at our own self-deceptions, habits, flaws, presumptions, fixed views, and fears. By acknowledging such vulnerabilities and flaws and accepting our own imperfections, we can connect to others in a genuine and heartfelt way, with less to hide and less need of armoring. It is by recognizing and accepting our faults, confusions, challenges, and distractions that we can begin to disempower them and let them go.

Qualities Cultivated by Contemplative Practice

Contemplative practice is designed to cultivate specific physical, mental, and psychological qualities. It is more than simply a form of relaxation. The following table gives a sample of some of the abilities and characteristics that meditative practices are designed to enhance.

Qualities Developed Through Contemplative Practice

MENTAL	EMOTIONAL	PHYSICAL
Concentration/ Stability	Gentleness	Stillness
Relaxation/ Expansiveness	Nonjudging	Postural dignity
Strength/ Resilience	Self-Acceptance	Well-being
Familiarization/ Self Knowledge	Restraint/ Self-control	Presence
Openness/ Spaciousness	Emotional honesty	Sensory refinement
Clarity/ Attentiveness	Genuineness	Grace
Insight	Lightness and Humor	Decorum
Nimbleness/ Pliability	Equanimity	Bodily awareness
Unbiasedness	Kindness	Ease
Wisdom	Compassion	Balance

Contemplative Forms / Contemplative Mindset

There are contemplative forms and practices and there is also a contemplative mindset. They are two different things. In terms of forms, the most commonly utilized in the context of end-of-life care are mindfulness practice, hatha yoga, and loving-kindness practice or *tonglen*. Although these practices have their origins from the Hindu and Buddhist traditions, all three can be practiced by people of any religious tradition as well as people with no religious affiliation. They are simple, practical, and beneficial.

The contemplative mindset is an approach to life that may include contemplative practice but is much broader in scope. It is based on the experience of interconnectedness of oneself, others, and the world as a whole, and the view of life as a path of continual challenges, learning, and growth. It is the attitude of a student, in which curiosity and inquisitiveness are valued, and even the most ordinary events of daily life are seen as potential teachers. Taking such an attitude changes the way a person relates to their work and to others. It changes the way one approaches EOL care.

Formal and On-the-Spot Practice

Contemplative practice is utilized in two main formats. In more formal individual or group meditation practice, you are taking time away from daily business in order to train the mind. You are taking a break from such activity to gain perspective and to develop qualities that you can then draw on when you resume your work.

On-the-spot practices are methods of touching into meditative awareness in the midst of whatever you are doing. They are a way of regrouping and coming from a fresh perspective. Such practices can be as simple as coming back into your body, slowing down, taking a pause, or remembering to breathe.

Contemplative Practice in the Context of End-of-Life Care

Recently there has been a growing interest in incorporating contemplative practice in the field of EOL care. The origins of this interest can be traced to the pioneering work of people who sought a more humanistic, holistic, and multidimensional approach to EOL care, and in fact, to healthcare in general.

In the 60's, Elizabeth Kubler-Ross opened the discussion of how we care for the dying in a daring and challenging way, by asking the dying persons themselves. Her example and her book *On Death and Dying* played a pivotal role in inspiring pioneers in the field.

Dame Cecily Saunders, was another pioneering figure. She not only established the first modern hospice, St. Christopher's Hospice in England, but she did significant research on pain management and published extensively on the need for a multi-dimensional approach to eol care that incorporated spiritual, social, emotional, economic, dimensions as well as the medical. Since the establishment of St. Christopher's, the modern hospice movement has expanded throughout the world, helping many dying people and their families.

In the 70's, Florence Wald, Dean of the Yale School of Nursing, inspired by Saunders, banded together with a concerned group of medical practitioners, activists and psychologists to create the first hospice in North America in Connecticut. Like Saunders, Wald and others vision was to re-situate the end of life as a human event, not simply as a medical challenge. Florence Wald convened a number of symposiums bringing together religious and spiritual teachers meeting with medical and hospice practitioners to explore the role of spirituality in helping both patients and caregivers and medical professionals dealing with the end of life.

Dr. Balfour Mount of the Royal Victoria hospital in Montreal was another pioneer in bringing spirituality and a more contemplative approach into EOL care. In a series of annual international palliative care conferences that brought professionals from around the world, Dr. Mount incorporated presentations on spirituality and of contemplative modalities as well as the arts into the context of a standard medical convention.

For more on the development of hospice and the early pioneers concern with holistic care, see the film *Pioneers of Hospice* (pioneersofhospice.org).

Historically, a number of forces converged in the 70's and 80's. The opening of the discussion of death and dying, the movement for patient empowerment, the rise of interest in meditation practice and the exposure to a wider range of religious traditions, the growth of the hospice movement, the resistance to the over-medicalizing of the human passages of birth and death, and the vision of a more holistic approach to health and healing, the AIDS epidemic—these all contributed to create an atmosphere open and receptive to the value of a contemplative dimension in EOL care.

As the country has grown more diverse, and as many more persons are unaffiliated with any particular religious tradition, the discussion of spirituality and care giving has changed. In the past, this aspect was mainly in the hands of a person's minister, priest, or rabbi, in the form of religious counsel. In more recent times, when people often say that they are spiritual, but not religious, there has been an interest in a more broad-based spirituality geared toward human needs, apart from religious affiliation. Because of that, many clinical pastoral education programs (CPE) now incorporate an interfaith chaplaincy option, and some now offer at least a basic introduction to meditation practice or tonglen.

Organizations that Support Contemplative Practice in EOL Care

At this point, there is a growing recognition of the value of contemplative training in EOL care. It is becoming more mainstream. As an example, the 18th International Palliative Care Conference scheduled for October 2010 in Montreal includes a plenary session on mindfulness in EOL care.

The list of organizations, people, and projects that follows is not by any means complete, it is only highlights, but it will provide a glimpse of the many organizations supporting this work.

- Being with Dying Training / Joan Halifax
- Zen Hospice San Francisco/founded 1987 by Issan Dorsey and Frank Ostaseski
- Metta Training Program / founded 2004 Frank Ostaseski
- Maitri Compassionate Care Project San Francisco / founded 1987
- Rigpa Spiritual Care Programs and Contemplative End-of-Life Care Training / Sogyal Rinpoche
- Naropa University Contemplative End-of-Life Care Certificate Program
- Naropa University Masters of Divinity Program
- New York Zen Center for Contemplative Care / Roshi Pat O'Hara Koshin Paley Ellison
- Mindfulness Based Stress Reduction Training U Mass / John Kabat-Zinn
- Brown University Contemplative Studies Initiative
- Dying Well / Ira Byock Dartmouth Hitchcock Medical Center, Hanover NH
- Center to Advance Palliative Care (CAPC) / Dr. Diane Meiers

There are a variety of web resources on EOL care and contemplative practice on sites such a beliefnet.com, dyingwell.org, zencare.org and others.

Demographics

The early adapters of meditative training and tended to be predominantly educated, white, and middle class; likewise, early proponents of hospice and the movement for more holistic approaches to the dying. Currently, there is growing diversity within the meditative traditions, culturally, geographically, and racially. Hospice, too, is gradually broadening its base. However, there is still suspicion and often misunderstanding as to what hospice is about and on issues of death and dying altogether. Death is a topic most people prefer to avoid.

Trends / Opportunities / Challenges

The trend over the past twenty years has been a steady but gradual increase of interest in, knowledge about, and exposure to contemplative practice in the general culture. Although there is still suspicion in some quarters, practices such as meditation and yoga have moved from the fringe to a more mainstream position in society.

There are many opportunities to strengthen the contemplative component of EOL care. Interest in meditation and its benefits is high. Research on neuroplasticity and the effects of meditation on the brain have created a powerful reinforcement to the subjective descriptions of experienced meditators. Furthermore, the population is aging and the baby boomers are at a point in life when they are beginning to take a personal interest in the quality of care available to them at the end of life.

A primary challenge in the further integration of contemplative training into EOL care is the lack of research on the various approaches and methodologies and documentation regarding their effectiveness. Information is scattered and anecdotal. Also, as the contemplative approach gains in popularity, there is the danger of losing the depth and power of such practices by presenting them in a shallow or formulaic way. It is important to distinguish the application of contemplative techniques and understanding as a tool in caregiving or as support to persons at the end of life from contemplative practice in the context of a specific religion or spiritual tradition. Along with that, there is a need to develop language and training in contemplative practice specific to the needs of EOL care. In addressing these needs, it would be a great benefit to find the means to gather and extend knowledge and resources by means of convening periodic conferences bringing together on a regular basis the key people and organizations active in this field.

The State of Contemplative Practice in the USA and Globally: Integrating Contemplative Practice and Leadership Development in Diverse Sectors of Society and Around the World

Walter Link

Every few hundred years in history there occurs a sharp transformation. Within a few short decades, society—its worldviews, its basic values, its social and political structures, its art, its key institutions—rearranges itself. We are currently living through such a time. — Peter Drucker

The most exciting breakthroughs of the twenty-first century will occur not because of technology, but because of an expanding concept of what it means to be human. — John Naisbitt

We will never have peace until men everywhere recognize that ends are not cut off from means, because the means represent the ideal in the making, and the end in process…the means represent the seed and the end represents the tree. — Martin Luther King, Jr.

Introduction to My Particular Perspective

You asked us to address a number of questions about the state of the contemplative movement in the USA. You asked me to do so with a particular focus on integrating contemplative practice into leadership development, i.e. how leaders and organizations around the world and across diverse sectors of society benefit from inner and interpersonal work practices to bring about a more effective and just, peaceful and sustainable world. In order to be transparent about where I am coming from in answering your questions, let me clarify a few things about my background and perspective:

Unlike most of my co-authors, I am not a US American but rather a European born in Germany who has lived and worked in many countries around the world, in particular throughout Western and Eastern Europe, South and North America and Asia. My work therefore is not predominantly focused in or on the US but rather internationally. When considering your invitation, I thought I might nevertheless be a useful addition to our gathering and this book, on one hand because during the past twenty years I have spent a lot of time in the USA and on the other because many of the contemplative perspectives and practices which we consider here originate in areas of the world where I have lived, studied and worked. These approaches have been significantly impacted by their adaptation to US audiences and are often re-exported in further developed or at least newly packaged forms. In my opinion we therefore can't fully understand the contemplative movement in the United States and elsewhere in isolation from the rest of the world. If ever there was a global movement, this is it.

Also you asked me to focus on the sub-field of contemplative leadership practice which I have increasingly specialized in after having been a student and teacher of various psycho-spiritual paths including Buddhism, the Diamond Approach and Transpersonal Psychology, training for example meditation teachers how to work with psycho-emotional issues and therapists how to integrate meditation and other spiritual practices and perspectives into their work and life. Now I primarily work with leaders and their organizations and movements in diverse sectors of society, ranging from business, civil society, the public sector to the media and arts, science and education in many countries around the world. This allows me to appreciate the underlying issues that differentiate us and are shared across sectors and cultures. In these diverse environments I adapt traditional and contemporary psycho-spiritual approaches, modern science and my own leadership experience to the particular people and circumstances I am working with—presenting the same essence in differing forms. I think that this "trans-formation" of practice and perspective is a challenging yet important trend in the development of contemplative practice in the Unitesd States and abroad, which is needed if we want to serve the mainstream of modern societies.

To illustrate my work in those regards, I offer a number of examples that can serve as mini-cases to point to the general opportunities and challenges for the contemplative movement, which you requested us to address. For example, in Europe I presently co-lead a two-year leadership development and coaching program for senior executives of Triodos, which in 2009 received the *Financial Times* award for Europe's most sustainable bank. They realize that sustainability in the broadest sense needs to go beyond "what" they do to "how" they do it and that the integration of appropriately adopted inner and interpersonal work will allow them to move towards their potential of organizational and societal transformation.

In Sri Lanka, I am engaged in a multi-facetted effort to strengthen the grass roots democracy and societal transformation movement initiated by Sarvodaya. The country's largest NGO, it today works with over 10,000 villages after being founded 50 years ago by Dr. A.T. Ariyaratne, who is often called Sri Lanka's Gandhi. While they are deeply inspired by both Buddhist and Gandhi's thinking, they wanted support in translating this even more effectively into the way they manage their organization and overall work, which Dr. Ariyaratne and I are also conceptualizing in a book on Buddhist economics and leadership. This follows *Leadership is Global*, which I co-edited as a dialog of 22 authors from around the world to demonstrate diverse approaches to integrate contemplative practices and perspectives into organizational leadership work and societal transformation.

To reach a broader audience I am also producing, with Brazilian and Dutch partners, a TV series in which I dialog with well-respected leaders from around the world who model how deep inspiration and contemplative practice can lead to outstanding success in sustainable business, social transformation, science and culture. With *Mega-Trends* author John Naisbitt and other colleagues I am presently developing an institute in China to support innovation in business, governance, education and other sectors of society. Finally in the US I founded the first fully accredited MBA in Sustainable Management that also attempted to integrate contemplative practice into its integrative curriculum. And I just co-taught the post-graduate Rotary Peace Seminar at Berkeley University where students from around the world who never participated in explicit practice acknowledged its usefulness. As the CEO and activist staff of ForestEthics, which after similar successes due to its outstanding negotiation approach is now working to create the world's largest forest conversation project.

These experiences and many I can't name helped to shape the perspective from which I make the following comments. They also let me to understand that each of us can only make a tiny contribution, if that. Therefore my work besides serving particular people, organizations and their constituencies is intended to co-create a movement around the world that allows people to recognize and benefit from the value of inner and interpersonal work not only to improve their personal lives but to co-create societies that become the expression for our potential for loving peace and dynamic sustainability.

Co-creating a Movement

Before following your request to offer a definition of "contemplative practice," I want to congratulate the organizers for convening this important and timely initiative. I have no doubt that in the US and around the world there is a strongly emerging movement towards what we call here "contemplative practice." As I will briefly mention below, I have directly experienced how creating gatherings and networks like this one have played a significant role in generating cohesion and critical mass for movements to enter and shift the mainstream of societies around the world, such as the movements for sustainability and human rights, corporate social and environmental responsibility and transformative leadership practice.

In support of that I also want to point to a key challenge that I think we face in this and other movements that are needed to evolve our civilization towards awake and dynamic sustainability. In order to communicate, we need terms that point to fields of meaning and activity such as "contemplative practice" (or "sustainability" for that matter). Such terms can help us to focus our expression and simplify communication. But they also introduce the potential for exclusion, which is particularly limiting in a field that is still widely met with disinterest and even rejection by the mainstream, and in which we ourselves can get quite attached to our own differentiating language and the particular "branding" of our approaches—many of which, I experience, have much more in common than is generally acknowledged.

Personally I like the term "contemplative practice" and your apparently very open definition of it, which is reflected in the diverse participants of this meeting. But if we want to co-create an inclusive movement that gains sufficient critical mass to accelerate societal transformation, we should be aware of this potential problem and intentionally invite others who use different terminologies and approaches that nevertheless share in the essence of what we choose to call "contemplative practice." We also must be aware that there can't be any single convener for such a movement. Movements generally arise around many kernels that gradually coalesce if organizers stay open enough to share their role with others who share their selfless intentions. Therefore let's see who else could join in this process to expand meaningful inclusiveness.

In my view and experience of working with many people from diverse backgrounds and cultures is that we share an essential nature, which in its manifestation includes both our oneness and our differentiation. Therefore I observe that all human development occurs according to the same underlying principles. Of course we come from different cultures. We have many distinguishing characteristics and histories. But ultimately we are all human beings who quite easily reveal their fundamental unity when we scratch the surface of our apparent difference. If we can both appreciate the uniqueness and also reach beyond the different forms and terminologies to discover what unifies us, we might help this movement, which still seems very disparate, to develop a stronger sense of cohesion without denying that genuinely diverse paths lead up the same mountain. As the Buddha pointed out, all suffering arises from the illusion of separateness. Having been around the US's and other cultures' contemplative communities for many years, I have observed how unconstructively critical some, maybe many of us, can be of each other and of each other's work. This leaves me wondering how we can honor differences and forgive limitations, which after all have been created by life's evolutionary process, which none of us can fully comprehend.

As I am writing this paper I find myself reflecting about the time when I was co-creating the movement for social responsibility and environmental sustainability in business, which included also sub-movements, ranging from responsible investment and micro-finance to fair trade, social entrepreneurship and new economics. At that time I had just sold my partnership in B.Grimm, a 130 year-old industrial group of companies in Asia and Europe to focus work on co-creating and co-leading business networks across Europe and the Americas to support this emerging movement that was not yet visible as an alternative to the mainstream of economic activity but that we believed wanted and needed to happen.

Many of my mainstream colleagues thought that I had gone off the deep end by leaving my company. And they didn't even know that spiritual development had by then already become the center of my life. In fact, only a few of us who were trying to catalyze this movement identified with doing spiritual work; the majority instead saw responsible business and economics as a movement for social transformation. However I always understood it also as an awakening of our collective soul to manifest our individual and collective potential. To me we felt like a community of practitioners who loved and inspired, supported and challenged each other.

Like in the field of contemplative practice, there was much that made us different from each other. And yet what allowed us to become so successful in co-creating a unifying movement that eventually gathered enough critical mass to cause significant transformation was that we generally put our commonalities above our differences. We became allies rather than competitors. We learned from and with each other rather than only criticize our many limitations. And we showed the world that a different form of business and economy was not only thinkable but doable. In both words and deeds we contradicted the mainstream conviction that responsibility and prosperity were mutually exclusive, and on the contrary demonstrated that a growing number of consumers and activists, investors and business people could co-create a large enough sample that demonstrated the viability of a real alternative.

Of course the full potential of this movement has not been reached by far. But I think that the contemplative movement could benefit from the collaborative lessons that were learned in the development of this and other movements that have led to significant transformation in societies around the world. I also believe that one of the great contributions of the contemplative movement could be to help those wanting to change the world of action to work and collaborate even more effectively. For that we need to practically demonstrate that we can do more than enhance individual enlightenment and personal lives but that our practices can optimize any kind of work and social transformation towards a better world. I believe we are increasingly managing to do exactly that. In this sense we are aligned with both Eastern and Western spiritual service traditions—from Kharma Yoga and Engaged Buddhism to authentic Christianity and ancient Western philosophies—which integrated "inner" and "outer" transformation.

Defining "Contemplative Practice"

You asked us for a definition of contemplative practice. While there isn't one that I regularly use, here are some that come to mind as we attempt to circumscribe this field:

- A generic version: "Any practice of doing and eventually of non-doing that supports us to deepen and broaden the realization of who we really are and that helps us to live that realization as we mature into the fullness of our potential."
- A shorter generic version: "Any practice that inspires and enables us to awaken, heal and serve."
- A culturally specific and yet universal version that I think gets to the point: "Anything that supports us to become a 'mensch'" (Mensch being the Yiddish term for a real, mature, world-wise human being, which adds the aspect of human potential to the more generic German word for "human being").
- A two-word version, which I sometimes use to describe my work: "Inspired Pragmatism." ("Pragmatism" because I my

opinion contemplative practice has to "work" in order to deserve that denomination. Real inner work works. "Inspired" because it originates from our deepest inspiration for self-realization and service, which are one with the path that leads us there.)

- I also love this quote from my dear teacher, colleague and friend Ram Dass who played such an important role in popularizing contemplative practice in the US without banalizing it: "We don't want to end up being expert meditators. We want to end up being free."
- And finally a version that is particularly close to my heart. It was offered by the amazing monkey warrior God Hanuman who is seen as the pure embodiment of Kharma Yoga, which uses service as a path. He says to the God Rama in the Ramayana: "When I forget myself, I serve you. When I remember myself, I am you."

Forms and Essence of Contemplative Practice

As you can see, I avoid reducing my definitions to traditionally codified practices such as various forms of meditation, prayer and inquiry, to name but a few. These traditional forms and the complete paths of which they are an integral part, are in my opinion of tremendous value. In my experience, the integrity of the complex interactions of the various practices and perspectives that make up of specific approaches to human transformation are often ignored to the detriment of the badly instructed practitioners, limiting their development. Simply said, the US "supermarket mentality," in which many people choose what they like (and ignore what they need) from a wide variety of partial and often superficial practice offerings, has created significant challenges to the maturation of practitioners and their instructors, who can suffer from the same limitations. In that sense our movement needs a more realistic understanding of what works and what doesn't to support real transformation.

On the other hand, the easy access to so many practices and the freedom to experiment with them has in my opinion brought much benefit, especially when it later leads to more focused forms of engagement. As I mentioned already, I also believe that a more essential, less formal approach to practice is one of the key trends in contemplative practice in the US and worldwide, especially in the very pragmatic world of individual and collective leadership work across the diverse sectors of action in which I work. Rather than wanting to practice in a particular traditional form, these "leaders" (a term that creates as much challenge as benefit) are inspired pragmatists. They somehow know that there is more to life, to their potential and their ability to be of service. They want to learn and do what works to develop toward the individual and collective potential on the closely interconnected level of personal, interpersonal, organizational and systemic levels of development.

Contemporary practice and conceptualization therefore are increasingly growing beyond personal development to include all aspects of life. While traditional paths and the monasteries in which many of them were originally practiced will remain important supports, I think that contemplative practice, especially in the US, will move more and more into new forms and day-to-day living, where it will be challenged and renewed in the cauldron of constant pressures and inspirations that strip it to its essential bones. In this process every formal aspect of contemplative practice will be rightfully questioned, and we will hopefully develop the wisdom to preserve both essence and essential forms while dropping unessential ones. In this process contemplative practice will increasingly help to transform the world, as the world will increasingly adapt and refine contemplative practice.

As someone who has gone through rigorous training in the forms as well as the essence of a number of Eastern and Western spiritual traditions and who greatly values their wisdom and integrity, I find this "essential approach" to be a fascinating challenge that continuously forces me to allow the essence of practice and view to take the form and language that is most useful in any given situation. Rather than being able to use age-old formulas, I have to continuously practice in order to refine access to and trust of my guidance so I can know how to best adapt to the specific person or group, in the specific situation and moment.

This makes the work on myself even more important because when leaving traditional forms I believe we don't only free up creativity, we also increase the risk of misunderstanding and distortion (which of course is also common within traditions). I notice that over the years of practice and service my humility continues to increase as I realize how challenging it is to deepen my own maturity and to guide others on their unique journey. I also appreciate more and more why so many traditions use the community of practitioners— optimally real friends on the path who also are able to tell us uncomfortable things about ourselves. And I appreciate the importance of teachers, teachings and their transmission, in whatever forms they arise. I hope that to some degree we can be this for one another as we co-create this movement that can empower so many other movements.

Some More Challenges

Before I elaborate further on some of what I perceive to be many positive trends and opportunities of the current developments in the field of contemplative practice, let me mention a few additional challenges. One of them is the question of "quality control" that we called "standards" and tried to address with new forms of accounting and auditing, with stakeholder engagement and quality labels in the movement towards changing the economy. If one wants to create an impactful movement it helps to distinguish between genuine contemplative practices and more or less empty forms that have little impact. As our field expands, I observe a kind of "inflation" in the use of terms such as meditation. While "real" meditation has of course the potential to bring about significant insight and transformation, many people who think they meditate are merely scratching the surface of rest and relaxation.

Surely even the ladder is of benefit in our hectic world and can serve as a gateway to deeper practice. But it also waters down the meaning of the term and its impact if it is not clearly understood and explained. Subsequently it risks undermining the interest in further practice, including real one and can in certain cases cause harm, such as when unskillful yoga instruction or inappropriate emotional work traumatize rather than heal the participant. It also doesn't help that many immature practitioners appear "weird" to many in the mainstream of society. On the other hand I observe that genuine development, while having extraordinary impacts, makes us ever more simple and ordinary to the point where people not involved in apparent practice don't perceive us as strange or different but rather as attractive and supportive.

Of course, as in so many things US American, there is also an important commercial challenge to the success of this movement. This is particularly true in the field of leadership and organizational consulting where certain practices are offered at 1 or 10 percent of effectiveness for 10 or 100 times the price of traditional teachings. For example, such profound terms as "presence" have lately become fashionable and attract business. Some of the consultants and coaches who now offer "presence work" have in my experience only a faint conceptual, let alone experiential understanding of what they read about in books or hear about during short workshops. While the use of such terms and practices can open the mainstream of business and other domains of action to the usefulness of inner and interpersonal work, it also can deliver them in such a way that the initial interest is disappointed, replacing genuine desire with disinterest and even cynicism.

A more honorable dilemma of the leadership component of our larger field is that even though many leaders and leadership process facilitators actually have deep psycho-spiritual development that allows them to be remarkably inspiring and effective, they have not been trained to instruct others. Therefore when they attempt to become teachers and coaches themselves their impact can be quite limited. We need to develop instruction methodologies that equal the kind of developmental practices and paths that have been refined in the traditions, sometimes for thousands of years with millions of practitioners.

Ancient and even some contemporary teaching traditions address these methodological and quality control issues with rigorous training programs that, as you know, typically last for many years, even decades. While serving on the boards of multi-denominational US institutions such as Naropa University, Omega Institute and the Institute of Noetic Sciences, I have experienced first-hand how we attempt to bring some level of quality control and training opportunities into the field. Of course also the "market" selects and promotes teachers and teachings, by the simple fact that people choose to join them. Unfortunately popularity is not always a good guide to quality. Indeed US attraction to and ignorance of charisma, transmission and certain spiritual powers can lead to the seduction of many hungry people into more or less awful cults or less dramatically to not very transformative practices.

Overall I see the greatest limitation to the genuine growth of the field of contemplative practice to be the number of qualified teachers, consultants and training opportunities that can effectively support the ever-increasing number of willing practitioners. In the field of contemplative leadership development we face the additional challenge that even well-trained instructors and consultants often lack specific experience of actual leadership in the world and are therefore removed from the experiential quality of the lives of leaders. While empathic attunement and a general understanding of the human condition can bridge many divides, I often hear from both coaches and clients how hard it can be to for people who haven't been involved in the day-to-day intensity of organizational and systemic leadership to fully appreciate the extent of loneliness and the weight of responsibility, the seduction of power and money, the need for courage and entrepreneurship, the pressure and exhaustion that leaders deal with on a daily basis. I therefore think that initiatives such as ours are well served by including not only "teachers" but also such "students," who then turn out to become our teachers.

Fortunately life, including human beings, continues to evolve, even if for times and in aspects it seems to devolve and result in unspeakable suffering. While I think we should seriously address these and other challenges, I also observe the ongoing development of people, organizations and societies that make great use of even the most limited resources and the most challenging situations to realize our human potential. Working with leaders in through-out professions and cultures, I find many who have the kind of development we look for even though they never received any formal instruction in con-templative practices but were just living life as it presented itself. In short, I am optimistic.

Is the Contemplative Movement Growing?

My short answer is yes for the US and for the parts of the world I have expe-rienced well enough. This is particularly true when we open up the definition of the term "contemplative" or any other inner- and interpersonal work-ori-ented terminology that is meaningful for only a small number of people and include the type of broad definitions that I offered above. Then I see that this development is very dynamic and inclusive, reaching into and across all professions and sectors in varying degrees of quantity and quality. This is even so in areas in which one might not expect it, such as in the military, where not only special commandos are trained in awareness practices but where, for example, tens of thousands of severely traumatized US soldiers return from battles in Iraq and Afghanistan with the urgent if not yet fully recognized need to be cared for in a holistic manner.

To date, more US soldiers have died from suicide than in actual battle. Eventually such situations tend to create a tremendous pressure to find an-swers, both in regard to curing trauma as well as to avoiding war and facili-tating peace, which as history shows will not be sustained without human maturation. We know that these answers can be found at least in part in contemplative practice. Accordingly my friends from Peace Direct that works with hundreds of peace initiatives around the world observed that those using contemplative practices and perspectives are more sustainable.

In this regard it is interesting to consider a society such as Germany, which until recently was one of the most war-prone not only during the 20th cen-tury but for many centuries before. Following the undeniable horrors of the Second World War and the Holocaust, Germans were forced to face their shadow to an extend that is rare if not unique in history. As a result it seems impossible that Germany would start a war again. It is only against continu-ously large majorities that German troops remain engaged in Afghanistan and Germany refused to join its close allies in Iraq. In a recent poll citizens from around the world ranked Germany as one of the most peaceful countries. Did "contemplative practice" play a role in this quite miraculous transformation?

In my opinion absolutely, even though this kind of contemplation fits more into the secular enlightenment and the values of humanism than into outright spiritual traditions. In fact, I suggest that especially Northern Europe, which is among the most secular regions in the world, has developed one of the most deeply "spiritual" societies if you join me in considering that environmental responsibility, the rule of law and social solidarity are the lived expression of mature contemplative practitioners. Of course Northern Europe, like the US, also suffers from rampant materialism and spiritual emptiness. The situation is more complex than can be explored here but I mention these points to open up our consideration of what the contemplative movement ultimately is and can be.

In addition to humanity's innate longing and opportunity for self-realization and service (which may be more or less accessible after years of often ill-guided "education"), it is also problems that motivate us to find solutions. And problems we have plenty. I don't need to go into detail with a group such as ours about the many crises that haunt every system humans are involved with. The resulting lack of sustainability severely challenges social and environmental systems as well as economic and financial ones, all of which are of course aspects of a unified and completely interactive field of life. At the same time, having worked in many sub-fields of inner and outer work—in mainstream and alternative business, in various sectors of non-profit work and social entrepreneurship, in health care and human genome technology, in psycho-spiritual teaching and integral leadership work—I have witnessed a dynamically expanding development of the demographic reach of our movement, especially if we use my wider definitions of contemplative practice.

From extensive research for a book about our evolving civilization and its relationship to contemplative practice that I have been working on for the past ten years I learned things such as these: Good cancer treatment increasingly involves both inner work and alternative healing modalities from around the world, advancing not only the use of "contemplation" but also helping us to realize the value of our diverse yet compatible cultures. Advanced sciences from physics to brain research are rediscovering and appreciating the insights of ancient contemplative teachings and are gradually opening to their practices. Appropriate technology choices, such as those involving human genome issues, also require ethical decisions. Activists, religious leaders and artists are involved in such contemplations, alongside scientists, business leaders and bureaucrats—bridging again the divides of modern specialization that often blind us to a holistic view. Leading innovation and design consultants such as IDEO, which helped to invent the (computer) mouse and increasingly help to innovate organizational processes, are using contemplative practices to stimulate creativity.

Companies ranging from Monsanto and Goldman Sachs to Google and Genentech are using such practices to support staff and strategy development. Inspired and burned out activists increasingly realize that their effectiveness requires being supported by contemplative practices, especially if they want to become the change they long to see in the world, as Gandhi put it. Education is experimenting again with its Oriental and Western roots of contemplative approaches to learning. In all of these sectors, terms such as "integrative" or "integral" point also to the inclusion of contemplative practice. And the list goes on and on, spreading to ever more areas in the mainstream of societies around the world, including, in my opinion, the person of US President Obama and the movement that arose around his election. Here is a quote of his that could serve as yet another definition of contemplative practice:

> ... I'm constantly asking myself questions about what I'm doing, why am I doing it... I'm measuring my actions against that inner voice that for me at least is audible, is active, it tells me where I think I'm on track... It's interesting the most powerful political moments for me come when I feel like my actions are aligned with a certain truth. I can feel it. When I'm talking to a group and I'm saying something truthful, I can feel a power that comes out of those statements that is different than when I'm just being glib or clever.

Of course the contemplative movement as well the societal transformation movements that I mentioned are still very far from reaching their potential. In fact, the movement towards the inclusion of contemplative practice highlights not only its benefits but also its limitations. The meditation practiced by the leadership teams of Monsanto also helped them refine their capacity to spread GMO technology around the globe. Yoga in its devolved form as mere physical exercise and relaxation technique practiced at Goldman Sachs didn't reduce their greed and fundamental amorality. And we could also expand this list significantly. In fact, in many regards it appears that we are taking more steps back than forward—with or without our current levels of contemplative practice. But as I already mentioned, I understand this as part of the mysterious yet irreversible process of evolution that obviously advances with much trial, error and suffering.

Leadership Development and Education

From countless conversations with people around the world, I sense that it is becoming increasingly clear to a growing number of people that the old "modern" ways of life don't work and that they logically lead to the negative outcomes we are facing today. When we take, for example, the present US and international economic and financial crises, we can easily observe that the leaders of the involved institutions have been educated and trained in the best schools, universities and training programs that the US has to offer. Yet they produced this crisis not by accident but from within the inherent logic of the system they are co-creating and co-leading. And they will do so again and again if we don't change the way we train people for individual and collective leadership.

This is not to say that Harvard and the like are not excellent learning environments. We certainly don't want to throw the baby out with the bathwater. But we also need to and gradually do realize that our ways of leadership education and development are both inadequate and incomplete. Among others, the important work of the Center for Contemplative Mind in Society demonstrates that contemplative practice is one of the missing if gradually developing links in education, which interestingly is one of our most conservative institutions.

I observed both this conservatism and emerging openness to the inclusion of meaningful contemplative work when I recently taught a post-graduate seminar for Rotary Peace Fellows from around the world at UC Berkeley. Unlike in most courses, we involved the students in deciding what would be most useful to learn for their careers, which ranged from international law to peace and sustainability oriented activism in the Niger Delta. In comparison to the work I do with senior leaders in companies and with social entrepreneurs, I offered a kind of watered down version of the leadership training and contemplative practice. Yet the comments of the students who found this work very useful and of other faculty members who asked to sit in on the course confirmed how even "contemplation-lite" pushes the envelop of major educational institutions, even one such as UC Berkeley that stood at the academic cutting edge of the transformation of consciousness in America.

At the same time my friend Americ Azevedo teaches a weekly mediation course on campus that is regularly attended by several hundred students. But clearly such courses are not integrated into the overall curriculum and even less do they inform the method of learning in other courses, where contemplation, as was confirmed by my mini-sample of students, can also lead to better exam grades.

To show that we can not only introduce the odd course of meditation, ethics or corporate responsibility but need to create integral programs to educate and train a new generation of business, non-profit and public service leaders, I co-designed the first fully accredited MBA in Sustainable Management in the US at the Presidio World College in San Francisco. The most interesting aspect in regard to the questions we are considering here is that we designed the program in such as way that while only 25 percent of the courses focused on sustainability and 25 percent focused on integral leadership, a full 100 percent of the courses were designed to integrate both with whichever other topic ranging from marketing to finance was taught according to ivy league standards.

We started seven years ago with 22 students. Today we have in addition to the original MBA, an Executive Certificate degree for professionals who can spend two to four years at school and a Master of Public Administration for about 600 students all together. At the same time we have received media and academic attention and are attracting more "mainstream" students, some of whom choose us over established Ivy League schools. In many regards the program has been a big success, and it certainly adds a little bit to the renewal of education in the US. However, a significant snag has arisen in regard to contemplative practice. While most of the early students were open to doing inner work, some weren't, and that number grew with the increasing number of mainstream students who primarily wanted to change the world around them rather then also themselves. And gradually, because we, much like other US educational institutions, are in my opinion too afraid of critical student feedback, the parts of leadership work that challenged students' personalities and invited them into deeper contemplative practice were diminished.

I recognize in this shift the power of systems to preserve their status quo that I have witnessed in other transformational movements in which I participated. First we were at the fringe of the system and thus didn't threaten its status quo. But when we moved closer towards its center, threatening to inspire wider change, the system "cleansed" itself. In that sense macro-systems are no different from the micro-system of our ego-personalities that allow a bit of contemplative practice as long as it doesn't really challenge who we think we are and brings up all kinds of resistances when it does. This is neither surprising nor evil. It is unconscious and logical and we need to work with and around that logic to really support the growth of the contemplative movement.

Yet the movement towards integral programs continues. For example with the Global Leadership Network—a network of senior leadership experts from around the world that I co-founded and co-chair—I studied thirty cutting edge leadership development programs from around the world, including several Ivy League and non-academic programs in the US. A core outcome of the study was that these programs are able to be so successful because they combine organizational and societal transformation with personal and interpersonal development. I believe that programs such as these show the way forward toward educational reform that addresses the whole of us and therefore supports us to become more effective leaders towards dynamic sustainability. This is also true in Asia, Africa and Latin America, where I have personally experienced the powerful impact of inner and interpersonal work.

Interestingly, also companies are increasingly integrating contemplative practice into their training programs. I believe this is happening because business people as well as social entrepreneurs and others who want to bring about change in the world can be very pragmatic. They really want to solve problems and take advantage of opportunities. They are willing to take risks in particular in the US where "just do it" is not only a marketing slogan but a way of life. The more we can demonstrate to these people and organizations that what we offer works for them and for the whole, the more likely it is that they will engage in contemplative practice en masse.

Let me give you another example from the work I been part of in that domain. A colleague and I currently are facilitating a two-year leadership development program for a transnational bank called Triodos. On average they have grown 27 percent a year over the past three decades and successfully mastered the recent financial crisis. In fact, their sustainable business model was so successful that it shielding it from the recent challenges of the financial crisis. For this reason Triodos has been studied by much larger competitors, Federal Reserve banks and government leaders. Its CEO is also wise enough to recognize that to continue down this line, their future top leaders whom we are training need to be deeply grounded in inner and outer reality. Therefore our program also works with deep personal transformation processes.

Based on the understanding of how human consciousness evolves, we have designed a process in which participants develop particular qualities or being and skills of doing. After an extended process of contemplation and practice this process can lead to actual transformation supporting these leaders to integrate certain leadership capacities that then manifest logically in different behavior. In my experience such developmental processes are much more sustainable and crisis resistant than methods that focus immediately on changing behavior before changing the person. We are also using "contemplative practice" based interpersonal processes to reinvent feedback mechanisms, corporate culture and stakeholder relationships as well as with topics relating to reinventing banking and society—all of which the participants increasingly recognize are intimately related.

In that regard I believe we don't only need a movement to bring about more contemplation but one that elaborates on how we can completely integrate all aspects of inner and outer work, resolving the unnatural split of what is ultimately one and the same—contemplation and action. If contemplative practice can't help us to redesign for instance modern economics, it has not yet reached its potential.

From my experience of designing and facilitating such processes over the past twenty years, I can say that such approaches do not only work in formal organizations in Western countries but also in companies and on the level of grassroots organizations and movements in societies of the Global South, where presently I am engaged in a multi-faceted project in Sri Lanka that offers an example of how contemplative practice can be integrated in a manner that respects local cultures and opportunities. In this short text I can only mention a few aspects of this complex leadership development and societal transformation program.

I am working there with a fifty-year-old organization called Sarvodaya, which was founded by a deeply inspired and pragmatic social entrepreneur by the name of Dr. Ariyaratne, whom many call "Sri Lanka's Gandhi." They work with millions of poor people in thousands of villages using an amazingly holistic approach. They combine Buddhist philosophy with infrastructure development and sustainable technology, microcredit and lifelong education, peace work and leadership development. For example, they help these villagers to develop their own autonomous governance councils, which always include children as young as seven years of age. This helps all generations to lead together and makes sure that the future of the village is represented in the decision making process.

When Dr Ariyaratne asked me to support them, Sarvodaya wanted a consciousness-based modernization of their organization and movement, using also further integration of inner and interpersonal work into its operation. Even though they subscribe to Buddhist philosophy and traditionally have used some rather ritualistic practices such as a few minutes of "meditation" at the beginning of each meeting, they felt that more was possible. After closely listening to their culture I designed, for example, a process for their leaders that integrated a variety of meditation, inquiry and movement practices throughout for example the schedule of a three day strategic planning meeting. As the managers and grass roots village leaders increasingly learned to stay present to their direct experience they recognized improved creativity, productivity and collaboration.

Now we are designing a leadership development program for tenths of thousands of their community leaders to help develop a holistic vision for Sri Lanka after thirty years of civil war and to shadow each of the country's 225 parliamentarians to support positive work and challenge corruption, rights abuses and environmental degradation. I am also writing a book with Dr. Ariyaratne in which we challenge ourselves with the above-mentioned task to come up with a pragmatic conceptualization of Buddhist economics and leadership that draws on current social-economic analysis as well as on the teachings of the Buddha.

Let me also briefly come back with two examples of how I think we can "train trainers" and those who because they work with many organizations and the countless people connected to them offer a tremendous multiplier effect in bringing contemplative practice into the mainstream of society. In this regard, I have been working for years with a corporate consultant and coach who when we started was already very successful but also unfulfilled, sensing that there was more to his life and work. As I inquired with him into what did satisfy him, he told me of becoming a world champion in sailing. When we explored that experience further, he re-experienced and realized that during the determining races he had opened so deeply into reality that he became one with his partner and the boat, the water and the wind. In his understanding he won not because he was the better sailor but because he knew exactly what to do and his body was able to do it. More importantly he felt profoundly alive and fulfilled. But at the time, as happens with many people's peak experiences, that door closed and he couldn't find his way back into the depth of his essential nature.

When we started to work together I suggested to him to experiment with sitting meditation, he said, "I can't sit still for longer than a few minutes." When I suggested that we could start with few minutes, he was willing to engage. A year later his half-hour morning meditation had become a high point and the ground for the rest of his day. We also found a way to turn his physical exercise into an awareness practice. Our regular contemplative coaching inquiries supported his overall development and subsequently his work with clients. They can't quite put their finger on what it is that makes his work so compassionate, creative and attuned to their needs. But it touches them, and they realize that it works better. At the end of a board process he recently facilitated, the tough chief financial officer of one of the world's largest multi-national corporations said to him: I don't know how this happened, but I have never been in a meeting that was so co-creative.

In the public sector, I am working, for example, with a regional representative of the Red Cross. After a period in which he increasingly learned to integrate contemplative practices into his day to day functioning, we recently engaged in a contemplative inquiry process to prepare a hostage negotiation with a much feared and reviled guerilla leader. He later reported that due to his practice he was able to perceive the underlying humanity of this man, who in turn felt met and respected. This sense of connection became a key to a successful negotiation, which led to the hostage release. Resting more deeply in his essential heart also helps when he frequently visits political prisoners in jail. Sometimes in the face of torture and despair, the only thing he has to offer is to be simply present. As you know this can be an incredible gift, especially when we feel most vulnerable and hopeless.

Not getting lost in the drama of such situations, but steadfastly working with them from the perspective of being integrates the personal and professional development of these leaders. After many years of working as a hands-on leader myself, I feel privileged to be available to people who are so deeply committed to service and help them discover its mutuality with their spiritual unfolding. I totally love doing that work. I want to find ever more skillful means to adapt it to particular circumstances. Many of them can't do several weeks of spiritual retreats a year and might have other reasons for not joining an inner work community. But if we look for flexible ways to make contemplative practice and perspective available to them, we can facilitate its generosity to touch them and those they touch. I also think that I and our community has a lot to learn from these people who in many regards are more mature and developed than many contemplative practitioners that I have met.

One important difference that I am discovering in working with these highly functional people is the need for a kind of reverse engineering of certain aspects of the developmental process. In many spiritual traditions, practitioners typically first gain self-realization of who and what they really are. Only then do they practice functioning from that depth of realization to develop what one can call called self-actualization, i.e. the integration of realization into action in the world. But many of these leaders already manifest such actualization—which is what makes them so effective—even though they lack the corresponding self-realization. This lack of realization, however, also tends to limit their effectiveness in other aspects of their lives. So, very simply put, they need support for self-realization, which in tandem with further self-actualization can significantly empower their development and functioning.

I think is this integration of self-realization and self-actualization that determines how we lead and where we lead to. Of course skills are also important. But they, too, are empowered by our underlying development. But the main question is: Do we come from ego-conditioning or from the depth of love and power and all the other qualities of our essential nature that help us to lead in truly creative and responsive ways? If we are closed to the aliveness of nature of which we are a part, how will we know what makes ecological systems sustainable? If we don't experience our humanity and the essential nature of justice and freedom, how will we be able to envision and implement a more humane, just and free society?

I think we are still very much in a learning process about how to help people mature in the midst of modern life. While there are plenty of books about the subject, nobody has found a perfect methodology of how to integrate contemplative practice with sustainable action in the world. But overall I think we are advancing in the right direction. This includes the leadership field, which is increasingly interested in inner and interpersonal work, even as it generally still ignores the complexities and practical implications of contemplative practice and truly integral approaches. But the experiment continues as more and more people understand that environmental, social and economic sustainability can't be reached in the same old ways that got us into the current mess, as also Einstein understood. Therefore our work is being supported by an increasing urgency in the system to find what works before it is too late.

As Peter Drucker, one of the godfather's of visionary leadership practice whom I quote at the outset of this article, said already quite a few years ago: "Every few hundred years in history there occurs a sharp transformation. Within a few short decades, society—its worldviews, its basic values, its social and political structures, its art, its key institutions—rearranges itself. We are currently living through such a time."

CONTEMPLATIVE LEADERSHIP IN ORGANIZATIONS

Janet Drey

Introduction

Leadership today requires a broad range of skills, including the ability to anticipate, innovate, question, and adapt. If we consider that the most important leadership tool is first and foremost the leader's self, it becomes critical to assist leaders in becoming more conscious of who they are, as well as the motivations influencing their leadership. Through purposeful, conscious direction of attention, we are able to see things that we might normally pass right by. For a leader, each conversation and exchange is an opportunity to gather valuable information about people, groups and cultures. When leaders become fully present and develop the awareness to notice subtle patterns of their own and other's behavior, group dynamics and organizational processes, they are better able to make decisions and manage situations simply because they see details and what is really going on more clearly. Among other things, contemplative leadership enlarges ones capacity for awareness, living with the unknowns of change, managing negative emotions, and staying grounded in one's values and purpose.

There are a growing number of leaders and organizations that are acknowledging the importance of contemplative leadership to overcome blind spots, promote consciousness, self-regulation, and problem solving. By deepening awareness and loosening the grip of old habits, leaders are freed up to think, relate, and act in new and more effective ways both individually and collectively. While contemplative leadership assists personal development and self management, it also seeks to enlarge leaders' capacity to influence and improve the human condition. Contemplative leadership intentionally focuses on strengthening four essential relationships as the source of a leader's awareness, influence, and vision.

In this paper, I will 1) describe contemplative practice and its relationship to contemplative living and leadership in organizations; 2) discuss lessons learned in exploring approaches to contemplative leadership; and 3) suggest opportunities, challenges, and future directions for contemplative leadership.

What Is Contemplative Practice?

Contemplation is primarily *awareness* to the present and to the stirrings of God (or however one names the transcendent) within and around us. It is the process of awakening, of developing habits of noticing, of experiencing ourselves as part of a larger whole, and of penetrating the illusions beneath what we identify as "self" and "reality."

Thomas Merton describes contemplation as "the highest expression of [human] intellectual and spiritual life. It is that life itself, fully awake, fully active, fully aware that it is alive. It is spiritual wonder. It is spontaneous awe at the sacredness of life, of being. It is gratitude for life, for awareness, and for being. It is a vivid realization of the fact that life and being in us proceed from an invisible, transcendent, and infinitely abundant Source. Contemplation is, above all, an awareness of the reality of that Source."[1]

Contemplative practice can be anything that helps us to penetrate illusion, wake up, and see the fullness, unity and sacredness of life. Examples might include meditation, centering prayer, lectio divina (meditative reading of scripture), being with nature, journaling, breathing, sacred dance, art, yoga, labyrinth, retreats, study and reflection, dialogue, etc. Contemplative practice supports a way of life called *contemplative living* and seeing that our everyday, active life is our spiritual life. Contemplative living calls us to unified relationships with self, others, nature, and God. Contemplative living calls us to responsible action in the world.

Meister Eckhart states that "what we have gathered in contemplation, we give out in love." Constance FitzGerald, OCD says: "...contemplation is not a validation of things as they are...but a constant questioning and restlessness that waits for and believes in the coming of a transformed vision of God...a new and integrating spirituality capable of creating a new politics and generating new social structures."[2]

"Contemplative" and "Leadership"

When considering a topic such as "contemplative leadership," it is important to acknowledge that we are bringing together worldviews, perspectives and experiences that seem initially incompatible and incongruent to many. There may be as many people who have concerns about "contemplative leadership" as have interest in this topic.

There are those who are naturally drawn to the "contemplative" aspect of this phrase because they have personal experience with contemplative practice or see the need for transformation in others and the larger society. Yet in this same population, I can encounter a resistance or negativity toward "leadership." The source of this resistance may be negative or limiting stereotypes about leadership or experiences of failed leadership. Resistance can also be more subtle—a preference for the inner and more subjective experiences of personal and communal living and a resistance to a strong external focus on behaviors, skills, processes, and structures.

Similarly many on the "leadership" side have concerns about "contemplative." For leaders in the public sectors, leadership means attention to performance, accountability, measurement, bottom line, and quality. Competition is fierce, and as one leader asked, "Who has time for introspection when I'm barely keeping my head above water"? Or the question asked by someone: "When I already deal with so much outer 'chaos,' why would I want to add to this chaos and explore my own?" Contemplation seems too "soft" and subjective to be useful for the complexities of organizational life. Some leaders fear that "contemplative" may be connected to religiosity and proselytizing, and really has no place in the post-modern social environments in which we work today. Or if it does, it belongs in the realm of one's personal life, spirituality, and/or religious practice, but not in the public arena of work so influenced by scientific materialism.

Yet it is the very contradictions that are created by contemplative leadership that seem to hold the potential to address the leadership crisis found throughout the guiding institutions of our society today. Beatrice Bruteau in *The Grand Option* writes, "Many people say that it is difficult to practice contemplation in our secularized society. But our society is 'secularized' precisely because contemplation is not adequately practiced. These two work in a circle: the general environment of our consciousness either supports or hinders our contemplative life, and our contemplative life (or lack of it) gives (or fails to give) spiritual dimensions to the surrounding world."[3]

Instead of trying to resolve the questions or resistance toward contemplative leadership in favor of one side or the other, contemplative leadership invites us to move beyond dualistic thinking about being either contemplative OR active, and to engage the tensions created. We are invited to live contemplatively in the midst of active daily life and leadership. Not possible? It is true that the ability to live within the tensions requires a human and spiritual maturity that many have yet to develop. Our natural tendency is to dissolve the tension prematurely before it can teach us. Yet successful leadership today requires a willingness to develop a level of inner growth and awareness capable of meeting the complexity of today's world. The promise and opportunity of contemplative leadership evolves as a new consciousness transforms our presence and intentional action in the world.

Lessons Learned While Exploring Approaches to Contemplative Leadership in Organizations

1. "You cannot enter into any world for which you do not have the language."   — Ludwig Witgenstein

When I began exploring approaches to contemplative leadership, I quickly learned the importance of language. The nuanced language of spiritual development and contemplative living has little to do with the day-to-day practical concerns of many leaders and complex organizations. Some leaders do not have a personal language for the religious, spiritual or contemplative dimensions of their lives. Further, there is great concern about religion and spirituality in the workplace. I began searching for language that was universal enough for the diversity of workplaces, credible enough to speak to the experiences of people who work in leadership and organizations today, faithful to the depth of contemplative spirituality expressed by monastic and wisdom traditions, and able to speak to people with different maturation levels.

I'd like to acknowledge the years of work by key members of the International Center for Spirit at Work[4] for laying the groundwork in this regard. I picked up many useful ideas from this group to get me started. The work of Ken Wilber and various Integral[5] communities, Integral Enlightenment and evolutionary spirituality provide important resources for developing a language that can connect many dots from human experience and practice areas. Authors and teachers of both contemplative spirituality and leadership practice (as well as other areas) continue to draw upon and further develop this work.

2. Integral Quadrants and the "Both-And" Paradoxes of Contemplative Leadership

The first element of Wilber's Integral framework—the Four Quadrants— speak to the contradictions and paradoxes that are created with contemplative leadership. The quadrants describe four lens of "reality," with quadrants 1 and 3 focusing on the subjective internal reality as experienced by individuals and groups, and quadrants 2 and 4 focusing on objective external reality as measured by individuals, systems and structures (see graphic on next page).

The quadrants remind us that in any situation, all four of these perspectives

Four Quadrants of "Reality"

	Individual/Internal "I"	Individual/External "IT"	
Quad 1	- Thoughts/Perceptions - Emotions/Interior states - Personal Beliefs/Values - Self and Consciousness - Psychology/Spirituality	- Behavior/Skills - Measurement/Performance - Rational & Material - Physical Organism/Brain - Sciences	**Quad 2**
	Collective/Internal "WE"	Collective/External "ITS"	
Quad 3	- Culture - Shared Worldview - Shared Symbols/Stories - Group Beliefs/Values	- Organization/Structure - Systems/Workflow - Policies/Procedures - Material, Economic, Social, Environmental, etc.	**Quad 4**

Ken Wilber, An Integral Approach

co-exist and are important to consider in creating a complete picture of "reality." Individuals and groups tend to have their favorite perspective, and often leave out or diminish the value of other perspectives.

For example, leaders and coaches who view reality primarily through quadrant 1 (individual/internal), tend to place a great deal of emphasis on introspection and awareness and may give less attention to developing behavior and skills. Similarly, leaders and coaches who see/act primarily from the perspective of quadrant 2 (individual/external) may focus primarily on behavior and skill practice, while giving little attention to reflective time or the consciousness that may be inhibiting a leader or group. Quad 3 leaders and coaches (collective/internal) may focus on lots of meaningful group work with little focus on developing personal awareness or individual practice. Quad 4 leaders (collective/external) may be great at designing systems and processes, but may ignore introspection or group culture.[6]

The four quadrants framework challenges all leaders and organizations to step back and view the lenses through which they perceive "reality." A helpful question that I am learning to ask myself and others within situations is:

What perspective(s) am I leaving out? This question points to contemplative practices of mindfulness; developing the habits of seeing our seeing, seeing our relationship with others and to the "whole;" letting go of attachments, illusions and worldviews that are limited; and moving toward more responsible or effective awareness with action. This is a useful contemplative practice for both individuals and groups.

Contemplative leadership recognizes that in order for leaders to effectively work with "reality," they must be aware of our own preferences and blind spots. Contemplative leadership promotes ongoing awakening, developing habits of noticing, and penetrating strong attachments to points of view and opinions related to favored external and internal "realities." Instead of protecting opinions, conclusions and certainties, contemplative leaders stop reacting, open, observe themselves and others, and seek to respond with greater consciousness, freedom and agility.

3. The Need for Greater Maturity: Engaging a Developmental Approach

In some circles, it is common practice to use different "stage" theories to teach about how children and adolescents are developing physically, cognitively, emotionally, psychologically, morally, and spiritually. Yet as adults, it is not a common practice to think/speak about aspects of our own development in terms of unfolding stages. Integral theory points to the importance of considering different "lines" of human development as well as the progressive levels or stages of adult development.[7] In each unfolding stage, an individual or group evolves toward greater complexity/maturity/capacity/capability. Different lines of development can be at different stages. For example, a leader can have a very high level of cognitive development, and at the same time a much lower level of moral or ethical development. Contemplative practice helps to promote adult development. (More on this below.)

In recent years, a growing number of developmental researchers who are working from an integral perspective are pointing to the increased need for individual and social development. In many situations, leaders and groups simply do not have the level of consciousness needed to deal with the complexity of issues before them. There is no "quick fix" to many of the problems we face. While cognitive development is often present in leaders, it has been shown that greater emotional development is key to successful leadership. There is growing evidence that spiritual development is more and more important in assisting leaders to reach higher stages of maturity.

Leadership, Change, and Contemplative Practice

In their book, *Immunity to Change*, Robert Kegan and Lisa Lahey describe a problem for leadership.

> ...We can learn and reflect as much as we want, but the changes we hope for, or that others need from us, will not happen because all the learning and reflecting will occur within our existing mindsets."[8] Kegan and Lahey go on to describe how a focus on adult development has "never been more important than the present, as leaders increasingly ask people to do things they are not now able to do, were never prepared to do, and are not yet developmentally well matched to do. The field of 'leadership development' has overattended to leadership and underattended to development. ...We ignore the most powerful source of ability: our capacity (and the capacity of the people who work for us) to overcome, at any age, the limitations and blind spots of current ways of making meaning. ...True development is about transforming the operating system itself, not just increasing your fund of knowledge or your behavioral repertoire.[9]

Susanne Cook-Gueuter, a renowned developmental and integral researcher began to notice in her studies of higher development, that "some individuals expressed a simplicity that emerges on the other side of complexity, allowing for integration and depth that she identified as a new order of higher development. The recognition of this higher-order simplicity begins to acknowledge a dimension of the self that goes beyond cognition, one that could be called spiritual."[10]

Other researchers and authors are helping to provide growing evidence of the importance of integrating contemplative practice with leadership. Bill Joiner and Stephen Josephs describe how the cultivation of attention and awareness impact leadership, in their 2007 book entitled *Leadership Agility*:

> Attention is the direct, non-conceptual awareness of the physical, mental, and emotional experience in the present moment. (Other terms sometimes used for attention are 'presence' and 'mindfulness.') Everyone has some degree of free attention. But our attention is usually so absorbed in our experiences and reflections that we're not cognizant of

it as a distinct mode of awareness. Yet it's by developing this capacity to live 'in attention' that you can move into and through the post-heroic [higher] levels of leadership agility. ...One of the most reliable ways to cultivate this quality of attention is through a meditation practice that emphasizes present-centered awareness. ...When you repeatedly cultivate a new level of awareness in the midst of your action, your mental and emotional capacities develop accordingly. These capacities, in turn, support more agile leadership behavior.[11]

In a September 2010 on-line issue of Harvard Business School (HBS) *Working Knowledge*, Harvard professor and leadership development expert, William George writes about the importance of Mindful Leadership and a recent Mindful Leadership retreat held in Minneapolis.[12] "Gaining awareness of oneself—our motivations, our destructive emotions, our crucibles, and our failings—is essential to being an effective leader. Based on my research into leaders, I have found the greatest cause of leadership failures is the lack of emotional intelligence and self-awareness on the part of leaders."[13]

Nearly all Wisdom and monastic traditions (both eastern and western) include a path to cultivating present-centered contemplative awareness. Through contemplative practice, we gain access to a deeper wisdom and reality not accessible through our rational minds or emotional attachments.

4. Emotional Intelligence

In 1995, Daniel Goleman published his groundbreaking book entitled *Emotional Intelligence*.[14] Since then a growing number of organizations and people use his framework as a measure for leadership success. Emotional intelligence is comprised of various skills that are grouped into four areas:

a) Self awareness
b) Self management
c) Social awareness
d) Relationship management

A basic premise in this framework is that we can't manage what we are not first aware of in ourselves and relationships. However, self-awareness and awareness of the worldviews of others are not skills that are well developed in all leaders. And the lack of these skills is often a cause for leaders failing to adequately serve others or accomplish goals. It is fair to ask how one develops "awareness." The answer is very much tied to contemplative practices and contemplative living as Richard Rohr suggests:

> The ability to stand back and calmly observe my inner dramas, without rushing to judgment, is foundational for spiritual seeing...The growing consensus is that, whatever you call it, such calm egoless seeing is invariably characteristic of people at the highest levels of doing and loving in all cultures and religions. They are the ones we call sages or wise...They see like the mystics see. Once you know that the one thing the ego hates more than anything else is change, it makes perfect sense why most people hunker down into mere survival...defended and defensive selves will do anything rather than change—even acting against their own best interests. Ego is just another word for blindness. The ego self is by my definition the unobserved self, because once you see it, the game is over. The ego must remain unseen and disguised to be effective in protecting itself. Most people have not been offered a different mind, only different behaviors, beliefs, and belonging systems. They do not necessarily nourish us, much less transform us. But they invariably secure us and validate us where we already are.[15]

5. Spiritual Intelligence

In 1997, Danah Zohar first introduced the term "spiritual intelligence" in her book, *ReWiring the Corporate Brain: Using the New Science to Rethink How We Structure and Lead Organizations.*[16] She and Ian Marshall later defined spiritual intelligence as "the intelligence with which we access our deepest meanings, purposes, and highest motivations."[17] According to bestselling author Steven Covey, SQ ["spiritual quotient"] is becoming a more mainstream component of leadership development and is the "central and most fundamental of all the intelligences, because it becomes the source of guidance for the other[s].[18]

In 2008, I discovered an integral assessment for spiritual intelligence developed by Cindy Wigglesworth, Conscious Pursuits[19]. I have been experimenting with approaches for how to introduce and teach spiritual intelligence to leaders. The model is very complimentary to the four competency areas of emotional intelligence:

a) Self/self awareness
b) Universal awareness
c) Self/self mastery
d) Social mastery/spiritual presence

The competencies of SQ tend to fall into two major categories: 1) expanding awareness (self, ego, others, Spirit, environment, etc), and 2) transforming ego-based behaviors into more effective, compassionate, and socially responsible behaviors). For those already familiar with emotional intelligence, the introduction to SQ is fairly seamless, and when blended with practices such as contemplative dialogue and short periods of silence to disengage the chatter of an active mind and attachments of various emotional states, can become an effective introduction to contemplative living.

In order to see, you have to stop being in the middle of the picture.
— Sri Aurobindo

6. How Do We Create Real Change?

An important question that exists at the heart of both leadership and contemplative spirituality is "how do we create real change"? This question is growing louder as we experience the breakdown of present ways of being, knowing, and doing personally, socially, and globally. I'd like to briefly address three areas that are important to contemplative leadership and its ability to transform:

a) Ground of Being: Wisdom and Monastic Traditions

From circles of interreligious dialogue, we discover spiritual seekers from many religious and wisdom traditions in search of a contemplative path that goes beyond belief to an experience of God (or however the transcendent is named) in everyday life. The experience and discipline of contemplation is less about our action and more about opening, accepting, and responding to what is already present. Through contemplative practice, we seek to disengage from our thoughts and emotions and move with courage into the unknown. Beneath the chatter of everyday life we discover a still place from which we can discover what Thomas Merton identified as the "true self" and a unity that we share with God, others, and the entire universe.

While some groups are using secular approaches to contemplative practice, there is a deep, rich resource in monastic and wisdom traditions that have stood the test of time and that are still relevant and important for today's world. In "The Common Heart," Father Thomas Keating describes Points of Agreement that emerged from spiritual teachers from a variety of world religions—Buddhist, Hindu, Jewish, Islamic, Native American, Russian Orthodox, Protestant, and Roman Catholic—dialoguing and meditating together in silence over a 20 year period of time.[20]

- The world religions bear witness to the experience of Ultimate Reality, to which they give various names.
- Ultimate Reality cannot be limited by any name or concept.
- Ultimate Reality is the ground of infinite potentiality and actualization.
- Faith is opening, accepting, and responding to Ultimate Reality. Faith in this sense precedes every belief system.
- The potential of human wholeness--or, in other frames of reference, enlightenment, salvation, transcendence, transformation, blessedness—is present in every human being.
- Ultimate Reality may be experienced not only through religious practices, but also through nature, art, human relationships, and service to others.
- As long as the human condition is experienced as separate from Ultimate Reality, it is subject to ignorance and illusion, weakness and suffering.
- Disciplined practice is essential to the spiritual life; yet spiritual attainment is not the result of one's own efforts, but the result of the experience of oneness with Ultimate Reality.

The work of the Merton Institute is guided by a rich Christian monastic tradition based on the Rule of St. Benedict and the writings of Thomas Merton, a Cistercian monk. Merton sought for himself and encouraged others to pursue ongoing spiritual transformation and a life of contemplation in a world of action.

b) The Modern Ego Is a Problem

The modern ego has become a big problem. In order to embrace change on a personal and social level, we have to find more effective ways to disengage the individualist "I" that has taken hold in so many ways and is almost snuffing out a perspective of "the common good." The problem of ego is actually a problem of motivation.[21] Individually and collectively, we lack the motivation to go beyond self preservation, comfort, safety, security and control to put ourselves in a relationship with life and God that compels us to do the inner and outer work that is needed in our time. At the heart of creating change and transformation is awakening a higher motivation that is more compelling than the ego.

Both the contemplative monastic tradition and the skills of spiritual intelligence provide ways to speak about the ego and concrete examples of how the "ego self" creates limits and drama. Whatever the approach, it is important to find ways to do the difficult work of moving beyond the ego or we will not get very far with the work of change.

c) Evolutionary Development

At the heart of creating change in our lives and for our times, is an ability to awaken an impulse to see our lives as part of a larger evolutionary whole that has been unfolding since the beginning of time. From this perspective, our values and motivations shift dramatically.[22] We engage in the difficult work of individual and collective transformation because we see that our lives and our leadership have a much bigger purpose than serving our own desires for comfort, safety, esteem, or power. From an evolutionary perspective, we begin to see from the perspective of co-creating with God and begin to realize that the work of transforming the human condition is ours to do. We see that personal transformation is the foundation for social and cultural transformation and that our spiritual formation cannot take place in isolation. Our spiritual formation is grounded in the experience of relationships and community. Leaders carry a special burden for engaging in this transformative work because of the power they hold to cast a light or shadow over many others.

Contemplative Leadership
Merton Institute for Contemplative Living

Goal of Contemplative Leadership

To influence the direction of leadership in all its manifestations, by integrating the principles and practice of contemplative living into mainstream leadership thinking and training.

A Description of Contemplative Leadership

Leadership can be described as the process of influencing the direction, actions, and opinions of others to achieve the purposes of a group or organization. If we consider that the most important leadership tool is first and foremost the leader's self, it is critical to assist leaders in becoming more conscious of who they are, as well as the motivations influencing their leadership.

Contemplative leadership is an approach to leadership that evolves from living in unified relationships with self, others, nature, and God. These relationships are the source and focus of a leader's awareness, influence, and vision. They guide a leader's ethical behavior, create trust, and provide the deeper meaning and purpose for achieving a group or organization's mission. Contemplative leaders seek to realize human potential and improve the human condition.

Guiding Principles

- Contemplative leadership begins with "self leadership," a focus on who the leader is rather than what the leader does.
- Contemplative leadership is grounded in relationships, including relationship with God.

Anticipated Structure and Approach

- Retreats
- Conference presentations
- On-site support for leaders/organizations
- Courses; seminars
- Creating awareness (articles, communications, group dialogue)
- Collaboration: forming non-competitive relationships that advance a shared vision for the greater good

- Online courses
- Webinars

Contemplative Leadership Retreats

Throughout 2009, a series of six pilot retreats were held as a means of exploring the concept of contemplative leadership and defining it; determining appropriate content and structure for a program; identifying the benefits to individuals and organizations; and determining for whom it is intended and where there would be interest in such a program. The thirty-eight participants came from a variety of backgrounds and leadership experience - business, military, religion, education, agriculture, law, healthcare, social services and the non-profit sector. Some represented organizations such as the National Alliance for the Public Trust and Christian Leadership Concepts.

The first Contemplative Leadership retreat was held in January 2010, with subsequent retreats scheduled. Retreats typically begin mid-day on the first day and conclude mid-day on the third day. Participants include leaders from healthcare, business, education, social science, and non-profit sectors. Ages have ranged from late 30's to 70. Participants tend to be professionals with higher education. The retreat process includes group contemplative dialogue sessions, presentation, communal contemplative experiences, and individual contemplative time to rest, reflect, read, walk.

Retreats serve the following purposes:

1. Providing renewal time for leaders to relax, reflect, awaken or reclaim their spirits, and renew themselves (typical things one might expect from a retreat to nurture ourselves right where we are at).

2. Experience and introduce the concepts of contemplative living and contemplative leadership.

3. Promote adult development and growth in contemplative awareness. (Built on the premise that we need more leaders today who are willing to awaken and develop an inner life of consciousness capable of addressing the complexities of today's world.)

Looking to the Future

In this paper, I have attempted to describe contemplative practice and its relationship to leadership in organizations, as well as lessons I have learned in exploring approaches to contemplative leadership. As we look to the future, what will be needed to nurture the growth and development of a contemplative movement in America, and specifically contemplative leadership? I suggest that attention is needed in the following areas:

- **Greater Awareness of Contemplative Living and Its Relationship to Contemplative Practice**
  Awareness of contemplative living will come through *experience*—not more information. We can't "think" our way to contemplative living, but rather we must learn to "live" our way to a new way of thinking and behaving. As we awaken to our true selves, bring an experience of God (or however we name the transcendent) into our lives through contemplation, and develop compassionate relationships with others and the environment, we experience a life of unity that reflects the undeniable and essential interconnectedness of life itself.

- **Attention to the Transformation of the Ego or False Self**
  The ego self has become a problem for individuals and postmodern society as a whole. Finding ways to explore this phenomenon together and awaken the personal and social motivation and courage to face ourselves and one another honestly is critical. Unless individuals and groups are willing to shift personal and collective motivations beyond ego, we will continue to act in defended and defensive ways creating more drama than shared understanding or solutions that serve the common good. The hope of contemplative leadership lies with our willingness to transform motivations and work together with greater emotional and spiritual maturity to improve the human condition.

- **More Collaboration Between People and Organizations Working with One Aspect or Another of Contemplative Living**
  By many indications, a contemplative movement is emerging in America. A growing number of people and groups are feeling drawn to various forms of contemplative practice and a unified way of living. As a means to provide the fullest support for this emerging contemplative movement,

it is important to deepen an understanding of what others are doing and explore where additional collaboration could better serve. The June 10-13, 2010 dialogue sponsored by the Fetzer Institute on the "State of Contemplative Practice in America" was an excellent starting point.

Notes

1 Merton, Thomas, *New Seeds of Contemplation.* Abbey of Gethsemane, 1961.

2 FitzGerald, Constance, OCD. "Impasse and the Dark Night." An article from *Living with Apocalypse, Spiritual Resources for Social Compassion* (pp 93–116). San Francisco: Harper & Row, Publishers, 1984. Quoted by Nancy Sylvester, IHM. Institute for Communal Contemplation and Dialogue. www.engagingimpass.org.

3 Bruteau, Beatrice, *The Grand Option*, Notre Dame, IN: University of Notre Dame Press, 2001.

4 International Center for Spirit At Work, www.spiritatwork.org.

   Our mission is to support global transformation by integrating spirituality and the workplace. Our Vision: We are the recognized global resource for integrating spirituality and the workplace. The International Center for Spirit at Work (ICSW) provides comprehensive world class, faith friendly and faith neutral, spirituality-at-work products, programs, tools and research that are practical and easily accessible.

5 See http://en.wikipedia.org/wiki/Integral_Theory for additional references and information. Also www.integralenlightenment.com.

6 Integral Coaching Canada, Laura Divine and Joanne Hunt.

7 See http://en.wikipedia.org/wiki/Ken_Wilber#AQAL:_.22All_Quadrants_All_Levels.22 for additional references and information.

8 Kegan, Robert, and Lisa Laskow Lahey, *Immunity to Change.* Boston, MA: Harvard Business Press, 2009, p. 6. *Note: Richard Rohr provides an excellent exploration of this dilemma from a contemplative*

perspective in his book, *The Nakend Now: Learning to See as the Mystics See*, Crossroad Publishing Company, 2009.

9   Kegan and Lahey, p. 6–7.

10 Debold, Elizabeth, EdD. The EnlightenNext Discovery Cycle, *Higher Development Research Project*, initiated summer 2009 to foster higher-order development individually and collectively.

11 Joiner, Bill, and Stephen Josephs, *Leadership Agility: Five Levels of Mastery for Anticipating and Initiating Change*. San Francisco: Josey-Bass, 2007.

12 George, William. Harvard Business School Working Knowledge, *"Mindful Leadership: When East Meets West."* http://hbswk.hbs.edu/item/6482.html?wknews=090710.

13 George, William. http://www.billgeorge.org/page/reflections-on-mindful-leadership-retreat.

14 Goleman, Daniel. *Emotional Intelligence: Why It Can Matter More Than IQ*. New York: Bantam Books, 1995.

15 Rohr, Richard. *The Naked Now: Learning to See as the Mystics See.* Crossroad Publishing Company, 2009. pp. 32–33; 90–91.

16 Zohar, Danah, *Rewiring the Corporate Brain: Using the New Science to Rethink How We Structure and Lead Organizations*. San Francisco: Berrett-Koehler Publishers, Inc. 1997.

17 Zohar, Danah, and Dr. Ian Marshall. *SQ: Spiritual Intelligence, the Ultimate Intelligence*, New York, Bloomsbury Publishing, 2000.

18 Covey, Stephen. *The 8th Habit: From Effectiveness to Greatness.* Simon and Schuster, 2004, p.53.

19 Cindy Wigglesworth, founder and owner of Conscious Pursuits, www.consciouspursuits.com now dba www.deepchange.com. *We build spiritual and emotional intelligence and create values-driven workplaces through our consulting, coaching, and training services. Based on many years of human resources and management experience, our consulting and coaching services support organizations in assessing core cultural issues such as values, principles, and spiritual and emotional intelligence. From our coaching and classes individuals learn*

how to increase clarity about what matters, handle difficult, stressful situations productively, and develop and apply their spiritual and emotional intelligence skills.

20 *The Common Heart: An Experience of Interreligious Dialogue.* Netanel Miles-Yepez, Editor. 2006. "The Points of Agreement", p. xvii by Father Thomas Keating.

21 Hamilton, Craig, Integral Enlightenment: Awakening to An Evolutionary Relationship to Life. "*The Key to Evolving Beyond Ego*".

22 Hamilton, Craig, Integral Enlightenment: Awakening to An Evolutional Relationship to Life Course. 2010.

CONTEMPLATIVE PRACTICE IN LAW: AN OVERVIEW

Rhonda V. Magee

More and more, lawyers are meditating across America. This white paper confirms that a contemplative movement has emerged within the legal profession, and is poised to expand its reach dramatically over the next decade. Numerous publications for legal practitioners and law professors, new law school classes on mindfulness mediation and contemplative lawyering, and post-graduate trainings for lawyers, mediators and judges are combining to create receptivity within the legal profession to contemplative practice as an aspect of effective lawyering. Even more exciting, the rise of contemplative practice within law may assist in answering the call of recent advocates of reform for legal education which better instills in young lawyers a sense of professional identity embodying self-reflective civic engagement and ethical judgment.

What follows is a summary overview of this movement, organized around the questions posed by the Fetzer Institute in convening this important dialogue.

1. How is "contemplative practice" defined by its practitioners in the field of law?

The core notion of "contemplative practice" in law derives from the definition of such practices common in the wisdom traditions at the foundation of the broader contemplative practice movement. In the field of law, much of the work to develop a common understanding of what is meant by contemplative practice, and to suggest how it might be apply to the practice of law has proceeded under the auspices of the Center for Contemplative Mind in Society's Law Program, and its San Francisco Bay Area-based Working Group for lawyers. The working group collaboratively developed its conception of contemplative practice through a document entitled "The Meditative Perspective."[1] In it, the concept is described as followed:

> Broadly defined, a contemplative practice is any activity that quiets the mind in order to cultivate the capacity for insight. Mindfulness meditation is a powerful contemplative

practice that is simple to learn and incorporate into one's daily routine. Mindfulness meditation is cultivated mainly through the practice of quiet sitting, with focus on breathing, not repressing thinking or emotion but simply allowing it to come and go within the field of awareness. Once such a practice is established it can be applied in informal ways during the day. Its essence is simply being fully and non-judgmentally present with what happens, on a moment by moment basis.

Examples of contemplative practices that have been offered to and embraced by the legal community in various workshops, retreats, and continuing education programs include sitting meditation, yoga, tai chi, chi gong, and contemplative journaling, contemplative dialogue, and contemplative walking. A recent small-scale study confirms that meditating lawyers have embraced a range of both formal and informal contemplative practices, including insight meditation, "ethically-engaged attention," the focus on developing compassion and empathy, mindful attention to communicating by telephone, yoga, etc.[2]

While many in the legal profession are drawn to contemplative practices in search of stress management techniques, the practices provide a bridge to deep reconsideration of how more meaningfully, ethically, and effectively to practice law in service to clients and community, and, if desired, to broader spirituality. Recent criticisms of legal education and the development of professional identity have highlighted the need for greater attention to increasing lawyers' capacities for self-awareness and ethical, civic engagement.[3] Thus, it behooves those who seek to broaden the acceptance of contemplative practice in law to underscore the capacity of contemplative practice not only to reduce stress but also to increase self-awareness and ethical engagement among lawyers. Beyond that, many have embraced the prudent objective of simply to point the door through which a practitioner may further explore the broader spiritual implications of these practices, or not, based on his or her own inclination.

By whatever definition and however differently framed, an avalanche of articles from practitioner oriented publications,[4] a growing list of for-credit courses among law schools, co-curricular initiatives by faculty, staff and students, as well as workshop offerings among state bars across the country confirms that a contemplative practice movement is on the rise among the legal profession.

2. Development of Contemplative Practice in Law over Past Twenty-Five Years

Perhaps the first systematic effort to introduce mindfulness into the legal profession occurred in 1989, when Jon Kabat-Zinn, director of the Center for Mindfulness in Medicine, Health Care and Society in Boston, offered a program on his signature Mindfulness-Based Stress Reduction (MBSR) to judges.[5] Subsequent efforts to introduce mindfulness into the legal profession included sessions on mindfulness for mediators and mindfulness meditation training at the 400-hundred lawyer home office of the nationally-regarded, Boston-based law firm Hale and Dorr[6] and perhaps a few other law firms. In 1999, Steve Keeva published *Transforming Practices: Bringing Joy and Satisfaction to the Legal Life*, a well-received book that contributed to the identification, both within the profession and in the broader public, of efforts among lawyers to change the practice and training of lawyers—often in ways reflective of contemplative or mindfulness practice.[7]

Nevertheless, legal historians will likely mark 2002 as the seminal year in the development of the contemplative lawyering movement. In that year, the Harvard Negotiation Law Review hosted a forum to discuss the implications of mindfulness meditation for legal practice and alternative dispute resolution, in conjunction with its publication of an article by Professor Leonard Riskin on that topic.[8] Professor Riskin's reports that his expertise on mindfulness and law developed in part through his collaboration with the Center for Contemplative Mind in Society, whose programs for law students, lawyers and law professors had previously been offered at Yale and Columbia law schools,[9] and whose annual five-day retreats for law professionals had been held, hosting increasingly broad audiences, between 1998 and 2002.[10]

As the first decade of the 21st century progressed, efforts to introduce contemplative practice to lawyers, law students and judges continued to increase. In addition to, and sometimes in conjunction with the work of the Center, a variety of individuals have introduced meditation and contemplative practice via myriad workshops and classes, and independent meditating lawyers groups have formed across the country, from Oakland to New York City, and Portland to Colorado.[11]

Perhaps most promising, since the mid-2000s, for-credit courses have been offered at a small but growing list of law schools.[12] The courses indicate the first efforts to experiment with introducing contemplative lawyering into the traditional law school curriculum, either as stand alone courses or as components of courses on alternative dispute resolution or other skills. They join no-credit and co-curricular offerings that expose students to mindfulness training in the law school environment, either directly, or through the resources of the larger University.[13] For example, at my own institution, I co-created a course on "Contemplative Lawyering," offered for the first time this Spring, after having assisted in leading guided meditations for students for the past three semesters.

Practicing lawyers, and even moreso mediators, are also benefitting from the increasing offerings of meditation training among continuing legal education (CLE) programs for credit towards the requirements of their state bar associations. Since the first CLE program for lawyers focused on mindfulness was offered by the Center for Contemplative Mind's law program,[14] mindfulness trainings have been increasingly offered among continuing legal education programs for lawyers and mediators.[15] In addition, Contemplative Lawyering groups have formed within the Bar Association of New York, and formally or informally in other major cities across the country.[16] Mindfulness training for judges, while still relatively uncommon, is also taking place in experiments across the country.[17]

Thus, over the eight years since the Riskin article appeared, interest in mindfulness and law appears to have grown annually. The Center for Contemplative Mind has sponsored annual retreats each year since the late 1990s. In addition, in the summer of 2008, the Center's Law Program sponsored a gathering of leaders in the Contemplative Lawyering Movement, at which about twenty invited participants from across the country (including the author) explored plans for developing a coordinated national law and meditation program. Followed by another such gathering in November, 2009, the Law Program decided to pause its retreat program in 2010, and instead focused its resources on planning what should be the first national conference on Meditation and Law—scheduled as of this writing to take place in October 2010 at the University of California at Berkeley's School of Law. This conference will be a defining moment in a movement marked by many such milestones over the past twenty-five years.

In short, since the late 1980s, mindfulness and contemplative practice has been increasingly, if somewhat unsystematically, introduced in a variety of settings and through a variety of programs, aimed at the full range of legal professionals: law students, lawyers, judges and paralegals. The 2000s saw the emergence of experimental additions to the standard law school curriculum in the form of courses devoted to the intersection of meditation and law, and co-curricular, no-credit offerings ranging from short trainings in mindfulness to weekly offerings of meditation or other practices, such as yoga. In some cases, experiments in more pervasive integration of contemplative pedagogy into the traditional law school courses have also been tried.[18] On the law practice front, members of law firms have introduced mindfulness meditation into their law firm settings on volunteer bases. And even judges have been exposed to mindfulness trainings and introduced the practices in nonobvious ways into courtrooms (although this is the area in which comparatively fewer inroads appear to have successfully been made).

Additional resources for training and development of teachers, classes, workshops and retreats are urgently needed to facilitate this energetic flowering of activity. In addition, both qualitative and quantitative empirical research assessing the activities thus far, and confirming the impact of these interventions on the lives and outlooks of lawyers and their clients, is urgently called for at this time.

3. Supportive Organizations

As the foregoing suggests, perhaps the single most supportive organization assisting the development of this movement to date has been the Center for Contemplative Mind in Society. The Center's Law Program began held its first meeting in 1997 and has provided support for the growing movement through a variety of resources and events ever since.[19] In addition, and quite notably, the American Bar Association has supported this movement, as part of its mission to improve lawyer's experience of law practice and the public's experience of legal professionalism.[20] Other organizations offer more regionally-based support for exposure to meditation and law. For example, Tail of the Tiger, a nonprofit educational organization that "presents seminars joining mindfulness meditation with the professions, business and the arts," provides support to law firms and law schools in the northeast.[21] There are also a number of websites and "one-person shops" which provide support for the development of mindfulness in law through a growing network that is itself a source of organizational support.[22]

Other organizations have been supportive of efforts uniquely suited to preexisting missions of their institutions. For example, at my own institution (the University of San Francisco, a Jesuit college), members of the broader campus community have encouraged the law school in its efforts to develop contemplative courses and co-curricular offerings to law students. In this connection, I was asked to co-present to the larger faculty community on the topic of contemplative pedagogy along with Jesuit priests. This effort has led to the formation of an ad hoc group of professors working across disciplines to develop and expand contemplative pedagogy at the University of San Francisco.

In short, there are organizations supportive of the contemplative movement in law within the legal environment. Still, the broad base of activity in the field suggests that further organizational and institutional support should be sought by leaders in the movement going forward, both to assist the movement's development along these diverse lines, and, perhaps, to assist in the development of more systematic approaches to the movement's goals, methods, and assessment strategies.

4. Demographics of Participants

To date, while there has been one published qualitative study focusing on describing the experiences of "Buddhist lawyers," published this year by Professor Deborah Cantrell, [23] there have been no large scale, reliable studies of the extent to which contemplative practices have been embraced by members of the legal profession. Thus, the demographics of the participants are not yet known. This is an area in dire need of additional research.

And as a source of information on the demographics of participants in the movement, The Cantrell Study provides only the barest starting point. In it, the author described interviews of fifteen lawyers who describe themselves as Buddhist and contemplative practitioners. Professor Cantrell's research indicates the meditating lawyers hail from a broad cross-section of the country,[24] a range of law practice backgrounds,[25] and various religious backgrounds and degrees of intensity.[26] The research does not, however, systematically track or report on the race, age, or socioeconomic status of the participants.

I have been working on a qualitative study of the effects of mindfulness in dealing with the challenges of practicing and working in diverse environments,[27] involving in-depth interviews with a number of contemplative practitioner lawyers and law students. I hope that this research will provide another starting point for further research.

Anecdotally, however, participants appear to be disproportionately white, and female. For example from my own institution, the nine students enrolled in the first Contemplative Lawyering class at USF, in the Spring 2010 semester, were six women and three men: four white women, one mixed white/Asian woman, one Latina, one Asian male, one Latino, and one man of mixed white and Asian descent. There were no African American students—although there was exceedingly strong interest on the part of one Black male who was, for administrative reasons, not accepted off of the wait list. Another Asian male not accepted off the wait list also expressed extreme disappointment.

While I continue to seek more information on the demographics of the participants in the movement, preliminary research indicates that this is an area in need of immediate additional research. Especially in light of the changing demographics of the nation's client and, to ultimately, lawyer population; the increasing globalization of law practice; and other winds of change blowing through the profession and the economy as a whole, it is important that such changes be kept in view as the movement develops. Merely calling attention to the need to track the inclusivity of the movement would at least assist participants to more routinely collect data that would be useful as we go forward.

5. Key Trends in the Coming Decade

Three significant trends are suggested by the foregoing, and appear certain to continue and gather steam in the coming decade. The first is the trend in favor of increasing acceptance of contemplative practice as at least an optional component of the legal educational environment, including both law schools and the continuing legal education industry offering training to lawyers, judges and paralegals. The second is the growing call toward legal educational reform and the movement to increase accountability through more effective assessment of the outcomes of legal education against stated objectives and norms. And the third is the increasing need to address the demographics of the movement, to ensure both diversity and inclusivity in the developments to come.

These trends create both an intensification of the call, and a unique opportunity for, the integration of the contemplative lawyering movement more pervasively and systematically within the legal profession, and doing so in a way that aims at promoting inclusive civic lawyering and social justice.[28] The high degree of energy around reforming legal education more broadly provides impetus and principled bases upon which members of the contemplative lawyering movement may specify contemplative lawyering skills as among those central to the development of a 21st century lawyer's sense of civic professionalism, wisdom, and sound judgment. I intend to develop this argument in a subsequent publication, and will seek to find support for this view among other legal educators and mindfulness trainers and advocates in the profession.

6. The Larger Contemplative Movement and the Role of Law

Myriad indications confirm that a broad-based contemplative practice movement is on the ascendancy in America. And while this movement creates the wind beneath the rise in contemplative practices *in law*, the impact will inevitably be reciprocal: the legal profession will no doubt play just as critical a role in the further development of the broader national movement. The profession's central role in lawmaking and leadership make the emergence of this movement in law a key indicator of the early success and breadth of the nation's broader contemplative practice movement. Perhaps more important, the broader movement may well depend for its success on the continued integration of contemplative practice into the central institutions of our nation's infrastructure, including, most centrally, law.

Notes

1   "The Meditative Perspective," available online at http://www.contemplativemind.org/programs/law/perspective.pdf. The Center for Contemplative Mind's Law Program is currently directed by Center for Contemplative Mind founder Charles Halpern, and Doug Chermak. The Working Group has consisted of 10–12 (mostly) law professionals (lawyers, law professors—including the author—and a former judge) who meet regularly for meditation and discussion of the intersections between contemplative practice and the practice of law.

2   *See* Deborah Cantrell, *Inviting the Bell: A Preliminary Exploration of Buddhist Lawyers in the United States,* available at: http://ssrn.com/abstract=1568953, hereinafter, "The Cantrell Study" at 42–6.

3   William M. Sullivan Et Al, *Educating Lawyers: Preparation for the Profession Of Law* 126–60 (2007).

4   *See* Stephanie West Allen, "Contemplative Lawyers: Some Mindfulness Resources," http://westallen.typepad.com/idealawg/2008/09/contemplative-lawyers-some-mindfulness-resources.html.

5   Jon Kabat-Zinn, *Full Catastrophe Living* at 125-26; Riskin, *infra* note 4 at 33.

6 Riskin, *infra* note 7 at 3.

7 Steve Keeva, *Transforming Practices: Finding Joy and Satisfaction in Legal Life* (1999).

8 Leonard Riskin, *The Contemplative Lawyer: On the Potential Contributions of Mindfulness Meditation to Law Students, Lawyers, and their Clients*, 7 Harv. Neg. L. Rev. 1 (2002).

9 *Id.* at 33–4 and accompanying notes.

10 Riskin, *supra* note 7 at 34.

11 For a short list of such events sponsored or co-sponsored by the Center for Contemplartive Mind's Law Program, see http://www. contemplativemind.org/about/history.html. *See also* Center for Contemplative Mind in Society Law Program's forthcoming Comprehensive Contemplative Law Survey (detailing hundreds of presentations and events focused on contemplative lawyering from the 1980s through the present) (preliminary draft on file with author).

12 *See* Leonard Riskin, Contemplative Practices in Law Schools, Prepared for the Association of American Law Schools (Janunary 4, 2005) (outline available at http://www.tailofthetiger.org/documents/riskin_outline.pdf.) (describing for-credit classes at The University of Connecticut, Hastings, Howard, University of Missouri-Columbia, William Mitchell, Washington & Lee). Additional courses have since been developed and offered at the University of Florida Levin, "Tools of Awareness for Lawyers," (Fall 2008); the University of California at Berkeley School of Law ("Effective And Sustainable Law Practice: The Meditative Perspective", Spring semesters, 2009 and 2010), Roger Williams School of Law, "Integrating Mindfulness Into Trial Advocacy,"(Spring 2009), The University of San Francisco ("Contemplative Lawyering," Spring semester, 2010); University of Miami, "Professional Responsibility and Mindfulness in the Digital Age" (forthcoming, Fall 2010); and The Buffalo Law School (forthcoming, 2011).

13 Riskin, *supra* note 11, *citing* Mindfulness-Based Stress Reduction courses at the University of Missouri-Columbia and the University of North Carolina. *See also* University of Southern California, Silent Meditation and Multi-Faith Prayer Group, http://wellness.usc.

edu/2008/09/silent-meditation-and-prayer-m.html; University of Miami, Eight Week Program on Contemplative Practices, http://www.themindfullawstudent.com/um.html. Yoga and stress-reduction training is becoming an increasing common feature of co-curricular offerings among law schools. *See, e.g.,* Fordham University law school weekly yoga and meditation classes, with links to guided meditation podcasts on the school's website, see webpage resources at http://law.fordham.edu/office-of-student-affairs/2822.htm. At the University of San Francisco, weekly guided meditation sessions have been provided by three members of the faculty since Spring 2009, and a two-unit course on Contemplative Lawyering was co-taught by therse three professors at USF in Spring 2010. *See infra* note 11. I will teach a course on contemplative lawyering perspectives at USF again in spring, 2011.

14 Maia Duerr, "A Powerful Silence: The Role of Meditation and Other Contemplative Practices in American Work and Life" (Center for Contemplative Mind in Society) (2004).

15 *See, e.g.,* Exploring our Inspiration for the Law: Mindfulness Meditation in Law Practice (The "Fourth Annual Retreat for Lawyers sponsored by the Vermont Bar Association and Tail of the Tiger, ") June 25, 2010, offering a one-day retreat and 6.25 CLE credits to members of the Vermont and New Hampshire Bars, http://www.tailofthetiger.org/documents/Lawyers_2010.pdf (webpage last visited May 17, 2010.

16 New York City Contemplative Lawyers' Group, (67 members), http://www.facebook.com/group.php?v=wall&gid=37848126423#!/group.php?gid=37848126423&v=info (webpage last visited May 17, 2010). Meditation and law events have recently been hosted by the Denver Bar Association ("Mindfulness for Lawyers," to be presented by Stephanie West Allen on June 11, 2010 for one CLE credit, http://www.denbar.org; the Massachusetts Bar Association, "Effective Lawyering with the Whole Person: Applying Mindfulness Meditation in Law Practice," co-sponsored a seminar with Tail of the Tiger on December 2, 2008, which describes its program as follows: "Lawyers face many stimulating challenges, whether in negotiation, counseling, advocacy, analysis, or office management; however, these activities can also be highly stressful and adversarial.

As a result, lawyers suffer from remarkable levels of stress, contributing to personal and professional difficulties, burnout, turnover, substance abuse, and divorce. But does law practice have to be so distressing? Mindfulness meditation, a practice of training the mind's natural alertness and presence, is today being practiced in law firms and law schools as a way of revitalizing careers and managing stress. This seminar will address how mindfulness practice can be useful for attorneys, how it enhances lawyering skills and enables lawyers to overcome the inflexibility of the adversarial mindset, find creative solutions to conflict, build confidence, and overcome knee-jerk reactivity in responding to challenging situations and people."

See http://www.massbar.org/for-attorneys/publications/e-journal/2008/november/11-20/cle-programs. Mindfulness training for mediators has become an increasingly common feature since the publication of Leonard Riskin's seminal article, see infra note 5, and has been well received, *see* http://www.realdivorcemediation.com/2009/05/mindful-mediation.html.

17 *See, e.g.,* "Harvard Doc Helps Judges Open Minds," May 5, 2010, Boston Herald (describing day of meditation training offered to Massachusetts state court judges in February 2010). Similar presentations have been offered to state court judges in Minnesota (by Robert Zeglovitch), and Kentucky (by Ron Greenberg).

18 As just one example, on two occasions last semester, I was asked by groups of my students to lead brief guided meditation sessions as part of my 120+ person first-year Torts class, and have also experimented with bringing a meditative perspective, and my mindfulness bell, into my upperclass seminars, such as Racism and Justice in American Legal History.

19 The Law Program's website provides links to a variety of supportive organizations at http://www.contemplativemind.org/programs/law/links.html.

20 The ABA has published articles and books which describe the value of contemplative practice to lawyers. *See, e.g.* George W. Kaufman, *The Lawyer's Guide to Balancing Life & Work* (2d ed., 2006). *See also,* Keeva, *supra* note 7 (including chapters on "contemplative practice," "mindfulness practice," and "the time-out practice" and

discussing the importance of these practices to lawyers and to their effectiveness as public servants).

21 *See* http://www.tailofthetiger.org/index.html (webpage last visited May 17, 2010).

22 *See* Scott Roger's The Mindful Lawyer, http://www.imslaw.com/Home.html; Stephanie West Allen's Idealawg, http://westallen.typepad.com/idealawg/; The Center for Contemplative Mind, http://www.contemplativemind.org/voices/index.html#law.

23 The Cantrell Study, *supra* note 2 at 20–49.

24 *Id.* at 20 (participants reside in New England, Northern California, Georgia, Kansas, Utah as well as Toronto, Canada).

25 *Id.* at 21 (seven participants representing a range of private practice areas and settings, and a former State supreme court Justice; four academics; three working in a "government setting").

26 *Id.* at 24 (including protestant, Catholic, "culturally Jewish," sustained Jewish training, and several who had been introduced to Buddhism at an early age).

27 *See* Rhonda V. Magee, *Mindfulness and the Management of Bias: A Qualitative Study* (work in progress, on file with author). For a preliminary effort to consider the intersections between diversity and mindfulness for lawyers, see Rhonda V. Magee, *The Mindful Lawyer and the Challenges of Diversity: The Benefits of Mindfulness in Differently Diverse Practice Settings*, available at http://www.contemplativemind.org/programs/law/TheMindfulLawyerandDiversity.pdf .

28 For an example of lawyering that seeks to embody this new approach, Angela Harris, Jeffrey Selbin, Margaretta Lin, *From the Art of War to Being Peace: Mindfulness and Community Layering in a Neoliberal Age*, 95 Cal. L. Rev. 2073 (2007).

"Point Vierge" (The Virgin Point): The Contemplative Intention in Community

Bobby William Austin

Foreword

> ...*But the joy is not for mere tourists. Our pilgrimage is more than the synthetic happy making cruise. Our journey is from the limitations and routines of "the given"—the Dasein which confronts us as we are born into it without choice—to the creative freedom of that love which is personal choice and commitment. Paradise symbolizes this freedom and creativity, but in reality this must be worked out in the human and personal encounter with the stranger seen as our other self ...*
>
> *Our task now is to learn that if we can voyage to the ends of the earth and find ourselves in the aborigine who most differs from ourselves, we will have made a fruitful pilgrimage. That is why pilgrimage is necessary in some shape or other. Mere sitting at home and meditating on the divine presence is not enough for our time. We have to come to the end of a long journey and see that the stranger we meet there is no other than ourselves—which is the same as saying that we find Christ in him.*
>
> — Thomas Merton, *Conjectures of a Guilty Bystander*

In the spring of 2001 I sat down in the corner of my dining room and there I sat for three months, unable to get up. All I could do was get from my bed to the shower to the chair in the corner of the dining room.

Eventually, I was referred to a wonderful doctor who was a practitioner of holistic integrative medicine, consisting mainly of tremendous massages, Buddhist thought and homeopathic medicine. Within three weeks I was better. In two months, I felt like myself again.

But much had happened in those two months. Things that started me down a path that I continue on to this day. I had been dealt a tremendous blow that almost took my life. I lost my future to two men, one a friend, the other a villain. The crisis left me without my dream that I had worked for and only a very few friends left I could count on.

I was broken and devastated. But here at this moment of what looked like complete demise, I was awakened, awakened to the fact that I had allowed myself to be defeated, by my own hands, or really by my own mind. Reading my Buddhist reading I gained insight into the "monkey mind" concept. There I saw myself. My mind had simply jumped all over the place, putting me in the most frightening place. My mind, which I could not control, was devastating my simple existence. Each day as I sat in my chair, my mind would torment and terrify me, never resting, always finding deeper pits for me to jump into.

The very Buddhist reading that mentioned monkey mind was helping me to gain control of my monkey mind. I developed a ritual each morning. I read from *The Path to Tranquility: Daily Wisdom* by the Dalai Lama and from the Psalms.

I had lost control of my life, and now I was in search of it.

> ...We are the prisoners of every urgency. In this way we so completely loses all perspective and sense of values that we are no longer able to estimate correctly what even the most immediate consequences of our actions may turn out to be. We know well; enough that if we do certain things, certain definite reactions will follow: but we lose all capacity to grasp the significance of those reactions, and hence we cannot see further than the next automatic response. Having lost our ability to see life as a whole, to evaluate conduct as a whole, we no longer have any relevant context into which our actions are to be fitted, and therefore all our actions become erratic, arbitrary, and insignificant. To the man who concerns himself only with consequences, everything soon becomes inconsequential, nothing "follows from" anything else, all is haphazard, futile, and absurd. For it is not humanly possible to live a life without significance and remain healthy. A human life has to have human meaning, or else it becomes morally corrupt.
>
> Hence we come to be forced into evil in order to avoid what seem to us evil consequences. We find ourselves more and more backed into a corner in which there seems to be no choice but that of a "lesser evil" for the sake of some urgency, some imaginary or desperately hoped for good. But an evil choice can never have wholly good consequences.

And a good choice can never have wholly evil consequences. But when one chooses to do *good, irrespective of the consequences*, it is a paradox that the consequences will ultimately be good, and the good that is in them will far outweigh the possible evil.[1]

— Thomas Merton, *Conjectures of a Guilty Bystander*

Personal Practice

The contemplative lets go of self to find self. I had begun my personal practice—as a way to restructure my interior life. I was not a contemplative. I was a poor frightened soul fighting for a way back. I had ritual readings—Buddhist and Christian (Psalms); Music—classical, religious chants, Negro Spirituals; meditations; quiet thoughts; and writing—fiction and nonfiction. I had given up trying to "hold myself together"—the monkey mind was too strong. In this situation Merton wisely counsels:

> …A personal crisis occurs when one becomes aware of apparently irreconcilable opposites in oneself. If the tension between them is strong enough, one can no longer "keep himself together." His personal unity is fractured. There are various pathological ways of trying to handle the fracture. For instance, reconstructing a unity built on one half of the opposition and projecting the unacceptable half upon the world and upon other people. Then the half of oneself that is still acceptable becomes "right" and the rest of the world becomes wrong. If the conflict is intense, then the outer world, other people, other societies are regarded s heretical, malicious, subversive, demonic, etc.
>
> A personal crisis is reactive and salutary if one can accept the conflict and restore unity on a higher level, incorporating the opposed elements in a higher unity. One thus becomes a more complete, a more developed person, capable of wider understanding, empathy, and love for others, etc. All this is familiar.
>
> What is less familiar is the fact that crisis becomes constant and permanent when a man allows himself to be preoccupied, before all else, with "holding himself together"—with his own inner unity. This is one of the great dangers of the enclosed contemplative life for weak and introspective

minds—precisely the ones who seem most drawn to it.

Basically, one who is obsessed with his own inner unity is failing to face his disunion with God and with other men. For it is in union with others that our own inner unity is naturally and easily established. To be preoccupied with achieving inner unity first and then going on to love others is to follow a logic of disruption which is contrary to life.[2]

— Thomas Merton, *Conjectures of a Guilty Bystander*

Rather than hold myself together I started to put myself back together. I did this with what I called "The Inward Journey." I can now define five elements of this journey of contemplation.

    a. the listening post: where I waited in silence to hear
    b. the singing thought: where I sung to myself (hummed)
    c. the music box: where I listened to beauty
    d. the prayer stream: where I meditated and prayed
    e. the drinking gourd: where I followed the spirit to
be refreshed

During this period I began and finished my book, *I'll Make Me a World: Bringing Wholeness to Fractured Lives After 9/11*. It was a meditation on 9/11. It was also my way of beginning my journey to my home of the soul. Here I asked each day, who am I? As I continued to go deeper trying to answer I was forced to ask about the people that I felt had harmed me. Who are they? Finally, when I could get far enough I could find the internal integration and ask, who are we?

Thomas Moore, in his introduction to Merton's *Conjectures of a Guilty Bystander*, tells us:

    ...Again and again Merton takes up yet another monkish paradox: *contemptus mundi*, contempt of the world, which he says needs to be reexamined and appreciated anew. He tells us that he doesn't mean fulminating against lax sexual morals, divorce, and pornography—the usual easy targets of religious moralists. He means something subtler: a giving up of the understanding of oneself that comes from identifying with society's aims. The monk has contempt for the world in the sense that he refuses to participate in its values and assumptions. It makes no difference if you live like a prince or a hermit; the point is whether or not you live out in your own life the unconscious and unconsidered principles of the society at large.

I have come to think that care of the soul requires a high degree of resistance to the culture around us, simply because that culture is dedicated to values that have no concern for the soul. To preserve our precious hearts, we may have to live economically against the grain, perhaps so as not to be forced into soul-maiming work just to place bread on the table or put our children through college. We may not want to be plugged into electronic media and have our thoughts laundered daily with biased news, superficial commentary, and "lite" entertainment. We may not want to contribute to disastrous pollution of nature or participate in the current value-empty philosophy of education. This *contemptus mundi* is not a misanthropic, superior rejection of life's pleasures but, rather, a compassionate attempt to find more grounded pleasure and communal fulfillment in deep appreciation for life relieved of ambition and control.[3]

That part of my practice that included writing and asking those three questions of my self, gave me the courage to want to be about something other than myself. I did not know the concept *contemptus mundi*, but I did know the effort that I was expending attempting to find grounded pleasure and communal fulfillment. So I wrote about what was going on around me after 9/11 rather than about my personal and professional problems. I created that space I called the inward journey[4] because it was time to lead myself toward wholeness. I did not and could not lead anyone else, just me.

The inward journey requires that we—

- dialog
- hear
- understand personally
- understand collectively
- script out

- use mental models
- act
- be in the present and at peace[5]

Good to Meet You, Father Merton

When I was finally introduced to Father Merton in book form, I read just about everything that he had written and added him to my practice. Even though we, Merton and I, do not see things always in the same way, he has a firm grasp on my thought process. I measure so much of what I say and do now by his towering narratives and majestic insight. His emotional and supreme vision of universal brotherhood at the corner of Fourth and Walnut Streets in Louisville is the epitome of the simple – complex visualization you come to expect from this modern day monk.

> ...In Louisville, at the corner of Fourth and Walnut, in the center of the shopping district, I was suddenly overwhelmed with the realization that I loved all those people, that they were mine and I t heirs, that we could not be alien to one another even though we were total strangers. It was like walking from a dream of separateness, of spurious self-isolation in a special world, the world of renunciation and supposed holiness. The whole illusion of a separate holy existence is a dream. Not that I question the reality of my vocation, or of my monastic life: but the conception of "separation from the world" that we have in the monastery too easily presents itself as a complete illusion: the illusion that by making vows we become a different species of being, pseudo angels, "spiritual men," men of interior life, what have you.
>
> Certainly these traditional values are very real, but their reality is not of an order outside everyday existence in a contingent world, nor does it entitle one to despise the secular: though "out of world" we are in the same world as everybody else, the world of the bomb, the world of race hatred, the world of technology, the world of mass media, big business, revolution, and all the rest. We take a different attitude to all these things, for we belong to God. Yet so does everybody else belong to God. We just happen to be conscious of it, and to make a profession out of this consciousness. But does that entitle us to consider ourselves different, or even *better*, than others? The whole idea is preposterous.[6]
>
> — Thomas Merton, *Conjectures of a Guilty Bystander*

I never had the luxury of perceiving myself out of this world. I was too stuck inside it. I took the opposite journey and so I took a different pathway. I went deep to find myself, so I could embrace once again, trust once again. I felt I had embraced too carelessly without real insight. Blind trust had cost me just about everything. At the time I found myself, and there are many, many voices of Merton I have come in contact with reading his immense body of work. But I am most in touch with the Merton quoted in "Bridges to Contemplation Leadership," produced by the Merton Institute in Louisville, Kentucky.[7]

War and Peace

I now know that my path along the inward journey is my contemplative intention. I call it intention because for me it is the desire to be and to do. It is my intention to seek wholeness in all phases of my life, most certainly in community and with others. The inward journey sounds lonely and self-centered on the face of it, and in some ways it is. But the outcome is to find oneself first, then to be of assistance to another. The problem with leadership today, if I may be so bold, is that people seek to lead when they themselves are profoundly lost. We have our motives for why we seek. Merton's narrative is fixed in his Christian discipline and belief. My narrative is centered in humanitarian and civil ideals framed in spiritual motifs.

I am very concerned about what can happen to others who are attempting good but are derailed by destructive forces. What can they do? I think they can do what I did, only earlier and better. They can begin to practice a way forward to calm the tone of the monkey mind leading away from a path of fractured pieces to a haven of wholeness.

Many communities are traumatized in America. Violence and fear is the order of the day. People are at war with themselves. I recently sat on a jury of a young man accused of murder of another young man, The accused could not tell us why he did it. There in the courtroom sat two families unable to cry but looking ancient and tired, one with a dead son and no explanation. The other family was about to lose a son to the death of prison. War. No winners.

There is something in this story that is reminiscent of *War and Peace* by Leo Tolstoy, the story of society in Russia during the Napoleonic era. According to critics, authors and literary experts, there are two main questions that this great novel ask:

- How should or does one live a moral life in an ethically imperfect world?
- Where is god in this amoral world?

The fact is there is only one answer to both questions, in the plot of the story as well as in life: the characters/individuals in community must work out "their own soul salvation." They must bother to take that inward journey. So today all must take the journey from the painful cry of a newborn baby until he reaches the embrace of his mother; from the noise of war and the quiet of peace; from the upheaval of chaos to the firmness of stability; from jangling disorder to harmonious order; from the fear of darkness to the clarity of light—we must, if we are to be whole, take the inward journey between the war and upheaval of the world around us and traverse along our own unknown path toward wholeness and peace. This path between pain and joy is the self-leadership of the modern contemplative.

Community Application

What then does this say about contemplative leadership? I have just been given the opportunity to do two things that bring contemplative intentions to practical application in a community. I host a weekly radio show called American Voices. On that show we tell civic stories as a way to create public kinship. Public kinship will, we believe, create public trust, which allows for wholeness. To our way of thinking all these civic elements are steps along a path that requires a contemplative intention. It is practicing thought that requires one to seek out and act with good intention toward another. It is personal action in which the two are involved in a personal act that can only be accomplished when one thinks about it. The idea is to cause people to think about their actions and the good that can come from that.

Secondly, I am working with a housing organization in Washington and we have two low-income housing projects in which we are soon to introduce the concept of "the assembly." The assembly was founded by Donald L. Anderson. According to Anderson, the assembly "is a means of encouraging low-income people to deal with their own individual and community problems." It is also a grassroots democratic process built on Jeffersonian principles that Mr. Anderson perfected. We are adding a contemplative model that we have developed to work along side citizens as they deliberate and make decisions about their community.

There are few grassroots organizations that do not begin with prayer or a moment of silence as they go about their work. We hope to infuse this moment with a simple practice of inward intention as a key practice in the deliberative work of grassroots decision making.

Point Vierge

I find Merton's *point vierge* (the virgin point) is my mantra for contemplative intentions. I find it in the hope that through American Voices and the assembly others will as well. Merton tells us that some species are who they are in their DNA. Man is who is by intention. He can awake in the spirit or he can awake each day as a captive of society and in control of himself (modern man). The revelation at the dawn of each new day is the eternal offering of a new day to find the path to wholeness.

> …The first chirps of the waking day birds mark the *point vierge* of the dawn under a sky as yet without real light, a moment of awe and inexpressible innocence, when the Father in perfect silence opens their eyes. They begin to speak to Him, not with fluent song, but with an awakening question that is their dawn state, their state at the *point verge*. Their condition asks if it is time for them to "be." He answers "yes." Then, they one by one wake up, and become birds. They manifest themselves as birds, beginning to sing. Presently they will be fully themselves, and will even fly.
>
> Meanwhile, the most wonderful moment of the day is that when creation in its innocence asks permission to "be" once again, as it did on the first morning that ever was.
>
> All wisdom seeks to collect and manifest itself at that blind sweet point. Man's wisdom does not success, for we are fallen into self-mastery and cannot ask permission of anyone. We face our mornings as men of undaunted purpose. We know the time and we dictate terms. We are in a position to dictate terms, we suppose: we have a clock that proves we are right from the very start. We know what time it is. We are in touch with the hidden inner laws. We will say in advance what kind of day it has to be. Then if necessary we will take steps to make it meet our requirements.
>
> For the birds there is not a time that they tell, but the virgin point between darkness and light, between nonbeing and being. You can tell yourself the time by their waking, if you are experienced. But that is your folly, not theirs. Worse folly

still if you think they are telling you something you might consider useful—that it is, for example, four o'clock.

So they wake: first the catbirds and cardinals and some that I do not know; later the song sparrows and wrens; and lastly, all the doves and crows.

The waking of crows is most like the waking of men; querulous, noisy, raw.

Here is an unspeakable secret: paradise is all around us and we do not understand. It is wide open. The sword is taken away, but we do not know it: we are off, "one to his farm and another to his merchandise"—lights on, clocks ticking, thermostats working, stoves cooking, electric shavers filling radios with static. "Wisdom," cries the dawn deacon, but we do not attend.[8]

— Thomas Merton, *Conjectures of a Guilty Bystander*

A FINAL INTEGRATION:
A CONTEMPLATIVE CIVIL RELIGION?

...The fruit of final integration in the contemplative life is peacemaking: the contemplative's being and behavior brings peace to every person or society with whom the peacemaker is in relationship.

Thomas Aquinas wrote that we cannot give what we do not already have. Unless the lion and the lamb can lie down together within our own hearts, we cannot bring peace to anyone else.

Becoming a peacemaker is the inner work of the day, the real labor of making incremental choices that transcend the small worlds in which we always find ourselves. Our personal heart-work for peace is never finished. We are always stretching forward and climbing upward toward that Love (as Dante envisioned it) "that moves the planet and the other stars."

The man who has attained final integration is no longer limited by the culture in which he has grown up. He has embraced *all of life* ... He has experienced qualities of every type of life: ordinary human existence, intellectual life, artistic creation, human love, religious life. He passes beyond all these limiting forms, while retaining all that is best and most universal in them, "finally giving birth to a fully comprehensive self." [Merton is quoting Arasteh.] He accepts not only his own community, his own society, his own friends, his own culture, but all mankind. He does not remain bound to one limited set of values in such a way that he opposes them aggressively or defensively to others. He is fully "Catholic" in the best sense of the word. He has a unified vision and experience of the one truth shining out in all its various manifestations, some clearer than others, some more definite and more certain than others. He does not set these partial views in opposition to each other, but unifies them in a dialectic or an insight of complementarity. With this view of life he is able to bring perspective, liberty, and spontaneity into the lives of others. The final integrated man is a peacemaker, and that is why there is such a desperate need for our leaders to become such men of insight.[9]

— Thomas Merton, *Contemplation in a World of Action*

The Final Integration: A Civil Religion

Wesley Hotchkiss, a former church executive with the United Church of Christ, aligns himself with the idea that religion is the quest for felicity. It is his understanding that the pilgrim quest for purity in this world was the transcendent message that catapulted those men and women who came to America to transform that wilderness into a promised land. Within that spirit, American culture and the American nation grew and developed. Daniel Bell is correct when he says that great cultures are geared toward or centered around a major religious belief, a belief in a God, an ordering spirit, a transcendence that brings the community together, shapes it, gives it focus, values, a past, and a future.

But our society has developed along the lines of separation of church from state, secular from sacred. It is not a tenet that Americans are inclined to give up, even though church is very much intertwined with the affairs of state and of the nation. What is not a part of this relationship is that one can tell the other what it must or must not do. It seeks to inform through dialogue, through values that interplay and intersect and the integration of those values into law or practice. Therefore, barring that a religion, a sacred religion, a religion of a God or a church or a priesthood is something that we will have at any time in the near future, it appears that there is need for some discussion of how our culture might be best served by contemplatives.

American culture is a multi-level culture. It has a political base, the structure that sets out the principles of government. It has a symbolic culture, which is the membrane for which various signs and symbols are sent back and forth. It then has a core which is called a common culture, the public arena where all Americans gather, contribute, view and understand our commonality and share with kinship a nation. Around that common culture live the ethnic communities that must move in and out of the common culture and the symbolic sphere. Then, we are, I believe, able to understand how a contemplative intention could be instrumental in organizing our thoughts and behaviors of an ethical, principled society.

In the March 11, 2004 edition of the *International Herald Tribune*, the headline on page three read "Religious Rhetoric: President Talks the Talk." The article, written by Gustav Niebuhr of the *Washington Post* wire service, sketches a somewhat faint scenario that Bill Clinton was "emerging as a canny practitioner of public religion." A few years later he could have added President George W. Bush, a born-again Christian. The idea was that Clinton, in using phases such as "heal this nation," and "almost a spiritual change" in regard to the idea of fighting violence, was using a rhetoric that is religious both in form and in reality. Of course various religious factions within the United States see it from their political points of view. Those who agree with him are comfortable. Those who do not, are still not comfortable. The point, however, was that President Clinton was using religious language to attempt to create an atmosphere in which the law, the ideas and concept of which are a part of our religious background, our heritage, become more recognizable in the public and secular life of the country. So in many ways, it is obvious that the president no less than other Americans feels that the key missing element in our culture at this time is some transcendent language that causes people to feel spiritually attuned and attached to their culture.

In Washington, DC, at Peoples Congregational Church of Christ, A. Knighton Stanley preaches a sermon called the "Sacred Canopy." And in this, he explains that the sacred canopy is where people of great and immense diversity come under a sacred or a spiritual covering, where they are allowed to simply tell their story, and, as they tell their story and as they listen and hear the stories of others, they walk into a different and special relationship. This relationship allows people of greatest diversity to be in contact one with the other. It is this sacred canopy, this sacred covering, where men can divest themselves of the mask of their lives in order to regain the sum of their souls.

This sacred canopy, however, in itself, does not call for a religious dogma. It simply calls for our own interpretation of this idea is that it does not call for a religious dogma. It simply calls for men and women of good will to come together and share under the covenant of spiritual connectedness. To me, this is a key idea that American culture must begin to consider, how to bring citizens into some kind of connectedness that does not rely upon a person professing a belief in a particular religion, but allows people to use their religion or at least their code of ethics to live in harmony one with the other. This will be our objective in our assembly work and American voices.

To my way of thinking, it would be under this sacred canopy, of the civil religion, that the ideas of civic storytelling, civic literacy, cultural citizenship, more responsibility and, most of all, public kinship could be worked out. It would provide a framework from which to flesh out the content and character of a new kind of social dialogue in the United States. It would in fact establish a set of moral and ethical principles that could be applied to each individual in everyday life. Principles that would come from the nation's religious communities, simple ideas such as "do unto others as you would have them do unto you." It would use the Ten Commandments. It would apply Ben Franklin's values for life such as thrift, sobriety, frugality, etc. These simple moral and ethic dictums, then, could be applied in everyday life as a part of the civil religion of the country that all men, women, boys and girls would learn, adopt and use as we each come within the sacred canopy of personal relationships to share our individual stories.

I believe this would generate mutual respect as a code of conduct, which is what a good culture does. It informs its practitioners of what is acceptable within that particular society. It could be the path which would lead us toward a more sane and civil approach to each other and to a public discourse that would provide our nation with a new sense of who we are and who we will be in the future.

Civil religion based on contemplative ideals and intentions is not something that one should discuss lightly. The idea that one prepares oneself first and then helps others is a major reframing ideal for leadership practitioners in America. And reframe we must. Communities are looking for authenticity today. They are requiring leaders be held to their own standards. contemplation will become a required element in the leadership bag.

And it would require far more discussion and thought than is possible at this point. Should we not begin to enunciate the idea that such is not only possible but probably necessary if we are to explore, enjoy, and expand our common culture and if we are to be a civil society in which the rule of law and respect of persons truly becomes a reality? Public kinship is the most needed feature that American life and culture can develop now. A contemplative civil religion could be one of the most effective ways to articulate these new relationships. Diversity in all of its many ramifications is causing Americans to dig deeper than ever before to understand who we are and what we are. But we are not alone. The whole world is involved in this process, the process of new people in the village who are no longer strangers, even though strange we may seem to one another. It is obvious that we must figure out the common will and we must act upon it if we are to create a common future that allows difference and diversity. Our future in America will be tied to our ability to take the contemplative journey as a part of routine practice in the art of community discourse and the art of democracy. We have begun to connect into that underground stream that flows beneath the consciousness of the American psyche toward the beginning of final integration.

Notes

1   *Conjectures of a Guilty Bystander,* Thomas Merton, Doubleday, New York, NY: 1965; p. 118

2   Ibid, p. 208

3   Ibid, p. VII

4   *I'll Make Me a World: Bringing Wholeness to Fractured Lives After 9/11*; Bobby Austin, p. 114–117

5   Ibid, p.107

6   Op. Cit. p. 154

7   *Bridges to Contemplative Living with Thomas Merton*; Jonathan Montaldo and Robert G. Toth; Ave Maria Press, Notre Dame, Indiana, 2008, p. 19

8   Op. Cit. p. 44–49

9   Ibid, p. 335

Contemplative Practice and Social Activism

Claudia Horwitz

We're Dying and We're Not Winning

When I graduated from college twenty years ago, I began work as an organizer on economic justice issues—namely homelessness, hunger, and affordable housing. After a few years, I began to worry. Almost everyone I worked with—both the young organizers we were developing and low-income partners we worked with—was struggling to stay healthy. People weren't getting enough sleep or eating well. Addiction was rampant. The postures of anger and righteousness were limiting our capacity for long-term success. It seemed like the entire future of our work to build a movement for social justice was in jeopardy. It dawned on me that people were dying (mostly figuratively but some literally) and we didn't seem to be winning. Soon, I hit my own wall in the form of depression and migraine headaches. It was in this context that I opened to the power of meditation and Kripalu yoga. This paper explores the role of practice in social change work through the lens of yoga in particular.

Yoga in the United States

Yoga is a 5,000-year old tradition, pre-dating Hinduism and Buddhism. By most accounts, yoga arrived in this country in the late 1800's, during the first Parliament of the Worlds Religions in Chicago. Swami Vivekananda, a disciple of Ramakrishna's, addressed the Parliament and sparked initial interest in the tradition. A couple of decades later, Paramahansa Yogananda arrived in Boston in 1920, began teaching meditation, and later established the Self-Realization Fellowship. He also wrote the famous text, "Autobiography of a Yogi." In the 1960's, Maharishi Mahesh Yogi (who had a brief relationship with The Beatles) introduced Transcendental Meditation to the west and also catalyzed the first wave of medical research on the benefits of yoga. During this decade other schools came into being including the International Society for Krishna Consciousness (ISKON), Swami Sivananda's yoga centers, and Yogi Bhajan's Kundalini community. The 1970's saw other teachers well-known to yogis including B.K.S.Iyengar, Pattabhi Jois (ashtanga yoga), Sri Krishnamacharya and his son T.K.V. Desikachar, as well as the establishment of Kripalu Center. In 1999, the Yoga Alliance formed and established standards for both a 200-hour and 500-hour teacher training. Currently, over 1,000 yoga teacher training programs in the country are registered.

How We Meet Suffering in the Body

Yoga offered me a window into the nature of suffering, transformation, and liberation. Rev. Walter Burghardt's definition of contemplation is "a long, loving look at the real"[1] and it's this understanding that still anchors me in these practices. As with many activists, I went through periods of prolonged anxiety, confusion and pain; not surprisingly, my tendency was to look for an escape route. The benefit of a sustained practice is that it opens us to whatever arises, to simply be with what is. This is a profound teaching: to surrender to the totality of the moment, whether it is grief over an act of senseless violence or anger with outdated public policies. And our suffering, in whatever form, can too easily eclipse our innate desires to be kind, to be whole. But instead of meeting crisis with "fight or flight" we can find an intelligent and expansive response that points us towards collective liberation. Many ancient Yogic and Buddhist texts embody this wisdom: mind-states obscure our capacity for clarity and compassion. The second of Patanjali's Yoga Sutras says simply this: Yoga is stilling the fluctuations of the mind so that the Self can abide in its true nature.[2] Contemplative practice wears this away, very slowly, enabling us to be present to what is actually unfolding. Once obstacles become known to us—whether it is anxiety in the body or the stories of the mind—they can become a messenger rather than an obstacle. With consistent effort, a contemplative practitioner becomes a witness. The veil of illusion is pierced and the roots of suffering have less power to direct our actions. In this way, distress, crisis, fear, sadness, and grief can serve as an impetus to discover truth; and discomfort becomes a springboard to greater understanding. We have a lens through which to examine and navigate our relationships to each other, to themselves, and to the ineffable.

Resourcing Activists from the Inside Out

In the U.S. and much of the West, many people think of yoga as an individual, physical practice. It has become estranged from much of its philosophical roots. But the core concepts of the tradition offer activists both inspirational and practical frameworks for our larger commitments. The body and the breath reveal much of what we need to know about our human experience. Blocks in our physical body can be great teachers. Through the asanas, or postures, we let go of what is no longer serving us—stress, information, anger, pain. Working with the breath enables us to focus our attention, to go deeper into a stretch, to hold a posture for a bit longer, to balance in unwieldy positions. With loving attention, we come into a fuller experience of the present. In yoga, we build asanas literally from the core of the body—the torso. The stronger the core, the more we can do—longer holds, greater flexibility, more fluidity of movement. The same holds true for our organizations, neighborhoods, coalitions and the like. If the core isn't hardy, it will fray everything else around it. When the core is healthy and strong, the energy moves more fully and the limbs stretch wider. It's from the vantage point as an organizer, spiritual practitioner and a yoga teacher in the Kripalu tradition that I engage with hundreds of change agents, activists and leaders every year.

My commitment throughout the past 15 years of running stone circles has been to help people see the deep and inextricable links between the collective liberation they are working for in the world and their own path of freedom. We have convened hundreds of retreats, workshops, training and conversations for thousands of individuals and organizations. In 2007, the organization purchased a 70-acre property in North Carolina where we have created The Stone House, a center for spiritual life and strategic action. The Stone House is weaving together three threads that we believe are crucial to our collective survival: a deep core of spiritual life and practice, strategic action for social change, and a sustainable relationship to the land. In a short time we have become an important gathering place and vibrant community. The Stone House offers formal practice in an atmosphere of radical hospitality, fellowship and an invitation to deep rest. People come for a variety of reasons. Some are interested in developing or deepening a spiritual practice but do not feel comfortable going to retreat centers that are mostly white and often out of their budget. We have a commitment to making all of our retreat programs at least 50% people of color, which we feel is required to provide a safe container for people of color. In addition, we make all of our programs available to anyone who wants to participate, regardless of ability to pay. We offer sliding scales and scholarships for everything we do and we never turn anybody away. This has been critical, particularly since our aim is to provide resources for people who need it the most and often get it the least. Most of the folks we see arrive weary from the world and their work. Some are suffering from fatigue or illness. Many have lifelong patterns of overwork and frustration that have begun to harden in the body. We give them permission to take care of themselves and follow their own wisdom.

The Yoga of Social Change

In this spirit, we have learned a tremendous amount about how to bring practice to a very broad range of people, folks who are a bit estranged from their bodies and even skeptical. I'm grateful that I began studying the Kriplau path many years ago because it is one of the most conducive yoga practices for people of varying body types and levels of health. I think of Kriplau as a tradition that does not leave anyone behind. We've developed specific ways of teaching meditation and particular posture flows that provide a gentle but deep experience that work for both the newcomer and the more experienced practitioner. We offer numerous forms of retreat at The Stone House—day-long practice retreats offered freely to the community, a 5-day refuge program for organizers and activists and longer practice retreats. In addition, we do leadership training that includes an emphasis on mindfulness through meditation and yoga, as well as other practices such as storytelling, art, writing, discussion and time in the natural world. Our intention is to explore the concepts of liberation and suffering in our movement building work.

We've also developed a retreat called "The Yoga of Social Change," which offers the teachings of yoga to activists in an explicit social justice context; we practice asanas, pranayama (or breath work), text study, group dialogue, individual reflection and meditation. In the practice of yoga, seeming "opposites" represent a place where we can begin to play with duality and dynamic tension. We are able to see a union of opposites—movement and stillness, expansion and contraction, back-bend and forward bend, holding and releasing, will and surrender. In our collective human experience, we tend to choose one side and demonize the other. Yoga can help us see intimate relationship inherent in every duality. It also enables practitioners to move beyond conditioning, a vital lesson for social change practitioners. We've all developed habits and patterns based on our cultural legacies, familial histories, personal experience and leadership challenges. When we are being triggered by something and reacting in a way that feels out of proportion, it's likely that a painful part of our past is being reactivated. These moments are opportunities to observe our conditioning. Over time, conditioned patterns are weakened through exposure, awareness, stillness and compassion.

Others are thinking about this as well:

- Sean Corne, one of the more popular yoga teachers in the U.S., has created "Off the Mat, Into the World," an initiative that uses yoga to ignite grassroots social change. The project offers leadership training, a network, local groups and opportunities for service.

- YogaActivist.org is growing a national network of teachers who serve marginalized populations, including the homeless, youth in detention, and trauma survivors.
- Studios have opened in many communities that aim for an explicit integration between the spiritual practice of yoga and the realities of the world. Sharon Gannon and David Life pioneered some of this work through their New York studio, Jivamukti. Others have followed suit including Studio 34 in Philadelphia, Yoga District in Washington, DC, and many more.

A Growing Call for Practice

The pressure on the frontlines of the struggle for social justice is tremendous. The work itself requires a proximity to injustice and that easily provokes sustained experiences of anger or sadness. The urgency can be relentless. As a result, the activist culture has left a lot to be desired; I've heard many younger activists express the desire to do things differently from their elders and mentors. And patterns of addiction, illness or exhaustion are common and the impact of these goes beyond the individual. These challenges also greatly limit the effectiveness of organizations. In a sense, the sector is ripe for contemplative and spiritual practice.

The demographics of this population have not yet been studied in a comprehensive way but they can be illustrated to some extent nonetheless. From 15+ years of working in this field, I would describe the group as spanning a wide age range (20s-70s) and class backgrounds. It is predominantly women, probably close to 75%. With regard to race and ethnicity, it is much more diverse than the demographics of those pursuing contemplative practice in the broader society, with the majority being people of color. Similarly, there is a much higher proportion of people who identify as queer. The geographic distribution of activists engaging in practice is complex. While I have visited and/or met with activists in every part of the country (33 states) who are bringing spirituality and activism together, the forms of this vary widely from region to region, from urban to rural settings. Much of the leadership in the growing field of spirituality and social change (or transformational movement building as many are now calling it) has come from the East and West coasts, which presents a series of juicy questions and challenges.

One thing is for sure—this work has come a long way. In the mid-90's, I was asked to facilitate a two-day roundtable (4 sessions total) on "Faith and Social Justice" at a large convening of the Black Student Leadership Network in Charlotte, NC. I'm a white woman so I asked two African-American male colleagues to co-lead these sessions. We worked diligently on an outline that would allow for more reflective and conversational time. We had no idea what to expect. When we arrived at the huge, downtown convention hotel and found the room for our session it was, without a doubt, the smallest room in the entire place. One long table, 12 chairs around and very little room for anything else. 15 people came to the first session, peeking a bit timidly into the room and speaking tentatively. We asked the hotel for a couple extra chairs. By the second session the crowd had ballooned to at least 25 people and the three of us facilitators were sitting on the window ledge. By the last session we had 50-60 people sitting on the floor and spilling into the hallway. The dialogue was alternatingly loud with laughter and quiet with poignant moments. People had found their tribe.

This mirrors the larger story I've seen unfold over the past 18 years. Social change activists, once tentative about their own needs and desires for some form of quieting or grounding practice have become forthright, even demanding. In the face of challenging times, many have turned to a range of practices to keep themselves sane and healthy. A vibrant subset has envisioned new forms of organization and organizing. These shifts stem as much from a hunger for new approaches to leadership and collaboration to strengthen social movements as they do from personal need. An inward path has become part of the activist's ability to see, to feel and ultimately to act from a place of wholeness. In the spring of 2009, we convened "Deep Change: Transforming the Practice of Social Justice." This was a gathering of 100 frontline activists, intermediary organizations and funders in partnership with the Movement Strategy Center and Rockwood Leadership Institute. We surveyed folks ahead of time on the questions below; the words appear at a size equal to their prevalence in the responses.

1. What is drawing you to this gathering?

2. Which transformational practices are part of your individual leadership work or life and with what frequency?

3. Which transformational practices are part of your organizational culture?

4. Are transformational practices part of your movement-building work? How?

Making the Movement Road by Walking

Many activists recognize the need to build stronger organizations from the inside out, because in the words of one organizer, "a healthy and honest organization or collective is the basis of everything we do." In order to sustain social justice work and increase its effectiveness on the ground, the culture of organizations has to be transformed to reflect the values that and love. This will require an expansion of infrastructure, vastly more trained practitioners, and more channels of distribution. And the training and infrastructure must be focused on the activist demographic and specific needs if it is to be useful.

I feel strongly that we are part of a much larger—and quickly growing—contemplative and spiritual movement in the United States. From ancient history through to more recent social movements there are compelling examples of how spiritual consciousness undergirds a compelling vision for the future of humankind. Spiritual wisdom sees beyond the mentality of "us versus them" to engage with the potential of commonality and radical equality. It has great potential to anchor visions of the good society in a commitment to concrete ethics and new forms of behavior, and to guide the actions of civil society groups as they labor to bring these visions to fruition. When I first started stone circles in 1996, I knew few other organizations that were thinking along similar lines. Over a series of gatherings from 2000-2010 the rich network of people bringing spiritual and contemplative practice began to reveal itself.

Recently, the Movement Strategy Center has completed a 65-page report, "Out of the Spiritual Closet: Organizers Transforming the Practice of Social Justice." It is an excellent and compelling look at how this movement is developing and I'm sure Brenda will share more about it at our gathering. There is a very comprehensive list of related organizations, including intermediaries, in the back of the report.

We've begun to capture much of the web on a map of spiritual activism, which will be integrated into a new site, www.liberationspirituality.org.

The site is not up yet but the map can be seen here; we still have many groups to add: http://spiritualactivist.org/strategy_map/index.htm.

The Opportunity Is in the Collective

Radical Catholic nun, Sister Joan Chittister, puts it this way: The question is "how to make private spirituality the stuff of public leaven in a world fiercely private and dangerously public at the same time; how to end our public crucifixions while we say our private prayers. The fact is that simple spiritualities of creed and community and co-operation are obviously no longer enough. We need now, surely, a spirituality of contemplative co-creation."[3] She is right. We need to be bold enough to bring this work into the collective realms, with all necessary protocols and steps to ensure safety and inclusivity. I am still in awe of the teachers who brought the Dharma here from the East. It's impossible for me to imagine my own life, my life's work or the world around me without the three jewels—the teachers, the teachings and the communities for practice—as they have taken root here in U.S. soil. But the evolutionary edge of contemplative practice is to apply it more fully and deeply to the work of organizational, community and social life.

Post-modern life entreats us to wander through a range of spheres, most unrelated to each other. We buy our food in one place, worship or practice in another, take our kids to play at the park, and find release in the darkened atmospheres of night life, all the while burning fuel, time and energy. The shrinking resource base and fragmentation of the planet demands that we envision a different way of living. People are feeling an increasing sense of instability and it's not surprising. The economic system that once brought unquestioned success or at least comfort to many is beginning to crack in visible ways. Climate change is a threat on a level that is hard to comprehend. To many, the war in Afghanistan lacks less viability with each passing month. I recently heard Keith Lawrence from the Aspen Institute's Roundtable on Community Change articulate the current landscape as one in which people value security most; he was referring to their economic prosperity, physical safety and the preservation of ways of life. This has great import for progressive movement-builders. In Keith's analysis, the majority of those holding electoral and policymaking power are attentive to the issues with the greatest emotional resonance for their constituency. Many have learned to define themselves as the public's protector rather than the custodian of our highest values. We see this in the tough on crime stances, the war on terrorism, the passing of SB 1070 in Arizona and the continued backlash and undermining of immigrant rights and dignity. It's in this light that we might best wrestle with the trends and possibilities for contemplative and spiritual practice. It takes on a new dimension and urgency. In their efforts to bring about real and widespread transformation, activists work in the aggregate, and experience even greater levels of the anger, grief and fear that are mirrored in wider society. In this context, what kind of glue will bind us together as we find our way?

One concern is contemplative practices will become a bit too precious, too relegated to a particular demographic. Yoga's meteoric growth is an old story but an important one. 2007 and 2008 studies from *Yoga Journal* and the 2008 "Yoga in America Study" (YIAS) on the growth of yoga reports three vital things:

1. The number of adults practicing yoga grew from 4.3 million in 2001 to 15.8 million in 2007, an increase of almost 400%.

2. 69% have a household income over $50,000; 48% have a household income over $75,000. Other data aligns with this. The YIAS reported 44% of practitioners in the US have a household income of more than $75,000; 24% over $100,000.

3. While data in both studies was collected on the age, income, geographic location and gender of practitioners, there is no correlating data on the race/ethnic background.

While *Yoga Journal* touts this information in building the case for the growing market of consumers, this data can, and obviously must, be read in other ways. And we need to remember that spiritual practice does not automatically inspire holistic or inclusive thinking. If they did, the world would be different. If inner work is undertaken in isolation from the reflective mirror provided by real communities, the spiritual path merely bolsters individualism. The path becomes too self-referential, and the opportunity to contribute to the common good is lost.

For activists—and I would maintain for most people regardless of vocation—practice aimed at individual freedom is simply not enough. People are seeing the opportunities to transform whole organizations and institutions. This is what we want. This is what we need. For activists, by necessity, the life of the spirit is both an individual and a collective enterprise. In nearly every successful social movement throughout history, there has been a significant role for contemplative and spiritual consciousness. The wisdom that can arise from deep practice is an anchor, At its best, a dedication to the spiritual life ushers in a new sense of spaciousness that encourages people to take on more responsibility for their actions and begin to choose new responses to old and familiar questions. As these attributes continue to manifest in practice, activists find themselves grounded in an increased self-awareness, a place of readiness and openness to change. They begin to know what is right in any given moment in time, and to trust that wisdom, whether it comes from within or from outside. Solutions can emerge at any time because the ground has been well-prepared. Marrying a rich inner life dedicated to the cultivation of loving kindness and compassion with the practice of new forms of politics, economics and public policy is the key to social transformation.

Notes

1 Burghardt, W. 1989. *Contemplation: A Long, Loving Look at the Real.*

2 Satchidananda, S. 1990. *The Yoga Sutras of Patanjali: Commentary on the Raja Yoga Sutras.* Buckingham, VA: Integral Yoga Publications.

3 Chittister O.S.B, J. 2000. *Spirituality and Contemporary Culture.* Paper presented at the 2000 National Forum of The Center for Progressive Christianity, June 1–3, in Irvine, California.

Appendix I

The State of the Contemplative Movement

Tom Callanan

From June 10–13, 2010, thirty spiritual leaders and practitioners from different faith traditions, practices, and professions gathered at a remote conference facility in Kalamazoo, Michigan. During the second day of the meeting, a tension point surfaced that had me sitting on the edge of my seat. "I'm concerned about the altar in the middle of the room," said a participant who is a spiritual director. "Many of us placed sacred objects there, and now I see that it's also become a place for note cards, pens and even insect repellant. This feels like sacrilege to me." Another participant, a spiritually-oriented radio personality, spoke up immediately, "I agree, and I'm also concerned about the rock that's up there. I know it means something to someone, but it worries me. I want to know more about that rock."

The intent of the three-day meeting hosted by the Fetzer Institute, a mid-sized foundation based in Kalamazoo, was to "assess the current and future state of the contemplative movement in America." Buddhist teachers and practitioners were in attendance from organizations such as the Naropa Institute and Spirit Rock Meditation Center as well as practitioners from other faith traditions including Christianity, Hinduism, Judaism, Sufism, and interfaith. (See attendance list attached). In addition to those working in religious settings, there were also those teaching in secular settings such as with Google, the University of San Francisco Law School and the US military.

Given the diversity in the room, I wasn't surprised by the discussion about the altar. For fifteen years between 1994 and 2009, I was a program officer at the Fetzer Institute responsible for attending, convening, and facilitating spiritually-oriented gatherings like this one. It was not uncommon at these events for questions regarding what was at the center of the room or who would lead the opening prayer or who would deliver to the keynote address to ignite the very conflicts that the gatherings were designed to preempt or heal.

Submitted to *Shambhala Sun*

Fortunately, at this particular gathering, the potential conflict was resolved as gracefully as I've ever witnessed. The facilitators announced a break; three participants quietly cleared the altar of note cards and insect repellant; and the participant with questions about the rock met over tea with the guy who'd brought the rock. Ten minutes later, everyone returned to their chairs and dove wholeheartedly into the next session of the gathering without so much as a glace backward.

How, I wondered, had this group so easily side-stepped issues that brought other meetings to a standstill? "I don't think we can attribute what happened here to any one person or element," said Mirabai Bush, co-facilitator of the event and Associate Director of The Center for Contemplative Mind in Society. "I think it's a reflection of the nature of the contemplative movement and a reflection of one of the gifts that this movement has to offer the world."

The "contemplative movement" described by Bush refers to approximately 1/4 to 1/3 of the adult population who are engaged on a regular basis with some form of contemplative, spiritual practice. Contemplative practice is defined broadly as that cluster of spiritual practices of all faiths that quiet the mind and bring body, mind and heart into alignment producing grater calm, insight, openness, receptivity, and connection to oneself, others, nature and the divine. Examples include forms of meditation, yoga, prayer, contemplative arts, contemplative movement and ritual.

Until just the past few decades, the number of people practicing contemplation was limited to small groups of monks and nuns living within monastic settings. With a few exceptions such as Emerson, Thoreau and 19th Century Trancendentalists, the idea of lay people engaging in meditation and contemplation wasn't considered until spiritual teachers from the east began visiting the west in the 1960s. When the Beatles took up meditation with Maharishi Mahesh Yogi in 1968, it was as if a spiritual Berlin Wall had come down and people of all ages and faith traditions began accessing powerful ancient practices, not just from within their own religious traditions but across many traditions.

Initially there were divisions and rivalries between practices mirroring the centuries-old divisions between religions. Those divisions, however, began to disappear as the practices were uprooted from their traditions and combined, often in secular settings, with other practices. Medical doctors such as Jon Kabat Zinn and Dean Ornish, for instance, began using Buddhist meditation and Hindu yoga techniques in hospital settings with reimbursement from insurance companies. In 1992, as awareness grew about the similarities between and benefits of such practices, The Center for Contemplative Mind in Society was created to support all contemplative practices. "We are committed to the value and insights of all spiritual and wisdom traditions and their associated forms of contemplative practice," says the group's website.

Although there's much that contemplative practices share in common, many at the Fetzer meeting questioned the idea of belonging to the same "movement." Most movements are defined by a sense of solidarity and shared commitment to a common element at the center. Given the group's discussion about the altar, there was no agreed-upon common center to rally around, at least not on the surface. "There's a transformation that I see happening within practitioners of all faiths that is birthing a new type of consciousness—a consciousness of interdependence and wholeness," said Dena Merriam, founder of the Global Peace Initiative for Women. "Perhaps it's this consciousness of wholeness that's at the center," said Merriam. "The consciousness is similar to the ocean, and each individual's practices and traditions are like harbors and bays that provide safe access to that ocean."

"The paradigm shift that we're experiencing here," said Mirabai Bush, "is that we're all moving toward the universal (the ocean) while still maintaining the integrity of our separate paths and traditions." The contemplative movement is thus one that is defined by a common goal of unity while acknowledging the validity of many ways of getting there. When this unity of consciousness is present, the items on the altar are representations of the different paths to that unity. "Though my primary work is in the domain of Sufism," said Pir Zia Inayant-Kahn, the spiritual leader of the Sufi Order International, "I'm moving out of my personal comfort zone of my spiritual tradition to support the larger movement for the transformation of consciousness that I see taking shape in so many seekers. The task here is to explore revelation as a planetary phenomenon in which all religions have a share but of which none has a monopoly."

As part of their participation in the Fetzer event, each of the thirty participants wrote 10-20 page papers describing the state of the contemplative movement within specific domains of action including education, leadership, law, social action, conflict transformation, end-of-life care, healing trauma, and online communities. When I read the papers and combined them with what was said at the meeting, a very clear and compelling picture of the movement and its potential effect on the spiritual landscape of America and the world began to emerge. The diversity and complexity of the movement as it develops within multiple sectors simultaneously can be described best through the following ten intersecting and interrelated trends and developments.

Ten Trends and Developments within the Contemplative Movement

1. A Radical Individuation of Practice: In most parts of the world, people's spiritual beliefs and practices are usually determined by their family of origin. We are born Hindu, Christian, Muslim etc. and that determines what we believe and how we practice. But now, with the dramatic increase and easy availability of contemplative practices of all kinds, we can choose our practices for ourselves without limitation from our religion of birth. "I was raised Jewish and I still consider myself a practicing Jew," says Claudia Horwitz, the founder of Stone Circles, a non-profit center dedicated to bringing spiritual practices to social activists, "but I also practice mindfulness meditation and yoga, and I sometimes participate in rituals inspired by indigenous traditions. I do what works best for me." This trend toward radical individuation is increasing as marriages continue to cut across religious, racial, and ethnic boundaries producing children who must necessarily choose those combinations of beliefs and practices that work best for them. "Of the 30 contemplative practitioners in this room," says Arthur Zajonc, professor of physics at Amherst College, "there are 30 different expressions of practice. And it's not just Protestant, Catholic, and Hindu. It's what particular kind of Catholic are you; and what particular type of yoga and meditation do you do?"

2. An Explosion of Contemplative Modalities: "During the past twenty years," says Michael Craft, the Program Director at the Omega Institute, "the list of contemplative modalities offered at Omega has literally exploded from a few meditation courses to now include a broad spectrum of techniques, practices and modalities oriented around self awareness and interior and even exterior experience." That list now includes such widely diverse activities as centering prayer, chi gung, journaling, breathing exercises, sacred dance, Zen flower arranging, and labyrinth walking. One participant at the gathering claimed to be experimenting with the idea of "mindful e-mailing." Despite this radical inclusiveness, the leaders of the movement are clear, if not always in agreement, around the boundaries that define the movement. Those practices most often excluded are faith-based forms of petitionary prayer, study and ceremony that tend to reinforce pre-existing religious, spiritual, and psychological beliefs versus focusing on direct experience and cultivating receptivity and openness. Following this line of thinking, one might best determine the line between contemplative and non-contemplative e-mailing by whether one comes away from the experience more righteous and willful or more open, expansive and creative. Regardless of where the line is drawn, "the variety of contemplative practices continues to expand dramatically," says Craft, "along with the public's interest in and demand for learning them and applying them in their lives."

3. Religions Are Adapting and People Are Returning Home: The exodus of westerners from mainstream religions during the sixties, seventies and eighties to embrace contemplative practices from the east is well documented. What is less well known is that mainstream religions are now opening to embrace these practices and people are returning to their neighborhood churches, temples, synagogues etc. Rabbi Rachel Cowan tells the story of a delegation of Rabbis who went to see the Dalai Lama in the early 1970s at his home in Dharamsala, India. "There are so many Jews here who are practicing Buddhism with you," they said. "Will you send them back to us?" His Holiness apparently responded, "They need a place to return to. Will you create that?" During the past twenty years Cowan's Institute for Jewish Spirituality has attempted to do just that by creating the movement for "contemplative Judaism." That movement has supplemented and revived/revitalized traditional Jewish practices with mindfulness meditation, yoga, spiritual direction, mussar, and contemplative prayer. "The Jewish community," explains Cowan, "more readily accepts that one can borrow practices from another tradition (acknowledging their source) and adapt them to the framework of Judaism without importing contradictory messages from another religion." The result, Cowan explains, has been a win-win, both for traditional Jewish synagogues who are finding people returning to their doors and also for those practitioners who reluctantly fled their synagogues and are now happy to return to their local communities and home religion.

Similar movements are happening in the other religions. Douglas Burton-Christie, Professor of Theological Studies at Loyola Marymount University and a leader in the Christian Contemplative movement describes the reciprocal process whereby those who've left the church return to breathe new life into traditional stories and practices. And for those who return after years of sampling practices from other faiths, the church can provide an integrity and continuity of practice. "What does it mean," says Burton-Christie, "to stand in a contemplative tradition and honor the integrity of the thought and practice that has unfolded over thousands of years? That doesn't mean we have to do it as it's always been done. But sinking one's practice into that rich ground can produce great benefit."

4. Finding Unity in Diversity through a Common Way of Knowing: One might predict that the radical individuation of practices within the contemplative movement would cause splintering and fragmentation, but that's not what's happening. Regardless of the tradition or set of practices, there's a growing recognition within the movement of a common mindset or way of knowing that all contemplatives share. "The contemplative mindset," says Buddhist teacher Judy Lief, "is an approach to life that may include contemplative practice but is much broader in scope. It's based on the experience of interconnectedness of oneself, others, and the world as a whole and the view of life as a path of continual challenges, learning and growth." Tobin Hart, the author of the Spiritual Life of Children says that contemplation is a "third way of knowing beyond the rational and the sensory." This way of knowing and experiencing the world is direct, intuitive, and non-conceptual. "Whether we find the contemplative in centering prayer," says Barry Boyce of the Shambhala Sun, "or in the zone we enter on a swift downhill ski run, in resting our mind on a sacred image, or while making art doing carpentry, the experience, or non-experience, if you like, is the same. There is a moment outside time, a suspension of any attempt to make permanent and solid what is dynamic and ever changing." To be a contemplative is to live with a certain kind of awareness that recognizes the unity in the diversity of all things. The contemplative movement is therefore a unique kind of club, the members of which include those who yearn to be part of a club where nothing and no one is ever excluded. "We're all working toward the same thing," says Brenda Salgado of the Movement Strategy Center in Oakland, California. "That's a vision of a world where there is no other."

5. The Movement Meets the Mainstream: The radical inclusiveness and creativity of the movement has helped to move its practices and its way of thinking into the mainstream in unexpected directions and sometimes at a rapid pace. A 2008 study of Yoga in America (YIAS) found that the number of adults practicing yoga grew from 4.3 million in 2001 to 15.8 million in 2007, an increase of almost 400% in just 6 years. "We're talking less about a movement," says Arthur Zajonc, "and more about an infusion." A 2004 study by the Center for Contemplative Mind in Society pointed to five sectors that were most influenced by that infusion. They include business, medicine/science, education, law, and prison work. Recent activity in the technology and military sectors warrants them also being added to the list.

In the technology sector, for instance, Google recently created a program for its employees called "Search Inside Yourself." And Apple has a new

"Meditate" application for its iPhone. In April, 2010, a conference was convened in the Silicon Valley titled "Wisdom 2.0" that brought together mindfulness practitioners working within the technology sector. In a talk at the conference on the "aesthetics of Twitter," Greg Pass described Twitter as an invitation to experience "a moment in time more deeply" so as to give "extraordinary attention to something in our lives that might otherwise pass us by."

In the military sector, programs such as the Military Care Providers Project and the Coming Home Project offer counseling and teach mindfulness, tai chi, and chi gung to Army chaplains, medics, and other care givers along with soldiers suffering from symptoms of Post Traumatic Stress Disorder. Although these programs focus on contemplative practices and their effect on behavior, their greater power rests in a more reflective way of knowing and being that promise a deeper and more lasting transformation. There was talk among the leaders at the Fetzer meeting of the notion of the contemplative family, contemplative education, contemplative law, contemplative journalism, and the biggest tent of all, the contemplative society.

6. Professionalization and Secularization: Social movements follow a fairly consistent developmental trajectory. Stage one typically begins on the fringes of society with a few charismatic leaders and small groups of followers who are focused on building their own identities, language, and practices with little awareness of other groups. Stage two occurs when groups begin enjoying wider popularity and recognize the advantage of joining with similar groups to form alliances, associations, collaborative publications and common ways of speaking. Stage three is characterized by further growth and acceptance within the mainstream. This brings greater popularity, resources, and attention but often threatens the integrity, depth and legitimacy of the individual groups and practices. At this point, various educational, research, and outreach organizations often position themselves between the groups and the mainstream so as to maintain the integrity of the individual groups but also to create a successful bridge and easier accessibility for those within the mainstream.

The contemplative movement is clearly moving into this third stage of development. For instance, a number of secular institutions within the mainstream have formed during the past two decades that are not attached to any particular practice but are clearly devoted to the study, application and dissemination of contemplative practices within the mainstream. These organizations include The Mind and Life Institute, The Center for Mindfulness Medicine, Health Care and Society at the University of Massachusetts

Medical Center, the Mindfulness Awareness Research Center (based at UCLA), and the Association for Contemplative Mind in Higher Education. Foundation support for the movement is now coming from many directions within the secular world including Fetzer, the Nathan Cummings Foundation, the Garrison Institute, the Templeton Foundation and the Seasons Fund for Social Transformation, a consortium of a dozen foundations.

This institutionalization of the movement has not been without its growing pains as secular organizations attempt to integrate contemplative practices once limited to the monastery into organizational life. "Bringing contemplatively-oriented individuals together into an organization is no guarantee of success," says Walter Link. "Some of the most dysfunctional organizations are the ones that claim to be contemplative." And yet, "we need organizations, memes, and ideas," continues Link, "to create an atmosphere and institutions where practice can be supported. It's a real challenge as we move from the fringe to a more active, organizational life that sometimes challenges the comfort of our contemplation."

7. The Marriage of Contemplation and Action: "The perceived split between contemplation and action is well established," says Patricia Jennings, Director of the Initiative on Contemplation and Education at the Garrison Institute. "The standard thinking has been that you're either a contemplative and removed from the world, or you're engaged in action and can't engage in true contemplation. What we're now seeing is that the movement is healing that split. You can do both. To be effective, we're realizing that you actually have to be both. True contemplation demands action, and effective action demands contemplation." A new report, "Out of the Spiritual Closet" developed by the Movement Strategy Center highlights how the split is being healed within the social justice movement. "Individuals are coming out of the spiritual closet; they are seeking transformative practices as a way to be more integrated, interconnected and whole. Across the country, in many different communities, frontline organizers are using a diverse range of practices as they seek to balance their commitment to political/outward transformation with spiritual/inward transformation. While there is great diversity in organizer's approaches, there is also profound unity. As organizers confront the disconnection, fragmentation, and objectification that defines dominant culture, they seek practices that will counteract, heal and transform those experiences. They are working toward deeper embodiment, awareness, connection, interdependence and a life-giving sense of power."

8. Science and Contemplation Become Engaged: The proliferation of scientific research on contemplative practices (particularly meditation and mindfulness) is one of the most remarkable trends of the past five years," says Maia Duerr, the author of "A Powerful Silence," a landmark study of contemplative practice in America in 2004. For instance, the number of clinical trials conducted on the effectiveness of various meditation practices increased from 12 between 2000 and 2004 to 72 between 2005 and 2009 (a 600% increase). Positive findings from these studies have seeded a few high caliber studies conducted by leading scientists including D. Clifford Saron (UC Davis), Dr. Richard Davidson (U. of Wisconsin/Madison), and Dr. Amishi Jha (University of Pennsylvania). The most promising elements coming from these studies relate to the notions of neuroplasticity and mental fitness. The studies point to the fact that our brains change and develop throughout life. We can exercise our brains and keep them young and fit (through contemplative practices) much as we can keep our bodies young and fit through physical exercise. "These studies are creating legitimacy for contemplative practices," says Duerr, "and they're providing people in leadership positions with excellent data to justify the application of these practices, not only in health care but in other fields as well." During a recent debate on Health Care reform within the U.S. House of Representatives, for instance, Ohio Congressman Tim Ryan presented personal testimony along with scientific evidence for the role that mindfulness practice can play in promoting health and well-being and thus reducing health care costs.

9. The Marriage of Personal, Organizational, and Social Transformation: Until recently, the contemplative movement has focused more heavily on personal transformation. The most common sensibility is that transformed individuals will create a transformed society. Unfortunately, current organizational, social, and cultural forms and structures are antithetical to contemplative practice. The circle of concern for those within the contemplative movement is now beginning to expand to include organizational and social transformation. The most promising work in this area is occurring within the domains of social action, law and politics. "Practice aimed at individual freedom is simply not enough," says social activist Claudia Horwitz. "People are seeing the opportunity to transform whole organizations and institutions. This is what we need. For activists, the life of the spirit is both an individual and a collective enterprise." Rhonda Magee, Professor of Law at the University of San Francisco, speaks about her experience working with a five-person team to organize the first national conference on law and meditation at the UC Berkeley

Law School. "We faced challenges right away," she says, "with group dynamics and navigating across real and imagined difference. Although we each had contemplative practices, we were challenged to apply the principles of that inner work to inter-personal dynamics and interactions with the field." "No one said it would be easy," says Horwitz, "but the key to social transformation is marrying a rich inner life dedicated to the cultivation of loving kindness and compassion with the practice of new forms of inter-personal and group interaction, politics, economics and public policy."

10. The Marriage of the Personal and the Environmental: "The environmental crisis is perhaps the most ominous crisis of our times," said teacher of socially engaged spirituality, Donald Rothberg. "The crisis makes problematic whether good conditions for contemplation will be possible in the long run (without confining contemplation to the enclaves of the few)." Michael Craft indicates a hopeful trend within the Omega Institute's courses on sustainability and the environment. "Our courses incorporate strong contemplative practice highlighting the inseparability of individual humanity and the wider web of life. We now believe that the internal experience of interdependence cannot be separated from environmental awareness." "Can we learn again to experience and express our deepest sense of affinity with the living world," says Douglas Burton-Christie, "to develop both the sensibilities and practices that allow us to engage the living world not merely as an object but as a subject—as Beloved Other? I believe such a vision of living is still possible. But we have yet to acquire the kind of moral and spiritual honesty required to bring it into being."

Where do the members of the contemplative movement begin to acquire the kind of moral and spiritual courage that Burton-Christie speaks of? "We don't know what our future will bring," says Arthur Zajonc. "How do we prepare for an inner security when all the outer security of our world is collapsing?"

During the closing circle of the Fetzer event, Barry Boyce of the Shambhala Sun received a phone call from U.S. Congressman, Tim Ryan who said to Boyce, "Washington needs mindfulness practice now more than ever. We need you and your constituents to knock on our doors and tell us how it will benefit the world." As Boyce relayed Ryan's message to the group, I was overwhelmed by conflicting emotions. First there was pride and wonder as I considered the movement's path from near obscurity to the halls of Congress in the course of my adult life. Then, I felt overwhelmed as I recognized the gulf that still existed between Ryan's world of constituents, knocking on doors and sound bites and the quiet, subtle, and persistent work of awakening consciousness. Where does one begin to start? "It's the immeasurables and subtleties of our contemplative relationship with each other and the world that will show us the way," said Arthur Zajonc during the closing circle. "We need our depth of commitment to our practice and to each other now more than ever." An hour later, as I walked to the parking lot to make my way home, I noticed two participants sitting on a bench waiting for a cab to the airport. Instead of talking and trading business cards as often happens at the end of these kinds of events, they were sitting close to each other—in silence—already doing their work.

Appendix II

Participant Biographies

STATE OF CONTEMPLATIVE PRACTICE IN AMERICA
Fetzer Institute / Seasons Retreat Center
June 10-13, 2010

David Addiss, MD, MPH, received his MD degree from the Medical College of Georgia in 1981, completed an internship at Valley Medical Center in Fresno, California, and was a general practitioner in a migrant health clinic in the San Joaquin Valley for two years. After completing a master's degree at Johns Hopkins University in 1985, he began his career in public health at the Wisconsin Division of Health, in Madison, where trained in infectious disease epidemiology. He completed a residency in Preventive Medicine at the Centers for Disease Control and Prevention (CDC) in 1988 and joined the Division of Parasitic Diseases, where he conducted research on the prevention and control of parasitic diseases, both in the United States and abroad. His work took him to countries around the world, including Haiti, Brazil, Switzerland, India, Pakistan, China, Sudan, Nigeria, and Malawi, among others. From 1997 to 2006 he co-directed the World Health Organization's Collaborating Center for Control and Elimination of Lymphatic Filariasis in the Americas, based at CDC. He left CDC in 2006 join the Fetzer Institute, where he served as Senior Program Officer for Science and Spirituality.

Bobby William Austin, PhD, is a sociologist and a consultant on American Culture, Leadership, and African American Men and Boy. Presently he holds, the General Hal G. Moore Chair on Contemplative Leadership at the Merton Institute and is director of the Alliance for Public Trust. He is a Mahatma Gandhi Fellow of the American Academy of Political and Social Sciences.

He was the founding editor of the Urban League Review for the National Urban League, President of the Village Foundation, Vice President for University Relations at the University of the District of Columbia, and Secretary to the Board of trustees of the University. He served as Special Consultant on American Culture to the Honorable Joseph Duffey, Chairman of the National Endowment of the Humanities. As the Executive Director of the Kellogg Foundation National Taskforce on African American Men and Boys he edited and produced the groundbreaking report *Repairing the Breach: Key Ways to Support Family Life, Reclaim our Streets and Rebuild Civil Society In America's Communities.* This report was called "the plan to save America..." by *Washington Post* Columnist Bill Raspberry.

Austin is the author of several books and monographs, including *I'll Make Me a World: Bring Wholeness to Fractured Lives after 9/11* and a fiction work called *Circus Clowns & Carnival Animals,* both in 2008.

He is a graduate of Western Kentucky University, BA; Fisk University, MA; and McMaster University, PhD (Canada) and received a higher education management diploma from Harvard University.

Barry Boyce is senior editor of the *Shambhala Sun* magazine, editor of the magazine's Mindful Society department, and a regular feature writer. He is co-author of *The Rules of Victory: How to Transform Chaos and Conflict—Strategies from the Art of War,* and editor of *In the Face of Fear: Buddhist Wisdom for Difficult Times,* and the forthcoming *The Mindfulness Revolution: Leading Psychologists, Scientists, Artists, and Spiritual Teachers on the Power of Mindfulness in Daily Life* (2011).

Mary Ann Brussat is an interfaith minister and the Co-Director, with her husband Frederic, of Spirituality & Practice, a multifaith website providing resources for spiritual journeys. The site has a database of 9,000 book, audio, and film reviews; profiles of spiritual teachers; and sections devoted to 37 essential spiritual practices of the world's religions. Their E-Courses are reaching seekers around the world who discuss applying their spirituality to everyday life in online Practice Circles. The Brussats are the authors of the national bestseller *Spiritual Literacy: Reading the Sacred in Everyday Life,* which has been made into a 26-part DVD series, and *Spiritual Rx: Prescriptions for Living a Meaningful Life.* Mary Ann is an initiate of the Mevlevi Sufi order and a member of a progressive Protestant Christian church in New York City.

Susan Burggraf, PhD, is a psychologist with a broad background in social, developmental, and clinical psychology. Her dissertation was about the appeal of horror movies under the supervision of social psychologist Clark McCauley. Susan taught at Mount Holyoke and Bowdoin Colleges for eleven years before coming to Naropa. Her recent research has been in the area of the effects of various kinds of meditation on empathy, altruism, and other social affects and behaviors. During her years at Bowdoin and Mount Holyoke, Susan began to integrate contemplative methods into her traditional Western psychology courses, and she is delighted to now be studying psychology in a community that is steeped in contemplative practice. She is a practitioner in the Dzogchen tradition of Tibetan Buddhism.

Douglas Burton-Christie, PhD, is Professor of Theological Studies at Loyola Marymount University where he teaches in the area of Christian Spirituality. He earned his Ph.D. in Christian Spirituality from the Graduate Theological Union in 1988 and his M.A. in Theology from Oxford University in 1980. His primary research interests are in the contemplative traditions of ancient Christian monasticism, spirituality and the natural world, and the discipline of Christian spirituality. He is the author of *The Word in The Desert: Scripture and the Quest for Holiness in Early Christian Monasticism* (Oxford), and the founding editor of *Spiritus: A Journal of Christian Spirituality* (Johns Hopkins Press). In 2008-2009, he was awarded a Henry Luce III Fellowship for his project, "The Gift of Tears: Contemplative Ecology and the Renewal of the Earth." His work has appeared in *Horizons, Cross Currents, The Anglican Theological Review, Weavings, Interdisciplinary Studies in Literature and the Environment, Cistercian Studies Quarterly, Studia Patristica, The Best Spiritual Writing*, and *Orion*.

Mirabai Bush is Senior Fellow and the founding Director of the Center on Contemplative Mind in Society, a nonprofit organization whose mission is to encourage contemplative awareness in American life in order to create a more just, compassionate, and reflective society. She has designed and led contemplative trainings for corporations from Monsanto to Google, led a survey of contemplative practice, and directed a Contemplative Practice Fellowship awards program with the American Council of Learned Societies to explore such practices in academic courses. She is currently directing a study for the US Army on promoting resiliency and performance among Army medical and chaplain caregivers through mindfulness training. The Center also sponsors a program to bring contemplative practices into social justice organizations and into the profession of law, engaging law students, law faculty, and attorneys in an exploration of the role of contemplative practice in legal education and the practice of law.

Mirabai formerly directed the Seva Foundation Guatemala Project, which supports sustainable agriculture and integrated community development. She co-developed Sustaining Compassion, Sustaining the Earth, a series of retreats and events for grassroots environmental activists on the interconnection of spirit and action. She is co-author, with Ram Dass, of *Compassion in Action: Setting Out on the Path of Service.* She co-founded and directed Illuminations, Inc., in Cambridge, MA. Her innovative business approaches, based on mindfulness practice, were reported in *Newsweek, Inc., Fortune,* and the *Boston Business Journal.* Before that she taught in the English Department at SUNY Buffalo.

Her spiritual studies include meditation at the Burmese Vihara in Bodh Gaya, India, with Shri S.N. Goenka and Anagarika Munindra; bhakti yoga with Hindu teacher Neemkaroli Baba; and studies with Tibetan lamas Kalu Rinpoche, Chogyam Trungpa Rinpoche, Kyabje Gehlek Rinpoche, Tsoknyi Rinpoche, and others. She was a student of aikido master Kanai Sensei for five years.

Tom Callanan is a writer, facilitator, coach, philanthropic advisor, and has been a senior advisor to the Fetzer Institute. He will be developing a synthesis report of the proceedings/papers of this meeting so as to assist Fetzer and the field in moving forward. For 15 years Tom was a program officer at the Fetzer Institute where he helped to initiate and support dozens of projects at the intersection of personal and social transformation. He is a former magazine and newspaper journalist and co-author of *The Power of Collective Wisdom and the Trap of Collective Folly* (Sept. 2009, Berrett-Koehler). He consults with a number of organizations and projects, many of which he helped found including: The Seasons Fund for Social Transformation, The Conflict Transformation Collaborative, The Collective Wisdom Initiative, the Powers of Place Initiative and Four Years Go.

Rabbi Rachel Cowan is the Executive Director of the Institute for Jewish Spirituality. She was named by Newsweek Magazine in 2007 as one of the 50 leading rabbis in the United States, and was featured in the PBS series *The Jewish Americans.* She received her ordination from Hebrew Union College-Jewish Institute of Religion in 1989. She has been Director of Outreach at the 92nd Street YMHA; and from 1990-2003 was Program Director for Jewish Life and Values at the Nathan Cummings Foundation. Her work has been included in Moment and Sh'ma as well as in anthologies, including *Illness and Health in the Jewish Tradition: Writings from the Bible to Today,* and *The Torah: A Women's Commentary.* She is the author, with her late husband Paul Cowan, of *Mixed Blessings: Untangling the Knots in an Interfaith Marriage.* Her training in mindfulness meditation has been with Sylvia Boorstein, Sharon Salzberg and Sheila Peltz Weinberg. She lives in New York City, near her two children Lisa and Matt, and three grandchildren – Jacob, Tessa and Dante.

Michael Craft is the program director of the Omega Institute where he researches and develops Omega's ongoing curriculum and works closely with its faculty. He was formerly program director of three leading West Coast retreat centers. A practitioner of Buddhist, Daoist, and Western spiritual methods since the 1970s, Craft has taught meditation, tai chi, and qigong at Omega for many years. A lifelong student of shamanism and comparative mythology, he is the author of *Alien Impact*, a study of the UFO-alien phenomenon.

Margaret Cullen is a Licensed Marriage and Family Therapist and a Certified Mindfulness-Based Stress Reduction Teacher, having trained extensively with Jon Kabat-Zinn. She has also trained with Zindel Segal in Mindfulness-Based Cognitive Therapy and in MB Eat with Jean Kristeller. For sixteen years she has been teaching and pioneering mindfulness programs in a variety of settings including cancer support, HIV support, physician groups, executive groups, teachers and Kaiser patients. For six years she has been involved in teaching and writing curricula for several research programs at UCSF including "Cultivating Emotional Balance" designed for teachers and "Craving and Lifestyle Management with Meditation" for overweight women. In 2008 she launched a mindfulness-based emotional balance program (SMART) for teachers and school administrators in Denver, Boulder and Vancouver, B.C. She has collaborated on the revision of mindfulness curricula for Kaiser, Northern California and for the Center for Compassion at Stanford. She has also been a facilitator of support groups for cancer patients and their loved ones for twenty years at The Wellness Community. A meditation practitioner for thirty years, she is a frequent contributor to "Inquiring Mind".

Andrew Dreitcer holds degrees from Wabash College (BA), Yale Divinity School (MDiv), and the Graduate Theological Union (PhD). He is Associate Professor of Spirituality, Director of Spiritual Formation, and Co-Director of the Center for Engaged Compassion at Claremont School of Theology, as well as Associate Professor of Religion at Claremont Graduate University. He was the co-founding director of a seminary program in spiritual direction, and served 15 years as a Presbyterian pastor. Studies with Henri Nouwen and a year spent at the ecumenical monastic community of Taizé significantly shaped his own spiritual life. Co-author of *Beyond the Ordinary: Spirituality for Church Leaders,* Andy's current interests lie in the exploration of contemplative practices across religious traditions, the relationship between Christian spiritual practices and neuroscientific understandings, (http://neurospirituality.blogspot.com/), and the ways in which contemplative practices form "engaged compassionate" (http://centerforengagedcompassion.word-press.com). He has recently co-led workshops on contemplative practice, compassion, healing, and reconciliation for pastors, tribal chiefs, and government officials in Zimbabwe and for US Congress members and staff (www.triptykos.com).

Janet Drey, MA, works with the Contemplative Leadership initiative of the Merton Institute for Contemplative Living, Louisville, KY. She brings experience as a program director, facilitator, consultant, and executive leader. For over 25 years she has created learning environments where critical reflection, dialogue, and transformation can occur for persons, groups, and organizations. Her interest in leadership and spirituality began as a search for more effective leadership practice in ministerial settings and evolved to exploring contemplative spirituality as a component of leadership development for a professional services firm. She holds a Masters degree in Pastoral Studies from Loyola University, Chicago. She is a certified coach for Spiritual Intelligence, a member of Contemplative Outreach of Central Iowa, and various integral communities. Janet lives in Des Moines, IA with her family.

Maia Duerr, MA, is a cultural anthropologist, writer, and editor. She is currently the principal at Five Directions Consulting, which offers qualitative research and communications services (www.fivedirectionsconsulting.com).

From 2002 - 2004, Maia was the research director of the Center for Contemplative Mind in Society where she led a study on the use of meditation and other contemplative practices in secular settings. She is the author of a number of articles on this topic, including "The Contemplative Organization," published in the February 2004 issue of the Journal of Organizational Change Management. Maia was a research associate in the Medical Anthropology Department at the University of California, San Francisco, from 1999 to 2002. She received a Masters in Social and Cultural Anthropology from the California Institute of Integral Studies in 1996.

Earlier in her career, Maia worked with people with chronic psychiatric disabilities as a music therapist and counselor. She is a student in the Soto Zen Buddhist lineage of Suzuki Roshi, and has practiced at the San Francisco Zen Center and Upaya Zen Center.

Liz Budd Ellmann, MDiv, serves as Executive Director of Spiritual Directors International. For more than twenty years, Spiritual Directors International has been tending the holy around the world and across traditions by providing educational programs and publications, including *Presence: An International Journal of Spiritual Direction*; *Listen: A Seekers' Resource for Spiritual Direction*; a series of books designed for use in seminaries, rabbinical colleges, and continuing education of spiritual directors; and *Seek and Find: an online guide of spiritual directors from around the world and across traditions, www. sdiworld.org.* Liz has co-led contemplative pilgrimages in Peru and Ireland, and she is co-leading an October 2010 interfaith pilgrimage in Israel and Palestine as a way to reconnect with and re-appropriate the ancient, contemplative spiritual direction heritage. Liz was featured in a February 2010 PBS *Religion and Ethics* television documentary about spiritual direction, which has helped to raise public awareness of spiritual direction. Before joining Spiritual Directors International, Liz founded SoulTenders, a multi-faith organization dedicated to tending the spirit of working people through the teaching and support of spiritual practices in the workplace. She has served as adjunct faculty in Seattle University's Executive Leadership Program and has extensive experience as a spiritual director and group facilitator. Liz earned a BA from Stanford University and a Master of Divinity degree from the Jesuit Seattle University. Liz is passionate about how spirituality and contemplative practices are fostered and integrated into everyday living, contributing to peace, justice, and right relationships with all of God's creation.

David Frenette has taught Centering Prayer in Contemplative Outreach since 1984, including as a trainer for long-term practitioners. He co-founded and co-led a Centering Prayer retreat community for ten years. He now teaches and gives spiritual direction at the Center for Contemplative Living in Denver and is an Adjunct Faculty in the Religious Studies Department at Naropa University.

Michele Gossman, MBA, is the Director of the Transformations Spirituality Center (TSC) in Kalamazoo, Michigan where she has served for the past 10 years. Under her leadership, Transformations has grown into a vibrant retreat and conference center serving seekers from many faiths as well as those searching for meaning outside of the context of a faith tradition.

Ms. Gossman came to this work after a 20-year career in banking and finance, and has been able to join her business background with a passion for the spiritual journey. She and the many gifted people she has worked with over the years have formed Transformations into a safe place of welcome for the spiritual seeker, with an operation that can support their needs. Her

BBA in Public Administration and MBA in Finance are both from Western Michigan University.

Her religious background is varied. Her family hailed from the South, where most of her relatives were actively involved with rural Southern Baptist or Pentecostal churches, which she attended with them when visiting. Her parents moved to Michigan in the 1950's and she was raised in the Christian Church, Disciples of Christ. As an adult, Michele finds community in the United Church of Christ and has been active in the First Congregational Church of Kalamazoo, Michigan for 25 years.

In that time, she has served both the Church and the community in small but meaningful ways. She was a founding Board member of the Kalamazoo Drop-In Child Care Center which offers free day-care for low-income families. She has served two terms on the Board of Missions, which allocates benevolence funds and one term on the Stewardship Board. She is currently serving as the Moderator of her Congregation.

As a quiet person who needs regular tastes of solitude, Michele finds Centering Prayer to be a place of profound refreshment for mind, body and soul. To her, this practice is like a well-worn trail through the woods – a path that can be found even in the dark of night.

Inspired by Thomas Merton's *Seven Storey Mountain*, Michele began reading on the spiritual life as a young adult. No longer young and, thankfully, less adult, she continues to be an avid student of this genre.

Linda Bell Grdina serves as a Program Officer at the Fetzer Institute. She develops, manages, and promotes projects that build community; promote community engagement; and foster awareness, understanding and application of love, forgiveness, and compassion in daily life. She has studied various wisdom traditions, including Buddhist, Christian, Shamanic, and Yogic.

Claudia Horwitz has been a leader in national efforts to integrate the power of spiritual practice and the work of social justice. In 1995 she founded stone circles, a nonprofit organization committed to sustaining activists and strengthening the work for justice through spiritual practice and principles. In 2007, the organization created The Stone House, a center on 70 acres of land in Mebane, North Carolina that welcomes people of all traditions for training, retreat, and fellowship. Her previous work includes developing youth leadership, supporting struggles for economic justice, and strengthening nonprofit organizations. She is the author of *The Spiritual Activist: Practices to Transform Your Life, Your Work, and Your World* (Penguin Compass 2002) is a practical guide to individual and social transformation through spirit and faith. Claudia has a master's degree in Public Policy from Duke University and was a Rockefeller Foundation Next Generation Leadership Fellow. She is a yoga teacher in the Kripalu tradition.

Pir Zia Inayat-Khan, PhD, is the spiritual leader of the Sufi Order International, a mystical and ecumenical fellowship rooted in the visionary legacy of his grandfather, Hazrat Pir-o-Murshid Inayat Khan. Pir Zia is also Founder of Seven Pillars House of Wisdom and President of the Suluk Academy for esoteric studies. Pir Zia holds a doctoral degree in religion from Duke University, is a recipient of the U Thant Peace Award, and is a Lindisfarne Fellow. www.sufiorder.org www.sevenpillarshouse.org

Patricia A. Jennings, MEd, PhD, is the Director of the Initiative on Contemplation and Education at the Garrison Institute and a faculty researcher in the Prevention Research Center at Penn State University. Dr. Jennings received her doctorate in human development from the University of California, Davis and completed postdoctoral training at the Health Psychology Program at the University of California, San Francisco (UCSF) where she directed the Cultivating Emotional Balance (CEB) Project, a randomized controlled clinical trial to assess the effectiveness of the CEB training. This training, combining contemplative practice with emotional awareness training, is designed to reduce destructive emotional responses, while enhancing compassion, and empathy.

She is currently developing a new training called Cultivating Awareness and Resilience in Education (CARE) based upon CEB that is designed more specifically for teachers and she is conducting research to examine how promoting social and emotional competence among teachers may translate into improved teacher-student relationships, increased student pro-social behavior, a more positive classroom atmosphere and improved student academic performance.

In addition to psychological research, Dr. Jennings has over 22 years of research and teaching experience in the field of education. After receiving a master's degree in education, she founded and directed an experimental school where she developed and field-tested curriculum for children from infancy through 5th grade, applying a variety of contemplative approaches that come from alternative educational approaches such as Montessori and Waldorf in her work. She later served as Director of Intern Teachers at St. Mary's College Graduate School of Education in Moraga, California, where she taught education courses, supervised student research, developed teacher-training curriculum, and supervised student teacher training.

Judy Lief was a close student of Ven. Chögyam Trungpa Rinpoche, who trained and empowered her as a teacher in the Buddhist and Shambhala traditions. Sakyong Mipham Rinpoche, his son and successor, recognized Ms. Lief as a senior teacher, or "acharya." Judy is the author of *Making Friends with Death: A Buddhist Guide to Encountering Mortality* (Shambhala Publications March 2001). She is a member of the Madison-Deane Initiative, which produced the award winning documentary, *Pioneers of Hospice.* She serves on the board and is a member of the faculty of the Clinical Pastoral Education program at the Fletcher Allen Hospital. In addition, Ms. Lief serves on the Naropa University Board of Trustees and is a member of the Contemplative Coalition formed under the auspices of the Global Peace Initiative of Women. She offers workshops and retreats internationally on the application of contemplative practices and insights to the care of the dying.

Walter Link works to integrate his hands-on leadership experience in international business and social entrepreneurship with being a longtime practitioner and teacher of inner work. Working in organizations and movements for economic and social transformation, Walter recognized individual and collective leadership as the major bottleneck of sustainable change. Therefore he decided to focus on leadership development, consulting and coaching for leaders, organizations and movements that work towards a more humane, peaceful and sustainable world. Walter now does this work primarily through the Global Academy, which he leads alongside the Global Leadership Network, an international community of senior leadership practitioners who innovate approaches for individual and collective leadership towards personal, organizational, and societal transformation.

Walter co-founded and co-led a number of international business networks and organizations, including the Social Venture Network (www.svn.org) in Europe—the first pan-European corporate responsibility network—and Empresa—the first such network across the Americas (www.empresa.org). He helped to create Human Rights Watch's European Union office (www.hrw.org), served on the board of Greyston Foundation (www.greyston.org), and founded a network connecting East and West Europeans through action and inner work. Walter is a member of the Club of Rome (www.cluboframe.org) and advised the United Nations leadership in the agenda development for the Johannesburg Sustainability Summit and the UN's general assembly at its

Global Summit in Istanbul. He is presently working with Sarvodaya (www.sarvodaya.org), which serves millions of poor people in several thousand villages integrating Buddhist philosophy with sustainability and economic development, peace and grass roots democracy work.

Rhonda Magee is Professor of Law at the University of San Francisco. She earned her JD MA (Sociology) and BA (with Distinction) from the University of Virginia. She teaches or has taught Torts; Insurance Law and Policy; Immigration Law and Policy; Racism and Justice in American Legal History; and Contemporary Issues in Race and Law and Evolving Notions of (In)equality; and Contemplative Lawyering. Prior to entering academia, Rhonda practiced as a civil litigator in San Francisco and as an associate in a Chicago-based law firm. Her articles and essays have appeared in journals such as the Law Reviews of the University of Virginia, University of Alabama, Temple Law School, and the San Francisco Chronicle, and the website of the Center for Contemplative Mind in Society, and some of these may be viewed on her social science research network author page, located at http://papers.ssrn.com/sol3/cf_dev/AbsByAuth.cfm?per_id=624519.

Born in North Carolina, Rhonda migrated to Northern California after law school and now holds the Bay Area to be her true home. Rhonda is committed to an open, ecumenical exploration of the spiritual nature of human existence, from an inclusive, spiritual-humanist perspective and to expanding this approach in education. She is a long-time practitioner of a variety of contemplative practices, including insight meditation, contemplative writing, and dialogue, supported by engagement in personal depth psychology work. She is a trained in the interpersonal dynamics of group dialogue and a member of a sensitivity training ("T-group") supported by Stanford University's Group Facilitator Training Program. She has been associated with the Project for the Integration of Spirituality Law and Politics, and a member of the Board of the Center for Contemplative Mind in Society, and its Bay Area Working Group for Lawyers. Through her scholarship, teaching, workshops, and coaching, Rhonda explores the inter-relationships among law, notions of justice and humanity. She proposes thinking, writing, and teaching from a relationally-aware approach she calls "Humanity Consciousness." Rhonda is committed to the development of contemplative pedagogy, and to a broad agenda of reform—reform of legal education and the development of professional identity, of substantive law, and of legal practice—guided by the insights of outsider jurisprudence (critical legal, gender and race theory) suffused with the compassionate heart of contemplative practice.

Dena Merriam, MA, began working in the interfaith movement in the late 1990s when she served as Vice Chair of the Millennium World Peace Summit of Religious and Spiritual Leaders held at the United Nation in New York. She subsequently convened a meeting of women religious and spiritual leaders at the Palais des Nations in Geneva and from that gathering founded the Global Peace Initiative of Women (GPIW) in 2002, an organization chaired by a multi-faith group of women spiritual leaders. The mission of this organization is to enable women to facilitate healing and reconciliation in areas of conflict and post-conflict, and to bring spiritual resources to help address critical global problems. Since its founding, GPIW has been working on programs in Israel/Palestine, Iraq, Sudan, Afghanistan, and Cambodia. GPIW also developed, in partnership with the United Nations, a global leadership program for young community leaders. GPIW's work in the area of peacebuilding has expanded to include fostering new models of development, inclusive and sustainable, and to changing attitudes toward the environment, regaining the sense of awe, respect, and reverence for earth and her life systems.

Through her work in the interfaith world, Ms. Merriam found that women and the Eastern religious traditions were very much under-represented at international inter-religious gatherings. She came to believe that the voices of these constituents are essential for greater world balance and for creating a new dynamic that will enable us to successfully address many of the global challenges we now face. Her work at GPIW has been devoted to creating a global platform for women religious and spiritual leaders, and to engaging the Hindu and Buddhist leadership more actively on the world stage.

For over 35 years, Dena has been a student of Paramahansa Yogananda and a practitioner of Kriya Yoga meditation. She is also a long time student of the great texts of the Vedic tradition. Ms. Merriam received her Master's Degree from Columbia University and has served on the boards of the Harvard University Center for the Study of World Religions, the International Center for Religion and Diplomacy, The Interfaith Center of New York, the Manitou Foundation, All India Movement (AIM) for Seva, Dharma Drum Mountain Buddhist Association, and Seven Pillars.

Tamar Miller, MA, consults to social change organizations and is founder of a new initiative, The PeaceBeat, whose motto is … *some good news, some of the time.* She was co-director of the New England region of The New Israel Fund; VP Education and one of three founders of American Higher Education, Inc.; and Partner in Middle East Holdings, a business development firm based in Boston and Dubai. Tamar was Director of Leadership Development and then Executive Director of the Institute for Social and Economic Policy in the Middle East at Harvard University. She directed social service programs in New York, Jerusalem, and Cambridge, MA for disturbed adolescents, pregnant and parenting addicts, and families of psychiatric patients. She also was a community organizer in Ethiopian, Yemenite, and Moroccan disenfranchised communities in Israel. Tamar holds a BA in Philosophy and Judaic Studies, a Master of Social Work from Yeshiva University, and a Master of Public Administration from Harvard University. She currently is active on the board of directors of Parents Circle – Bereaved Family Forum, IPCRI (Israel Palestine Center for Research and Information), and the Alliance for Middle East Peace. Tamar is a long-time practitioner of vinyasa yoga and karma yoga.

Eric Nelson earned his MA in organizational and interpersonal communication and a BS degree in social psychology, both from Western Michigan University. He serves on the board of the Interfaith Strategy for Advocacy and Action in the Community, and co-founded several networks, including The Holistic Health Network, Southwest Michigan Greens, and The Global Meditation Group. He was previously a program officer at Fetzer Institute, where he developed programs in religious traditions and spiritual pathways, including the meeting for which these papers were written. His projects fell into three major categories: research on religious resources of love, compassion, and forgiveness; interfaith engagement; and contemplative practice.

Wayne Ramsey is the Director of Research Design and Evaluation at the Fetzer Institute. Prior to this appointment, he supervised Fetzer-supported scientific research studies and inquiries into spirituality, love and compassion, forgiveness and reconciliation, and positive transformative processes.

Richard Rohr, OFM, is a Franciscan of the New Mexico Province. He was the founder of the New Jerusalem Community in Cincinnati, Ohio in 1971, and the Center for Action and Contemplation (CAC) in Albuquerque, New Mexico in 1986, where he presently serves as Founding Director. He founded the Center to serve as a "school for prophetic thinking," to encourage lay leadership, and what he calls "a new reformation from within."

Father Richard is probably best known for his writings and numerous audio and video recordings which are distributed by St. Anthony Messenger

Press, Crossroad Publishers, and Orbis Press as well as through The Mustard Seed, the C.A.C.'s resource center. He is often introduced as "the most taped and recorded Catholic priest in America". Some of his more well-known books include *Everything Belongs, Simplicity, From Wild Man to Wise Man, Quest for the Grail, Adam's Return, Things Hidden,* and *Job and the Mystery of Suffering.* His most widely distributed talks are his recorded conferences on *The Enneagram, Breathing Under Water,* and *The Great Themes of Paul.* Many of these books and conferences have been translated into German, Czech, Spanish, Italian, and other languages. Articles authored by Fr. Rohr regularly appear in *Radical Grace,* the quarterly publication of the CAC, and the Jewish journal, *Tikkun.*

Richard was born in 1943 in Kansas. He entered the Franciscans in 1961 and was ordained to the priesthood in 1970. He received his Master's Degree in Theology from Dayton that same year. He now lives in a hermitage behind his Franciscan community in Albuquerque, and divides his time between working at the CAC, and preaching and teaching on all continents. He considers the proclamation of the Gospel to be his primary call, and uses many different platforms to communicate its messages. Scripture as liberation, the integration of action and contemplation, community building, peace and justice issues, church reform, contemplative prayer and non dualistic thinking, male spirituality, the Enneagram, and eco-spirituality are the principle themes of his teaching.

His latest book, *The Naked Now: Learning to See as the Mystics See* was published by Crossroad Press in September of 2009.

Diana Calthorpe Rose is President of the Garrison Institute, a non-profit organization located in Garrison, New York whose mission is to apply the transformative power of contemplation to today's pressing social and environmental concerns, helping build a more compassionate, resilient future.

The Garrison Institute's Program Initiatives develop rigorous, evidence-based ways to apply contemplative methodologies to key social change fields —education, ecology, and trauma care—redefining their core issues, connecting them to a larger context of systemic change.

Mrs. Rose is a leader in helping to build a bridge between spirituality and social action, and her career reflects her commitment to creating linkages between individual transformation and social transformation. Reflecting on her own spiritual practices and commitment to social action, she has served on the Boards of several national Buddhist organizations in America.

Diana is also President of the Lostand Foundation, a private charitable organization she and her husband founded in 1997. The Lostand Foundation supports a wide variety of organizations involved in social action, land conservation, and sustainable development.

Diana Rose was educated at UC Berkeley and has a professional background in art, design, event production, and gallery management. She is an accomplished dressage rider who trains and competes successfully at the highest levels. She is married to Jonathan F.P. Rose, a real estate developer and planner, and has two daughters.

Donald Rothberg, PhD, (Philosophy), is a member of the Teachers Council at Spirit Rock Meditation Center in the San Francisco Bay Area, has practiced Insight Meditation since 1976, and has also received training in Tibetan Dzogchen practice and the Hakomi approach to body-based psychotherapy. Formerly on the faculties of the University of Kentucky, Kenyon College, and Saybrook Graduate School, he currently writes and teaches classes, groups, and retreats on meditation, daily life practice, spirituality and psychology, and socially engaged Buddhism, in the San Francisco Bay Area and nationally. An organizer, teacher, and former board member for the Buddhist Peace Fellowship, he has helped to guide three six-month to two-year training programs in socially engaged spirituality through Buddhist Peace Fellowship (the BASE Program), Saybrook (the Socially Engaged Spirituality Program), and Spirit Rock (the Path of Engagement Program). An editor of *ReVision* for ten years, he is the author of *The Engaged Spiritual Life: A Buddhist Approach to Transforming Ourselves and the World* and the co-editor of *Ken Wilber in Dialogue: Conversations with Leading Transpersonal Thinkers.*

Deborah Rozelle, PsyD, is a clinical psychologist and trauma specialist with over 30 years clinical experience. She currently serves as Senior Fellow at the Garrison Institute's Transforming Trauma Initiative, Garrison, NY; Senior Advisor to the United States Office of Refugee Resettlement-Unaccompanied Minors Trauma Program based at Latin Health Institute, Boston, MA; Senior Advisor for Occupational Therapy Associates in Watertown, MA; and Guest Faculty for the Institute for Meditation and Psychotherapy in Wellesley, MA. Dr. Rozelle presents nationally and internationally; and she is a certified EMDR therapist, an EMDRIA-approved consultant, and a registered art therapist.

From 1997-2007, Dr. Rozelle offered clinical supervision and was on faculty at the Trauma Center at JRI in Boston, MA. While there, Dr. Rozelle helped design and implement a UNICEF-sponsored, school-based psychosocial training program for Turkey earthquake victims; and she served on Dr. Bessel van der Kolk's clinical team for his ground-breaking NIMH-funded EMDR research study that compared EMDR, Prozac and placebo conditions. Dr. Rozelle also served two years as a board member for the New England Society for the Study of Trauma and Dissociation.

Dr. Rozelle has been a practicing Tibetan Buddhist for the past 20 years, and is an active member of the Jewel Heart (www.JewelHeart.org) community. Dr. Rozelle integrates Buddhist psychology concepts and practices in her psychotherapy practice, teaching, and consulting work.

Brenda Salgado joined MSC in 2009 and has 10 years of experience in the nonprofit sector. She believes that visionary movements for social change are rooted in the experience, vision, and transformative practice of grassroots and community leaders and those most impacted by injustice. She sees interconnectedness and transformative practice as important pathways for embodying and constructing equitable, thriving, healthy, and ecologically sustainable communities locally and globally.

Her areas of interest include movement building, youth and community organizing, environmental health and justice, women's health, and health equity issues. She served as the Program Manager at Breast Cancer Action for 5 years, where she was responsible for campaigns, media and communications, and legislative and policy work. Prior to this, she was the Associate Director at Literacy for Environmental Justice, a youth environmental justice organization. Prior to her social justice work Brenda studied howler monkeys, directed a field research center, and developed conservation education and community development programs in Central America.

She serves as a volunteer with KIDS for the BAY, Building Futures with Women and Children, the East Bay Meditation Center, Unity Church, Coffee Party USA and her local neighborhood association. Brenda is a native Californian with Nicaraguan heritage and she holds a deep appreciation of her family for the spiritual and cultural values that have led her to environmental and social justice work. She finds joy in gardening, nature, and appreciating the beauty in those she meets on her journey.

Robert Toth, MA, was the Executive Director of the Merton Institute for Contemplative Living in Louisville, Kentucky from 1998 to 2010. He is currently serving as The Institute's Director of Special Initiatives and is responsible for developing the Contemplative Leadership and Contemplative

Family Initiatives and for planning a Center for Contemplative Living and Leadership on forty acres at the Abbey of Gethsemani. He is the co-editor of *Bridges to Contemplative Living,* a series designed for small group dialogue.

He received his AB in Classics and MA in Education degrees from John Carroll University. He taught English in secondary schools for six years and worked in healthcare administration for twenty-two years before joining the Merton Institute.

Deborah Yeager provides assistance to Rob Lehman, Chairman of the Board of the Fetzer Institute. Deborah's work focuses on projects aimed at exploring and articulating the Institute's spiritual foundations in the areas of mission, guiding purpose, deep engagement, and deep collaboration. She spent nine years on staff at GilChrist, Fetzer's contemplative retreat center, and is a grateful student of Buddhist meditative practices.

Arthur Zajonc, PhD, is Director of the Center for Contemplative Mind in Society and professor of physics at Amherst College, where he has taught since 1978. He received his BS and PhD in physics from the University of Michigan. He has been visiting professor and research scientist at the Ecole Normale Superieure in Paris, the Max Planck Institute for Quantum Optics, and the universities of Rochester, and Hannover. He has been Fulbright professor at the University of Innsbruck in Austria. His research has included studies in electron-atom physics, parity violation in atoms, quantum optics, the experimental foundations of quantum physics, and the relationship between science, the humanities, and the contemplative traditions. He has written extensively on Goethe's science work. He is author of the book: *Catching the Light* (Bantam, 1993 & Oxford UP, 1995), co-author of *The Quantum Challenge* (Jones & Bartlettt, 1997), and co-editor of *Goethe's Way of Science* (SUNY Press, 1998). In 1997 he served as scientific coordinator for the Mind and Life dialogue published as *The New Physics and Cosmology: Dialogues with the Dalai Lama* (Oxford UP, 2004). He again organized the 2002 dialogue with the Dalai Lama, "The Nature of Matter, the Nature of Life," and acted as moderator at MIT for the "Investigating the Mind" Mind and Life dialogue in 2003. The proceedings of the Mind and Life-MIT meeting were published under the title *The Dalai Lama at MIT* (Harvard UP, 2003, 2006) which he co-edited. He is author of the books, *Meditation as Contemplative Inquiry: When Knowing Becomes Love* (Lindisfarne Press, 2009) on contemplative pedagogy, and a volume on the youth program PeaceJam, *We Speak as*

One: Twelve Nobel Laureates Share their Vision for Peace. His book on higher education with Parker Palmer is in press and is entitled, *The Heart of Higher Education: A Call to Renewal* (Jossey-Bass, 2010). He currently is an advisor to the World Future Council, and directs the Center for Contemplative Mind in Society, which supports appropriate inclusion of contemplative methods in higher education. He has also been a co-founder of the Kira Institute, General Secretary of the Anthroposophical Society, president/chair of the Lindisfarne Association, and was a senior program director at the Fetzer Institute.

Made in the USA
Lexington, KY
23 May 2014